THE LAST SOUVENIR

The Battle for Okinawa - 1945

Jack Carroll

DEDICATION

I dedicate this book in three ways. The first is to my children, Susan, Jack, and Dan. For years, when they were young, we used to gather in the living room or around a campfire where they would listen to the yarns of my travels in the great Pacific War. It was their urging that inspired me to pick up my pen and

Secondly, my dedication goes to my dead comrades who fell, never to know the joys of fathering a family.

And lastly to my wonderful, sensitive mother, whose beautiful blond hair turned gray during the two years I was away at war.

THE LAST SOUVENIR

The Battle for Okinawa - 1945

Jack Carroll

ipicturebooks
New York

ipicturebooks, 2009

© Jack Carroll, 2002

All rights reserved under the International and Pan-American Copyright Conventions. Printed in the United States by J. Boylston & Company, Publishers, New York. No part of this publication may be reproduced, stored in a retrieval system, or transmitted in any form or by any means, electronic, or otherwise, without the prior written permission of the copyright holder. The Brick Tower Press colophon is a registered trademark of J. T. Colby & Company, Inc.

Carroll, Jack
The Last Souvenir, The Battle for Okinawa - 1945

ISBN 978-1-876963-04-0

Library of Congress
    Control Number: 2009943252

First Edition, January 2010

Jack Carroll

INTRODUCTION

When a boy leaves the warmth and security of his home and marches off to war, his head is filled with impossible dreams and false illusions. He is truly ignorant of the violence ahead, yet this has no bearing on his intelligence quotient. The stories and pictures he has seen and heard seem vivid enough, leaving the high spirit of his youth to carry him through it. In this great new adventure he hopes to find his manhood and attain a permanent identity in the adult world. The nucleus of friends and relatives he leaves behind will be proud of him and he will stand above the crowd at last.

Next he will don a uniform and take up a weapon, joining a sea of other youthful faces. These are his new peers and he finds solace in their numbers. He is now a foot soldier, subject to a higher authority and mass movement. There is no turning back. A divine providence has marked him for war, and soon he will be fed into the fray. On occasion, his thoughts will turn to the tenderness of his mother's love, or his father's counsel, but this is not the time to look backwards. The excitement swelling in his breast reaches an intensity he has never known before.

The shock comes in the opening minutes of his first battle, when all of his predetermined fantasies are shattered. He wasn't told it would be this loud and furious, simply because there are no words to describe it. The sky opens to rain artillery and mortar shells and the unsuspecting earth is literally ripped apart. He can hear the shrieks of mortally wounded men, or watch a severed leg hurtle through the air. The panic that grips him brings on awareness of the frailty of his own body. The fierce patriotism he once knew is drained away and replaced by the terror of the moment. To make it worse, there is no place to run and hide. The new struggle is with his own cowardice, and not the enemy.

 The magic word is truth. Now he knows the true meaning of war and its carnage. He must reach deep into his soul to find courage and pride in himself. Other men are advancing now and he will join them, hoping he doesn't hear the sickening thud of a bullet entering his body. The force that drives him forward is a combination of duty and the fact that there are no other alternatives. This is his war and he is stuck with it.

 At day's end, when exhaustion sets in, he will live where he stops. Digging a hole is first, where he can sit and draw sustenance from his pack and the canteen on his hip. He has just become an important link in a long front line. There is no shelter from wind and rain, and henceforth he will live in the ground like a burrowing animal. A strange numbness sweeps through him, and he starts his swift climb to new heights of maturity. The keenness of his senses is sharpened to a fine edge, giving him instincts he never knew existed. It becomes necessary to see in the dark, or identify the sound of a whistling shell or a zipping bullet. Even an evening breeze can carry the musty smell of an enemy uniform. The boy doesn't know it, but these gifts are increasing his prospects of staying alive. Step by step he is turning into a veteran.

 Good news is relative, and must fit the occasion. When his badly decimated unit is no longer capable of front-line service, they are ordered to the rear for rest and replacements. The pathetic handful of a once proud company will straggle away and seek a defilade haven where only limited danger lurks. Their filthy, sweat-stained uniforms, and bloodshot eyes give testimony to the ordeal they have endured. The boy is older now, and he will never see his fragile youth again. He will always remember the faces of the enemy dead, realizing that they too are from his own age group. He can't afford the luxury of sadness. There is no more room in his heart for remorse. However, if it means anything, it appears his side is winning.

The suspended animation of a long sleep overcomes his weariness, and a new strength urges the boy to awaken and count faces. A wonderful revelation tells him these are his new comrades, and there is no delineation between the rich kid and the ghetto boy. This brotherhood of survival has bonded them together like Siamese Twins, joined at the shoulders forever. Fear is a terrible monster, and it was their togetherness that conquered the beast. The exclusive club has no password or secret handshake, and now the boy is a member. The entrance requirements are simple. The boy was there with them, he saw it, and he survived.

They will fight together again and more will die, yet this only strengthens their ties. In the years ahead, when peace comes, they will travel hundreds of miles to share their brotherhood once more. To the outsider, these odd rituals of reunions defy logical explanations. The wives and sweethearts who are dragged to these events will usually issue the same comment: 'What makes these guys tick?' Now, it is the women's turn to carry a pack. It is the burden of tolerance.

The chapters that follow will tell, in part, the story of that comradeship. It has been said, and rightfully so, that a war is never over until the last veteran has passed away.

The Last Souvenir

PREFACE

The last great battle of the Second World War was fought on the island of Okinawa, and this is where the reader will be taken. Situated about three hundred miles southwest of the Japanese mainland it is bordered by the China Sea on the west and the vast Pacific Ocean to the east. On a map, the island resembles a large pod full of irregular peas, lying at an angle pointing northeast. Being less than sixty-five miles long, and eighteen miles at its widest point, it is ringed by multi-colored coral reefs and lined with sandy beaches reminding one of granulated white sugar. Breathtaking beauty would be a fitting description.

The topography abounded with small streams and low-lying mountain ranges and coral ridges punctuated rivers and the green valleys. The fields were hand-hewn into checkerboards of rice paddies and sugar cane patches, tended by a populace that used the same antiquated farming techniques for centuries. Even the hillsides were terraced into hand dug rice paddies. Available water sources were carefully diverted to complete the miracle.

Each valley had a central village of wooden houses with red tiled roofs. Here and there, a stone wall marked the family territory. The omnipresence of vegetable gardens behind the dwellings demonstrated the need for self-sufficiency. Neatly lined rows of sweet potatoes and other small tubers showed the main staples of their diets. Short-horned milk goats could be seen everywhere, staked to the ground, while chickens serenely pecked the soil around them. Fenced corrals housed Shetland-sized ponies used for pulling little horse-carts along narrow dirt roads connecting the villages.

The people were small in stature and could be likened to

the Lilliputians from Gulliver's Travels. The men stood about five feet four inches in height, while the women were four to five inches shorter. Their features were oriental with a smattering of Chinese and Japanese. Clothing was a common, calf length kimono, hand carved wooden sandals, and a woven straw head covering. Everyone had a predetermined workload. Farmer, fisherman, dressmaker, and wood carver were typical professions on this quasi-socialistic environment. Bartering was the key and cash money was rare.

When the Japanese Empire established the island as a colony in the late 1800's, the old ways put up a resistance to change. The invaders created a limited educational system and gave the people a new language, but the culture remained ancient. They had never seen war, but they were soon to receive their baptism of destruction and horror.

The Allied forces had been battling the Japanese Empire in the Pacific War since 1941, flattening island after island for three and a half years. Now, it was Okinawa's turn. The Japanese engineers had scarred the paradise by building three major airfields, affording a tempting morsel for the American juggernaut. On April 1, 1945, ironically April Fool's Day and Easter Sunday, the rape of Okinawa began. Thousands of warships and aircraft appeared, dumping tons of high explosives on the pristine little island. Tens of thousands of American infantrymen stormed their beaches. Within the flick of an eyelash the quaint little villages were reduced to rubble. The beautiful fields of rice and sugar cane looked as though a giant heavenly shotgun had blasted them into a quagmire of mud and broken debris.

Fortunately, the islanders were warned in advance to dig caves in the mountainsides where they could seek refuge. This they did, and this is where they hid for three months as the battle raged over their heads. For tactical reasons, the Japanese commander decided to make his stand in the south. Thus, the

The Last Souvenir

lower end of the island was demolished, leaving the north unscathed. Perhaps fate stepped in and decided to preserve at least half of this wonderful civilization. Many of the riflemen who survived the flames of combat in the south were sent north and allowed to mingle with these gracious people. This story belongs to them.

CHAPTER ONE

The idea of sending American boys to wage a war with the veteran Japanese Army was ludicrous at best. On a Christmas day an American youth is given a baseball glove or a fishing pole, and the process begins. Thousands of miles away, a Japanese child is handed a toy sword or Kendo stick as soon as he sheds his diapers. He learned to maim or behead his enemies and die by sacrifice. For centuries the Samurai warrior was held in the highest esteem, tantamount to our Babe Ruth or Daniel Boone. The Samurai swordsman, returning home from combat, would cradle the severed head of an adversary under his arm, displaying his trophy with pride. Ancient art scenes of Japan depict these grisly parades.

To the Japanese General Staff, the American boy was too weak and pampered to offer any resistance. He would soon roll over and accept the point of a bayonet at his throat. The Imperial Army of Nippon had rolled up the map of Asia like a scroll of paper. For over a decade their triumphs ran from Manchuria to Burma, the East Indies, and the Pacific Ocean ranging from Alaska to the Gilbert and Solomon Islands. The next stop was Pearl Harbor and California, the nice plums ripe for picking.

Alas, this was a classic under estimation of American anger and industrial might. Like a sleeping giant, an entire nation of over a hundred million patriots rose up. Men and boys enlisted and women went to work. But there was more bad news. The United States of America was not only shocked, it was unprepared for an island war, or any other war for that matter.

The Last Souvenir

The stepping stones to a victory over Japan were the islands themselves. Thousands of miles of ocean, dotted with land masses and coral atolls, lay ahead. This painstaking task was assigned to the US Army Infantry and the newly christened Fleet Marine Force, Pacific. The US Navy would be reclaimed from the bottom of Pearl Harbor and fight by their sides, the largest amphibious armada in history.

Factory smoke stacks began to billow. Training camps sprang forth, echoing the sounds of a million pounding boots. Mothers wept and wives tried desperately to hide their sorrows. The worst was yet to come, but the purpose was firm. If sacrifice was their game it could be matched.

Until now, the Japanese steamroller was invincible. They had never swallowed defeat, and surrender was not in their manual of arms. These traditional warriors had no fear of the spoon-fed Americans, and would die to the last man if ordered. The rude awakening was an electric shock to their inflated egos.

Island after island began to fall in a chain of conquests. Grim faced Marines and soldiers pounced on the supermen from four directions at once. The Americans were learning the art of slaughter and were ready to apply it. Their own book of rules was written on the way up the ladder.

The big island of Okinawa was the last bloody rung. For eighty-two days and nights the battle raged, with each side pounding the other. On the last day, when the end was in sight, the battle cry became: 'Next Stop, Tokyo!'

CHAPTER TWO

"Take a look at that, Jake, down by the cliff. The Nips are jumpin' off that ledge."

The hill before them was riddled with a network of enemy caves. Sergeant Jake Carter was preoccupied, rewiring the terminals on his field telephone. Watching high ranking enemy officers commit suicide was not on the top of his list of priorities. His observation post was the critical link to the Intelligence Section in the rear. Somehow, while fighting off a counter attack in the night, a big boot had kicked away the wires.

A light morning breeze from the west cleared the last traces of battle smoke, and the big guns were silent. Even the rattle of rifle fire and the popping of hand grenades had stopped. Everything reeked of burnt powder and picric acid. Once green hills and valleys had changed to a gray beige and the scorched tree stumps were pointing accusing black fingers at the sky. The silence was a backdrop for the buzzing of flies, already massing on the dead bodies below.

The infantry lines had moved as far south as they could advance, and only a few hundred yards remained on the southern tip of the island. The view ahead was water, where the China Sea on the west merged into the dark blue of the Pacific Ocean. The last military communication issued to all field units was brief: 'Okinawa secured, stand by for further orders.' It was finally over, and a reserve regiment would move through to round up any stragglers who might surrender. This was possible, but highly improbable. Last night's puny and futile Banzai charge had taken the junior officers and staff personnel. As it was from the first shot fired, the Japanese soldier would die to the last man for his Emperor, and the fanatical code of Bushido.

"Do ya think we'll be pullin' out, Jake?" Corporal Johnny Bowman lowered his field glasses for a better view of the enemy dead. "The sun's comin' up and it's gonna get kinda ripe around here."

"Keep your shirt on, Johnny." Sergeant Carter and his telephone were almost ready. "I'll see if I can raise the command post. They probably think we got blown up last night."

The front lines were extended in a zigzag pattern along a low-lying ridge. A rifle platoon from Fox Company, 2nd Battalion, occupied the crest with the usual two man foxholes. High on a rise to their right, Carter and his two men had set up observation post number five, or by simple designation, OP-5. This by itself was hazardous duty, spotting for the artillery and observing enemy activity night and day. It was sight by day and listening by night.

Every infantry regiment, in its headquarters, had an Intelligence Section, known informally as R-2, or the 2 section. These were the scouts, trained and experienced in reconnaissance, map reading, and manning observation posts scattered across the width of the infantry lines. An OP was a prime target for Japanese artillery. Only a master of camouflage would survive. Stated succinctly in the Oriental philosophy: 'It's easier to kill the beast if you put out its eyes.'

The third member of their team was Corporal Moe Chernikov, asleep in a connecting trench leading down the reverse slope. He had taken the last night watch, and it was his turn in the rotation of rest. The normal number in a scout group was four, but they were reorganized. Three months ago they landed with sixteen, and now only six were fit for duty. The rest were either dead or wounded, and no replacements were available.

The fourth member was worth more than a mere mention. He was Private M. O. 'Arkie' Jonas from the mountains of Arkansas. A spontaneous and real backwoods humor provided a comic relief for everyone who came within his range. Once he was asked about his hometown, and he replied, 'The town I come from is so small, you can throw the newspaper up in the air, and read it before it hits the ground.' His favorite cuisine was 'Bull Dick Stew,' referring to the genitals of a male steer. Two weeks before he had been wounded, stitched across both legs by a lone machine gunner. A final tribute to his rural wit would linger in their hearts: 'I wonder what the Arkie would say about that.'

The Sergeant made contact with the CP, his command post. He placed the receiver back in its leather carrying case. "Good news, Johnny. We're being relieved by the Eighth Marines today. Lieutenant Chandler's gonna call us back."

"At least they ain't shootin' at us anymore. Looks like they've had it."

Jake looked at the sleeping Chernikov with disgust. "Get rid of Moe's empty bean can. He's attracting every fly in the neighborhood."

"That crazy bastard can sleep anywhere. Look at him, covered with 'em and he's out cold." Bowman scooped up the green container and flung it over the back-side of the hill. The hungry little pests spiraled after the missile, intent on finishing their morning repast.

In a few minutes they would receive an interesting and welcome visitor. In a swail on the ridge below, a young Lieutenant was climbing out of a foxhole to make his way up the slippery incline.

"Hello. Anybody home up there? May I come up?"

Jake looked over the side. "Sure, come on up. You're just in time for the cocktail hour."

"Thanks, make mine a dry martini." The officer slid into

their position. "I'm Lieutenant Lyons, Joe Lyons from Fox Company, and that's my platoon down there."

Moe was awakened and sat up while Jake made the introductions. "What brings you to the penthouse, Lieutenant?"

"We're pulling out soon, and I just came up to thank you." Lyons removed his steel helmet and scratched his matted hair. "Your artillery fire direction is the best I've seen, and last night.... hell, I've never seen that many parachute flares."

Bowman glanced sideways to scan the scores of white silk patches lying between the shell holes. "We like to see what we're doin', sir. And your boys did some mighty fine shootin'."

The Lieutenant had mixed emotions about the carnage. "Yes, we do what we have to do, but it seems like such a waste."

"The whole damn war is a big waste if you ask me, Lieutenant. How long have you been out here?"

Second Lieutenant Joseph P. Lyons was a typical reserve officer, deferred from active duty to finish his studies at the University of Oregon. Because he was enrolled in the ROTC, the Reserve Officer Training Corps, he was allowed to graduate before reporting to the Platoon Leader's School at Quantico, Virginia. After spending three months at Quantico, he received his gold bars and was immediately dubbed a 'ninety day wonder' by the enlisted men. He was young and new, just like the boys in his command. The masses of officers and men had been loaded on troopships and sent across the Pacific as infantry replacements. Many died on their first day of combat, while the remainder pressed forward, hopefully maturing into veterans. For the most part, the men in Lyon's platoon were all newcomers, boys in their late teens.

"Let me see." Lyons was counting with his fingers." We landed about two weeks ago. Been on the line about ten days."

There was something about the man and his intellectual mannerisms that intrigued Carter. "Where you from, Lieutenant? What did ya do back in the States?"

"Just another college boy, from Portland, Oregon. I was studying history. Hope to be a history professor someday."

Bowman threw in his own reality. "Ya won't be studyin' history out here, sir. You'll be makin' it."

"Yes, I know." Lyons reached into his pocket and withdrew a note pad and pencil stub. "I'm keeping a journal. I'd like to record your names, if you don't mind."

"Did ya hear that Moe? You're gonna be in the history books, just like Napoleon."

Chernikov was awake, stirring a cup of cold instant coffee. "Yeah, but that son of a bitch made more money than I do."

The historian was scribbling on his pad like a secretary taking dictation. "I became interested in the Japanese, and I've done extensive research on their culture, especially the Samurai Warrior. Last night we saw the Banzai sacrifice, and this morning the ritual of Hari Kari."

"Ya mean harry carey, Lieutenant? Those generals jumpin' off the cliff?" Jake craved specific answers, and the expert was seated before him. "The three of us been together for a year and a half, and we still can't figure it out. They want to die for their country and we want to live. It's crazy. I wonder if the people back home know what we've been up against?"

"Of course they don't, and most of them never will." Lyons paused to explain. "You see, to the Japanese soldier, capture or failure is a disgrace. His holy spirit could wander forever in humiliation. If he dies in battle, or apologizes in Hari Kari with his life, he goes to his Imperial Heaven as a god."

"Then we done 'em a favor. Their heaven is full of new recruits." Bowman leant back, his brow knitted in thought. "My mom ain't never going to believe this story. She'll just be wondering what the Japanese mothers are thinkin'."

"The civilians aren't allowed to think about politics, Johnny. They do what they're told. It's the Bushido Code of absolute obedience."

The Last Souvenir

"Yeah, I know, Lieutenant. When we hit Japan, even the old ladies will be waitin' for us with pitchforks."

Lyons dropped his pad and stared at the sea. "After studying the Samurai philosophy of death before dishonor, I shall offer a prediction. The war will go on for at least one more year, maybe two. When it's over, there will be no more Japan. The Japanese Empire will cease to exist."

The philosopher found agreement from his audience of three veterans, but not sympathy. The fiery Chernikov had the most resolve.

"Yeah, and a million more dead marines. They asked for it, but they ain't gonna win, we are."

The ensuing discussion fell to the lowest of political levels. They were far below the scope of policy making. No matter what kind of master strategy evolved, they were stuck doing the job. They were riflemen and nothing else. Whatever meaning there was in their civilian lives was meaningless out here. Many questions arose with no answers forthcoming. The final solution was too terrible. It had to be painted with a hard crust of fatalism and a light-hearted sense of humor.

"I'll have to get back to my men pretty soon." Lieutenant Lyons sharpened the pencil with his utility knife. "Do you have a special story you can tell me? You know, a little vignette for my book."

"Jake, tell him about the time that Jap officer blew himself up right in front of you."

The Sergeant shook his head. "Naw, that's a grim story. Nobody's gonna believe it."

"I will. Tell me in your own words, this is what history is all about."

Carter was usually modest about his exploits, but this time he relented. "OK, Lieutenant, but first you gotta know things happen so fast it's kinda hard to remember the details when it's all over."

"I understand. Please continue."

A sudden lack of oxygen gripped the Sergeant, and he sucked in a deep breath. "Anyway, about a month ago we were on patrol lookin' for infiltrators. You know, the suicide squads that sneak back into the rear areas and raise hell. Well, we found 'em in a patch of sugar cane. I'd fired my last round so I went down on one knee to reload my rifle. Well...." He paused.

"Go on, Jake."

Jake nodded at the Lieutenant and continued. "Like I was sayin', I was shovin' a new ammo clip in my rifle when a Jap major holding a smokin' grenade jumps up about ten feet in front of me."

"Oh my God, he had you cold turkey." Lyons was writing feverishly. "Then what happened?"

Jake hesitated again, almost overwhelmed by the memory, and the clammy fear he had experienced. "I thought for sure my time was up, like I'd just bought the old wooden cross. I slouched down in the sugar cane and, like I told you, things went kinda fuzzy. Anyhow, I could see the Jap through a gap in the cane and he musta been wounded 'cos he fell forward and slammed the grenade into his gut. He just blew up. Blew himself right in half. The concussion was so bad I was half deaf the rest of the day." Jake leant back and looked up at the sky as if he was reliving the ordeal.

"That's an incredible, but not an unusual story." The Lieutenant shook his head and finished writing.

Sergeant John H. Carter was a California boy, born and raised in southwest Los Angeles. From the age of six his first love had been sports, excelling in track, football and swimming. He looked the part too. Not pretty, but with his blond hair and blue-gray eyes, together with a five foot ten inch, one hundred and eighty pound frame, he presented a sports magazine image of an athlete or an ocean surfer. His features were,

The Last Souvenir

in fact, a rubber stamp of his Scandinavian heritage. In High School, his life became complicated when he fell in love with Tokiko, a second-generation Japanese-American girl and sister of his best friend. To further confuse the matter, the war with Japan had started. Tokiko and her entire family were taken into custody and shipped to an internment camp. They were farmers, and their land was quickly confiscated under a new federal law. They lost everything and were gone from his life. Jake had severely mixed emotions about fighting the Japanese when he enlisted in the Marines, yet he was young enough to overcome them and strong enough to look to the future.

Soon after being shipped overseas a new side of his personality developed. He was a class 'A' businessman, constantly sniffing out deals ranging from dry clothing and extra rations to beer and whiskey. He used battlefield souvenirs as a medium of exchange. There was always a swap to be made or a deal he could close. He never actually stole anything, and yet there were times when this seemed doubtful. One day he arrived in a jeep loaded with ten cases of warm beer. He claimed he traded a Japanese Arisaki rifle to a Naval Construction Battalion for the loot, and it was the truth. In the end, whatever he scrounged he shared with his buddies.

Jake's real forte was staying alive in combat, seemingly able to spot an enemy ambush a mile away. When asked how he did it, he'd simply reply, 'Hell, that's where I'd hide if I were them.' His stealth and craftiness quickly got him elevated to the rank of sergeant and chief scout, passing older and perhaps more deserving men. No one complained and the word became: 'Stick with Jake and you'll stay alive.'

The story of the Japanese officer and the hand grenade spread through the Headquarters Company, achieving the dubious title of 'Jake's Lucky Day.' Moe Chernikov couldn't resist telling the gory details.

"You should'a seen Jake when we hauled him outta that

cane patch, covered with blood and guts."

"Don't mind him, Lieutenant." Bowman felt it wasn't a necessary addition to the story. "Moe's OK. It's just that sometimes he lacks class."

"Who needs class?" Chernikov was there and he wanted to add his version. "Let me tell you what happened when we went ghoul huntin'."

Lyons began writing again, his appetite for news undiminished. "What's ghoul hunting?"

Moe realized the young officer was green and he loved a good listener. "Ghoul huntin' is searchin' dead bodies for maps and papers. We were checkin' the pockets of what was left of the Jap Major.... what the hell, that's our job. Well, this newspaper guy tossed his cookies all over the sugar cane. He was throwing up for about twenty minutes."

Moe told the story for reasons of his own. He didn't like correspondents in his patrols. His bleat was they weren't trained for combat, hence they became a liability. He was wrong but he didn't care. Jake was tolerant of his buddy, and yet he still flinched whenever the tale was retold.

Corporal Lawrence W. Chernikov was a native New Yorker of pure Russian descent. His parents had immigrated from the Steppes of Central Russia, literally chased out because their ideologies conflicted with the new Communist regime. Moe was born an American citizen in Schenectady near the banks of the Mohawk River. As a boy he was given the nickname 'Cossack', which he hated. As he grew in height to six foot five inches even the bravest of jesters began to back off. His high cheekbones and thick black hair, growing low on his forehead, gave his squinty eyes a menacing look. Long, lean muscles and stringy arms supporting a pair of huge powerful hands added to 'big Moe's' 'no-nonsense' appearance. He was one of those rare but true war lovers, volunteering for anything that would put him in the thick of it. He was fascinated by Carter and

Bowman, trailing after them like a hulking mascot. Smart and loyal, he was very protective of his smaller buddies. It was generally understood that, 'If you mess with Jake or Johnny, you'll have to deal with Moe.'

It was time for Lieutenant Lyons to leave, and he raised himself to a crouch, taking one last look at his new friends. He saw them as the real veterans who carried the burden of war on their backs. Unlike himself, and his young replacements with new equipment, their uniforms were faded almost white from months of hot sun and inclement weather. The cloth of their once green dungarees was ripped and torn by numerous bouts with barbed wire and sharp coral. Lyons felt a ground swell of comradeship sweep through him, as though he had been invited to join a very exclusive fraternity.

"I sure hope I see you fellows again. Where can I find you?"

Jake shared the same sentiments. "We're in the 2 section, Headquarters Company, Lieutenant. Just ask anybody."

"Do you have any last words of wisdom for a rookie Lieutenant and his brood of chicks?"

It was Bowman's turn to play sage. "There's one thing we learned, sir. Heroes die the quickest. Tell your kids not to take any dumb chances."

"That's good advice, Corporal. Thanks." With a final wave, Lyons was gone.

"Seems like a helluva nice guy, Johnny."

"Yeah, sure is." Bowman spoke with a tinge of sadness. "Hope he makes it so he can write his book."

John C. Bowman was an upstate New Yorker who liked to brag about the beautiful apple orchards and flowering countryside. He was nicknamed Johnny B to distinguish him from two other prominent Johnnys in the Company. Six foot tall and lean of body, the long-striding, slightly pigeon-toed Johnny B was the handsome one with Cary Grant-like features. Being intelligent and smart could have made him vain but hadn't. Like the rest, he had endured three months without a decent haircut, and at least a week with no shave. Shaving with no lather in the front lines was not to his liking. Johnny B was a budding con man. Because of this, he was attracted to the off-duty scams of Jake Carter. Jake would hatch an idea and Johnny B would quickly jump on it, adding his own twists and turns. He was a perfect henchman and the two were inseparable.

A light buzzing from the field telephone caught their attention. Carter raised the receiver. "OP-5, Jake speaking." The developing smile on his face and nodding head told of good news. "Wilco, Lieutenant, over and out."

"Whats'a story?"

With the telephone back in its case, Carter began disconnecting the wires. "That was Lieutenant Chandler. He's calling OP-4 right now. They'll pick us up on the cart path about a mile back, two trucks, in one hour."

The announcement was overdue. Bowman and Chernikov started to stuff sundries in their field packs, bringing a warning from their sergeant.

"Not so fast, boys. First they want us to stick around a few minutes and observe the Eighth Marines movin' through."

Chernikov pointed east. "Here they come, through the pass about two hundred yards to the left."

A long column of Marine riflemen with fixed bayonets was filing through the gap and fanning into a wide skirmish line. Only a pitifully small handful wore faded uniforms that marked them as old-timers, most probably corporals and sergeants. They marched slowly in two waves toward the silent ridge ahead. As a precaution, two machine gun crews planted their weapons on the high ground, providing covering fire in case of an eruption. Below them, a mortar section was ready with smoke shells. A platoon of engineers waited for the riflemen to reach the ridge. These experts carried packs of C-

4, an explosive powerful enough to blow off the top of a mountain. The caves would be sealed, entombing the last of any reluctant enemy survivors forever.

A loudspeaker truck showed its nose, blaring surrender instructions in Japanese. The most gruesome sight came last. A bulldozer and burial detail rounded the corner and began gouging a long furrow in the already mutilated soil. This would constitute a mass grave, the final resting-place for the dedicated enemy dead. In military parlance, this was casually called a mop-up.

From their perch high above, Jake and his buddies watched the grisly performance in silence. Not a shot was fired. Bowman finally summed up his nausea.

"Come on, Jake, we've seen enough. Let's get the hell outta here. This place is startin' to give me the creeps."

CHAPTER THREE

The sky was clear and a gentle breeze swept across their faces as the three men walked through the fields. The front lines no longer existed. Each man was pondering on the events of the last three months as he trod along the narrow path between the shell holes. The whole thing seemed like a dream.

To their left the China Sea was calm with only a soft rolling motion. On the horizon the big warships cruised, alert and still fearful of another air attack from the Japanese Kamikaze Corps. The battle was over, but the war was far from finished.

Johnny B, in the lead, turned his head and looked over his shoulder. "Hey Jake, there's the cart path. It ain't much. Hope our trucks can make it."

"Course they can make it, they've got four wheel drive. Find a place to squat and we'll break out some rations."

"Here come the guys from OP-4." Moe pointed and began waving wildly.

The OP-4 group waved back. They had also lost a man and only numbered three. Corporal Del Stack was in charge. Del, a salty veteran of three major campaigns, was in his mid twenties and the oldest of the lot. He was followed by Corporal Russ Keeler and private first class Bill Hull, the former milkman from Indiana. The fourth member, Private Clary Berg had been killed by a sniper four weeks ago.

When the two groups met by the road it was like old home week. They were grinning and slapping each other on the back as they piled their equipment by a small embankment.

Jake walked up to Del Stack and shook his hand. "Haven't got your ass shot off yet, Del. What's your secret?"

Del laughed. "Clean living my boy, clean living. Speaking of which, you're filthy. Why don't you take a bath and set a good example for your men?"

"A bath? What's that? Isn't that some kind of strange ritual they have back in the States?"

The two men smiled as Russ Keeler piped in. "Hey Johnny, you guys got any chow?"

Johnny B. glanced at Keeler and looked away. "Russell, don't you ever think of anything but food?"

"Not out here, what else is there to think about?"

Moe suddenly pointed across the fields. "Something coming at us, way over there."

The men instinctively grabbed their rifles and began to take cover. The wily Jake Carter stayed upright, his hand shielding his eyes from the sun. "Put down those damn guns you idiots. It's a jeep, one of ours."

"Can you see who's drivin'?"

Jake continued to stare in the direction of the approaching jeep. "It's the Chaplain, Padre Turner. Wonder what the hell he's doing way up here."

"You know our padre, he's liable to pop up anywhere."

Popping up everywhere was his style for sure. Lieutenant William R. Turner, the regimental chaplain, was by far the most popular man in the regiment. Catholic by faith, he had been warned by his commanding officer to stop going so close to the front. 'That's where I'm needed the most,' he would say, 'and that's where I belong.' Giving comfort to the wounded and reading the last rites over the dead.

Once, when accompanying stretcher-bearers to the rear, he was accosted by the Colonel who shouted angrily, 'Lieutenant Turner, step over here!' When the padre complied, Colonel Mason began to chew on him. "I've told you before and I'm going to tell you just once more. The Manual states clearly that every man in my regiment will carry a weapon in the combat area, and this includes you. You were issued a pistol, now wear it!"

The padre looked sheepishly at the ground. "But Colonel, it's not just my religion I'm concerned with, I don't even know how to shoot a gun."

The Colonel relented when he saw the look on Turner's face. "O.K. Padre, you don't have to shoot anybody with it. Just wear it as a favor to me."

"Yes sir, as a favor to you I'll wear it. God bless you." With that he spun on his heels and ran to catch up with the stretcher-bearers. The story about the Padre and the pistol spread throughout the regiment and became a constant source of humor to his boys.

The men stood in the road waving cheerfully as the padre drove up and parked his jeep. "Hi ya padre." They gathered around the young priest, jabbering away. "Ya got any idea where were going?" "Has the mail come in yet?" "Have ya heard anything about our new rest camp?"

"Hold it, hold up a minute." He held up his hands for quiet. "First of all the engineers are building a big camp for us up north, just east of Motobu. Second, there will be a mess hall with three hot meals a day. Third, we'll have hot showers and clean uniforms. Fourth, we'll have tents, cots and new blankets. And last but not least, the mail came in." Smiling broadly as his 'boys' cheered and clapped each other on the back. The padre was out of his jeep by now and removing a large wooden box from the back seat. The box was full of tropical chocolate bars and the padre passed them around. The candy bars were large, about the size of a big cake of soap, and molded hard to prevent melting in the hot sun. The men had the wrappers off and were gnawing away at the sweet taste. They broke into groups of twos and threes and began to speculate about their new lifestyle.

"Jake, I have something special for you." The padre put

The Last Souvenir

his hand on Jake's shoulder and steered him to the other side of the jeep. He reached into a small bag and pulled out an oversized pink envelope. The envelope smelled of perfume and was addressed to him in care of Father Turner.

"For me padre? How did you get it? Who's it from?"

"Jake, do you remember when we first landed, you were sent out to search the bodies of all those dead Japanese boys?"

"Yeah, I remember, padre. It was down by those old barracks."

"And one of those boys had a pin-up picture of Shirley Temple in his pocket. You brought it back and gave it to me."

Jake nodded. "Sure I recall that. He was young and only a private. Didn't have any maps or anything but he was carrying little Shirley Temple's picture around with him. Seemed kinda weird to me. I've often wondered where he got it and why he kept it."

"You know they showed her movies all over the world. She was a big star. Well anyway, I took the liberty of writing her a letter about you and sent her the picture as a souvenir."

"How the heck did you do that, padre? How did you know how to reach her?"

The Padre smiled. "I addressed the envelope: Miss Shirley Temple, Hollywood California; trusted in God and prayed for the U.S. Post Office."

"You're beautiful padre. So she wrote back and you got her letter. Amazing."

The padre handed the pink envelope to Jake. "She sent a picture too. She's a grown up young woman now and very beautiful. I suggest you read the letter first so you don't get side tracked. I hope you don't mind I've already opened and read it."

"No problem padre, it's addressed care of you anyway." He pulled out his letter and unfolded it. It was written on pale pink stationary with tiny yellow and white flowers for a border.

The handwriting was obviously feminine. It started:

> *Dear Sergeant Carter:*
> *It was wonderful of you and Father Turner to think of me and take the time to send me this unique souvenir. It has become one of my most treasured things.*
> *My family and I send our hearts and our love to all of you boys who are so far away from your homes.*
>   *God's speed and good fortune.*
>   *Warmly,*
>   *Shirley Temple*
>   *P.S. I hope you like the picture. I would like to meet you in person someday.*

"WOW PADRE! She says she wants to meet me. Now for the picture." Jake stared at the enlarged snapshot in disbelief. Shirley was no kid anymore. It was taken in a farm setting with a white rail fence in the background. She had one hand on a fence rail and the other hand on her hip. Her tight blue jeans were rolled up just below her knees and showed a pair of penny loafers with no socks. She wore a sleeveless plaid shirt with three buttons open in the front. The Shirley Temple look was still obvious but a mature woman showed through. Her hair was medium length and slightly curly, and her smile revealed her famous dimples.

Jake continued to stare as the padre looked over his shoulder. Suddenly big Moe edged in. "You guys talking about Shirley Temple, that little kid movie star?"

"She's no kid anymore, Moe."

"Let me see that," and with his big paw he snatched the picture out of Jake's hand. "Hey you guys. Check this. Shirley Temple's got tits now."

The men crowded around Moe's big frame, straining to see the young woman. "Yeah, she's got a nice fanny too."

The Last Souvenir

Jake barged in and grabbed back his picture. "Don't you gorillas have any respect for American womanhood? Knock it off. And show a little respect for the padre too."

"That's O.K. son," the padre responded, putting his hand on Jake's arm. "Even though I'm an ordained priest of the Holy Catholic Church and a devout celibate I am fully aware of the biological urges of the young human male."

Jake blinked as he turned and looked at Father Turner. "If all those big words mean horny, padre, you hit the nail on the head."

The young soldier was admiring the picture again as the Chaplain looked into his face. "Do I detect a little water in your eyes? I don't see tough marine sergeants cry very often," he joked.

"Naw, it's just that I've forgotten what home was like. Someday, maybe, I could have a pretty girl like that."

"I can't answer that one, my son. Nobody can. I just put my faith in God and pray that we'll all get home safe someday."

"Put in a good word for me padre. I'm inspired again." Jake smiled and turned back to his men.

It is very difficult for a young rifleman to adjust to peace after months of warfare. His senses are so acutely tuned to sounds or sudden movements that they can't be easily turned off. Learning to sleep with one eye open is a bad habit to develop if you want to live in a happy, peaceful world.

The first real signs of peace had come. Many species of native birds were gingerly making their way south. One loud-mouth resembling the American Mocking Bird sat on a burned bush across from the men, squawking his head off. Moe threw a rock at him but the obstinate bird stood its ground and squawked louder. A little fly-catcher zoomed in and out of the shell holes, gorging itself on the big ugly black flies. Overhead, seagulls and white-tailed terns were swooping down, ripping up and turning the earth to provide all kinds of seeds and other goodies.

The fascinating acrobatic show was interrupted by Del Stack. "Here comes another jeep." He pointed his finger down the road and stood up. "It's a gray jeep."

"Yeah, it's navy. Couple of sailors too. Where do they think they're going?"

The Jeep slid to a stop in front of them. The letters USN were stenciled in black on the bottom of the windshield frame. The driver was an older man wearing the cap and visor of a chief boatswain's mate. Stuck in his unshaven face was the stub of a half chewed cigar. The other man wore no cap. He was young, in his late teens and sporting a neatly trimmed blond crew cut. They were both wearing the light blue denim dungarees of the U.S. Navy.

The younger sailor stood up in the jeep and spoke first in a high-pitched voice. "Hey, you guys been up to the front?"

Moe looked at the kid with mild annoyance. "Naw, we're a troop of boy scouts working on our merit badges."

The older man still sat behind the wheel sizing up the marines. "Looks more like you've been playing mud pies in a pig sty."

"Very funny swab jockey. Where do you people think you're going?"

"We're looking for souvenirs. Ya got any souvenirs?"

Moe turned sideways and patted his backside. "Ya see this big ass? This is the only souvenir I want to take home." Jake was strolling up, furtively stroking his chin with his thumb and forefinger. Something he always did when he sensed the possibility of a scam. Johnny Bowman's antenna picked up the gesture immediately and felt the exhilaration of a new con game. He sidled up to Jake's elbow. "What's up pal, what you thinking?" he whispered.

The sergeant held up his hand. "Let me think a minute." After a brief pause he was ready and sauntered casually up to

The Last Souvenir

the gruff old chief. "I'm Sergeant Carter, Jake Carter, and this is my buddy Corporal John Bowman."

The chief didn't offer a handshake. "Muldoon, Chief Motor Machinist, and this here is Seaman Henderson. We're off a repair ship anchored up north."

"We're looking for souvenirs, you know, something to send home," the young seaman added. "The only Japs we ever see are diving their planes at us from ten thousand feet."

The rest of the men kept glancing down the road for a glimpse of their trucks. Not Jake. He stared fixedly at the two sailors, like a spider tending his web. He knew there were thousands of men at sea who wanted mementos of combat. He also knew the rear areas had been picked clean by non-combatants. Jake finally spoke, looking at the Chief Machinist. "Muldoon, you're in business aren't you? You can pick up a lot of bucks selling souvenirs to the fleet. I happen to know those guys are loaded with back pay."

Muldoon tried to look shocked. "Sergeant, how can you think such a thing. Whatever I find, I send home to my kid brother."

"Bullshit, Muldoon." Jake's eyes turned to flint.

The old chief's face sobered. "OK, OK, I can see you're a hard man to deal with. Let's cut to the chase. I've collected a few coins from my shipmates and I told them I'd see what I could scrounge up."

Jake knew it was time to strike. "Johnny, gimme that Jap canteen hanging on your cartridge belt." Johnny B. reached around his waist and produced the canteen. It was a dark khaki colored oval shape, with Japanese writing on the flat side. "Look it's got writing on it, probably the Nip's name." He held it up for the sailors to see. The young sailor was hooked.

"Wowie, that's a real one. I'll give you five dollars for it."

"Fifty." Jake was hard and fast.

"Fifty bucks? That's almost a whole months pay for me." The kid sat down in his seat.

"Listen junior, you might as well know we're the last store in town. All the dead Japs are buried. The engineers were here three days ago. They bulldozed 'em to keep down the flies. I'll give you my price and you can take it or go home empty." Jake's monotone was deadly. "One more thing. We take the risks of booby traps, land mines, and any other devious tricks those little bastards can come up with." He looked Muldoon straight in the eyes. "In other words, we take the chances and you pay."

The young sailor was stunned, but the salty old Muldoon had melted down to reality. "OK Carter, fifty bucks it is. What else you got?"

Private Hull stepped forward, unbuckling the straps on his pack. He pulled out a packet wrapped in wax paper containing four eight by ten inch glossy pictures. "Ain't these beauties? Jap pin up girls. I took 'em off a dead sergeant. He must have been a real ladies man, they're all different and autographed."

Muldoon took the pictures and carefully scrutinized them. After pondering for a minute he looked up. "I'll give you two bucks apiece."

"Ten each. Forty bucks, all or nothing." Carter didn't even blink.

"You're a tough cookie Sarge. You're not going to bend. I can smell it. Alright, now what else you got?"

Jake nodded his assent as he glanced both ways, looking out for their transportation. He turned to Chernikov. "Moe, grab my pack for me. It's right there by your heel."

The big man bent down and tossed the pack to him. Johnny B. was next to him, gleefully scribbling notes on a candy wrapper. The master salesman was about to administer the coup de grace. He produced a neatly folded piece of white raw silk and began to open it. He had a genuine Japanese battle flag, the most prized souvenir of the fleet. The large red meatball in the center signified the Rising Sun, the symbol of the Japanese Empire. Radiating from the sun, like spokes of a wheel, were hundreds of Japanese characters written in black ink. These denoted good wishes and signatures of the owner's closest comrades.

    Young Henderson was standing up again in the jeep. "Holy Mackerel, where did you get that?"

"Got it from a dead captain."

"Has it got any blood on it?" The kid revealed a maudlin curiosity.

  "Nope, you can tell your kid brother he took a bullet in the head." Jake was ready to strike again. "Muldoon, your tab is up to ninety bucks. Make it an even two hundred and I'll throw in the flag."

Jake was firm and the Chief knew it. Poor Muldoon was breathless. In his bracket it was almost two months pay. He also knew he could sell it for more money to the fly boys on the aircraft carriers. He really wished he could lay his hands on a hundred of the damn things.

"OK Carter, two hundred bucks for the whole bunch." The men cheered and began back-slapping their sergeant's back. The spider had stung again. The old sailor was happy too, already figuring out his profits as he groped in his pocket for the cash.

    Padre Turner had a big grin on his face as he watched Muldoon fill Jake's hand with greenbacks. "Jake my son, if you ever come to one of my masses when we get back to the States, I want you to pass the collection plate for me."

    Muldoon finished counting and smiled at the chaplain. "You got that right padre. Give this guy a mask and a gun and you'll own the whole parish in a week." Then he turned to the sagacious sergeant. "Boy, now that the dealin' is over, I have to admit I like your style. I wish we were shipmates." He extended a hand and they shook on it.

"We can do business again, Chief. There's more where that came from. Look me up. I'm in headquarters company, First Regiment."

"You got a deal buddy." With that the two sailors drove off, waving as they disappeared over the hill.

Private Bill Hull was the first to speak as he counted his money. "How did ya do it, Sarge? I only make fifty bucks a month as a private, and you conned those swabbies out of four months pay."

"Very simple, my dull witted friend." Jake was in a contented mood. "First, that fleet out there is bulging with back pay and no place to spend it. Second they never get ashore and everyone wants some kind of souvenir. Third, the whole island has been picked over, especially by the Sea Bees." He referred to the Naval Construction Battalions and their nickname. "Fourth, right now we happen to be the only game in town. But most of all Muldoon made a big mistake. He had a big wad of money in his pocket and I could see the bulge."

Hull was scratching an itch on the back of his neck. "You make it sound like an old Sherlock Holmes movie."

"Elementary my dear Watson." Jake got serious again and looked at Bowman. "Johnny, remember that Jap supply dump we found up by Machinato airfield?"

Johnny B. nodded. "Yeah, the one with all the camouflage. Why? That was two months ago."

"That's right Johnny. I told Lang the quartermaster sergeant about it and sent him over with a truck. Well, he stashed it for us, and there's a whole truckload of enemy equipment headed north right now."

"No shit Jake. You're a genius."

"Thanks but no thanks, Johnny my boy. Let's just say opportunist." With that he strutted to the center of the road and faced his men. With hands on hips and a smile on his face he smugly announced. "Gentlemen, me thinks we are going into the souvenir business."

CHAPTER FOUR

First Lieutenant James B. Chandler had troubles of his own back at the CP. CP or Charlie Peter was the military acronym for Command Post, Headquarters Company, First Marine Infantry Regiment. Maps, papers, aerial photos and other documents had been piling up at an alarming rate. They were not to be thrown away. Everything had to be crated and shipped to the Main Intelligence Base at Pearl Harbor for further dissection. Paperwork was a drag and he knew it, but he was stuck.

Chandler was not a typical line officer, but a natural intelligence man. He could put a magnifying glass over an aerial photograph and spot a flea on a hound's back. With use of map overlays and captured documents, and the Colonel looking over his shoulder, he would pinpoint enemy strong points with astonishing accuracy. At times, the whole regiment would move on his word alone. The responsibility was enormous.

He was constantly struggling with obesity. Even the rigors of front line duty couldn't bring down his weight. His most pronounced feature was his guttural voice. When he spoke, he sounded like his words were coming from the bottom of a deep water well. His laughter erupted with a hollow, 'Ho Ho Ho', as though emulating Santa Claus on Christmas Eve. He was a perfect bass singer for a barber shop quartet.

Chandler was born in New Hampshire, giving him the ethics and mores of a Down East Yankee. When his family moved to Philadelphia, he attended and graduated from the University of Pennsylvania with honors. His high IQ was quickly acknowledged when he enlisted, and he was immediately transferred to intelligence work.

The Last Souvenir

'Lieutenant Jimmy' was more like a mother hen than an officer. He loved his men and they respected him. He hated casualty lists, almost taking them personally. He once said; 'Sometimes I wish I could trade my commission for a set of Corporal stripes, just to be with you guys.' He was a devout Christian and family man, and wrote home often. During mail call he would be besieged by letters from his wife and five year old daughter. The little girl could only scribble for her daddy but Jimmy loved it.

The two main men in Chandler's 2 section were 'Boston Leo' Beauchamp and George 'Mike' Michaelson. They were his draftsman and map experts. Leo was actually from Framingham Massachusetts, but 'Boston Leo' was easier to say. He was a small powerful man with USMC tattooed on his upper left arm. His facial features were fine and his piercing eyes showed an ever present sense of humor. A side view of his face showed a long protruding nose, giving him a hawk-like profile.

One famous story about Leo Beauchamp would return to haunt him for the rest of his days. He was standing on a high ridge with a pair of binoculars, staring off at the distance. Mike was next to him. They were watching a squad of riflemen clearing the enemy out of a patch of sugar cane. Leo put down his glasses for a moment and turned his head to speak to his buddy. Suddenly, a half spent grenade fragment hit him on the side of his nose. He let out a yelp and sat down with his hand up to his face. "Shit, I'm hit! Right on the nose."

Mike instinctively removed the compress bandage from the first aid packet on his cartridge belt. He pried Leo's hand away and slapped the bandage on his face. When the pain began to subside, the two men stood up. Mike looked down and saw the small fragment lying at his feet. He bent over and picked it up, handing it to Leo. "Ya see, I told you some day you'd get shot in that big beak of yours. Here's a souvenir for ya."

"Blow it out your ass, you bastard. Can't you see I'm dying?"

Mike laughed. "Come on pal, I'll help you down to the aid station."

Leo sported a large white bandage on his nose for two weeks. His left eye stayed black for a month, but he refused to be evacuated to the rear. They even offered him a Purple Heart Medal, but he refused.

Mike Michaelson hailed from the southern tip of Florida, the other end of the eastern seaboard. Burly in stature, he took a pragmatic approach to everything, especially humor. He seemed to find a way to laugh at anything. He and Leo became comrades on the first handshake. Mike too had a distinctive nose. It had been smashed to one side years ago in a high school football game, and never properly straightened. He had the countenance of a seasoned prize fighter, which belied his kindly nature. The men had dubbed Mike and Leo with the dubious distinction of having the most famous proboscises in the regiment. Nothing is sacred in the closeness of an infantry outfit.

Mike had his combat story too, but it was grim and gave him a deeper respect for the riflemen at the front. It happened on night guard duty weeks before. Even though the command post was more than a mile behind the front, it was within easy walking distance. The Japanese infiltrator could crawl that far on his belly for a chance to commit suicide and take a few marines with him. The veterans knew this and so did the Colonel, who always went by the book.

A wide defense perimeter was established around the command post each night with foxholes every fifteen or twenty feet. Every marine, even the non-combatants had been basically trained as riflemen, thus accepting the mandate of an occasional stint at night guard duty. Mike the draftsman was no exception. Even the cooks from the field kitchen would

The Last Souvenir

take their turns.

On the night of Mike's brush with death, he drew a midnight to two a.m. watch. There was no moon and even the stars were shrouded by black clouds. He felt like he was trapped in a giant black box as he groped his way to the assigned gun pit. He heard a low rasping voice hiss; "Halt, what's the password?"

"Fertile," Mike squeaked like a mouse with a sore throat.

"Myrtle." This completed the two word password. The other man was private Johnny Cobb, the Colonel's orderly. "Is that you Mike?"

"Yeah." Mike could only move by voice direction.

'Fertile Myrtle,' was the perfect password, containing two L's which the Japanese could never pronounce. If the Japanese had the password and tried to respond, it would sound like 'Fertah Murtah and he would be shot. The code was brutal, but efficient.

Mike slid into the hole and relieved Cobb, who spoke in a low whisper close to Mike's ear. "There's someone out there but it's too damn dark. Can't see anything. Once in a while there's a scratching noise, then nothin'. My eyes are so bugged out I'll never get them stuck back in my face."

Mike usually had a good sense of humor but this time the levity escaped him. "What'ya got here Johnny?" The adrenaline was beginning to pump through his body.

Cobb felt for Mike's hand. "Feel around the bottom of the hole. There's one flare grenade and four 'frags'," referring to the lethal fragmentation grenades. "See ya buddy, good luck." Cobb made his exit and began to slither back to the CP.

Mike was alone in the dark now as he placed his rifle on the parapet in front of him. The pupils of his eyes had shrunk to mere pinpoints as he stared futilely down the gun barrel. Suddenly he detected the same noise that Cobb had heard. It sounded like an object slowly sliding over dirt. 'What's the matter with our mortar crew?' he thought. 'They're supposed to fire a flare shell every five minutes.' An eternity passed. Suddenly a loud thump shattered the silence and Mike almost jumped out of his skin. It was one of those mortars. A star shell streaked over his head and popped, sending the metal casing whistling to the ground. The burning can of magnesium was suspended on a white silk parachute, and began swaying its way to earth. The terrain in front of him was bathed in a ghostly white as though someone had just thrown on the main switch in a football stadium.

Mike was petrified with fear as he saw the flare wafting slowly downward. He committed a cardinal sin and stuck his head up, craning his neck for any sight of the enemy. There seemed to be nothing. The flare dropped to the ground and burned out, flooding the position with darkness again, like a tidal wave of black ink. A few more minutes passed and the scratching began again. Mike looked at the luminous dial of his wristwatch. It read ten minutes after one. He'd been there for over an hour. Panic gripped him. He pulled the pin on his last flare grenade and tossed it into the open ground in front of him. The flare ignited and revealed the silhouette of an enemy soldier. He was on his hands and knees, his face only three feet away from the muzzle of Mike's rifle.

For a split second the two men were dumbfounded as they stared at each other in the eerie light. Mikes reaction was instinct alone as he closed his eyes and pulled the trigger. His shot rang true.

The next morning, after the patrols had cleared the area, a small group of marines stood around the body, viewing it with morbid curiosity. They were rear area people, unaccustomed to such a spectacle. The dead man had a neat hole in the front of his forehead but the back of his head was gone. He was lying on his side with his right hand still clutching a long samurai sword. The stainless steel blade was beginning to glisten in the morning sun.

The Last Souvenir

One of the men turned to Mike and drawled; "You got lucky, Mac. That guy was gonna hack your head off with that pig sticker." Mike gulped as he nodded in agreement.

Leo bent over and pulled the sword away from the dead man's grasp. Unbuckling the scabbard from his belt he slid the sword into it. A chaplain elbowed his way into the group and knelt beside the corpse. After making the sign of a cross he blessed the departed soul of the unfortunate man. Was this hypocrisy? Absolutely not. All chaplains were like that, living in a private world of their own.

The chaplain arose and turned to face Mike. "Try not to let this bother you, my son. Just consider it God's will and press on."

The only reply Mike could make was; "I think I'm going to be sick." He turned and walked away. Leo was on his tail, carrying a rifle in one hand and the Samurai sword in the other.

Mike had no problem telling the story in the weeks that followed. He even injected a strange form of infantry humor, but only about the fear he felt. This would be the only shot he fired in his entire military career, but the memory would hound him until his own final judgment day came.

Mike and Leo were both helping Lt. Chandler load boxes of paperwork on the two big trucks. Chandler was spluttering under his breath and shaking his head disdainfully. "This reminds me of the paper drives we used to have back home when I was a kid." They were scheduled to vacate the Command Post in fifteen minutes and head for the front where the scout groups were waiting.

Sergeant Lang was nearby at the quartermaster dump, shouting orders at a group of straining men. Chandler spotted him and trotted over. "Lang, I'm going to commandeer two of your trucks. My boys are waiting to be picked up and there's no place for them to ride."

"No problem Lieutenant. Take those two, they're both only

half loaded." Lang pointed at two big ten wheelers.

"What's in them now?" Chandler asked.

"Just a few boxes of rations, blankets, and some medical supplies. They can sit on those."

Chandler yelled at Leo and Mike. "Grab your gear and come over here." When the two men arrived he spoke in his deep voice. "I hope you two know how to drive a truck. You're both drafted as truck drivers."

"Yes sir, I love to drive these big babies. So does Mike."

Chandler nodded. "OK, let's pick up the rest of our crap and move out."

"Wait a minute, you guys got any room for a couple of hitchhikers?" It was corporal John Kovak, the interpreter and Japanese language expert. Walking with him was the Medical Corpsman, Frenchie Labeau.

"How about it Lieutenant? I'm supposed to ride shotgun on those medical supplies?"

Chandler had a wide grin on his face. "Sure, hop in. We might as well make it a real gang bang. The more the merrier."

Frenchie jumped into the lead truck with Leo and Chandler while Mike and Johnny Kovak brought up the rear. The little caravan cranked up and trundled away.

CHAPTER FIVE

Leo was having a tough time wrestling the steering wheel of his huge truck. Potholes and shell craters were everywhere. The road from the CP to the front lines had only been traveled by jeeps and a few tanks. Chandler had a big map in his lap, pointing left and right while hanging on to the dashboard. Mike carefully followed in Leo's tracks. If there were any stray land mines, Leo would blow up first.

Finally, from the top of a small hill, they could view the valley and cart path below. Jake and his boys were waving wildly. "Here. Over here!" The trucks ground to a halt and Leo was the first to dismount. Moe walked up and looked down at the little man. He was almost a foot taller than Leo.

"We knew you were coming, Leo. Saw your big nose come over the hill first."

Leo folded his arms across his chest and confronted the big man. "How would you like to get knocked on your ass, you big tub of shit?"

The two men glared at each other with fierce hostility. Then they broke into laughter and embraced. This was a game they played, like a banty rooster trying to provoke an ostrich. They were long time pals going back to boot camp in the States.

Frenchie Labeau remained in his truck while the others climbed down. He enjoyed watching their displays of comradeship in spite of the raw profanity that made him flinch. Jake broke away and walked up to the young corpsman. "Heya Frenchie. How's my favorite medico?"

"Still at it Jake, practicing meatball medicine."

Jack Carroll

Gaston Jean Claude Labeau was Jake's favorite unsung hero. Born French-Canadian out of Eastern Canada, he spoke fluent French with some knowledge of Latin. His family had migrated to Northern Michigan to farm winter wheat when Frenchie was a small boy. As a youth he began to show a deep compassion for all living things. Before he was ten he was busy mending broken wings or treating sore paws. Old 'Doc' Shiller, the local country doctor, recognized his latent talents immediately, and began to groom him as a protege. Somehow, Shiller knew that someday Frenchie would replace him as a trained medical doctor. Frenchie read every book he could borrow, including a Latin primer.

As a medic, he was awarded the Silver Star Medal for bravery under fire. Once, in the heat of combat, he raced across the battlefield to tend a wounded man. With machinegun bullets splattering around his heels he literally dragged the unconscious man to safety. With his left hand on the scruff of the man's neck, and his right hand holding a bottle of blood plasma, he towed him over two-hundred yards through the mud.

When asked about his citation he remarked humbly; "I'll always wonder if the kid made it."

Frenchie was smiling as he looked down at Jake. "I've got some good news for ya, buddy."

"Great. I can always use some good news. Lay it on me."

Frenchie climbed down from his seat and faced the sergeant. "Last week I took an ambulance load back to III Corps hospital and I saw Arkie Jonas. He's doin' fine an' bitching his head off. He's worried about his guitar; wants Lang to ship it back to Arkansas."

"I'll talk to Lang. What about his legs?"

Frenchie lost his smile. "The poor guy will walk with a limp for the rest of his life. One of the bullets severed a tendon in his knee."

"Shit! Welcome to the war." Jake could say no more.

The Last Souvenir

Chandler was stirring around. "Come on you prima donnas. It's show time. Get on board, we're headed for Shangri-La." The men split up into groups and mounted the two trucks.

"Mind if I ride with the padre, Lieutenant?" Jake pointed to the Chaplain's jeep.

"If he can stand it, it's O.K. with me. Go ahead"

Mike stood up on the truck's floorboards and announced in the tradition of the Indianapolis Speedway; "Gentlemen, start your engines." The three vehicles lurched into motion and began to feel their way down the very uncertain road.

"It's nice to have your company Jake. It gives us a chance to talk. You're thinking about Arkie, aren't you?" The padre's jeep was bringing up the rear.

"It's not just that, Father. It's the whole mess in general." Jake gestured towards the fields with his open palm. "We totally creamed this place and lost a lot of good men doin' it. Is this land really that important?"

"You're probing the mysteries of ages, Jake. The Bible says the meek shall inherit the earth."

Jake emitted a soft laugh. "The meek better hurry up, padre. Looks like the birds are goin' to beat them to it. They keep peckin' away like nothin' ever happened."

The chaplain took his hands away from the steering wheel for a moment, then re-grasped it. "My son, you've just given me a wonderful idea for my next sermon."

The men were somber as the convoy passed through the silent battlefields. Every ridge and valley jogged a personal memory. The fury of fire had switched to the futility of waste. 'Purchased, one piece of real estate, price paid in full.'

"See that, padre, that's Shuri Ridge and what's left of the old castle. That's where I got nicked."

"I didn't know you were wounded. What happened?"

"Wasn't that bad, sir. A bullet blew off the top of my boot.

The leather saved me but it sure hurt like hell. A corpsman put a patch on the cut and I went back up with the boys." Jake was minimizing the seriousness of the event, but that was his way.

"What about your boot? How could you possibly get another one?" the Chaplain asked.

"Off a dead man."

Turner's insides turned over. How can young men adapt to this kind of life? Necessity is truly the mother of invention in this front line environment. He was sorry he'd asked.

The trucks were passing through the road cut that bisected Shuri Ridge. The once glorious castle and its moat had been reduced to a heap of blasted stone blocks, a monument to accurate artillery fire. It was hopelessly beyond restoration, and would remain an eyesore for years.

"That's Wana Draw comin' up Father. That's where Clary Berg got it." Jake was pointing ahead like a tour guide. "Do you remember him?"

"I sure do. He was that nice boy from the Midwest. As I recall he was a Lutheran. Didn't he pitch for your softball team back at the Pavuvu rest camp?"

Carter nodded, and lapsed into a soliloquy of sadness. He felt personally responsible for the boy's death and a wave of guilt engulfed him. It really wasn't his fault but even his buddies couldn't convince the young sergeant.

Jake and his men had been in an observation post high above the village of Wana. Two platoons of riflemen from Charlie Company were in the ruins, preparing to move forward in a skirmish line. Johnny B. spotted a hidden 47 millimeter cannon about five-hundred yards ahead, and pointing right down their throats. Carter was on the field telephone, screaming for support from the tank battalion. Moe was on his feet, exposing himself and waving frantically for the men to wait. This was to no avail. The noise was too loud and the smoke too thick.

Jake turned to Berg. "Do you think you can get down there and warn those guys?"

"Hell yes, I'm on my way." With that Berg climbed out of the OP and began sliding down the slope. They never saw him again.

It was almost a week before the whole story came out. Jake got it from one of the sergeants in C Company.

Berg had arrived in time and the assault was delayed. Only God knows how many lives he saved. He was hiding behind a stone wall with a squad of riflemen while the tanks were moving into position. When the rifle fire stopped he heard an old woman crying in the rice paddy directly ahead. With complete disregard for his personal wellbeing he jumped over the wall and ran forward to save her. He carried her back and deposited her safely over the wall when a bullet struck him in the side of the head. He never knew what hit him.

Jake was relating the story to the Chaplain and shaking his head. "I never should have sent him, padre. The kid was too gung ho. I should have gone myself."

Father Turner accepted Jake's melancholy as a form of confession. "You mustn't let this become a complex of guilt, my son. He was doing his duty and you were doing yours. Only God can be the final judge."

"Thanks Father, you've been a great help. I'll try to see it differently."

The little motorcade was sweeping down into the Wana Valley now, and the ruins of the village were approaching on the left. A silent pall hung in the air. Jake slowly sat erect and turned his head.

"I have a crazy idea."

"I'd like to hear it."

"Well," Jake continued, "I was wondering. If I can get Chandler to stop, do you suppose you could go down there and hold a religious service? You know, like a delayed last rites?"

"Of course." The Chaplain's face broke into a wide grin. "That's what I'm in business for! How are you going to stop the trucks?"

"Just start leaning on the horn, Padre"

'Beep, beep, beep.' Turner wasted no time as he punched the little button on the steering column.

"What the hell is that?" Chandler looked back and saw Jake standing in the jeep, waving his arm. "Pull up Leo, it looks like those guys have gone nuts."

The trucks were parked as Jake trotted up to Chandler's side. "This better be good, Sergeant, I've got a schedule to keep!"

It only took a few moments for Carter to explain the request to Chandler. The Lieutenant looked down with a pensive expression on his face, letting the request sink in. Jimmy was a religious man, constantly being saddened by the loss of one of his boys. He glanced at the men in the truck and saw them nod their approval.

"To hell with the schedule, let's do it!" He beckoned the Chaplain to join them.

The men dismounted their trucks and stood by the roadside, awaiting their next move.

CHAPTER SIX

Moe unslung his rifle and held it in a ready position. "This place looks spooky to me, Sarge."

"You're right. We better go down first and take a look."

The little village of Wana was spread out below them with the valley extending to the left. On the right was a steep cliff with a small creek trickling along its base. Footpaths seemed to wander everywhere. The once picturesque little houses had been reduced to so many piles of junk, like a tornado had twisted its way through. Broken boards, tiles, and timbers were strewn about.

By some miracle, one tiny house in the center had remained intact. It was badly scarred by bullet holes and shell fragments, but it stood alone like a sore thumb protruding from a bloody bandage.

The men were veterans of Japanese treachery and took a dim view of getting shot by a bypassed enemy soldier. The campaign was over but there's always someone who doesn't get the word.

Lieutenant Chandler sensed the caution in his sergeant's voice. "Do you want to take a patrol down there, Jake?"

"Not this time, sir. Moe and I can handle it better alone. We'll leapfrog it." Carter was alluding to the tactic of one man moving ahead while the other gave him cover. By rotating this procedure there was less chance of being caught in the open.

"The rest of you guys hit the deck. I'll take the first leg, Moe." With that Jake took off on a dead run, stopping at the end of the village. Then, Moe followed.

The two men worked their way through the little town and

started back. "Think I saw someone, Jake. Over there by that pile of rocks."

"Don't get trigger happy, I saw it too. I think it was a small boy."

In recon school both men had been trained in a smattering of Japanese phrases. Carter was about to use one. *"DEY TAY KOI, SHIM PAI SHI NAI DEY!"* Jake repeated the sentence three times. It meant, 'Come out, don't be afraid..

Moe interrupted. "Let me try this one, *CHOCK-O-LOT, CHOCKO-LOT."* The two scouts crouched and waited as the tension started to mount.

Jake spoke again in a more reassuring tone. *"DE TAY KOI, DE TAY KOI."* More moments dragged by.

Abruptly, like a puppet on a string, a native boy of about nine years popped up, his mouth shaped by half fear and half smile. He was wearing a ragged kimono, no shoes, and a crude bandage on his left forearm. It was plain to see he was starving.

Jake laid his rifle on the ground and extended both hands. "Come on little fella, we won't hurt you. Come on."

Moe was next to him by now, and held a bare chocolate bar in his hand. The boy clambered over the rock pile and gently took the candy bar from Moe. Then he backed off a pace and bowed from the waist. The huge Marine returned his bow, which somehow broke the tension. All three were smiling now.

Jake walked to the center of the road and looked up at his buddies at the top of the path. He cupped his hands around his mouth and began barking orders. "O.K. you guys, fan out and come on down. Del, take your group and check the cliff. Mike, bring a box of rations. The rest of you move out through the valley. And no shootin' unless you have to."

The men took off with their usual clockwork efficiency. Jake had a second thought. "Kovak, I need an interpreter.

The Last Souvenir

Hot foot down here on the double."

Chandler shrugged his shoulders and sidled up to Chaplain Turner. "You know, Padre, sometimes I wonder who's in command here, me or Sergeant Carter."

Turner laughed. "You're lucky to have him Jimmy. He's a good man."

Kovak had already spotted the little Okinawan boy, and was anxious to talk to him. Corporal John D. Kovak grew up in the outskirts of the Japanese settlement in San Francisco. He spoke flawless Japanese. Many of his childhood friends were Japanese-Americans, and they played together as children. The military had picked a nice plum when Johnny K enlisted.

"What do we have here Jake? He's a cute little fella."

Johnny K stood watching the boy chomp vigorously on the hard candy bar. "There sure is nothin' wrong with his teeth. I never could chew one of those damn tropical bars."

"I need you to talk their lingo. There's got to be more civilians scattered around here. See what you can find out."

Kovak talked to the child in Japanese. "Are there any more children? Where are your parents? Where are the grown-ups?"

The little boy was elated, and chattered away like he and Kovak were old pals. "Come out," he shouted, "these are my new friends. They have candy."

A wonderful sight unraveled before Johnny K's eyes. Little faces stuck up everywhere, and soon he was surrounded by a clamoring throng. The beautiful naivete of children must be universal. They respond so quickly to kindness and new adventure.

"Hey Padre, ya better bring that extra box of chocolate bars down here. I've got a bunch of new customers for you." Jake was motioning to the two officers who had remained on the road by the trucks.

The Chaplain gave the affirmative sign of the circled thumb and forefinger with his right hand. "Comin' up. Tell Kovak to

ask if any are Catholic." He chuckled and headed for his jeep.
The children numbered ten in all, boys and girls ranging from three to twelve years old. They were a bedraggled lot, but their youthful spirits were high, in spite of the adversities they had suffered. Kovak told them the 'candy man' was coming, and their spirits were lifted even higher. They giggled and snickered with expectation as they watched the Chaplain carrying the big wooden box down the path. Their exuberance had literally erased the terrors of war. It was like being home again with the joys of a family picnic.

The first little boy edged in next to Johnny K's side. "My name is Hideo. What's your name?"

Kovak looked down fondly at his smiling face. "They call me Ja Ni," translating to the phonetics of Johnny.

"Ja Ni?" Then he repeated, "Ja Ni." His face now covered with chocolate as he proclaimed to the rest of the children; "This is my friend, 'Ja Ni'."

Kovak's eyes became moist. It was impossible to be a hardbitten soldier with little children around.

Del Stack and Russ Keeler were standing with their backs against the cliff, pointing at a row of caves they had discovered. The openings were crudely camouflaged with brush and broken planks. Jake stood by the edge of the creek, evaluating the situation.

"No grenades boys. Those aren't military caves. Hold up a minute." Jake turned and shouted across the road; "Kovak, bring Hideo over here."

Kovak took the boy's hand and led him to the sergeant, speaking to him in Japanese. "Would you like to do us a big favor little buddy? Are the grown-ups hiding in those caves?" The little boy nodded eagerly. "Would you please go over there and tell them to come out? Tell them it's safe now and we have food for them."

Hideo was off, bounding over the creek and racing for the

cliff. He stripped away the brush and boards and climbed inside one of the caves. Del and Russ could hear him jabbering inside. Then he reappeared, running from cave to cave like an Oriental Paul Revere. A few moments passed. Then the horrifying sight began. The bedraggled entourage, twenty in all, filed into the daylight, blinking their eyes against the bright sun. They were thin and wizened, obviously pushing starvation. Their fear of the Americans was no secret, but their weakened condition left no room for politics. Mostly old people had remained, as the Japanese had conscripted the young ones for labor.

The Americans were appalled. How could any form of humanity be allowed to sink so low? Their kimonos were filthy and most were shoeless. Many were crawling with black fleas and too weak to brush them away.

Chandler became a titan of activity. The spectacle was so disgusting that something snapped inside of him and he began screaming orders in a way never seen before. "You men form a work party. Bring every box of rations we have! Beauchamp, get those cans of fresh water! Hull, you and Bowman, jackass the crates of blankets down here. Empty the trucks! Move it!"

Father Turner was the only one who understood Chandler's tirade. The man was only venting his anger while showing a deep empathy for his fellow man. It was actually turning into a marvelous sight.

Frenchie Labeau was the first to brave the storming Chandler. "Sir, may I set up an aid station in that little house? I'll need the medical supplies too. If you'll step over here there's something I'd like to show you."

The Lieutenant glared at the corpsman. "What is it Labeau? I'm busy!"

Tactfully, the medic lead Chandler to a pair of children standing by the house. A young girl had a dirty rag wrapped around the knuckles of her left hand, while the other was holding the hand of her little brother. "She's lost half of her little finger, sir."

"Oh no! She's about the same age as my little daughter back home. Can you help her?" Jimmy was beginning to soften.

"Yes sir, but look at this." Frenchie bent over and pulled aside the little boy's kimono, revealing his right leg. A piece of shrapnel had opened a four inch gash in his thigh. The open sore was teeming with maggots.

"Good lord, scrape off those little bastards. This is terrible!"

"Yes sir, but first you should know those worms probably saved his leg. It's one of the oldest forms of medicine. They eat the dead flesh and prevent gangrene."

"I don't care how old the cure is. Can you do anything now?"

"Yes sir, with disinfectant, sulfa powder, and clean bandages I can do the job," Frenchie replied with quiet confidence. "What about your schedule?"

"To hell with the schedule. We'll stay here till doomsday if necessary!"

"Yes sir." Labeau began herding the children into his new hospital. Leo and Mike were already hefting the medical supplies into the hut.

Chandler decided to air his frustration on the Chaplain. "Why has this place been ignored, Bill? Where's the Medical Corps? Where's the Military Government? Where's the Red Cross? Where is everybody?"

"I don't know, Jimmy. But what I can see is that you've missed your calling. You shouldn't be a line officer, you should apply to be in Military Government.."

"I couldn't leave my boys, but I suppose you're right. Better to help people rather than blowing up the world. I'll think about it."

Carter and Chernikov had preceded Labeau and his little patients into the house. At the end of the room stood a rock fireplace, reaching from floor to ceiling. In front and over the hearth was a waist-high barbecue grill. Overhead a tapered flue absorbed the smoke, which was already drifting over the valley. The hut was surprisingly well equipped with pots and utensils. Five large GI cans of meat and beans were simmering away while Jake stirred with a long wooden spoon. Moe was on his knees feeding the fire.

"Come on in, Doc." Jake pointed to a large cauldron of warming water at the far end of the grill. "Thought you might need some hot water."

Frenchie looked around in amazement. "You guys think of everything, thanks." He moved a table to the center of the room and began spreading out his surgical instruments. "I could use some of that hot water."

Jake handed him a wok. "Here, use this."

Little Hideo walked through the door grinning like a kid watching a cartoon. He was holding a box of chopsticks and porcelain bowls, probably stashed in one of the caves. He bowed and handed the box to Jake.

Jake looked down and tousled the boy's hair. "This makes everything perfect. Arigato. Thank you." Hideo backed away and bowed again.

Kovak and Johnny B. stuck their heads in the door. "Need anything, Sarge?"

"Yeah." Jake pushed them both outside and pointed to the supplies from the trucks. "Break out those blankets and spread out a couple in the street. Set up a picnic. Kovak, round 'em up and sit 'em down. Everybody eats."

Within ten minutes the villagers were seated on the blankets and the beans were distributed. They held their bowls up to their faces and the whole scene was a blur of flying chopsticks.

"Jeez, look at 'em go." Moe was looking down wagging his head. "They're really goin' for those beans. Ugh!" Meanwhile Chandler had his men busy opening crates with their utility knives. Blankets and cans of rations were in orderly stacks on the roadside. Two boxes of waterproof ponchos and a box of hand tools were also found. Saws, hammers, and nails were included, and chandler decided to leave everything.

"What are you going to tell the supply officer when this stuff turns up missing?" the Chaplain asked.

"He's a friend of mine," Chandler replied. "I'll tell him we ran over a mine and he'll write it off."

The padre walked over to Sergeant Carter, who was watching the feast. "You know Jake, this is a wonderful sight. I wish I had my camera."

"You don't need a camera, father. Just keep this picture stamped on your brain. We Americans aren't so bad after all."

CHAPTER SEVEN

The banquet was winding down and the older people were wandering away. The marvel of their rejuvenation was heart warming. Many had gone to the ruins of their respective homes, picking through the debris for salvage. It was pitiful to see, but at least it was a beginning.

The children remained seated, working on their fourth helpings. The pre-lunch chocolate bars had in no way spoiled their appetites. Their eyes were sparkling as the Marines watched in astonishment. "How could they hold so much?"

Father Turner watched Jake strolling slowly down the road. His head was turned and he was scanning the remains of a long stone wall. Turner jogged up and took a place by his side. "You're thinking about Berg, aren't you?"

"Yes Father, according to that sergeant from Charlie Company, he got it somewhere around here." The sergeant knew his quest was morbid, but he was still compelled to see. "It was right here, Padre." Jake was pointing at a large dark spot on the ground next to the wall. The bloodstain had turned black from weeks in the hot sun. Suddenly, Jake bent over with his hands on his knees, his body retching as his brow broke into a clammy sweat. Saliva was drooling from his mouth as he gasped for air. "I think I'm gonna puke. What's wrong with me? I've never done this before!" His body was heaving violently but nothing came.

The chaplain had seen this happen before. It was something common to the frontline rifleman, and his heart went out to the sergeant. The sadness and frustration in him had been building for months until his psyche opened like a dam bursting. The brutal fact was he would feel a hundred-percent better when the release was over. He was enduring nature's therapy.

The priest softly patted Carter's back. "You're going to be alright, my son. Let it come out. It's God's way of lifting your burden."

"I don't know whether to feel shame or anger. All I know is I don't want my buddies to see me like this." The sergeant was standing straight again, his composure returning.

"There's nothing to be ashamed of, I've witnessed this before. Believe me you'll feel better."

Jake's face was pale and his eyes were watery, but his breathing was returning to normal as Moe and Johnny B appeared.

"You OK, Sarge? What's going on?"

"Nothing fellas. This is where Father Turner is going to have his service for Berg. Please tell the men to gather down here." His tone so low it was barely audible.

"Sure, Sarge." As the two men turned and went striding off, Bowman turned to his companion. "What's wrong with the Sarge, Moe? He sounded subdued."

"How the hell should I know, I ain't a sergeant."

The men filed down and formed a half circle around the priest, who was standing bareheaded beside the bloodstain, a purple stole around his neck, his left hand clutching a bible to his chest. The men edged closer and doffed their steel helmets. Everyone was present, including a few of the villagers. Though they were Buddhists, they sensed the solemnity of the occasion and wanted to be part of it.

Father Turner raised his right hand and made the sign of a cross, while the men bowed their heads. "I shall begin by reciting the Twenty-third Psalm, as it applies to us all, the standing and the fallen. 'The Lord is my shepherd, I shall not want. . . .'" The priest recited from memory, with some of the men mouthing the words silently, waiting apprehensively for the part that would reach out to touch their souls. "Yea, though I walk through the valley of the shadow of death, I shall fear no evil . . ."

Each man had his own mental image of this valley, having walked through it many times. A thousand words would be needed to describe their own brand of 'fear', and even those would not do justice to the memories racing through their minds. If it were possible to pry the raw truth from the depths of a man's soul, it would be revealed in all its ugliness. 'I'm glad it was him and not me.' Some men will freely admit to this psychic phenomenon while others will close up forever, and allow a serious guilt complex to ferment. The infantryman will simply shrug it off with the words; 'His luck just ran out.'

As usual, the chaplain's service was poignant and brief, and he ended with a whispered; 'Amen'. "Thank you Father," some of the men muttered, while the rest walked away in silence, swallowed up in their thoughts. Labeau returned to his aid station.

Bowman took off in the opposite direction with Chernikov at his heels. "My feet are killin' me, they're itchin' like mad."

"Your feet are always itchin'!"

"I know. Feels like I got that green fungus growin' between my toes, like we used to get in the jungles." Johnny B reached in his pocket and pulled out a sliver of soap wrapped in toilet paper.

"Son of a bitch! Ya been holdin' out on me! Where'd ya get that?"

"Quit squawkin' you big moose, I'll share it with you. Come down to the creek."

Bowman and Cherrnikov descended the embankment to where the villagers had constructed an earthen dam and a small pool. The brownish water flowed in, forming a slow eddy in the center. It was dirty but wet and that was all Bowman needed.

Suddenly, they heard a low moan from their left and downstream. Both men dropped to a crouch and drew their pistols. "Did you hear that?"

"Yeah, I heard it," Chernikov nodded as the sound came again. "Sounds like a woman."

Under normal circumstances they would take cover and toss a grenade. They had been tricked so many times by the Japanese that it didn't pay to be foolhardy. The school of war had sharpened their senses to the keenness of a razor blade, but a temporary peace had come and they were struggling to adjust. One side of the coin held the instinct of survival, and the other showed compassion, not an easy spot to be in.

Chernikov, by far the most daring of the two, stood first. "It's comin' from those bushes down there. Come on, let's take a look."

The moaning intensified, overcoming Bowman's reticence. "It's a woman alright. Even the Japs ain't that good at play acting." Both men were aware that the islanders, being basically passive in nature, had never committed an act of violence against them. To the contrary, they had only shown fear and bewilderment.

The two scouts slowly and carefully worked their way downstream, their big .45 caliber pistols at the ready. And then they saw her, a girl in her late teens, lying on a pile of rocks at the far edge of the thicket. The signs seemed to indicate she had slipped on the bank and injured her side in the fall. She was clutching her baggy black kimona and squirming with pain.

"Hell, Johnny, she ain't no older than my kid sister. Looks like she busted her ribs."

The young woman looked up at them, her face a mask of terror, holding up her hand as if to say, 'please don't hurt me.' The Japanese had brainwashed the islanders into believing

The Last Souvenir

that when the Americans came the women would be raped and murdered. The fear was too much for her and she fainted.

"What'll we do? We just can't leave her here!" Moe looked down, his mind filled with images of his little sister lying there.

"Well don't just stand there, Tarzan, pick her up. We'll take her back and let Frenchie take a look." They put away their pistols and Moe bent over, scooping her up in his powerful arms.

"Hey, Moe, you remind me of King Kong climbing a building in New York City." The big man was scaling the bank like an ape climbing a tree.

"Shut up you fool. Can't ya see this is serious?"

Bowman smiled as they both made it to the road and headed for the village.

Frenchie Labeau was standing in front of his makeshift hospital, wiping his hands on a dark green towel. He had finished with the last of his patients and was sizing up the approaching duo. "That's some souvenir ya got there, Moe. What's up?"

"Found her down by the creek. Think she broke some ribs," Moe said breathlessly. "She passed out but she's startin' to come around. Can ya take a look at her?"

"Can do, take her inside and put her on the table."

Moe ducked his head and carried the girl through the door, noticing an old woman standing by the stove. She was busily stirring a pot full of boiling rags and appeared to be right at home. It was her house before the devastation came. When Moe placed the young girl on the table, the old lady turned her head and started chattering frantically in Japanese.

Frenchie, following close on Moe's heels was disturbed by the intensity of the outburst. "Johnny B, you better find Kovak right away! I can't understand a word she's sayin' but it sounds drastic. Moe, you get the hell outta here. I'm gonna examine her now and the little lady deserves some privacy."

Johnny B was outside yelling for the interpreter when Moe joined him, followed soon after by Frenchie poking his head out the door.

"Broken ribs eh? Only thing that's broken is her water and she's startin' to dilate!"

"Water? What water?" Moe had a dumb expression on his face.

"To put it in plain saloon talk, so you two clowns will understand, she's knocked up, she's havin' a baby."

Moe was shocked. "A baby? She can't do that HERE! She's gotta go to a hospital."

"Sorry buddy but I think God has other plans. Go find the padre. Tell him I need him on the double!" Frenchie went back inside.

The young woman was writhing and groaning on the table when Turner arrived. "They told me I'm needed here, is there something I can do?"

"Plenty Father! You're going to assist me. You can start by taking these scissors and cutting off her underwear." The corpsman was hastily sterilizing his instruments.

The chaplain looked down at the half naked girl. Her kimono was open and her legs spread apart as the older woman held down her shoulders. He began to falter. "But this is a very personal situation. I'm not sure a priest should be putting his hands down there."

"This is no time for piety, Padre! You don't want me to call in one of those bumbling marines, do you? Besides, this is God's work, isn't it?" Frenchie was at the stove now, fishing out boiling rags.

"I guess you're right, my son, when you put it that way." Turner reluctantly picked up the scissors and snipped at the crude muslin panties. The contractions were increasing rapidly.

"Good job, now pull 'em off!"

The Last Souvenir

The priest was blushing red as he fought off a wave of modesty and tried to get a grip on the emergency at hand. He turned his head away and gave a tug, exposing the girl's lower body.

Labeau nodded with satisfaction. "You're doin' fine, now grab a hot rag and wash between her legs. She's probably crawlin' with germs."

"Good heavens no! That's too much!" Turner backed off and shook his head. "Maybe I'd better change places with the old lady."

"Aw come on Padre, I want to take a picture and send a print home to your Bishop."

"THAT'S NOT FUNNY, Labeau! Don't even THINK such a thought!"

Frenchie laughed. "Sir, you'll have to admit, even a lowly corpsman has a right to a little humor once in awhile." He waved to the old lady and the two switched duties.

By now the whole gang was crowding in front of the hut, attracted by the sounds of anguish. Chandler was pacing back and forth like he was the expectant father. "This reminds me of when my little girl was born. I musta walked a hundred miles that night."

Hull was busy drumming up bets on the baby's gender while Johnny B and Moe sat on the ground with their backs against the house. They both looked like they'd just been shot. Labeau had mentioned he thought it would be a fast delivery and possibly a rough one. He had no anesthetic and had to rely on the mother's native knowledge of natural childbirth. He was right, it didn't take long.

An unearthly scream froze the men in their tracks. Frenchie had nailed a blanket across the open door and they could only guess what kind of witchcraft was occurring inside. After a brief silence they heard the slap of a hand on naked flesh, followed almost immediately by the squeal of a new baby piercing the air.

A cheer went up as the men tossed their helmets in the air. The stoic villagers could only smile as they nodded their approval. The older women were entering the house as Padre Turner emerged. He was white as a sheet and on the verge of collapsing.

"I never want to go through that again, but God bless Gaston Labeau. It's a boy."

Private Hull reacted to the news with a groan. "Oh no! I just lost my ass." In his impromptu bookmaking scheme everyone had wagered it would be a boy. He was obliged to take the other option. "There goes the forty bucks I got for those souvenirs." Grimacing as his customers lined up to get paid. "Oh well, easy come easy go."

Inside the house, the old women were working with an efficiency passed down through centuries of native culture. The dinner party had filled their bellies and virtually brought them back to life. A bed was made, diapers were cut, and the room was swabbed clean, leaving nothing more for Frenchie to do. The mother was lying quietly in the corner, covered with new blankets and holding the baby in her arms.

Unbeknown to his comrades, Gaston Labeau was not a newcomer to childbirth. Before he was seventeen he had assisted Doc Shiller dozens of times, and even with farm animals. Some divine hand had plucked him from a tree and destined him to become a physician. When the corpsman finally showed his face in the daylight he was met by a barrage of questions:

"How's she doin' doc?"

"How in the hell did you know what to do?"

"Can we see him now?"

Labeau wiped his face with a towel and held up his hand for silence as the men pressed in. "She's a brave girl and the baby is healthy. Everything went smoothly, I guess I got lucky. She only needed a few sutures."

"Ya mean ya had to sew up her. . . . ah, you know what I mean?"

Frenchie smiled knowingly as the men hung on his next words. "Yes, I had to apply a few stitches, but I left the best part open."

They roared with laughter as they patted him on his back.

To an outsider this form of humor might seem in questionable taste but it was well within the scope of front line jargon. To them life was raw and sometimes short. The more graphic it was the better they liked it.

Chandler pumped the young medic's hand. "Labeau, if it was within my power, I'd recommend you for the Congressional Medal of Honor. Congratulations!"

"Thanks Lieutenant, but they don't give out that medal for just doing your job. But anyway, everything's squared away here, we can shove off now. There's one more thing. If we can find a telephone I'd like to call the hospital for an ambulance. She needs more care, and especially antibiotics. Can we get on that?"

"You betcha! I'll personally call up the Military Government people. I'm going to light a fire under their asses about this whole damned village." Chandler turned to Jake Carter. "Get 'em loaded on the trucks Sergeant, it's time to take off!"

CHAPTER EIGHT

The sad little village of Wana was slowly vanishing behind them as the big trucks headed North. The men gazed back passively, each with his own special memories of the power of kindness. The basic desire to show affection beats in the heart of every human being, but is somehow suppressed in the violence of war. The Wana experience had awakened a flood of long-dormant emotions. The gratitude of the old people and the smiling faces of the children would remain on their minds like a lithograph of hope. There had to be more to life than kill or be killed.

Like the snap of two fingers the bumpy cart path had been transformed into a two-lane highway. The Navy Seabees had been busy again, grading and back-filling with their fleet of bulldozers and skip loaders. The surface was neatly topped and rolled with a thick layer of crushed coral, wending it's way over the terrain like a pale orange ribbon.

Mother Nature had also been creative. The heavy rain and winds of the May monsoon had eroded the sharp edges of the shell holes and practically filled their craters with fine silt. The mud was hardened and baked by the warm summer sun, giving the land a variegated profile resembling the old washboard that Grandma used to scrub her laundry. Stubborn little grass seeds had germinated in the once tortured soil, poking their green blades skyward.

The riding was easier now. With the truck beds empty, the portable side benches were dropped, affording more comfortable seating as the men rode facing each other. Other roads were feeding into theirs now, forcing their vehicles to brake

The Last Souvenir

and stop. An endless convoy of dark brown trucks with 'U.S. Army' stenciled on their doors was merging in ahead, starkly contrasting with the forest green color of the U.S. Marines. Scores of truckloads of haggard army riflemen passed them, both sides smiling and waving at each other.

"Hiya Dogface! Where ya been, pickin' daisies?"

"Hello Gyrene, where the hell do ya think you're goin'?"

"Home I hope."

"Yah, you should live so long! Dream on sucker!"

The friendly banter continuing until the road was clear again. In spite of the high spirited rivalry, the common bond of comradeship in the infantry remained unbroken. The sweetness of survival always takes the highest priority. Early reports rumored of the badly decimated army ranks in their fight along the eastern coastline.

The big brown trucks were high-balling far ahead as the two-section convoy waited for the light orange dust to settle. Moments later they were kicking into high gear again, following the road as it began to bend westward. The scenery changed abruptly on both sides of the road. Engineers and Seabees on huge bulldozers were grading plats of land in a pre-construction phase of future building sites. Building materials were stacked everywhere in high piles.

Suddenly the China Sea came into view and the stark reality of war slapped their faces once more. As far as the eye could see the water was dotted with every type of vessel imaginable, with a predominance of fuel tankers and cargo ships anchored just beyond the reefs, in the shallows. Smaller landing craft were buzzing around the mother ships like bees around their hives. The pregnant supply ships were busy disgorging the contents of their bellies into the boats below, high-masted booms swinging cargo nets overboard, supported by heavy steel cables.

On the shore a hyperactive beach-master was directing

traffic. Trucks, jeeps, and anything else with wheels was pressed into service, even the amphibious tractors. From the sea a long queue of various sized landing craft made its way through a passage in the reef, marked by large gray buoys. At the water's edge a mammoth tractor-crane unloaded the little boats as soon as their prows hit the sand.

"Look at all them boats!" Moe Chernikov was the first to speak. "Bet you could walk on 'em all the way to China and not get your feet wet!"

Del Stack the philosopher saw it a different way. "Well boys, what we went through in the South Pacific is going to seem like child's play compared to this. They're setting us up for the big one."

Del didn't know it but he had just coined a new acronym: 'The Big One.' The magnitude of the invasion of the Japanese homeland was too mind-boggling for the ordinary rifleman. His war had always been his foxhole and the few hundred yards of dirt around him. Slugging it out eyeball to eyeball for an island was one thing, but this defied description.

Heavily laden supply trucks were scurrying away in three directions to assigned destinations. Everything from shoelaces to carburetor jets was coming ashore. To the right, about a mile from the shore road, an ominous high barbed wire fence protected a gigantic five-acre fuel dump. Fifty gallon drums of highly inflammable gasoline were stacked end on end and clearly stenciled for use in either aviation or trucks and jeeps. A direct bomb hit could spell disaster, hence their strategic isolation.

Beyond this, and barely visible to the east, lay the ammunition dumps, guarded by sandbagged machine gun posts at all four corners. A line of trucks, steered by nervous drivers, was delivering a wide spectrum of artillery and mortar shells, along with .30 to .50 caliber cartridges for rifles and machine guns. This too was a ticklish place to be if an enemy air-raid came. Fortunately, the chances of an air assault were getting slimmer by the day. The best of the Japanese Air Force had been shot out of the sky by the dedicated fighter pilots and surface gunners. The Imperial Navy was all but sunk, its once proud fleet of warships now enjoyed a private suite in Davy Jones' locker. Even if a stray survivor attempted a breakthrough to shell the shore, it would be like a sick mouse attacking a kennel of hungry cats.

Stacked at random by the roadside were cases of rations, shoes, dungarees, and the thousand other sundries needed to support men at war. If given a second thought, the logistics of the coming operation would frighten even the most experienced supply officer. The quartermaster people struggled daily with checklists resembling the size of a city telephone directory.

One big box struck the men with an envious ripple of humor.

"Hey Russ, check that one!" Johnny B. pointed as he read from the label. "TABLECLOTHS, LINEN, STAFF OFFICERS MESS."

"Yeah, wonder if they get lace doilies too," Russ responded wryly. "We wouldn't want the Generals to get their fingers dirty while they're eating their broiled lobsters. The men burst into laughter. Even Lt. Chandler got a kick out of that one.

The powers of sea and air were converging on the Western Pacific Theater from all points of the compass. Ships and planes with their manpower were coming from as far away as New Zealand and Australia. From the east, Pearl Harbor was committing the massive reserves they had been accumulating for the last three years. In the north-east the triumphant forces in the fight for Alaska were poised and ready to strike. In the west the China, Burma and India campaign was winding down, releasing machines and men from a multitude of nationalities. To the far west, with the war in Europe concluded, millions of men and equipment were being diverted for the final coup de grace in the Northwest Pacific.

The men who had been fighting the fanatical Japanese in the island slaughtering of the South and Central Pacific had brought their feelings to one final scenario. The entire focus was one huge extermination crew. The civilian gentry had been force fed with the Samurai code and they would face the infidel invaders to the last man, woman, and child if necessary. Dying for their Emperor would assure their passage to the eternal reaches of their imperial heaven, transforming them into gods. Never in history had a nation and a way of life this size been wiped off the face of the globe. A thick gossamer cloud would envelope their sacred homeland and Japan would no longer exist.

Boston Leo had thoughts to share. Still steering his truck, he half turned his head to the right and spoke from the corner of his mouth. "We got some preliminary reports from III Corps Intelligence last week. When we hit Japan we'll be in the first five waves, somewhere in the center. They're expecting around a million casualties in the first two weeks."

Del Stack felt a cold shiver cross his shoulders and up the nape of his neck. "I like the way the top brass use the word 'casualties,' meanin' us. Feels like I'm livin' in a meat locker."

Moe sounded almost cheerful when he added; "Aw come on Del, look at it like a great adventure. Maybe you'll get a 'million dollar' wound and they'll ship ya back to Iowa."

"That's what Gabe said the day he got his hand shot off."

"I remember that day." Johnny B. had been there. "He was lying on a stretcher waving his bloody stump in the air and yelling; 'Look fellas, I got me the million dollar wound. I'm goin' home!'"

"He was out of his gourd. The corpsman probably had him doped up on somethin'. Maybe he'll drop us a line and tell us how he's doin'."

"Sure, when he learns to write left-handed."

Mike was honking the horn loudly as Frenchie waved his arms to attract Chandler's attention in the lead truck. They were passing the immense bomber base at Yontan on their left and a cluster of buildings lay ahead at the far end of the runway. Chandler caught on immediately. An Air Force hospital stood by the edge of the road, a large red cross marking its side. He ordered Leo to pull up by the emergency entrance.

The corpsman leaped out of his seat and sped to Chandler's side. "I think we can get an ambulance here, sir for that little girl back in Wana. You'd better come in with me, I might need some juice from a commissioned officer."

"I'll bring more than juice, Labeau. How about a blow torch?"

Frenchie grinned with relief. His thoughts had constantly been with the young mother and her baby. "Great, let's go." The two men pushed their way through the emergency door and disappeared inside. This time the procedure of waiting was far from dull. The men were awe-struck by the drama that was unraveling on the wide sweeping airstrip to their left. Lines of parked B-29 bombers stood like winged behemoths on the steel-matted tarmac. Fuel trucks were everywhere, pumping their plasma into the thirsty wing tanks. Armorers were hoisting long belts of .50 caliber ammunition into the waist and turret gun ports. A fleet of jeeps was making its way down the line, towing strings of bomb loads on little wheeled trailers.

To the infantryman this was another world, a shocking contrast to their pitifully small rifles and bayonets. To him a pack and a few hand grenades was a heavy load to carry. The Air Force dealt in destruction by the ton, reducing the rifleman's cartridge belt to a mere toy.

As luck would have it, an aerial tragedy was developing overhead, in plain view of the bewildered ground soldiers. A flight of B-29's had circled above them and turned into the wind to make their final approach. It was easy to surmise they were coming in from a bombing mission, probably over a major Japanese city or seaport. The lead ship was belching billows of smoke from its outboard starboard engine, while the second was dropping flares signaling wounded crewmen aboard.

To add to the deafening roar of the engines, sirens began screaming like a thousand banshees. Ambulances and fire engines shot out of the hangers on their grotesque errands of mercy. High above, a squadron of gull-winged escort planes made one last circle, prior to seeking out their respective fighter strips.

"Ya know, I've never seen anything up close like this before. What'a show!" Bill Hull was shouting to be heard. To hold a conversation over the crescendo of the engines was impossible. The men could do no more than wait and watch in reverence for their fellow comrades with wings. War to them was no fun, no matter how you sliced the thing.

Thirty minutes passed before Chandler and Labeau returned to the parked trucks. The lieutenant held up his thumb in a victory sign, then plunged his fingers into his ears. "Lets get the hell outta here," he shouted, motioning up the highway.

Jake Carter was still riding in the Chaplain's jeep. The din of the airstrip was subsiding behind them and the outskirts of the sprawling base at Motobu Bay were coming into sight.

"Do you notice anything peculiar, Padre?"

Father Turner turned his head. "I see a lot of things. What kid of peculiar?"

"This place has hardly been touched. No shell holes or beat up houses, or anything. Looks the same as it must'a been a hundred years ago."

"Beautiful isn't it?" the priest agreed. "I guess the Japanese

General decided to make his stand in the south so he took all his soldiers down there."

A native man and his wife stood ankle deep in a rice paddy, waving and grinning under their broad straw hats. Shoots of rice were protruding from the muddy water. The surrounding square earth-berms were brightly colored by the light green summer grass. A midget-sized pony, nodding his head in a silent tribute, and harnessed to a little two wheeled wooden cart, stood behind them. Beyond them a dozen small houses huddled together, their red-tiled roofs shining in the early evening sun, blue-gray smoke curling from the rooftop flues and corkscrewing across the valley. Kimono clad children ran and frolicked between the structures, adding to the peaceful setting. The women inside were preparing evening meals, probably rice and sweet potatoes, or fish perchance.

"You know, sir, I'll betcha Wana looked like this once. What'a shame. Only a few miles separates the sublime from disaster. It's like the flip of a coin."

"You're right, Jake, you just gave me a wonderful. . . ."

"I know padre, I just gave you a wonderful idea for your next sermon," Jake interrupted.

The undaunted priest could still find a smile. "Am I that obvious? I must be getting redundant in my old age."

"Uh oh, padre, here it comes, civilization. Look at all those signs."

"I like that one." Turner indicated with his finger and read; 'SPEED LIMIT 35 MPH.' I haven't seen a sign like that since I left Hawaii almost two years ago."

Half-domed quonset huts lined both sides of the road. The prefabricated structures of curved corrugated sheet-metal were bolted together in lengths of fifty to a hundred feet, and stood in military rows. Strange looking men in clean pressed uniforms stood gawking at the passing parade of filthy ragged riflemen.

"Look at those guys, they're even wearing neckties. These rear area Joes really have it made. To them we probably look like men from Mars."

"I know how you must feel, Jake, but you must remember it takes hundreds of rear area people to back up one man in the front lines. They have their problems too, my son."

"I'd trade with any one of 'em right now. I'd rather choke on paperwork than stop a bullet anytime."

"Sorry, Jake, you're too good at what you do. You're stuck!"

"Hey Father, there's one sign for you. 'CHAPLAINS OFFICE'. Look what else it says; 'OFFICE HOURS, M THRU F 8AM to 5PM'. Sounds like the old boy is really organized."

"That would be Commander Ryan. He was a Bishop back in the States. I'll report to him tomorrow."

"Shall I tell the Bishop the story about you cutting off that little girl's panties?"

The super-shy priest blushed a pale pink. "Not you too, Jake. It was bad enough putting up with Frenchie Labeau."

"But Father, doesn't this give you a wonderful idea for your next sermon?"

Turner rapidly changed the subject. "There's our turn off. Chandler's turning right."

The sign they passed was short and simple: 'HQ 1st MARINES 2 MI'. The trucks rolled smoothly on the tightly compacted road, the men craning their necks for a glimpse of their new home. It was dusk and a city of dark green pyramid tents was approaching dead ahead. Their high pointed tops formed a series of razorbacks against the waning light of the evening skyline.

The wide road sliced straight through the center of the new tent camp. A well secured guard tent protected the entrance, a white sign with red letters announcing STOP HERE staked

The Last Souvenir

in front. A baby-faced sentry stood by the door flaps, his rifle slung casually over his shoulder. In the middle of the road, holding up his right hand, was a tall skinny officer wearing clean new dungarees. His fatigue cap, with a shiny silver bar on its front, was pulled down securely over his blond eyebrows. The clipboard in his left hand a symbol of some kind of authority.

"Better pull up Leo. Maybe I can find out what the scoop is."

Leo hit the brakes and stopped, leaving the motor idling. The second truck and the Chaplain in his jeep followed suit as Chandler climbed down and strode towards the tall officer in the fading light.

It was First Lieutenant Hans Van der Slice, the regimental transportation officer who recognized Chandler first. "Hello Jimmy. Where the hell have you been? Sightseeing? You're almost nine hours late. The Colonel has been on my ass like a bloodhound!"

"Hiya Dutch, it's a long story, believe me!"

"Oh goody! I just love war stories."

Chandler looked down at the officer's clipboard. "Come on buddy, you Motor Transport guys have forms for everything. Isn't there something there for 'unavoidable delay'? I'll square off with Colonel Mason tomorrow."

"You know me, Jimmy. I frankly don't give a damn one way or the other. For all I know you guys found a cat-house somewhere." He thumbed his paperwork painfully, and after a few moments broke into a toothy grin. "Here it is! 'Mechanical breakdown due to enemy fire.' You'll have to do something to fake the bullet holes though."

Chandler drew his pistol and pointed it at the truck as though he was going to blow a few holes in the hood.

"No, no, I was only kidding. Put that damn thing away!"

"Hey Dutch, is that a mess hall I see over where the lights

are on?"

"Right on. The First Engineers put it up about two weeks ago. Three square meals a day and all you can eat!"

"Great! Listen, can you meet me for breakfast tomorrow morning? I've got a helluva story to tell you. I'm a new godfather."

Dutch looked skeptically at the smiling Jimmy. "Godfather? You boys haven't been away long enough to get anybody knocked up. The last time I heard a story like this, three wise men walked over the hill."

"Nope, this is for real. I think I grew up a little more today. I'll see you at chow tomorrow early. Now what about my men? Where do we go?"

The Dutchman turned and pointed through the camp entrance. "Your First Sergeant is waiting for you by that first line of tents on the right. You're two down from the Colonel. Look for the sign that says 2 SECTION. Good luck, see ya tomorrow."

The big ten-wheelers moved through the entrance and traveled the short distance to where their guide was standing. It was Master Gunnery Sergeant L. B. 'Gunny' Stebbins, a salty old career marine with a rock-like square jaw. The weathered features on his tan face were etched like a road map on a scroll of leather. The six chevrons on his sleeves completed the majesty of his presence.

Gunny Stebbins snapped to attention by Chandler's side and brought up a smart hand salute. "Good evening, sir. Everything is squared away and ready."

Chandler returned a sloppy salute as Jake Carter walked up. "Ya know Jake, this is the first salute I've returned in three months. I guess it's time for spit and polish again."

"You'll have to admit, sir, it's a damn sight better than livin' in foxholes."

Master Sergeant Stebbins started to point in four directions

The Last Souvenir

at once. "That's officers country across the road, that's your tent, Lieutenant. Padre, you're next to him, right across from communications. The mess hall is there and the quartermaster dump is behind it. You men will all draw new gear in the morning." Retaining his ultra military manner he turned his attention to Jake.

"Sergeant Carter, how many scouts are left?"

Jake was not happy with this matter of fact attitude toward survival, but he considered the source. "Six scouts Gunny, and with Leo and Mike it comes up to eight."

"Good. You're in luck. Around that corner I've reserved the first two tents on the right for you. Only four men to a tent. You men can shove off now." With that he turned and marched away.

Carrying their rifles in one hand and packs in the other the men rounded the corner of the new company street. Johnny B. was grumbling half under his breath. "In luck he sez. Ya know Moe, sometimes I think Stebbins wasn't born, he was issued. He's gettin' more chicken-shit every day!"

"Yeah. Wait'll they give Jake six stripes. I'll put in for a transfer."

"I heard that you knucklehead, you should have it so good." Jake lowered his head and moved through the flaps of the big square pyramid tent. A long wooden pole in the center supported the green canvass structure. The side flaps were down giving an aura of privacy for the first time in months. A twenty watt light bulb dangled from a cord on the ceiling.

"How about that, electric lights and everything. I thought I heard a generator out there." Jake grabbed the socket and pressed the switch, illuminating their new quarters.

Jake, Johnny B, Moe, and Del Stack would inhabit the first tent. The four men entered and looked around, dropping their packs and clunking their steel helmets on the dirt floor. Moe chose the far end while Jake picked a spot by the entrance.

Jack Carroll

The others trailed away to the sides.

In the far corner stood a pile of collapsible wood and canvas GI cots, a veritable nightmare to assemble. The little six-legged beasts had to be unfolded, stretched, and put together with the ingenuity of a mechanical engineer.

"Oh no! Not GI cots again! Those things ain't long enough for me, my feet stick out over the end." With his hands on his hips Moe stared mournfully at his new bed.

Johnny B. couldn't resist a cheap shot. "Ya know Moe, I pity the poor guys that have to build a coffin for you. When they get it finished it'll probably look like a railroad freight car."

"Listen you bonehead, they ain't gonna get me. I'm gonna make it out of this clambake, wait and see."

Del was gesturing for Jake to look through the door. "Don't look now Daddy, but I think your little family just arrived. You've got yourself a brand new boy scout troop."

Jake turned around. "Oh no, the replacements already. Where do they get these kids? They just keep coming."

Eleven new boys, wearing the thick new herring-boned dungarees and rough-sided field boots, crowded around their tent, maneuvering for a first glimpse at their new heroes. Their eager young faces were barely visible in the dim light emanating from the door of the tent. A million questions were bottled up behind their innocent faces.

Jake walked outside and faced them, scratching the crusty hair on the back of his scalp. "Welcome to the First, boys. Are you guys assigned to the 2 section?"

A freckle-faced young man who seemed to be their leader stepped forward. He was of medium height, the top of his head adorned with close-cropped red bristles. "Yes sir, we're your new replacements. Are you Sergeant Carter?"

"That's me, at least what's left of me. Any of you boys from California?"

The Last Souvenir

Whatever tension existed was broken, unleashing a staccato of states. "I'm from Texas, sir." Then Ohio, Tennessee, South Dakota, Vermont, Illinois, Georgia.

"Hold it boys! OK, OK, you'll wake the dead!" Jake was holding up both hands as he confronted the freckle-faced young man. "What's your name Marine?"

"O'Malley, sir."

"Well O'Malley, welcome aboard. Just out of curiosity, how old are you?"

"Nineteen sir, but I'll be twenty in December!"

"Nineteen eh? Well after you've been in this outfit for a while you'll feel like you're a hundred like the rest of us. What kind of training did they give you?"

"We all graduated from the Scout Sniper School at Lake Cuyamaca in California, sir."

Carter smiled, shaking his head. "You mean that old place at Green's Farm up in the mountains? That's where I went to recon school two years ago. It's still cranking 'em out huh?"

"Yes sir, twenty four in a class."

"Well I'll be damned. What's the name of that little hick town down below where they used to have barn dances every Saturday night?"

"Julian, sir."

"That's right, Julian. Do the boys still go down there on weekends?"

"No sir, two of the farmer's daughters got pregnant and everybody got pissed off. They made the place off limits."

Jake wasn't surprised, remembering the raucous times he had there with his buddies. "OK, let's break it up for now. You boys'll probably get sick of hearin' my voice over the next few weeks. I know you all have a thousand questions."

Jake felt the presence of Moe and Johnny B. standing by his side. They had been taking in everything. "One more thing. These two scroungy looking specimens are John

Bowman and Moe Chernikov. Graft yourselves to their tails and listen to everything they tell you. Out here the Marine Corps Manual is going to seem like a first grade reader. You're in a new ballgame now. And another thing, you can stop calling me 'sir,' this is no boot camp. Just call me sergeant, or sarge. OK, you got that?"

"Yes sir. . . . I mean Sarge."

"That's better."

Master Sergeant Stebbins was rudely brushing his way into the little crowd. "Alright you new cherries, scatter. Sergeant Carter, if you and your men want hot food, get your asses up to the mess hall on the double. The mess sergeant stayed late just for you so move it! You won't need your mess gear, he has trays and utensils. That's all." Stebbins whirled and disappeared in the dark.

"Ya know Jake, that Gunny doesn't have one polite bone in his head. I think he has a ramrod up his ass."

"Forget it Johnny, we don't have to be told twice. I'm so hungry I could eat a dead caribou. Let's go." As the rest of the men heard the good news and poured out of the tents Jake had an afterthought. "Hey O'Malley. Come back here!"

The young redhead came trotting back. "Yes sir, Sarge, what can I do for you?"

"You and your boys can assemble our cots for us while we go to the mess hall."

"Can do Sergeant. We'll get on it right away."

Jake nodded and joined his motley little group heading for a late supper.

Cookie the chef was waiting patiently behind the counter of steaming pans. His formal title was Master Technical Sergeant George Watts, but no one knew it. Every chef on any military base in the world was just plain 'Cookie'. The kitchen was his domain and in it he was God. However, no matter how fine his cuisine, the verbal abuse never ended.

The Last Souvenir

"Hello Jake, long time no see. I hear you guys had it pretty rough. Good to see you back in one piece."

"Thanks Cookie, what's on the menu."

"Chipped beef on toast, sliced peaches, and all the hot coffee you can drink."

Moe stepped up first with a tray in his hands. "Come on Cookie, not shit on a shingle again?"

"You know Moe, someday you're gonna get your head blown off and I'll have one less thorn in my paw. Where's the chow hound?"

"If you mean Russ, he's right over there with drool on his face."

"Hello Russ, it's good to see you too. Hungry?"

Russ moved up, shoving his empty tray under the cook's nose. "My needle's on empty, Cookie. Load me up double, with some extra slices of that toast too. Got any of that canned butter to go with it?"

"This is a first class joint, Russ, if I've got it you can have it. Comin' up!"

The scouts sat eating in silence as they stuffed themselves on the creamy beef and sawed away at the fresh toasted bread. The cook stood back in quiet wonderment as their forks clinked on metal trays. To him these men were special. They piqued in him a silent admiration, and he always felt a personal loss when he heard of their casualties.

When the cramming match was over an insurmountable drowsiness crept over them and they headed for the door with cries of; "Thanks for staying open Cookie, thanks for everything."

The canvas cots had been perfectly assembled by O'Malley and his boys when they stepped inside their tents. There were no sheets or blankets yet but the bare canvas looked wonderfully inviting to them. They were lifted off the cold ground at last and too exhausted to remove their clothes and boots.

Jake was the last standing as the other three stretched out, covered only by ponchos. He flicked out the light and made for his bed. His words were the last spoken. "Man, I'm bushed! It's been a long day." Just before he sank into a deep coma.

CHAPTER NINE

"Alright you sleepin' beauties, REVEILLE, everybody hit the deck. Roll call at O' six hundred. Everybody OUTSIDE!" Master Sergeant Stebbins was in the company street, bawling orders and strutting like a crowing rooster. His brusque manner was the indelible stamp of over two decades of regular military service. His erect posture and polished boots served as a frame for the perfect soldier.

Dawn was breaking over the tent camp. Orange spikes of sunlight were punching their way through the low lying cloud-bank on the eastern horizon. Sleepy eyed young men in their underwear were stumbling out of the tent flaps, heading for the field toilets at the end of the street.

Stebbins was unhappy with the snail like exodus and backtracked to the tents of Carter and his scouts. Peering inside, he was shocked by the direct disobedience of his orders. Mike and Boston Leo were up and gone, but the other six lay stretched out like bodies in a mortuary.

"Alright you goofoffs, you heard me! REVEILLE! Roll call in thirty minutes!"

Jake was the first to move, pulling his poncho over his head and rolling over. Chernikov's big feet twitched as they hung heavily over the end of his little cot, but that was as far as he got. The men were completely exhausted after months of front line duty.

Stebbins was furious as the other sections of Headquarters Company lined up for the morning accounting. The Communications Section was first as he blew out the names from his clipboard. Quartermaster and Personnel Sections followed, saving the scout groups for last.

"Six absent from the morning roll call! This is unheard of!" Stebbins was muttering angrily as he dismissed the remaining men. The company broke ranks and made for the mess tent, unaware of his dilemma. "They'll pay for this! They all go on report!"

Chandler kept his breakfast date with Dutch Van der Slice at the officer's mess. He related the long pause in Wana village, extolling the wonders of childbirth in the wilderness. The Dutchman was a family man too, sharing memories of pacing the floors of a maternity ward. Even war can produce great moments. Dutch had covered Jimmy on the paperwork, and everything was well with the world.

Chandler left the field kitchen and headed for his domain in the intelligence tent. Colonel Mason was approaching from the opposite direction and he knew that it was time for the resumption of formal courtesies. He whipped up a snappy salute.

"Good morning, Colonel."

He returned Chandler's salute. "Good morning, Lieutenant. I want to meet with you and your scouts soon. I'll inform you through my orderly."

Chandler was a contented man when he entered his canvas office. Leo and Mike were standing at their drafting boards, fingering through new stacks of maps and aerial photos.

"Good morning, men."

"Good morning, sir." Both men answered in unison.

Leo was apologetic as he pointed to a large box in the corner. "You'll have to use that for a desk, sir. You can have one of those crates for a chair."

"That's it?"

"Yes sir. If you don't mind my askin', how come the Army and the Navy get all kinds of new equipment, and we Marines don't get doodlie shit?"

Chandler was unruffled. "Maybe they think we're too tough for comfort."

Leo forced a smile and continued. "III Corps sent down the personnel records of the new men, sir. They're on your box... I mean desk."

Chandler planted his backside on a tiny crate and began the procedure of reading the folders on his new people. In five minutes he was half way into the reports when a loud voice startled him off his seat.

"Sir! Master Gunnery Sergeant Stebbins requests permission to speak to the Lieutenant, Sir."

"What is it Sergeant? You just scared the hell outta me! This better be good."

Gunny Stebbins stood stiffly at attention, his left hand holding a clipboard along the seam of his trousers. He stared straight ahead in his own private oblivion and blurted out his report. "Sir, you had six men from your section absent from roll call this morning. Sir, I wish to put them on report for insubordination and direct disobedience of orders from a superior non-commissioned officer!"

Chandler had a good idea of what was happening, but he squelched a desire to smile. "Pull up a box and have a seat Sergeant, I need to hear more."

"No thank you sir, I'd rather stand."

"Well, suit yourself, I suppose you have the names of these culprits?"

"Yes sir, I do." The Master Sergeant raised his clipboard and read off the names: "Bowman, Chernikov, Stack, Keeler, Hull, and Sergeant Carter, sir."

Chandler could no longer contain himself. He let off a series of his famous deep-throated guffaws and reared back on his seat.

"Sir, I do not follow the Lieutenant's humor." Stebbins was alarmed by the officer's unmilitary reaction.

Chandler recovered from his loss of control and gave off an unexpected belch from his morning breakfast. "I'm sorry Sergeant, I realize you have a serious charge. I think I have your personnel folder here, somewhere. How long have you been in the Marine Corps?"

"Twenty-three years, sir." Stebbins was openly proud of his longevity.

"Twenty-three years eh? Ah, here it is." The Lieutenant had his file and was scanning it carefully. "It says you enlisted when you were seventeen?"

"Yes sir, I was an orphan and underage, so the County authorities had to sign for me."

"Stebbins, I must say you have an excellent service record. I'm very impressed."

"Thank you, sir, the Marine Corps has always been my home."

Chandler was reading while he talked. "It says that you've served all over the world, and your last peacetime post was in China?"

"Yes sir, Shanghai Legation in '36."

"Stebbins, as far back as I can remember as a kid I've looked up to the regular Marines. I even enlisted because of men like you. I wanted to be a part of your pride and esprit de corps. I'm still proud, can you understand that?"

"Yes, sir. Thank you, sir."

Leo and Mike remained standing by their map boards in silence. They both had been in close quarters for a long time with the tactful officer, and knew when a punch line was forthcoming. They were right. The fatherly love Jimmy felt for his boys was no secret.

"There's just one thing missing, Sergeant Stebbins. I don't see any front line duty in your record. Have you ever been an infantryman? Have you ever served in a line company? Have you seen any combat against the Japanese?"

For the first time Stebbins had an inkling of what was coming. "No, sir." He felt a rash of prickly heat on the back of his neck. "If you don't mind, sir, I think I'll accept your offer to sit down." He was basically a good man with an open mind, and he somehow sensed he was in for a new learning experience.

"Stebbins, how long have my boys been asleep?"

The Master Sergeant raised his left hand and peeled off the dust cover of his wristwatch. "Thirteen hours, sir."

Chandler was chortling again. "That's typical of those jokers. Let 'em sleep some more. The only problem is their bladders are so full by now they're ready to burst and they're too zonked to know it. They'll probably piss their pants and not even care."

"I've never known an officer like you, sir. You really seem to care for your men, sir."

"Stebbins, I'm going to give you a big lump to swallow. You cannot lead men like these by jabbing them in the ass with a pitchfork. Why hell, three years ago they were playing football in a sandlot somewhere back in the States. They volunteered to fight because their country was attacked. They're not regular Marines like you, they're civilians in uniforms, and so am I. Those boys are in a meat grinder where nasty little pieces come out the other end. Do you have any idea how long it's been since they've had a full nights sleep?"

"Not really, sir." Stebbins was on the spot and he knew it.

"At least three weeks. They've been catnapping in slit trenches, foxholes, caves, ditches, and God only knows the rest. We face a clever, vicious enemy, but our guys are beatin' 'em. Someday you'll be proud to say you served with them, am I getting through?"

The salty old sergeant could only manage a weak rebuttal. "But sir, I was always taught to run a tight ship. It's the only way I know."

"Dammit man, this isn't some peacetime navy yard! We're in a gut ripping war! If you want to go to Tokyo, these are the boys who will take you there."

"Sir, are you ordering me to throw away 'the book'?"

"Not at all sergeant, just file off some of the sharp edges. Get to know the veterans, especially Carter. Watch him and see how he leads. He has an uncanny instinct for survival. He has eleven men to break in and you can help. Make 'em tough and hard but for God's sake don't break their spirit. It's a fine line, but I'm confident you can walk it."

"Sir, I think I've just walked into the new Marine Corps and it feels good to be here."

"That's wonderful Stebbins, you're a good man and we're happy to have you with us. Let's shake on it!"

"Lieutenant, I've never shook hands with an officer before, but here goes." He accepted Chandler's hand and broke into a wide grin.

Stebbins stood outside in the bright sunlight, his mind whirling with new concepts. Lieutenant Jimmy had opened the door to a brand new set of challenges and he was ready for them. A feeling in his inner soul was telling him he never really bought the chicken-shit approach to leadership, and it took a reserve officer like Jimmy to expose it. 'I can fit in,' he thought, 'my experiences with men and weapons could make me a real asset to this regiment.' A strange combination of happiness and relief crept through him as he went striding away.

Jake Carter opened his eyes and brushed the poncho away from his face. Chernikov was lying on his side, watching him with half shut eyes.

"You awake, Jake?"

"Yeah, except I feel like I've been drugged. What time is it?"

"Moe glanced at his watch, "Eleven-thirty." He swung his

The Last Souvenir

feet to the floor and stretched his arms. "Man, I gotta piss so bad I could blast a bird out of a tree."

"Me too." Johnny B was awake. "Where's the head?" using the Navy slang for latrine.

"Down the street." Del had been in a semi-doze for the last half hour. "Gotta get the hell outta here!"

The four men left together and stiffly wobbled down the company street. Keeler and Hull had preceded them and were walking up from the other direction.

"Hey look Russ, it's the Marx Brothers," pointing at the disheveled quartet.

"You ain't no rosebud yourself. I thought I smelled somethin' funny around here." Moe had no time to pause. He was ready to burst.

The sun was directly overhead when they re-entered their tent. Russ and Bill joined them, and the six scouts sat in a circle on the cots, reflecting on their thoughts. Jake rubbed his chin with his thumb and forefinger, his conniving mind seeded with a master scam.

"It's lunch time, I gotta see Lang right away. He's got all that enemy equipment stashed away for me and he's probably getting itchy. We've got some horse tradin' to do. Time to shove off for the mess hall."

CHAPTER TEN

The mess tent was crowded as usual but seating on the wooden benches was plentiful. Jake filled his tray with frankfurters and beans, and a large side helping of canned peaches. He grabbed four slices of fresh baked bread and turned away, his eyes traveling around the scores of faces hunched over the tables. Quartermaster Sergeant Lang was at the other end of the big green tent, standing and motioning for Carter to join him. A small group around him had left, leaving ample space for Jake and his buddies.

"Hiya Jake, I've been lookin' for ya. I heard ya slept over fourteen hours this time. Some kinda record huh?"

"Hello Lang, you ready to talk some business?" Jake and his boys gathered around and placed their trays on the table.

"Man, you get right to the point in a hurry!" Lang lowered his voice to a whisper. "That Jap equipment I've been holdin' for ya has been classified as contraband. Nobody knows about it 'cept you and me, but I'm gettin' kinda antsy!"

"Aw bullshit Lang! If those guys at III Corps get a'hold of that stuff they'll split it up and sell it. That ain't gonna happen. Everybody's got the right to collect souvenirs and that's how I see it. Don't worry, you know me, I'll find another home for it. Did you make up that list for me?"

Lang nodded and produced a piece of paper from his jacket pocket, handing it across to Jake. Carter unfolded the list and quickly read the inventory.

"Excellent! This is better than I thought. Rifles, bayonets, uniforms, helmets, and even ammo. Holy shit, is there a case of pistols too? Those babies are worth a fortune!"

"You got it pal, the whole magilla. But I gotta get rid of it. I ain't about to go to Mare Island Prison for a bunch of Jap doodads!"

"OK Lang, I'll take it off your hands, just give me one more day. We'll work out a split later."

"Sounds good to me, Jake." Lang stood and headed out the door with his empty tray.

The nefarious Johnny B watched Jake rub his chin and could no longer contain himself, chewing so furiously the beans were drooling from his mouth. "Did we hit the jackpot, Sarge? What do we do now? What's next?" The excitement of a new con had launched him into seventh heaven.

"This is the way it's gonna be boys." Jake motioned for them to crowd in closer, holding his finger to his lips for secrecy. "Russ, where the hell are you goin?"

"Back for seconds. I operate better on a full stomach." Russ took off at a fast walk.

"Nix. Here comes Gunny Stebbins."

Stebbins spotted his men and rapidly moved in behind them. "Good afternoon men, did you all have a nice lunch?" The men looked at each other in puzzlement. Nobody spoke but their thoughts were of a common thread - 'Since when does he give a shit?'

Jake finally broke the silence. "Just fine, Gunny. It's great to have hot chow again."

"Good, I'm glad to hear it." The Master Sergeant's voice was low and almost patronizing. "I ran into Sergeant Lang outside. He forgot to tell you he has your new gear laid out and ready. You'll get socks, boots, dungarees, and a list of anything else you might need. I've arranged with the Sergeant of Engineers to fire up the boiler for hot showers at 13:00. I'll drop in later and see how you're doin'." He spun around and sauntered away, a noticeable lack of pomp in his bearing.

"Did you hear that? The old ramrod must be constipated

or somethin'. He actually sounded human!"

Jake shrugged. "Dunno, beats me." Russ was back now with a mountain of frankfurters and sliced bread and Jake returned to business. "Here's the deal. We got a big milk cow by the tail and we're gonna cash in. Chances are, in three, four months we'll all be blown to hell, so until then we're gonna live in comfort. Nothing in the book sez we can't live like kings in the meantime. Right?"

The men bobbed their heads in total agreement. Johnny B. summed it up simply. "What's the setup, Sarge?"

"The setup is this. Del, I want a private telephone in my tent. Get a'hold of your buddy Eddie Gallo in the comm section. Promise him anything, but get it! Johnny, check with Leo and pick up topo maps of the whole area as far south as Yontan Airfield. Plot in every QM dump, post exchange, officer's club and anything else with food and equipment. Moe, check with Motor Transport. Find out what it takes to check out anything with wheels. Russ, you and Bill reconnoiter every inch of ground south and southwest of us, no more than a mile and a half out. Find us a house, barn, or even a cave where we can move our stash. Make it look like a security recon patrol, so climb into light packs and helmets, and take your rifles. Check with Johnny B. and plot in what you find. Any questions?"

A perplexed Bill Hull threw in the only question. "Not sure I get it, Jake. What's the master plan?"

Carter was standing, a wry smile lighting up his face. "Well, to put it bluntly, my ponderous friend, we're about to skin the Army and the Navy! Let's shove off for the QM and the showers."

The men wasted no time. Forty-five minutes later an atmosphere of sartorial splendor filled the drab, olive green tent. Jake, Del, Johnny B. and Moe stood staring at each other in disbelief. Showered, shaved, and shampooed, with their hair

The Last Souvenir

slicked back over their ears, they were complete strangers to each other.

"Hey, even my dungarees fit." Moe was admiring his long legs. "Lang said he had a helluva time findin' my size."

"I like the new blankets." Del smoothed his hand over the thick green wool.

O'Malley appeared. "Hey Sarge, you've got company. He's been waitin' for you in my tent." A familiar figure rudely elbowed him aside.

"Carter, it's me, Muldoon. I had a tough time findin' you. The First is a big regiment."

"Glad you did, Chief. Pull up a cot and sit awhile."

Muldoon sat across from Carter and lit a monstrous brown cigar. "Sarge, I'll give it to ya straight. This whole island has been plucked like a Christmas goose. There ain't a souvenir to be had for fifty miles. I'm out'a business."

"Not quite my comrade, not quite. But first, you remember my buddies, Johnny B., Moe, and Del?" Jake gestured around the tent with an open hand.

"Yeah sure, hiya fellas, what'ya mean, not quite?" Muldoon's eyes narrowed.

Jake was prepared, reaching under his cot and producing a long object wrapped in a green towel. "Take a gander at this, buddy." He handed it to the anxious old sea dog.

Muldoon's eyes bugged out like a hungry blow fly. "Holy shit, a brand new Jap infantry rifle. Where'd ya get it? Ya got any more?"

"Not so fast, my seafaring friend. Just tell me what you can get for it."

The old Chief gave a poor imitation of playing coy. "Well, I dunno, maybe fifty bucks."

"Muldoon, as one businessman to another, you insult my intelligence. I say between two and three hundred. Those flyboys down at Yontan look pretty fat to me."

"Jake, ya got me over a barrel, but I have to admit, maybe you're right."

"OK Chief, we are beginning to understand each other. I'm gonna give you this rifle and you can keep all the cash!"

"Now wait a minute, Sergeant Carter don't give nuthin' away. What's the hook?"

"No hook, a small favor is all."

The Chief's cigar hung down from his jaw at a dangerous angle. "How small is this favor you're askin'?"

"Well Muldoon, let me put it this was. You Navy boys have been kind enough to ferry us Marines all over the Pacific. You and your bunkmates live like royalty, and we live like slobs. Look around!"

The old sailor had to go along with him. "Yeah, it is pretty bleak."

"Can you get us some Navy mattresses?"

"Mattresses? I might be able to scrounge up a few. How many do you need?"

"Thirty."

"Holy jumpin' swordfish!! Thirty? You call that small?" Muldoon squirmed like he was sitting on a hornet's nest. "Come on Carter, business is one thing but rape is somethin' else."

"I have a lot of faith in you buddy, you haven't heard the rest of it yet. Two more rifles like that one will be handed to you on delivery. I reckon that comes to between six and nine hundred bucks. Is that too small for you to handle?" Jake was letting out his line, playing him like a trout.

"Hell no, let me think a minute. I've got a good friend at the supply dump by the bay. He's a chief like me. I'll need to borrow a truck. OK, you got a deal." His eyes were almost pink with greed.

"Super, now there's just one more little thing."

"Oh - oh, here it comes. What next?"

"We want pillows, mattress covers, and sheets to go with 'em. Pillow cases too."

Muldoon fell back and slapped his knees with his gnarled hands. "Nope, I gotta draw the line somewhere. You're askin' me to practically clean out the whole damn warehouse. I'll end up in the brig."

"Naw, not a slick old salt like you. There's more to come." Carter reached under his cot again and slipped him a shiny new long bayonet. The large hook on its wooden hilt was the trademark of the Japanese rifleman.

Muldoon ground down hard on his cigar stub. "Ya got three of these too?"

"Yep."

"Alright, Carter, if I get on it right away I can deliver tomorrow. Can you fix it up with the guard so I can pull my truck in here?"

"Sure Chief, I'll put Johnny B. on it."

"Well Jake, so long for now. I still say I wish we were shipmates!"

"So long, Chief." Jake walked outside with him.

Moe and Johnny B. were soon by his side again. Del stayed inside in a prone position, using his new blankets as a headrest. Bowman's brain was brimming with eagerness.

"Thought you almost lost him when you pressed for the sheets and pillows."

"Not a chance! Muldoon let the cat out'a the bag when he told me the island was plucked. Business is supply and demand, and we might be the only supply. It's like playing poker, you gotta watch for the clinker."

"I see what you mean."

"Do me a favor, Johnny we have work ahead. These guys know what to do so get them moving. I want their reports by chow-time tonight." Jake was off for the QM dump and an inventory with Sergeant Lang.

CHAPTER ELEVEN

The bugler was blasting reveille, jarring Jake into a sitting position. He felt woozy but refreshed after logging another ten hours of sleep. The new blankets were wonderful, but his mind was on mattresses and pillows. A heavy mist hung over the camp, shrouding the tents in a gray silver hue. Master Sergeant Stebbins was not deterred as he stuck his head through the flaps.

"Good morning, Sergeant Carter. Can you have your men ready for roll call in thirty minutes?"

"Yeah, sure Gunny. I'll roust 'em out on my way to the head."

Chernikov sat up, rubbing the sleep dust from his eyes. "What's with the ole ramrod? Why the sudden change?"

Carter shook his head. "Dunno, maybe he don't have the rag on anymore. Ya better stop next door and roll out Russ and Bill. They'll sleep in if you don't kick 'em in the ass."

Stebbins was a happy trooper when his roll called a hundred percent present. Before he dismissed the company he confronted Jake. "Sergeant Carter, the Colonel wants you and your section to fall-in in front of your tents at o'nine hundred for orders."

"Willco, Gunny. Ya got any idea what he's up to?"

"Maybe he's going to pin a medal on you Jake."

"Yeah, the Purple Shaft! We'll be there."

The morning sun was slowly burning off the gray mist as the 2 section trailed back from breakfast. Jake joined O'Malley and struck up a casual conversation.

"What's your first name, O'Malley?"

"Sean, Sergeant."

"Sean O'Malley eh? Sounds as Irish as 'Paddy's pig.' I

The Last Souvenir

suppose they call you Red."

"Not if I can help it, Sarge. I'll come out fightin'!"

"I like your attitude, Sean, I'm proud of my heritage too. My folks are from Norway. I feel the same way if I get called a Swede."

They laughed together as they spied a gang of forlorn looking young replacements mulling around O'Mally's tent. Colonel Mason wasn't due for at least another hour, and Jake seized the opportunity to get acquainted with his new brood.

"What's the matter with you guys? You look like the cook just poisoned your peaches."

A tall, thin young man in baggy dungarees ventured forward. "Well Sergeant, we were just wondering, when are we gonna fight?"

"Good Lord, another gung-ho bunch of heroes. We'd better go inside and talk about the birds and bees." Jake slipped into O'Malley's crowded tent and sat on one of the cots. "Come on boys, everybody inside and grab a seat."

The new recruits shouldered their way into the tent and squeezed themselves together on six little cots. The naive willingness in their expressions gave Jake a queasy feeling in the pit of his stomach, feeling empathy for these fine young men. They were the true virgins of war. Basic training had brought them this far, but the horrors they must face cannot be written in a military manual. Each man must learn to deal with his own personal destiny, and no two sets of circumstances would be alike. Jake fought to erase the meandering melancholy in his heart, and opted to douse them with a bucket of cold water.

"Men, I'm gonna shoot from the hip. In a few weeks were goin' to Japan, and some of us ain't comin' back! You're gonna see more ships and planes than you can imagine. Everything that can fly or float is pointed straight at the Nips, and you boys are going to be stuck right out on the point. You enlisted, you asked for it, and you're gonna get it!"

A spray of questions erupted, hitting him in rapid-fire succession.

"How many grenades do we carry?"

"Do we wear field packs?"

"Do we need to carry blankets?"

Jake felt like a third baseman trying to field too many grounders. He held up his hands, waving for attention. "Colonel Mason will be here in a few minutes and I'm sure he will announce the new training schedule. You can forget most of the bullshit you were fed by those strutting peacocks back in the States. You're gonna learn some rotten tricks that would even make a Hollywood pimp blush. The Jap soldier is clever and deadly. He fights twenty-four hours a day and can live a whole week on a bowl of rice. He's been fighting in China and Manchuria since the thirties, and he's out to cut off your nuts! We've been whipping the little bastard at his own game, and we're gettin' better. You guys are young and tough or you wouldn't be here, so don't worry about it."

Jake continued for another half-hour, outlining the fundamental functions of a front line scout. It was clear that their sponge-like brains were soaking up every drop, a typical and happy sign for a training sergeant. He glanced at his watch and cut it short.

"I remember an old sergeant I had in boot camp, his name was Thompson. He lined us up and said; "Men, we're in a war now. We don't have time for you to grow up, so I'm gonna jerk you up.' I didn't know how right he was 'til I came out here. Anyway, one last word about Colonel Mason. He's strict, but he's fair. He got the Navy Cross at Guadalcanal back in '42, and took a piece of shrapnel in his shoulder. He's on his second tour overseas, and the best part is he's a Mustang. Anybody know what a Mustang is?"

They all knew, and O'Malley spoke for them. "Yes sir,

Sergeant. He came up through the ranks as a private like us."

"That's right, Sean, like us. He knows the ropes so don't even try to lie to him. He likes clean uniforms and straight lines so look as sharp as you can. Formation is in ten minutes." Jake exited the tent and turned left, unable to hear the hushed tones of their conversation.

Del, Moe, and Johnny B. were waiting as Jake entered their tent, beaming like cats looking in a fish bowl. "How was the pep talk, coach? Are we gonna win the big game?"

"They're a great bunch of kids. Glad they're on our side. As usual they're green as hell but that's the way the ball bounces." Carter was looking nervously at his wristwatch. "If I know Mason, he'll be here at nine sharp." He straightened and walked to the center of the Company Street.

"2 Section fall in! Everybody outside!"

Within a minute a long line of green uniforms faced him, each man staring dead ahead.

"Straighten out that line!" They lifted their left arms and spaced themselves in perfect position.
"All's well, don't move. Stand at ease."

Colonel Mason, the robot, was exactly on time as Jake watched him turn the corner. He was clad in a clean new field uniform, creases pressed sharply in the trouser legs. A silver eagle on his cap alerted everyone to his almighty presence. A pair of parachute wings were pinned above his left breast pocket, while on his feet he wore jump boots with the pant legs carefully bloused inside their tops. In his right hand he carried his famous bamboo swagger stick. The tip was a hollowed brass .30 caliber cartridge, balanced on the other end by a leather holding strap resembling a riding crop. He habitually tapped the stick against his right leg, keeping cadence with his steps.

Carter wheeled around. "A TEN-HUT!"

The men snapped to attention as Sergeant Carter

performed a precise about face.

Mason was moving at a rapid gait, followed by Lieutenant Chandler and Master Sergeant Stebbins. Chandler always felt the same apprehension when the 'Old Man' came to inspect his section. Being loose on discipline, he never knew what to expect from his rambunctious charges.

When Colonel Mason stopped and faced him, Jake saluted. "Good morning sir, all present and accounted for!"

The colonel returned his salute by touching his stick to the brim of his cap. "Good morning, Sergeant, it's been quite a while since I've seen you. Are these your new replacements?"

"Yes sir. On your left sir."

Mason turned his head and ran his eyes along the line of young faces. "A fine looking group of new Marines, sergeant. I'm trusting in you to shape them into the finest reconnaissance team in the division."

"We'll give it our best shot, Colonel. Do we have new orders, sir?"

"New orders, yes, and that's putting it mildly. The landing on the main Japanese Islands will be the biggest show in our history. We'll need every man sharp and ready." Mason changed the subject as he drew scraps of paper from his pocket. "I have here some past communiqués received from my field commanders. This one from C Company struck me, and I believe in giving praise when it's due. It reads that you and your men saved two of his rifle platoons from being wiped out. Do you recall the incident?"

"Yes sir, I do. We were on Wana Ridge. It was Corporal Bowman and Private Berg, sir."

"Well done, Carter, are these men here today?"

"No sir, not all. Berg was killed, but Corporal Bowman is standing directly behind me. He's the one that looks like a movie star, sir."

Mason gave him an unexpected smile, looking around his

shoulder and nodding to Johnny B. "I'm putting these messages in your care, Sergeant. I want you to read them to the new men as soon as possible. I'll say a few words later, tell the men to stand at ease. Chandler, take over."

Jake complied as Lieutenant Jimmy stepped forward carrying a large manila envelope. He withdrew a sheet of white paper and began to read. "Attention to orders! Regimental order number 865. Subject, promotions. To Platoon Sergeant: Carter, John H." He reached in the envelope and handed Jake a pair of four striped chevrons. "Congratulations, Sergeant. This puts you in the top three pay grades now."

"Thank you, Lieutenant." Jake knew his responsibility had just stepped up another notch.

Chandler continued. "To Buck Sergeant: Bowman, Chernikov, Keeler, and Stack."

Johnny B. moved his head slightly and whispered to Moe from the corner of his mouth. "Since when do they pin three stripes on a big baboon like you?"

"What about you, blubber butt! I think we just lost the war!"

Chandler applied a stern facade, maintaining discipline for the benefit of the Colonel. "No talking in the ranks," and read on. "To Corporal: Beauchamp, Hull, and Michaelson." He passed the manila envelope to Carter. "See that these chevrons are distributed, Sergeant."

The Lieutenant moved in closer to his men as Mason backed away. "You will be split up into four groups of four men each, and each group will be headed by a sergeant. Hull, you'll fill in with Sergeant Stack's group. Platoon Sergeant Carter will be in overall command and I'll back him up. This is the new training schedule. I will read it to you so pay strict attention. No questions until I'm finished." Chandler held up a sheaf of papers and exhibited them for his men to see. He read methodically, covering everything from map reading to ghoul hunting. The plan was so thoroughly prepared that the men had no questions, only suppressed groans.

"If there are no questions, the schedule will take effect at o'eight-hundred tomorrow morning. Colonel Mason has some last words to say. Colonel!"

Mason stepped forward again, highly gratified by the professionalism displayed. "Thank you, Lieutenant. Men, I have a brief closing comment to make. This regiment is..." Mason was cut off at the tonsils by an overloaded truck turning the corner and rolling down the company street. The uncouth driver loudly honked the horn three times and hit the brakes just short of the formation, raising an irritating cloud of dust. A tall mound of tightly lashed down bundles filled the oversized truck bed.

It was Muldoon. The Chief Motor Machinist hadn't shaved for a week, and his light blue uniform was splattered with engine grease. He slid out from behind the wheel and plucked a cigar stub from his mouth. "Hey, where daya guys want me to put this stuff?"

At first, the pop-eyed Colonel was awe-struck, erupting into a volcano of rage. "WHO IN GOD'S NAME IS THAT? How did he get in my camp? Chandler, do you know anything about this Neanderthal?"

"N' No sir. It looks like a Navy truck, sir."

"I can see that Lieutenant. What about you, Stebbins?"

"No, sir."

Mason rotated slowly to his left and pointed his swagger stick straight between Jake's eyes. "Carter, I should have known, you're at the bottom of this. Step over here, Sergeant"

Jake was thinking fast as he stood stiffly to attention before his red-faced commanding officer. 'Why did Muldoon have to pick this exact time to show up?' His brain was spinning at 2000 RPM'S at least. Colonel Mason was too crusty to fall for a scam. He decided to tell the truth by seasoning it with tact and hoping the Old Man would go along.

"Well sir, that's my friend Chief Muldoon from the United States Navy. I got a chance to do a little swappin' with him so he's delivering his end."

"Damn it, Sergeant, this is an infantry regiment, not a flea market! What in the hell do you mean swapping?"

"Sir, I got a chance to trade some Jap souvenirs for Navy bedding. I'm just trying to take care of my men, sir."

"What do you mean *YOUR MEN*? They're my men too! Do you have requisition forms for this equipment? I don't remember signing anything."

"Colonel sir, could we talk in private for a couple minutes?"

"Private is a good word right now, Carter. That's what you'll be if this doesn't wash, a *PRIVATE*!"

Jake had one thing going for him and the old Colonel knew it. He had a long and excellent combat record, and this meant a lot to the gray-haired Mustang. Mason condescended to listen and the two men paced away, out of earshot.

"Colonel sir, this is the way I see it. The Navy has it all and we Marines have nothing. They have hot chow and we eat cold beans. They have soft beds and we sleep on the ground. They have laundries and we have buckets. Why sir, it's an old marine tradition to beat the Navy outta anything we can get!"

Mason was beginning to get the picture, but most of all he liked the young Sergeant's initiative. He had fought the battle of supply since he received his commission. Now, he led a light infantry regiment that was always on the move. Top Brass didn't deem it necessary to over-burden him or his men with luxurious comforts, hence they lived in the fields like migrant farm workers.

"What's on that truck, Carter?"

"Thirty mattresses sir, with pillows and linen to match."

"*THIRTY?* My God, Sergeant, are you trying to get the

Military Police on my rump? What about requisition forms?"

"We only need forms to pick-up new equipment, Colonel, not receive it! Let the Chief worry about that. Besides, I have a mattress and pillow for you too, sir."

Mason furrowed his brow and looked skeptically at Jake. "For me too? Why?"

"Because you're my Colonel, sir. We're all in this war together."

"Don't soft-soap me, Carter, just move the gear up to my tent, and get that truck out of my camp! I don't know whether to give you a medal or throw you in the brig. Dismiss your men."

Mason went striding away, holding his swagger stick in front of him with both hands and thinking, 'I'm really proud of those boys, I really am. I wonder if I've just been had?'

CHAPTER TWELVE

Jake sat down on his cot with both hands up to his face. "Whew! That was a close one!" Johnny B. sat next to him, putting his hand on his buddy's shoulder.

"Nice goin', Sarge, you pulled it off. I thought the Old Man was going to boil you in oil!"

"I learned something today, Johnny. The Colonel's all right. I don't want to push him too hard, but I think, if we use our heads, we can get around him. I hope!"

Bowman rose to his feet. "Muldoon's pulling his truck up. What do you want us to do?"

"Come on, let's hit it."

Jake and Johnny B. watched as the Chief tugged at the lines securing the merchandise. He had tied them in tight navy slipknots. Every time he yanked another rope fell off.

"You better count 'em Johnny. That's gonna be your job from now on."

"Wadda ya mean count 'em, Carter? I'm an honest man." Muldoon was feigning hurt feelings.

"Just routine, Chief, just routine."

The tent camp of an infantry regiment is a small community, circulating rumors like native tom-toms in a jungle. Every story, whether large or small, will travel through the air with the rapidity of electric current flowing through a copper cable. A crowd of gawking Marines was gathering around Jake Carter and his mobile circus.

"How come you bums get all the breaks? How do we cash in?"

Jake sized up the situation with the acumen of a top

business executive. He turned and faced the crowd, holding up his hands for silence. "OK men, pipe down and listen up. This setup is strictly business and we're all partners. First of all, this dapper gentleman on my right is Chief Muldoon of the U.S. Navy."

The scruffy old sailor puffed up his chest and took a place by Carter's side. A born opportunist in his own way, he could sense the coming of a large and profitable organization. His admiration for the enterprising Sergeant was growing by leaps and bounds.

"If you men have any Jap souvenirs you can trade, don't go off half-cocked and get screwed by some fast talking con man. Make up a list and bring it back here. Be sure to add your name and unit, and spread the word. Are you tired of living like dogs while the Army and Navy get all the cream?" Over a hundred faces were turned his way.

"Yeah, they get everything and we get the shitty end of the stick!"

"What about beer and whiskey?"

"Can ya get us a juke box?"

Jake called for silence again. "What do you say, Muldoon?"

The old chief began to fidget. Carter was pressuring him again, driving him to new heights of scrounging. The tentacles of greed and profit had a tight grip on his spinning brain, and the only avenue left was forward.

"OK you mud hens, show me what ya got and I'll see if we can pluck some fat turkeys for ya!"

A cheer went up from the veteran riflemen as they turned to their new champion. Jake was ready and spoke a few final directions.

"My name is Carter, and this is my assistant Sergeant John Bowman. Bring your lists to him and we'll get back to you. Now, break it up and go back to your outfits. Give us some room to unload."

The Last Souvenir

The smiling mass broke away and filed off in four directions. A familiar figure remained and walked up to confront Jake and Johnny B.

"Remember me, Sergeant? Joe Lyons from Fox Company?"

"Sure Lieutenant." Jake extended his hand informally. "You're the historian from Oregon, right?"

"That's right. I've been taking notes. You're getting to be famous. You seem to be some kind of a pipeline to your people."

Bowman couldn't resist a comment. "That's right Lieutenant, he's a regular Marine Robin Hood. He robs the rich and gives to the poor."

"Say, I like that." Joe Lyons was writing again. "If this story builds like I think it will I may write a book about it. I could call it 'The Robin Hood of Okinawa'."

Jake's reaction took an ironic twist. "If we all survive the landing on Japan you can call it;'The Miracle of the Century'."

He had taken the concept of a redistribution of wealth and put it back into perspective. They were living on borrowed time and nothing more. He had, common to the combat veteran, swept his fatalism back into the far corners of his living space. He had given his comrades something to do and something for which to look forward. His motives were not entirely without selfishness. The thrill of accomplishment was taking his mind off his plight.

"Would you like to stick around for awhile, Lieutenant?" Jake felt compelled to continue his new friendship.

"I sure would, if you don't mind. You guys have more stories than Aesop's Fables."

"Be with you in a minute. O'Malley, I've got a job for you and your boys."

"Sure Sarge, name it."

"Here's a delivery list. Make sure everybody gets a mattress and all the trimmings. You new men get one each.

Pile 'em on everybody's cot, including Leo, Kovak, and Mike. Then take one each to the Colonel, Lieutenant Chandler, the Padre, and Frenchie Labeau. Then detour to Lieutenant Dutch in Motor Transport, Cookie in the mess hall, Gunny Stebbins and Sergeant Lang at QM. That should leave two extras. Put 'em on the floor in my tent. Sergeant Bowman is in charge."

Johnny B. spoke through a twisted grin. "Do I detect a little ass-kissing here, Jake?"

"Not a bit, call it patronage. One favor always deserves another. Politicians do it all the time. As soon as you get these guys movin', round up Moe, Del, Russ, Hull, and Leo. Get 'em in our tent right away for a meeting and join us as soon as you can."

Johnny B took the list and strode up to the big Navy truck. The replacements were already gathering their loot.

Jake beckoned to Joe Lyons to follow into his tent. Chernikov and Stack were ahead of them.

"This is Lieutenant Lyons from F Company. You men met at the front in the OP. This old man here is Sergeant Del Stack. He's a Joe College like you. University of Iowa."

Lyons shook hands with Del. "As I remember that makes you a Hawkeye."

"That's right, sir, have a seat."

Before they could seat themselves O'Malley and his work party were muscling mattresses through the door, followed by another young Marine with pillows and linen. Without asking questions they were flinging blankets and ponchos from the cots and spreading out the big pads.

"You'll have to make up your own sacks, Sarge. We're pretty busy!" O'Malley was gone.

Moe Chernikov was bouncing lightly, testing the density of his new luxury. "Shit Jake, this is heaven, and all for three crummy rifles."

The alert historian had his pad and pencil poised. "What

was that about three rifles?"

Moe and Del together unraveled the transaction for Lyons who couldn't seem to write fast enough. "I didn't realize the souvenir business was so critical. This is a hell of a deal."

"There's a lot more to come, Lieutenant." Jake paused and turned to Moe. "Don't look now but I think you've got mice under your bed."

A scratching noise was emanating from the tent flap behind Moe's cot. Moe quickly went to his knees to investigate. A hand appeared, lifting the canvas a foot above the ground. A grunting face showed itself sideways in the narrow opening.

"It's me, Eddie Gallo from communications. Is that you Jake? I got your phone."

Del stood first. "Hiya Eddie, let me give you a hand. You're early."

"Thanks buddy." Gallo handed him a field telephone and connecting wire, slithering after it.

Joe Lyons' mouth dropped open. "Now what? A private phone in your tent? Does a sexy secretary go with it?"

Eddie Gallo now stood in the center of the tent, brushing the dust from his dungarees. "OK Jake. You're hooked into a special line at the main switchboard. My boys all have the word to give you any line you want... any place on the island."

Carter was delighted. "I don't know how to thank you buddy." He stopped and looked down at his new bed. "Men, I think Sergeant Gallo should have a new mattress. What say Eddie?"

"I'll take it, Jake with pleasure, but since Moe saved my life you know I'd do anything for you scouts. You're tops in my book."

The young historian flared his nostrils again. "What do you mean saved your life? I have to record this."

Gallo looked across the tent at the stranger. "Who is this

guy, Jake? He looks like an officer!"

"He's OK Eddie, he's a friend. He's writing a book and you'll be in it."

"Me, in a book? Sure I'll tell it. I was stringing wire up to their OP on the front lines on Dakeshi Ridge. I was bent over, splicing the wire when a Jap officer jumped up behind me and pointed a pistol right at the back of my head. This big son of a bitch right here was watching the whole thing." He pointed at Chernikov. "Moe blasted him, shot him right in the ear. I got the piss scared outta me. I still shake when I think about it."

Chernikov turned serious, remembering what a close call it was. "Ya still got the pistol Eddie?"

"I sure do! That's one souvenir I'll never give up." Gallo hoisted the mattress on his shoulder and headed for the door. "Gotta go now, I've got the duty. Thanks for the pad. I'll send someone for the pillow and linen."

Leo, Russ, and Bill Hull passed him in the company street, turning right into Carter's tent. "Ya wanna see us, Sarge?"

"Yeah, squeeze in and have a seat. This is Lieutenant Lyons from Fox Company. He's a writer and he wants to meet you heroes." The men nodded him welcome and Carter opened the meeting. "Russ, let's hear from you and Bill first. Did you scout the area south of us?"

Russ Keeler was a natural woodsman, born and raised in the Pacific Northwest. To him, map reading and the outdoors came second nature. He took the contour map Leo was holding and spread it on the floor at Carter's feet. With his forefinger he retraced his steps. "Here's our camp, Jake, follow this path due south through the sugar cane to this horse pasture. Southwest is a little village marked with an X. They have a community warehouse half full of rice and sweet potatoes. The town mayor is an old man and he's in charge."

"How do you know all this?" Carter cut in.

The Last Souvenir

"Hull came back to camp and got Johnny Kovak to interpret."

"Good thinking. Go on."

"Well, it seem the old man loves our American cigarettes so Johnny K offered him two packs a week for rent. He countered with four packs, so we settled on three."

"What about security? Can we lock the place?"

Russ scratched his head. "That might be up for grabs, Jake, but the old man has two sons, and he claims nobody ever steals. They watch the place like a hawk."

Jake was decisive. "I can believe the old man. But nights might be a problem. Yes, set up a cot in the warehouse. The new men can take turns sleeping there, sundown to sunup. See that they're armed. If the old man bitches about it, take Kovak and offer him an extra pack of butts."

Moe nodded. "Gotcha Jake."

"Leo, what about military bases?"

Beauchamp crossed the tent floor and knelt beside the big map. "They're all marked, Sarge, red for Navy and blue for Army and Air Corps. I know I print pretty good so it's all there: supply dump, officers clubs, post exchanges, Red Cross, hospitals, and everything else you can think of. There's even an Army sawmill on the main road south of Motobu."

Jake began to stroke his chin with his thumb and forefinger. The men knew his conniving mind had kicked into high gear. Johnny B felt a tingling excitement as his mentor studied the map with more than a mild intensity.

"Aw come on, Sarge, let us in on it. What are you hatching?"

Carter was coming out of his semi-trance, his words slow and deliberate. "That sawmill interests me. I saw it on our way up. They ship in big timbers and cut them up into 2 X 4's and 1 X 6's. Keep this under your hats boys, we're going to pull off a big heist."

The men were in a state of shock over the magnitude of his statement, except for Bowman.

"Why lumber? How big a job will it be? Am I hearing you right, we're gonna highjack Army lumber? Isn't most of that wood reserved for officer's clubs?"

The smirk on Carter's face was almost sinister. "How would you like to have wooden floors in your tents? Aren't you guys getting sick of dirt everywhere we go? There's a way to do it and we'll go by the book. We'll play by their rules."

Chernikov was quick to respond to the daring idea. "I'm with ya buddy. It's either get shot by the Army or the Japs."

"Nobody's gonna get shot. I'm wearing four stripes now, and that means I have access to company jeeps anytime I need one. After this meeting is over Johnny, we're grabbing a jeep and heading for that sawmill. We'll park across the road and check out their routine. Bring your field glasses." Jake was anxious to move forward. "Del has already set us up with a telephone, Leo has the maps covered. That leaves you, Moe. What about trucks?"

"It's easy now that you're a regimental big shot. That fourth stripe on your sleeve did it. When you sign out a ten-wheeler you can say you're movin' troops on a training mission, no sweat."

Carter was more than satisfied. Everything was falling into place with a minimum of hitches.

"Moe, take O'Malley and four of his boys and check out a truck in my name. Take 'em over to QM and load up with as much Jap equipment as you can. We'll move it tomorrow. Leo, you and Mike will give lectures in the afternoon on map reading and aerial photos. I want those kids to be able to give artillery fire direction in their sleep. That's it, you can scram now."

Johnny B and Lyons remained. The history buff had a bushel of questions but none seemed to come out. "Sergeant

The Last Souvenir

Carter, you have dazzled me with your footwork. In all my time in the service I have never been in a meeting like yours where so much ground was covered in such a short time. Am I still welcome to come back as a visiting historian?"

"You bet, Lieutenant. Come on Johnny, we're goin' shopping at the lumber yard."

CHAPTER THIRTEEN

Truckloads of new replacements were pouring through the main gate, steering into the heart of the sprawling tent camp. Their young faces were wide-eyed with expectation as the months of training and indoctrination in the States were coming to fruition. The long boat ride was over. At last they were smack in the middle of the big war. They were headed for their new homes in the infantry battalions, unaware that their own private hell was just around the corner.

Noon chow was over as the veteran Marines filed from the mess hall and lined the street to view the familiar parade. They stood waving in a waist high cloud of coral dust.

"You'll be *SORREE*...!"

Colonel Mason stood on the other side in front of the communications tent. He watched with pride and foreboding as the awesome responsibility filled his thoughts. His regiment was bulging with combat readiness. Whatever the final victory might be, these were the young men who would take him there.

Padre Turner had joined Mason, standing by his side. "They all look so young, sir. I wish I could bless every one of them."

"I know what you mean, Father. The next time you talk to your boss I wish you'd put in a good word for me too."

Turner smiled as he turned his head, noticing the tightness in Mason's features. In the past he had detected an inner flinch in the Colonel's reaction to casualty lists. A seasoned infantry officer is trained to steel himself against such things but the trickling stream of compassion and humanity still must flow.

The enlisted men rarely consider this side of the coin but the Priest could feel it.

"I wish I could say I understand, Colonel, but I'm not in your shoes. I can guarantee a special prayer though."

Mason nodded, only half listening, an ominous mist shading his future. "I'll take all the help I can get, Padre. Thank you."

Mason was attracted by the humming of a jeep engine as the vehicle turned out of the motor pool and into the main gate. Jake was at the wheel with Johnny B in the passenger seat.

"It's Sergeant Carter and his sidekick. Dammit, they're up to something, I can smell it. Every time I see that man I don't know whether to kiss him or spank him."

Father Turner suppressed his grin for the benefit of the frustrated Mason. "You'll have to admit sir, every regiment has its operator."

"Operators yes, but I think I've inherited the master crook of the entire Marine Corps." The Colonel held up his hand and Jake ground to a halt, sitting at attention and whipping up a brisk salute.

"Good afternoon, Colonel. Hiya Padre."

The suspicious colonel waved his swagger stick across his face. "Just where do you think you're going, Sergeant? I suppose you have specific orders?"

"No sir, I'm on my own initiative. I've scheduled a training mission for tomorrow. Sergeant Bowman and I are going to reconnoiter the terrain, sir."

Mason squinted his eyes. "Reconnoiter eh? Are you sure you're not going to reconnoiter some Army supply dump instead?"

"Don't you trust me, sir? I'm just doing my duty, sir."

"Carter, I wouldn't trust you across the street, but I'm stuck with you, God help me. Excuse that last one Padre."

Padre Turner was still fighting off the humor of the love-hate relationship between the two men. "No offense taken sir."

By now the idling jeep was attracting men from all directions. Lieutenant Van der Slice crossed the street with the cook trailing him from the mess hall. Gunny Stebbins came striding up with Frenchie Labeau on his tail. Quartermaster Sergeant Lang was bounding between the tents in a fast dogtrot. The men seemed to converge on Jake within a few seconds of each other. Lieutenant Dutch had the first words.

"Thanks for the mattress and pillow, Sergeant, you've made my day!"

Frenchie Labeau was next. "Jake, I haven't had sheets in months. Thanks buddy!"

The clucking continued like hens in a chicken coop. Jake was almost overwhelmed, acknowledging their gratitude with his usual modesty as Lang patted him on the back.

Colonel Mason broke away and disdainfully walked toward his tent with Padre Turner at his side. "Why is it that every time I leave that man, he's the hero and I end up the villain?"

"Every family has a problem child, Colonel."

"You're right, Turner. I think I'll go back to my tent and write a letter to my wife. I always feel better afterwards."

"Will you be sitting on your new mattress, Colonel?"

"That was a cheap shot, Lieutenant." Mason quickly reconsidered. "Never mind Father. I'll put it down as left-handed humor. Forget it."

The little crowd around Jake was dispersing, except for Gunny Stebbins.

"Hold up a minute, Carter. I've got something I wanna get off my chest."

Jake slipped the gearshift into neutral and took his foot off the clutch pedal. "If you're gonna ream my ass make it quick. I'm in a hurry. If it's good news, take you time, Gunny."

Stebbins bowed his head and cleared his throat. "I know

you and your guys don't like me. I got off on the wrong foot, but I want to put that behind us. You and your people have shown me the new Marine Corps and I like it. I want to be a part of it."

Aghast at first, Johnny B rebounded with a facetious quip. "Why Sergeant Stebbins, I do believe you're buckin' for human being at last."

"Shut up Bowman, let him speak. Can't you see he's serious? Spit it out Gunny!"

Stebbins went on. "I want to be part of your training schedule. Why hell, I'm a Master Gunnery Sergeant. I've been teachin' kids about weapons for almost twenty years. Right now I'm nothin' but a sheep herder in this company."

"Ya know Gunny, I think you're really leveling with me."

"You bet your ass I am, Jake. I want to do more than fit in, do you savvy me?"

"OK Gunny, take it easy. Remember, we're just a bunch of civilian kids in green uniforms. We're not a bit like you regular Marines."

"Jake, I'll have to admit I was more than jealous of you when you got promoted. Why shit, it took me fifteen years to earn my fourth stripe. You got yours in less than three, can you blame me?"

"Gunny, we're fightin' the Japs, not each other. Let's bury all this horse dung and start over." He extended his hand.

The Master Sergeant clasped his hand and wrung it vigorously. "Done! Where can I start?"

Stebbins didn't know it but Jake was far ahead of him. Though the man had broken the ice, Carter had him slated as an integral part of his schedule. He was too valuable to let pass. " Gunny, these kids need to be drilled on every weapon we've got till they're sick of lookin' at 'em. Also, I want them to be able to pick up a Jap grenade or rifle and use it like it was one of ours. Can you handle it?"

Stebbins face was serious. "Piece of cake!"

"Good! Set up your lecture schedule and give it to Lieutenant Chandler for his OK."

Carter paused and came up with an afterthought. "Another thing Gunny. Blindfold 'em and make 'em sit on their asses like they were parked in foxholes. Slap mud on their weapons and teach 'em to work in the dark. There's no street lights where they're goin'!"

"These kids are going to be all thumbs, Jake. How far do you want me to go?"

"Gunny, when you get through with them they'll be slick as brain surgeons. But do me one favor. Teach 'em but don't ride 'em. They're a high spirited bunch so skip the chicken shit."

"Sergeant Carter," Stebbins had a new-style smile on his face. "I'm getting the message."

"Great." Carter vaulted out of the jeep and grabbed the Master Sergeant by the arm. "Let's take a walk. I've got a little scheme for tomorrow. This is just between you and me."

Johnny B turned to watch, resting his arm on the back of his seat. Jake was on another of his walks, holding Stebbins' arm with one hand and gesturing with the other. The Gunny was nodding, smiling with glee as he absorbed the words. Suddenly, the two parted, waving their goodbyes.

"What was that all about?" Johnny B asked as Carter climbed back into the jeep.

"I just cut him in on tomorrow's training patrol. You'll see." Carter liked his little secrets and Bowman said no more.

The jeep was in high gear, rolling smoothly on the crushed coral road. Johnny B took off his cap, slanting his head to allow the wind to blow against his face. It felt good. "Ya know Jake, I thought we'd never get outta there. You're like a juggler with too many plates in the air."

"Not a chance, pal. You ain't seen nothin' yet."

The Last Souvenir

Brand-new prefabricated structures lined both sides of the road marked with ostentatious signs. Half-round Quonset huts were the most prevalent, hooked together with connecting hallways. Sweating men on ladders were busily painting camouflage patterns on the dull metal.

The bay, and the China Sea beyond, teemed with cargo ships waiting patiently for their turns to be unloaded. The average man would have been overcome by the industrial might on display, but not Carter and Bowman. They were like pirates sailing into the middle of a rich merchant fleet.

"Pull up Jake, look over there." Johnny B was pointing at a huge brown building marked - US ARMY QUARTERMASTER, KEEP OUT. A brightly painted Army jeep was parked by the door, a plaque on its front bumper contained two white stars denoting the property of a Major General. A young sergeant was seated behind the wheel, casually reading a magazine.

Carter veered off the road and parked beside the blasé soldier. The two Marines dismounted and sauntered to his side.

"Don't they teach you Marines to read? That sign says KEEP OUT. Ya wanna get your asses in a sling?"

"Do you work here, Sergeant?" Jake was playing the salesman putting his foot in the door.

"Naw, I'm just the General's driver. He sends me over to pick up supplies for his officer's club."

Jake and Johnny B were eyeing the wooden cases stacked in the back seat. The black stenciled letters were clear: Gordon's Gin, French Vermouth, and stuffed green olives. Two Army privates appeared carrying cases of smoked oysters and canned Australian lobsters. A small carton on top was labeled: toothpicks.

Johnny B's eyes were bugging out as the jeep driver spoke. "I told you guys to clear out but it's too late now. Here comes the top sergeant and he's a mean son of a bitch!"

The short, chunky man with six stripes on his sleeves came blustering up. A handlebar mustache twitched under his bulbous nose. His eyes were badly bloodshot from the stress of his responsibilities. "What in the hell are you two birdbrains doing on my post? Can't you see this place is strictly off limits? If you're not outta here in two seconds I'm callin' the Military Police!"

Bowman was blown back by the outburst, but Carter remained unruffled. "We don't mean to intrude, Sergeant, but we just came in from the front lines. We're not familiar yet with rear area protocol. We're a little short of supplies and we thought we might do a little tradin'."

The old top sergeant moved in, sticking his face close to Carter's nose. "I don't care if you're the Wizard of Oz, you're about to get your head blown off by that guard over there!"

"Well, I guess you're too busy to talk about swappin' for some souvenirs."

The quartermaster backed off and began circling the General's jeep as if double-checking the inventory. "Waddya mean souvenirs? What kind of souvenirs?"

"Jap Army."

The squatty man remained silent for several moments, rounding the jeep for a second time. Jake could sense the old boy was taking the bait but it was too early to set the hook. In the art of con there are times when silence is golden.

"You guys are riflemen aren't you? I used to be in the infantry myself back in '38. Come on inside." The tight squeeze was over. The three men walked together as the top sergeant led them over to his cluttered desk. He seated himself and placed his hands palms down on the desktop. "What's the name of your outfit?"

"I'm Platoon Sergeant Carter and this is Sergeant Bowman. We're in the First Marines."

The Last Souvenir

"I heard about the First. You people had it rough. Now, down to the nitty gritty. My older brother and his wife have a couple of shoe stores back in Des Moines. They want some of them Jap split-toed shoes for their window display. I'd like to send a Jap helmet to my ten-year-old son in Frisco too. What do you say?"

Jake knew now was the time. The law of supply and demand was about to be enforced. "Those are prime items Sarge. The whole damn fleet is lookin' for 'em but I think I can come up with what you want."

"You ain't kidding me?"

"Nope."

"Well, lay it on me, what do you want from me?"

Carter's eyes were clear as he leaned over and planted his own palms on the desk. "The same thing the general has in his jeep: gin, vermouth, oysters, olives and toothpicks."

"Holy jumpin' shithouse mice!" The old man shot out of his chair and stared at the ceiling. "Are you tryin' to get me busted down to buck-assed private after twenty-nine years in the Army? Get the hell outta here!" He grabbed a clipboard and stomped toward the rear of his warehouse.

Johnny B was crestfallen. "Shit Jake, I think you lost him. You're askin' the guy for the moon!"

"Play it cool buddy, start walking out, slowly."

The two men reached the front door, noticing the General's jeep had left. The bright sunlight fell upon them once more. A loud voice shattered the quiet. "Hold it you birds. Freeze right there!" The quartermaster approached, puffing slightly after running the full length of his warehouse.

"Carter, you bastard. Ya got me in a vise and you know it. This is all imported stuff. The general's aide keeps track of every toothpick."

"You can jockey those books, Sarge. Maybe it's your turn to be the Wizard of Oz."

"OK Carter, tell me again what I'm gettin'."

"Two pairs of brand new split-toes, one helmet, and I'll throw in two pairs of hobnailed Jap infantry boots."

"I forgot to tell you, I'm Master Technical Sergeant Hicks. I'll have to deliver the goods myself. I can't trust anybody else. Gimme some directions."

Jake grabbed his clipboard and scratched out the necessary notes. "Call me at this switchboard, you'll get piped right through." The two men shook hands, and the old sergeant disappeared back into the pit of his problems.

Carter steered the jeep back onto the main road with Bowman looking back over his shoulder. "Ya know Jake, that old crybaby is full of bullshit. Did you see the gut on him? I think he's been sampling the general's lobsters."

"Yeah, I noticed. He should be happy we relieved him of some of his temptations."

The young men broke into laughter together, their happy moment cut short by the whirring sound of a giant saw blade.

The Last Souvenir

CHAPTER FOURTEEN

The road south narrowed sharply, confined by rows of flooded rice paddies. The July sun glanced off the water, giving the impression of reflecting mirrors. The afternoon traffic had slowed to a snail's pace, barely escaping scraped fenders as they passed each other.

The little sawmill loomed on the left, less than a mile ahead. A three-acre patch of sugar cane had been bulldozed flat to accommodate the structure and its adjoining storage yard. Surrounded on three sides by water, and completely ringed with a high barbed wire fence, it stood like a modern fortress.

A long flatbed truck of the Army Engineers stood by a raised loading platform, laden with heavy bridge timbers. A short crane was efficiently plucking the raw material from its bed and feeding it into the screaming blade. The sawyer inside was hidden from view, adjusting his saw for the sizes of board footage required.

From the front of the building a clanking conveyor belt was disgorging a finished product of fresh cut lumber. A detail of sweating men performed the grueling task of pulling the sticks from the belt and stacking them on storage pallets. They were clad in prison uniforms with large white P's painted on their backs. The Army had emptied the guardhouse of its bad boys and put them to work. A disinterested guard sat on a folding stool in the shade, watching the boring process.

The main gate by the road was clearly marked for no admittance. A wooden guard-shack stood off to one side, a telephone wire leading through the side window, its narrow front porch with an overhang providing limited protection from the sun. An armed guard with a threatening sub-machine gun had his eyes fixed in the passing traffic. Joining him was a sergeant of the Military Police, a black and white MP armband stretched around his sleeve. A wide red sign with white letters carried a simple message: ALL VEHICLES STOP HERE.

Directly across from the main entrance was another graded area, a parking lot for heavy equipment. There were no posted signs but the Marines knew by the dark brown paint on the vehicles that they belonged to the US Army. A young private with peach fuzz on his face stood guard, a small carbine slung loosely over his shoulder, faded khaki uniform indicating he had been overseas for more than a few weeks. He was leaning against the tread of a huge tractor, cleaning his fingernails with a switchblade knife and watching nonchalantly as Jake pulled his jeep off the road.

Carter boldly wheeled his jeep around and parked it between two bulldozers in full view of the sawmill operation. The empty flatbed was leaving as another one, fully loaded with timbers, was halted at the gate by the cautious sergeant. The guard stared at his clipboard as the driver handed him a piece of white paper, most likely a written requisition order. Jake was already making mental notes when the young soldier strolled to their side.

"You guys are Marines aren't ya? Ya don't look like Jap spies, what the hell are ya doin' here?"

"Hiya, Mac. I'm just curious. I worked at a sawmill once during summer vacation back home in California." Jake was not lying. Due to the wartime shortage of labor he had gone north to work as a lumberjack in the Redwoods of Eureka. The pay was good and the work was hard, getting him in shape for varsity football next season. He told his buddies that work in the sawmill was the toughest job he ever had. He gained fifteen pounds in three months, all muscle.

The young Army man was more interested in asking questions than performing his guard duties. "Have you guys seen much action?"

Johnny B nodded his head. "Yeah, we're riflemen. Came in with the assault waves back in April."

The soldier engineer was bug-eyed. "No shit! Ya lucky stiffs. I enlisted to fight but they stuck me in the Engineers. The only thing I ever do is lean on a shovel or stand guard duty. I put in for transfer into the Infantry twice but they turned me down."

Bowman looked at him with a frown darkening his face. "You gotta be kiddin'. What are you, some kinda nut? You're ridin' the gravy train and don't know it."

Carter remained silent, watching every detail of the lumber yard. Bowman was holding up his end, keeping the kid occupied. A picture was clearing in his mind but he needed more information. Getting a truckload of lumber out free and clear would be a ticklish task, but possible. Finally, he turned his head and spoke to the guard. "Hey Mac, are those guys in your outfit?"

"Yeah, why?"

"Just askin'. What's the sergeant like?"

"Aw, he's a great guy. He's on limited duty. Got hit in a Jap air raid down on New Georgia."

Carter carefully pressed for more. "I suppose he's a family man?"

"Naw, he's not married, but he has a little sister who writes to him all the time."

Jake's eyes lit up but he tried not to show any emotion. The part about the little sister could be very useful, and a plan was taking shape. This had to look like an inside job and bribery was the answer. It always worked if one pushed the right buttons. The key to the front door was the MP Sergeant, and he was taking first things first. Getting in was the problem and getting out was another. Jake needed to know more. Once again he spoke to the talkative young soldier.

"Who's in charge over there? I don't see any officer."

"Oh, you mean our Lieutenant? He's there, checkin' the paperwork on all pickups. He sees that the trucks are loaded and ships 'em out."

The simplicity of it all seemed almost childlike to Jake. The Sergeant checks the trucks in and the Lieutenant checks them out, a typical military format. He remained cool but his heart was beating faster, like he was awaiting the kickoff in a big game.

"What's your Lieutenant like?" Jake was conjuring small talk. "Does he get a lot of mail too?"

"That's a joke. He's a gun freak. Only mail he gets is magazines about handguns, ya know, pistols. He always brags he has the best collection in Texas."

BINGO! A light bulb lit up in Carter's head. His memory took him back to the conversation he had with Lang and the box of enemy pistols he had stowed away. These highly coveted prizes were extremely rare, worth their weight in platinum bricks in the souvenir trade. P-38's by name, they were a remake of the famous German nine millimeter Lugar. A real gun collector would give his soul to own one. Would he go so far as to swap a truckload of precious lumber for such a small firearm? Greed and pride are two powerful motives, and fit right into the scheme of things for Jake. The answer went off like a gong in his thoughts. 'No doubt about it.'

Carter began to break away from his mind trip, becoming aware of the droning conversation beside him. The young man had latched on to Bowman's coattails like a little brother pumping him for stories about the rigors of combat. He had no way of knowing he was a small cog in the caper that was

The Last Souvenir

unfolding and probably wouldn't care. Bowman was telling the kid how he and Chernikov had slain five enemy infiltrators in a cane patch south of Naha. Jake smiled as Johnny B embellished the tale to befit the occasion.

"That's enough boys, time to shove off." Jake turned the key in the ignition, slipped the shift into low gear and slowly pulled away.

"So long Marines. You all take care of yourselves." The soldier waved slowly as they rolled away.

"Ya know Jake, he's a nice kid. He and his buddies are bored stiff. This whole thing is crazy. He wants my job and I envy him for the soft touch he has. I must be gettin' the Asiatic fever or somethin'."

"Why Sergeant Bowman, how you talk. Don't you know the folks back home look up to you as their local war hero? They'll probably put up a statue of you in the town-square."

"Yeah, somethin' for the pigeons to shit on."

A long truck convoy heading north was blocking their entry on the road. Carter had his eye on the guard-shack by the entrance to the lumber yard, impatiently seeking a gap in the traffic allowing him to dart through. Finally a small break came in the creeping caravan and Jake made his move. He jammed the jeep into low gear, cut through and careened left, his spinning wheels spewing a rain of coral pebbles on the following truck's hood and windshield. The driver was furious, shouting profanities and waving his middle finger at the two Marines. Carter ignored the epithets, grinding his little car to a halt parallel to the wire fence.

"OK Johnny, no names please. From now on you're Hank Blake and I'm Fred Brokaw."

"You mean like those two kids that got wounded down at Machinato a couple of months back? Why the secrecy?"

"Never mind, 'Sergeant Blake', let me do the talking. I'll explain later."

Jake climbed down from his seat and circled the rear of his jeep, peering through the wire as he walked. According to his plan the guard should show up any minute. His calculation was correct. When he glanced to his right he saw the MP Sergeant approaching, smiling and applauding as he walked. "That was a helluva maneuver, Gyrene. You almost turned into a jeep sandwich. What the hell are you two guys doin' way out here?"

Carter shrugged his shoulders. "Just curious, I guess. Worked in a sawmill once and it brings back old memories."

"Well stay away from the fence, it's charged with electricity. You'll get your shorts fried."

"Thanks for the tip." Carter pointed to a stack of fresh cut lumber. "What are you going to do with all that wood?"

"That's a special order for the General's Staff." The guard's face took on a disgusted look. "They're gonna build a clubhouse for Generals and Admirals only. They're even expecting some Senators. I get a call every day from some big shot asking for progress reports. It's a buncha bullshit."

"Ya know, you're not such a bad guy, for a cop."

"Hell, I'm no cop. I'm just another dog face stuck in a boring job." The Sergeant sounded indignant. He stuck out his hand. "The name's Noonan, what's yours?"

The man was so affable that Carter hated to lie to him, but his plan was already set and it was too late to vary. "Call me Fred, and that jarhead in the jeep is Sergeant Blake."

Johnny B left the jeep and joined them. They shook hands and the next ten minutes were spent reminiscing about home and their native states. It soon became obvious that the guard-sergeant didn't give a whit about the Generals and their lumber. The GI contempt for Staff officers and their lifestyle seemed to be universal throughout the ranks. Jake broke the chain of conversation.

"We would sure like to get our hands on some of that

lumber, Noonan."

"You can have it all as far as I'm concerned." Noonan paused and broke into a beaming grin. "Wait a minute. You two jokers got some kind of scam in mind." He paused again and tugged at his earlobe. "Aw what the hell, why not, long as I can keep my skirts clean. Watcha got in mind?"

"It's very simple. How do we get a truck in and out?"

Noonan began stamping his feet with excitement. "Oh man, I love it. Them Generals are gonna piss their pants. Here's what you do. Call me on the phone before you come. Give me your name and unit, and the officer who's doin' the signing. Make a list of what you need and I'll put it on my clipboard. When you show up have a signed requisition form and I'll let you in. You'll have to figure out how to con the Lieutenant and get your truck loaded but that's your problem."

"I've already got that base covered, pal."

The mind-numbing boredom was broken for Sergeant Noonan, and he was striking a blow for the enlisted man at the same time. The three men stood grinning at each other as if to say, "that's what comradeship is all about.'

Jake had one more thing to say. "The kid across the road told us you have a little sister."

"Yeah, her name is Melissa. She's seventeen now, a real beauty and she writes to me often. I guess I'm her hero."

"Do you think Melissa would like to have a Jap kimono?"

Noonan's face lit up. "Would she? You bet. You mean a real silk one like the geishas wear? I'd give my eye teeth if I could lay my hands on one."

Jake grabbed the man's elbow. "You can keep your teeth buddy, here's the story. About two months ago our regiment captured a Jap headquarters. When we searched the place for papers I found a chest full of kimonos. Ya know, their officers had Geisha girls to entertain them. Anyway, I kept one for myself and it's in my seabag. It's yours now, you can send it to your sister."

"No shit. Really? What's it like? What color is it?"

"I'll try to describe it. It's hundred percent white silk with a brocade flower pattern. The lining is purple and it turns down at the collar. There's a gold and red obi sash that goes with it. Hope she likes it."

Noonan was ecstatic. "Like it, she'll love it. She'll probably wear it to school."

Carter looked at his watch. "It's 3:30 now, we gotta go. The next time I see you will be at your gate. I'll slip you a package with a note inside. You'll get a call in a couple of days from a Captain Manhoff. The signing officer will be Colonel L. B. Puller. Leave the rest to us, and remember MUM's the word."

"OK Marine, so long for now. Maybe when this is all over you can tell me your real name. I'd like Melissa to know."

"What do you mean by that crack?" Jake was stunned.

"When you took off your cap to wipe the dust off your face I saw the initials JHC stenciled on the inside."

"Why you sneaky bastard, you would make a good cop."

The two Marines drove away feeling the warmth of satisfaction in their breasts. Noonan was still waving as a cloud of coral dust enveloped their jeep.

The Last Souvenir

CHAPTER FIFTEEN

Lieutenant Chandler was beside himself with frustration and anger. His makeshift desk was piled high with a deluge of maps and aerial photographs from III Corps, all pertaining to the pending invasion. Colonel Mason was on his tail for a report on the progress of the new training schedule. New equipment forms had to be read and signed.

"Where in the hell is Carter? If that crazy son of a bitch is out lollygagin' with some nurse I'll have him shot."

Gunny Stebbins sat on a box beside the irate officer. He wanted to calm him but didn't know where to start. Pressure was mounting from all directions and the old Master Sergeant had seen this happen before.

"He'll be OK, Sir. Besides, he's got Sergeant Bowman with him."

Chandler straightened slowly. "Oh, he's got Johnny Bowman with him, eh? Carter's going to corrupt that nice kid. Why that's like sending him to medical school with Jack the Ripper for a professor."

Across the tent Mike and Leo began to giggle, which triggered a big smile from Gunny Stebbins. The momentum carried them into gales of laughter. The tension was broken and even Chandler was caught up in the contagious roar.

Leo was gasping for air. "That's real funny, Sir. I mean comparing Jake with Jack the Ripper. Maybe you should be a writer someday."

Chandler was, by now, laughing so hard his deep voice began to choke from lack of oxygen. He stood up with tears in his eyes and wiped his face with a handkerchief. A good laugh was perfect therapy, he thought, even if it was at the expense of poor old Jake. They had been through so many tribulations together he felt almost akin to the man. He just plain needed him and that was that.

"You're in luck, sir." Stebbins was pointing his finger through the tent flaps. "Carter and Bowman just drove by. They're probably headed for the motor pool."

"Let's call it a day, men." Chandler was stuffing maps and papers into a strongbox. He closed it and snapped the lock shut. "Let's get the hell out of this pressure cooker."

Jake and Johnny B parked the jeep and signed out. They were crossing the road, heading for the company street when they spotted Chandler coming at them from the direction of the 2 section tent. "Wait up men, I want to talk to you."

The two scouts exchanged questioning looks. "What do you suppose the old boy wants, Jake? At least he has a smile on his face."

Chandler came puffing up. "Mind if I walk with you? I need an up-to-date report on the training schedule. I've got Colonel Mason on my ass."

Carter was reassuring. "I've set up everything with Sergeant Stebbins, sir. We fall out at 8:30 tomorrow morning for a simulated recon patrol. Stebbins and I have a little surprise cooked up for the boys so keep it under your hat, sir."

"OK, I'll trust your judgment, Sergeant, but have something on my desk by tomorrow afternoon. Mason is a stickler for going by the book and he's breathing down my neck."

"Will do. Sir. I'll see if I can take the heat off."

They were interrupted by the shouts of Del Stack, standing in front of their tent, waving his arms and yelling at Carter. "Hey Jake, telephone. It's some guy named Sergeant Hicks. He's called three times already."

"Telephone? Did he say telephone?" Chandler was straining to keep pace with the fast striding young men. "Do you have a private telephone in your tent?"

"Yes, sir." Carter ducked his head and entered the tent. "Come on in Lieutenant, have a seat."

Jimmy couldn't believe his eyes. A new field telephone was placed on a wooden box next to Jake's cot. A pad and pencil were next to it with several messages scribbled on the paper. The bewildered officer sat down on the soft mattress, watching Jake pick up the receiver, thinking, 'This I gotta see.'

"Hello Hicks, this is Carter, what can I do for you? You what? Twenty minutes? Sure. OK, I'll have someone at the gate. We'll have it ready for you when you get here. Thanks Sergeant, goodbye."

"What in God's name was that all about, Carter?"

"Stay right where you are, Lieutenant, sir. There's a surprise coming and we want you to be part of it. Del, read the Lieutenant a couple of Betsy's letters. Moe, in about fifteen minutes get up to the main gate and watch for a fat old Army Sergeant driving a brown jeep. Bring him back here. Johnny, hotfoot up to QM and fill the order. Can you remember what Hicks wants?"

"You know me, I write everything down. Four pairs of boots and a steel helmet."

Chandler's jaw sagged open. It was like sitting in the middle of a whirlwind. This new dream world had already erased the stress of his day and he was too fascinated to leave. Was this the Marine Corps or some kind of a bawdy burlesque skit?

"Gotta go now, you stay right there Lieutenant." Jake was repeating himself as he flew out the door.

Chandler took a deep breath and turned to Stack and Chernikov. "Do you boys have any idea what's going on?"

"Not a clue sir, but I'll bet it'll be worth checkin' out, and you're sure as hell welcome to stay, sir, anytime." Del too had been with Chandler for a long time and he meant it.

Jake busted into the mess hall looking for Cookie. A messman was carefully mopping the floor between tables. He anticipated the nature of Carter's visit and yelled toward the kitchen. "Hey Cookie, come on out, you got company."

The cook appeared through the kitchen door and walked around the long counter. "Hiya Jake, hey, thanks again for the mattress. It's better than sleepin' on a cloud."

"Hello Cookie, come on over here and let's talk. I gotta favor to ask of you." Jake led him to the far end of the mess hall. "You're a drinking man aren't you?"

"A drinking man? I'd say a boozehound is a better description. Watcha got?"

"Can you get one of your men to run this place while you're gone?"

"Sure Jake, I'll put one of my corporals on it. They're all buckin' for sergeant. What's up?"

"Be in my tent in about thirty minutes for martinis and hors d'oeuvres."

"Are you shitting me? Martinis out here? You might as well come up with a glass of water in the Sahara Desert too."

Carter laughed at the skeptical Chef. "You've got a new ice maker and I know it's worth its weight in gold. I'll need three of your big, steel pitchers full of ice. I'll help you chop it. Also, I'll need a couple of trays. If that crate over there is empty, I'll borrow that too."

"Wait a minute, the pitchers and trays are no problem, and you can have the crate. I was going to throw it out anyway. But the ice, that's different. Most of it goes to the officer's mess."

"Screw 'em."

The cook stared at Jake for a moment before flashing a twisted smile. "Jake, I've always liked your style. Screw 'em it is. Let's get to choppin'!"

Bowman was the first to return to the tent. He jockeyed his burden through the flaps and deposited the order on his cot. Chandler arose immediately and walked over to gaze into the box.

"My God, that's captured enemy equipment. III Corps has classified that as contraband. Are you trying to get us all thrown in the brig?"

"No sir, Lieutenant, there's no law against collecting a few souvenirs is there?"

"I'm beginning to smell a rat. If you and Carter are behind this it's got to be shady." Chandler returned to Jake's cot, putting his face in his hands. "Well, there goes my commission."

"Cheer up, sir, Jake and I have everything covered. All you've seen is some boots and a helmet."

Jimmy grinned. "Guess you're right, I'll let it go at that, but I don't want to know anymore."

Moe looked at his watch and jumped to his feet. "Time to go. Gotta date with a fat man." He bolted through the door, passing Jake on the way out.

The Army Quartermaster Sergeant was right on time, meeting Moe simultaneously at the front gate. The young sentry had him stopped dead in his tracks. Mason had stiffened the gate security. Moe walked up to the passenger side and spoke to the guard.

"It's OK Sonny. He's with me."

"Yes sir, Sergeant," and he waved him through.

Hicks looked sideways at Chernikov as he put the jeep in gear. "Are you one of Carter's men?"

"Yep. They call me Moe. Go straight ahead and take the first right."

"What kind of a man is Carter? Is he trustworthy?"

"Trustworthy?" Moe was slightly annoyed and didn't mind showing it. "We're foxhole buddies. I've trusted him with my life. Does that answer your stupid question?"

"No offense Moe, your loyalty just answered my question. I have some more business for him and I don't want to get my butt caught in a bear trap."

"You won't." Moe was no diplomat, over-protective of his pal. He wasn't cut out to be a salesman. "Pull up in front of that first tent."

Moe climbed out of the quartermaster's jeep and went inside. Carter came out and walked around the jeep to shake hands with the old Sergeant. "Hello Hicks. Thanks for coming."

Hicks was apprehensive as he shook Jake's hand. "Who is that big ape, Carter? He's kinda testy. Looks mean enough to chew roofing nails."

"Naw, not Moe. He's a pussy cat when you get to know him, kinda like a self-appointed bodyguard."

"OK Carter, if you say so, but I'm sure glad he's on our side." Hicks stayed in his jeep, leaning closer to Jake and speaking in a hushed tone. "Do you remember my telling you about our two family shoe stores? Well, we have clothing dummies in the window. Can you get me a couple of Jap uniforms and two more helmets?"

"Can do Sergeant. Same deal as this one?"

"OK Carter, the price is pretty stiff, but the same deal. Whatever you do, keep this whole thing quiet, I got my neck stuck out a mile already. Ya better send one of your men to my place for the pick-up next time."

O'Malley had edged close to the jeep, craning his neck to view the contents, with no success. The sly Sergeant had everything covered with a tarp.

"Can you drive a jeep, O'Malley?"

"Sure Sarge."

Carter turned back to Hicks. "I'll send this man. With his red hair you could recognize him anywhere."

With the deal consummated Jake swung back to O'Malley. "Sean, get this stuff unloaded and stowed in my tent." Then he called to Bowman. "Hey, Johnny, bring that order for the Sergeant."

Hicks was happy as a child with a new toy when he drove away. The merchandise was stacked neatly in the corner of the big pyramid tent. Russ and Bill had found their way inside along with Leo and Mike. An eerie silence hung in the air as they read the exotic labels together. They could not believe what they were reading. It was all there in large black stenciled lettering. Jake and Johnny B just stood to one side, grinning from ear to ear. It was Bill Hull who severed the silence.

"Is that a mirage or is it two cases of Gordon's Gin I see?"

"Yep."

Leo was next. "Smoked oysters too?"

"Yep."

Chandler, in peacetime a gourmet diner, found his own words. "Carter are you going to stand there and tell me you have three cases of canned lobsters?"

"Yep."

As if by spontaneous combustion a rousing cheer went up. It was no secret now, the noise was heard at least twenty tent rows away. If ever a group of men needed a morale boost it was there for them now. The memories of eating cold beans at the front were washed away. Even if it was only a small piece of civilization it was enough.

"I see it, but I don't believe it." It was Padre Turner who had elbowed through the crowd, attracted by the noise.

It was time for someone to take charge. Carter raised his arms for quiet. "Hull, didn't you tell us once you used to be a bartender?"

"I sure was, Sarge."

"Well there it is: Gin, vermouth, stuffed olives and toothpicks. Over there are pitchers and ice. How about whipping up the biggest batch of martinis in the world?"

Another cheer erupted as the men scurried away in search of their canteen cups. Moe and Johnny B pried open the wooden cases while Del worked his can opener. Within minutes cups were being filled while trays of toothpicked hors d'oeuvres were passed around.

Cookie arrived and quickly poured himself a double. Chandler and the Padre had canteen cups shoved in their hands. Kovak and Frenchie Labeau were next. Most of the crowd found itself pushed into the company street. Of the replacements, only O'Malley and two others imbibed, and they were present. The non drinkers were there too, wasting no time spearing the smoked oysters.

Chandler and Turner had worked their way outside and were observing the merriment from the fringe. "You know, Padre, an hour ago I was down in the dumps. Now I'm back up high in the sky. Carter must be some kind of magician. I don't know if he's a saint or the Devil in disguise."

The Padre put his hand on Chandler's shoulder. "Jimmy, he's certainly not the Devil. He - oh no, don't look now. Here comes Mason."

The men saw him too. Someone shouted, "A-TEN-HUT!"

Those in the street snapped to attention. The bedlam inside the tent continued uninterrupted.

Mason was walking alone, banging his swagger stick against his right leg. "Lieutenant Chandler," he bellowed "what's the meaning of this?"

"Colonel Mason sir, it's just a ..."

"Never mind, Lieutenant, Carter's at the bottom of this. Get Sergeant Carter out here on the double!"

"Yes sir." Chandler pushed his way into the crowded tent and dragged Jake through the melee. Jake looked the fuming officer in the eye, shifting his canteen cup to his left hand so as to execute a hand salute.

"Good evening, Colonel."

Mason wouldn't dignify his salute by returning it. "Put your hand down Carter and stay at attention. Once more you've disrupted the discipline of my camp. Do you realize we have rules against drinking on a military base? You've stretched my patience too far this time."

"Are you going to have me shot, sir?"

Mason's eyes traveled around the circle of young faces. Jake was on the spot and they didn't dare smile. He turned back to face Carter. "Carter, are you crocked?"

"No sir, not yet, sir. I mean no, sir."

"Sergeant Carter..."

Before the Colonel could finish his announcement Jake interrupted. "Colonel, before you have me dragged away may I say something?"

Mason bobbed his head once, condescending to let Carter continue. Jake raised his cup.

"Men, no matter what happens to me, I propose a toast. Yes, a toast to the finest commanding officer in the entire United States Marine Corps. Gentlemen, I give you Colonel A.T. Mason."

The men responded in unison, raising their cups high in the air. *"TO COLONEL MASON."* They sipped their drinks and returned to attention.

Mason was touched by the sentiment and the reaction of his men. He was caught between the proverbial rock and hard place. It had been many months since he had seen morale soar this high. He also remembered the same thing happened to him over two years ago on Guadalcanal when his boys got stoned on 'Jungle Juice.' There is a fine line between respect and villainy.

"Carter, I'm going to bend this time. You can thank your combat record for that. Now get rid of that booze and get your men up to the mess hall."

Mason turned abruptly and went marching off, muttering to himself. He had gone about thirty paces when he heard the pounding of boots on the crushed coral. A young replacement had reached his side, saluting as he walked.

"Colonel Mason, sir, Sergeant Carter told me to give you this. He said to tell you it's a tribute from your scout section, sir."

"Gimme that thing. Dismissed Private."

The colonel held up the bottle and read the label. "Gordon's Gin, eh. At least he has good taste."

CHAPTER SIXTEEN

Platoon Sergeant Carter read the luminous dial on his wristwatch. '*Oh no*, it's only 4:30 in the morning.' He had been plagued with a panorama of terrifying dreams and now he was wide awake, a torrent of thoughts pouring through his mind. The dawn would bring the first day of the new training schedule, charging him with responsibility for preparing his little brothers for war. Uncle Sam had just given him a raise in pay and the time had come for him to earn it.

The remnants of a half-moon still hung in the western sky, affording a dark gray hue on the company street. In the dim light the big tents stood like monuments in a ghostly valley, offering shelter to thousands of young warriors. 'How come they sleep and I can't?'

Clad only in a pair of dark green shorts he swung his feet from the cot, feeling the cold dirt floor with his toes. 'What in the hell is the matter with me?' He heard the heavy breathing of his tent mates as he strained his eyes against the darkness. The copious martinis from the previous night had filled his bladder, making a trip to the head his first priority. He slipped bare feet into his field boots and groped for a towel and shaving kit. 'Shaving in the dark at 4:30 in the morning? The boys are going to think I blew my cork.'

Jake felt his way through the tent flaps, orienting himself with the soft light coming from the toilet shed at the end of the street. He turned right and clopped along in his untied boots. A sleepy-eyed sentry accosted him, armed with a rifle and cartridge belt.

"Mornin' sarge, trouble sleepin'?"

"Naw thanks, I'm OK." He found his way to the latrine and stood complacently urinating into the metal trough below. 'It's those boys, those young boys. Some of them are going to be killed but *by god* they're not going to die half trained. I'll see to that.' He felt a swelling of dedication in his throat. 'Good old Moe and Johnny B, they'll help me. The kids have so much to learn... so much.'

Fumbling outside, he faced the washing counter, turning the spigot to feel the cold water in his cupped hands. The cool liquid felt good on his face as he worked up a lather with a new cake of soap. Cold water shaving to him was simply a way of life. Suddenly his thoughts went to visions of his mother. She wrote to him about her new friendship with the postman and how delighted he was when she received a letter from her son overseas. They would stand together on the front porch while she opened his letters and shared them. He wasn't kidding himself and neither was she. They both dreaded the possibility of that final message that her son had been killed in action. Every month, thousands of these crushing telegrams went out to a nation of brave mothers. Jake's awareness of this was becoming keener.

The whole package was formulating in his mind and his resolve was climbing. 'By heavens, if my mother can find the courage, so can I.' He gathered his toilet articles and hurried back to his tent. With the aid of a small flashlight he read his mother's last letter with renewed interest, trying desperately to scan between the lines, feeling strength and love flowing through him. He was ready now.

The sunrise came on schedule, shooting its yellow rays between the tents. Jake was fully clothed in a field uniform, sitting on his cot with a contour map spread across his lap. The debris of last night's cocktail party still cluttered the empty crate in the corner. Rude blaring from the company bugler was greeted by the usual groans and turning bodies. Mechanically, and with a smile on his face, Gunnery Sergeant Stebbins forced aside the tent flaps.

"Good morning, Sergeant Carter, I see you're up early. This is a surprise."

"Hello Gunny, is everything set?"

Stebbins nodded with assurance. "All set. Roll call in thirty minutes."

A curious Johnny B raised himself to lean on his elbow, yawning as he spoke. "What's with you and the gunny, Jake? How come the buddy-buddy shit?"

For now, Carter could only smirk. His inner batteries were recharged from another direction, abounding with enthusiasm and a new sense of duty. "You'll see John, my boy. Hit the deck, we've got work to do." With that he was up and gone. His new challenge was both inspiring and deadly. He roamed from tent to tent, counting noses and urging his men to arise and face the new day.

The morning formation came off without a snag. Sergeant Stebbins faced the company, listening to the attendance reports from the section leaders. Gratified by another perfect roll call he lowered his clipboard. "Platoon sergeants, dismiss your men for chow."

Jake spun around and stayed back, in full view of his scout section. "Before we break up, I'm going to lay out today's training problem." He began describing a lesson on map reading and the use of a compass. Reconnaissance and observation came next as he outlined their predetermined line of march. The men, young and old alike, were both surprised and impressed by his transformation. The image of a smiling con artist was slowly brushed aside, replaced by the form and substance of a real fighting Marine. The young replacements responded first, soaking in every word with a new confidence. 'If anyone could teach us it was Sergeant Carter.'

Even the veterans were soberly contemplating the

meaning of their new responsibilities. They had seen a new side to their old buddy Jake. An astrological forecaster would explain it as a split personality of his Gemini sun sign. A military psychiatrist would diagnose it as 'acceptance of leadership'. To Carter it was simple; a perfect synopsis is nobody gets killed and everyone goes home unscratched, unreal as that may seem.

The other sections had long since broken away and headed for the mess hall. Jake was getting anxious to close. "OK boys, that's it for now. I want everybody back here at 8:30 with the whole works: Helmets, rifles, cartridge belts, and light field packs. You new Sergeants, meet me in the mess hall in ten minutes. That's all."

Jake was off first, striding rapidly up the street, headed for the 2 section tent. Leo had told him a box of the new field compasses had arrived and he wanted to inspect them. Lieutenant Chandler was alone in the tent when Carter entered.

"Good morning, Sergeant. Are the boys ready to go?"

"Yes sir, I just came in for that new box of compasses."

"Right over there." Chandler pointed to a carton on the floor next to a drafting board. "Well, what have you cooked up? I realize you're on your own initiative, but don't you think your commanding officer deserves at least a preview?"

Carter picked up the box and examined the contents. "Excellent, these are great, ten times better than our old ones." He moved closer to the waiting Lieutenant. "Sir, the Gunny and I have hatched up a surprise for the men. Last night Stebbins went out and planted five dummy land mines on our line of march. He also strung a couple of trip wires. Everything is camouflaged. We'll see if the boys can spot 'em."

Chandler emitted one of his famous deep-throated chuckles. "That's a good one, Jake. Sneaky but good. Be sure to give me a report on the outcome."

"Will do Lieutenant. I'll see you tonight." Jake departed

with the box under his arm, heading in the direction of the mess hall, where his four buddies were waiting for him, having secured a table by the door. Johnny B was the first to see Carter approaching. "Here he comes now, get ready."

When Carter entered the mess hall his four buddies sprung to attention with smart hand salutes.

"*Good morning, General Sir!*"

Over a hundred faces turned to observe the red-faced Carter. "At ease you shitbirds. Guess I deserve that one. Shut up and sit down, I've got a plan and I need your help."

Carter sat next to kindly Del Stack, who put his hand on Jake's back. "No offense buddy, we're just havin' a little fun. We all think you're doin' fine, just fine. Tell us what you need.

Bowman sat across from him, shoving a tray of breakfast his way. "Here you go, Jake, I made up an extra tray for ya. Scrambled powdered eggs, fried Spam, and bread. Lovely isn't it?"

"Here, you'll need ketchup to go with it." Chernikov shoved a gallon can of the red glop in front of his tray.

Jake ignored the spartan nature of the menu, covering the Spam with dark red sauce as he ate, resigned to the fact that anything was better than a cold can of beans. His mother would be appalled by the raw basics of the fare the boys were enduring, but that story would have to wait for a better time.

"Do you guys remember how green we were when we joined this outfit back in the Solomon Islands? Russ, you and Dell were there."

Russ Keeler assented. "Yeah, I remember, you were like street punks itchin' to start a fight."

"You're right Russ. Del, you sat me down on a log and talked about dead heroes, remember?"

Del smiled. "It musta worked, we're all still alive. It's been almost two years."

Carter was making his point. "Boys we've got a whole crop of new kids just like we were. I want you to tell 'em every war story you can think of. Tell 'em every nasty trick the Nips have thrown at us. They're a fine bunch of young men and they deserve the best we can give. Remember Charlie Manhoff? He used to say, 'I don't want your mother to get one of those telegrams for nothing.' Charlie was right, I feel the same way. How about you Moe?"

Chernikov was in solid agreement. "OK buddy, if that's what you want I'll give it to 'em good." A response that triggered an avalanche of thought. The seminar lasted almost an hour with rapid-fire comments crisscrossing the table. The five veterans willingly accepted the heavy pack of duty on their shoulders. They left the mess hall together with a fresh attitude on the awesome task ahead.

Carter was deep in thought, walking with Bowman and Chernikov on the crowded company street. His concentration was interrupted by an excited O'Malley emerging from their tent.

"Hey Sarge, I answered the phone like you told me. Ya got three messages." He held up a scrap of paper and waved it in the air.

At first, Jake was reluctant to switch away from his plans for the day but he slowly reconsidered. "What the hell, a little business as usual couldn't hurt anything. Good work Sean, read 'em out loud."

"Well Sarge, the first is from a Sergeant Miller at the Yontan airstrip, somethin' about souvenirs for the pilots and crews. He runs the officer's club. The second is from Sergeant Hicks at the Army QM. He wants us to pick up another load of gin and lobsters. I told him I'd be there like you said but you would call first. The third is the best, I think, it's from Chief Muldoon. He said he heard someone talk about a Juke box and he's found one."

The Last Souvenir

"A Juke box?" Jake and Johnny B looked at each other and broke into smiles. "Does it work? What about records?"

O'Malley was sheepish but remained positive. "Well, Muldoon says it needs some work but I've got that base covered. My buddy, Private Levine, used to work in his father's drug store in Brooklyn. One of his jobs was to fix the box when it broke down. He makes his own parts and hops up cars too. He's a good mechanic. I asked him about it and he said 'no sweat'."

"Sounds like you've been busy, Sean. What did you tell Muldoon?"

"Well Sarge, I've heard you talk so I tried to think like you. He wants five new Arisaki rifles for it, but I told him since it was busted it was only worth three. He bitched at first. Claims it cost him over five-hundred bucks but I don't believe him. Do you Sarge?"

Carter laughed. "Ya know kid, I believe you've got the makings of a real operator. What did you tell him?"

"I offered him three rifles and he finally went for it. I hope you don't mind my taking the liberty, but it sure would be swell to have a jukebox in the mess hall. The chief said it has Glen Miller and everything. Did I do OK?"

Carter couldn't resist the young man's exuberance and the way his eyes sparkled with expectation. "You did fine Sean. Be sure to bring three rifles to my tent, and get those boots and stuff for Hicks too. After the training lecture this afternoon I want you to check out a jeep in my name and make the pickup. Sergeant Bowman will give you the directions. Be sure you get there before five o'clock. Is there anything else?"

"Gee thanks Sarge, real stateside music. There is one more thing. Chief Muldoon will be here at four o'clock with the juke box and Private Levine is ready to go to work. He has his own tools." O'Malley handed the messages to Jake and hurried away to tell his pals the good news.

Johnny B stood watching the excited young redhead duck into his own tent, spreading the news like a town crier. "Jake, the Colonel's gonna crap his pants when he sees Muldoon pull up with that juke box."

"Don't worry about Colonel Mason. I'll put Padre Turner on this one. We'll chalk it up to morale."

Moe Chernikov exited the tent, a steel helmet on his head and a submachine gun slung on his shoulder. "It's after eight o'clock Jake. Almost time to move out."

"You're just in time Moe, roust out the men. Inspect their weapons and check their gear. Issue the new compasses and grab that contour map on my cot. Show 'em how to orient the map on the new magnetic north. They've all been trained in map reading but show 'em again. We're on a new grid."

The huge Marine was the perfect choice for training new men. The replacements would soon be introduced to one of the toughest and most experienced men in the regiment. To Chernikov, war was a serious business. His stern appearance and blunt delivery would imbue them with enlightenment and a new purpose: Kill the enemy and stay alive.

Inside the tent, Carter and Bowman carefully donned their combat gear, yanking at the bolts on their weapons. Gunny Stebbins had prepared a special pack for Jake and left it under his cot. He reached for it and slipped his arms into the straps, adjusting it high on his back. He briefly discussed the contents, all pertaining to advanced training, and Bowman nodded.

Carter stuck his thumbs under his pistol belt and gave it one last hitch. "Come on buddy, it's time to go to work."

The Last Souvenir

CHAPTER SEVENTEEN

Like the cast of a Broadway show in full costume, assembled on stage and awaiting a last dress rehearsal, the young men stood ready in front of their tents. The menacing look of a combat platoon had materialized in the morning sun. With camouflaged helmets pulled low on their foreheads and .30 caliber M-1 rifles in their hands they were armed and dangerous. They were the solid building blocks. It was Carter's job to apply the cement.

Jake wasted no time, circling the group with his experienced eyes scrutinizing pack straps and first aid pouches. Canteens were full and new compasses were securely attached on the right front of their cartridge belts. He stopped and removed a utility knife from its scabbard, testing it for sharpness. He felt satisfied and proud when he looked into their determined faces.

"We'll move out in single file. I'll take the lead until we clear the camp, then I'll fall back to the rear and observe. Sergeant Bowman's group will take the point. Sergeants Chernikov and Stack will follow. Sergeant Keeler's group will trail as rear guard."

An unexpected Lieutenant Chandler had appeared, standing a short distance away, raising his hand as Jake led off. He watched the spotted helmets as they bobbed along, following his platoon sergeant. Carter's off duty antics would be an enigma to any commanding officer, but he was a first class fighting man and Chandler felt good when Jake was in charge. When his scout section disappeared he turned away and shuffled up the street, wishing that sometimes he could take off his silver bars and go with them.

New replacements always seem to arrive with near perfect physiques. Months of hard physical conditioning had brought them to a peak of readiness. Breathing without strain under the weight of their heavy equipment they trod lightly along the narrow path. The urban-like tent camp fell far behind them, opening the countryside.

After climbing a small rise, Carter raised his left hand. "OK boys, we'll stop here." He motioned for them to gather on the high ground. "There's today's recon problem between here and that little village. I want you to grow eyes in the back of your heads, memorize every blade of grass, count every beetle if necessary. You may be asked to draw sketches if they're needed."

The valley was spread below them like an old oil-painted mural. Water filled rice paddies lined both sides of the path, retained by neatly spaded earthen squares. Patches of greenish brown sugar cane fields added intermittent colors, with ankle-high grass growing on the edges and across the trail. Occasional outcroppings of white coral punched through the reddish brown soil, dwarf pine trees growing between them. Almost out of sight, next to a barn like structure, two ponies grazed in a pasture confined by a low stone wall. The village was beyond and completed the picture.

Carter had a few more things to say. "Looks peaceful, doesn't it, boys? Well I've seen valleys like that turn into a slaughterhouse. That's why they send us in first. We're supposed to be the eyes of the Regiment. As graphically as possible Jake spoke of the perils they would face: artillery fire, snipers, mines, and a dozen others. The force of his delivery and experience came surging into their open minds, a new type of mental plasma. They were drinking a cocktail mixture of fright and patriotism. The wonderful high-spirited courage of youth was in them and Jake could sense it.

"There's one last thing before we move out. Every step you take from now on, pick out the next best place to take cover. Usually there will be plenty of shell holes. If not, a small ditch, or even a fold in the ground is OK. Trouble strikes fast so ya gotta move on instinct. OK Johnny, lead out. Stay behind your boys so you can watch 'em."

The single file started down the gentle slope with rifles at the ready. The group sergeants spaced them at ten pace intervals, warning against bunching up. They looked like they were walking on fresh eggs, but they were learning. When Russ Keeler's group passed, Jake brought up the rear. The line now was strung out over fifty yards, Jake being only partially impressed. He climbed atop a small coral head and shouted at the top of his lungs. *"MORTAR ATTACK, TAKE COVER. TAKE COVER."*

The replacements froze in their tracks, stunned and confused. The veteran Chernikov was on them immediately, shouting loudly. "You heard the Sergeant, take cover!"

Panic ensued, men racing in four directions like patrons leaving a flaming movie theater. Some sloshed through rice paddies while others crashed into the sugar cane. Three tried to worm behind a coral rock barely large enough to hide one. At some time in the future they might find humor in this comic opera, but for the present it was pathetic.

With hands on hips, Chernikov remained on the path, shaking his head as Johnny B joined him. Carter trotted up and stood with them as they gazed at the exposed bodies of the frustrated young men.

"Well boys, it looks like the kids need some work. You know what to do."

Carter paced back along the path and stopped, raising his hand to the side of his mouth. "Alright men, you can come out now. Don't feel bad, this is only your first dance. You'll get the hang of it."

He was neither apologetic nor cruel, and the men appreciated his empathy. When they reappeared, their once clean uniforms were soggy with mud and dark water. Also, the affirmation of reality had drenched their brains. More determined than ever they continued their march.

In less than forty-five minutes the patrol reached the pasture and filed along the inside of the stone wall. Across the field two pint-sized horses stared at them with bored looks on their shaggy faces. Carter ordered the men to stop and take a seat on the wall. "Well men, I want a full report on everything you've observed. Who wants to be first?"

"Me, Sarge." Sean O'Malley stood and shoved a fat cigar in his mouth.

"Where'd you get the cigar, Sean?"

"Chief Muldoon gave it to me for helpin' out."

Carter shook his head and smiled. "Normally I'd tell you that thing'll stunt your growth, but right now it doesn't matter. Over half of you guys are dead." Eleven pairs of wide eyes looked at Jake in shock, with the long faced O'Malley at the top of the list.

"Waddya mean dead, Sarge?"

"I mean dead, like in corpse." Jake was purposely testing, dropping a bomb in their laps to stress urgency. It worked. A buzz of conversation broke out and a barrage of questions were fired his way. The hubbub was subdued by a confident young man who stood and moved up to face Carter, staring directly into his eyes.

"I beg to differ with you, Sergeant, but your premise is not entirely correct."

Jake was startled by the man's flawless diction. He spoke with the eloquence of an English professor, yet with the softness of a nursing mother. His politeness seemed out of place in the hard-bitten infantry. Swarthy skin and wide set cheekbones, topped off with a crown of jet black hair, gave him the

The Last Souvenir

countenance of an American Indian.

Carter stared back. "So you beg to differ? What's your name Marine?"

"Hightree, Private Jesse Hightree, sir."

"Well Hightree, it sounds like you do have something to say. You appear to be Indian, are you a Navajo?"

"No sir!" The young private took an emphatic stance. "Full-blooded Sioux from the Dakotas. My Great, Great Grandfather fought against General Custer at the Little Bighorn."

Silence hung heavily on the men as they weighed his words. Moe Chernikov threw in his own ideas. "Ya know, that old dogface son of a bitch Custer wudda won if he'd taken Marines with him."

A hail of laughter came down but the laconic Indian was unmoved. Carter was anxious to hear the man's reaction to Moe's analysis. "What do you say to that, Jesse?"

"Sergeant Carter, the pride in our tribal heritage is timeless. However, after serving a few short months in the Marine Corps, I am inclined to agree with Mr. Chernikov."

Clapping their hands with delight the men applauded their new champion. The usually non-verbal Hightree was restoring a new confidence in their lives.

"Well Jesse, why don't you tell us why you beg to differ with me?"

The young brave looked away and gestured back across the valley. "Along the path there were five places where the dirt had been disturbed and replaced, denoting the possible presence of land mines. In the grass, two pieces of green trip wires, probably grenade traps."

Jake could hardly believe his ears. Hightree was a gem of a discovery. "That was very good, Jesse, almost too good. Did they teach you that in recon school?"

"No, Sergeant, from my father. He's a tour guide and

tracker. He's been teaching me trail signs since I was three years old."

"I see, is there anything else you can add?"

"Yes sir, that bush over there." Hightree pointed toward a clump of foliage in the center of the pasture. "I've been around horses all my life. By now they would have consumed it, eaten it down to a stubble. It's wrong, out of place."

"Do you hear that men? Private Hightree doesn't like that little bush."

By now, the men were too apprehensive to answer. The Indian had called the shots and they thought best to quietly wait. Jake turned his head and shouted across the field.

"OK Sergeant Stebbins, you can come out now."

The bush began to rise, revealing the camouflaged form of Gunny Stebbins. In his hands he held a Browning automatic rifle. He pointed the light machine gun upward and fired two long bursts at the sky, demolishing the morning silence. Their brush with death was only simulated, but the noise brought cold shivers along the spines of the trainees. O'Malley was choked with remorse.

"You were right, Sarge. We walked right by that damn thing. We'd all be dead."

"Cheer up Sean, there's always an answer. Never trust the Jap. If something doesn't look right tell your buddies. Take cover and toss a grenade. It's better to blow the patrol and play it safe."

Sean looked around and saw the veterans nodding in agreement. The teenager felt he had just grown up a notch. His respect for the reclusive Hightree was mounting, and a new comradeship was about to be born.

Sergeant Carter placed himself in front of his men, noticing each had a firmer grip on his rifle. This was a good sign. He held his pack in his left hand as he reached inside to reveal a gray hand grenade. Its elongated shape resembled an oversized beer can with rounded edges. On the top end a ringed retainer pin held the handle and firing mechanism in place. He held it high in his right hand for all to see. "Gentlemen, this is a white phosphorous grenade. It's one of the most dangerous weapons we have. It's too dangerous to be used in stateside training. When you pull the pin and let this spring handle fly off it ignites a powder-train fuse. You've got five seconds to get rid of it before all hell breaks loose."

Awe spread across the faces of the recruits as they viewed the menacing gray bomb. They had never seen their Platoon Sergeant so serious before, hanging their attention on his next words. Carter paused a few seconds before he continued.

"When this sucker goes off, it's like the Fourth of July. It blows a fountain of burning phosphorous in four directions. Each piece is about the size of a marble and it burns through everything it touches. The nasty part is it will burn clean through a human body and nothing can stop it. Hold up your questions. I'm turning this lecture over to Sergeant Chernikov. He has an arm like a quarterback. He'll show you how and when to use it."

Moe came forward, taking the grenade and hefting it in his hand. The grim look on his face would frighten the bravest of men. He only knew one way to deliver a war story, blunt and to the point. "Jake's right. This baby is murder, sheer murder. Ya gotta toss it at least twenty yards or you'll be sorry. Ya throw it roundhouse with a stiff arm like this." He simulated a wide sweeping arc with his arm.

"You shudda seen Jake the time a wild piece flew into his sock. He jumped like a stuck pig." Johnny B couldn't resist telling the story on his buddy.

Carter nodded. "Sergeant Bowman is right. He had to scrape it off me with his knife." He peeled down his sock and showed a dime-sized scar on his ankle.

"Couldn't you pour water on it ,Sarge?"

"Hell no! Water has oxygen. It just burns harder. You have to cut it out."

Chernikov was anxious to get on with the grisly business. "The Nips love to hang out in sugar cane. They crawl in during the day and hide. We send out patrols to root 'em out. When ya get close enough, toss in a couple of phosphorous grenades. That sets 'em on fire and they jump up. Then everybody throws frag grenades and blows 'em up. Ya move in with rifles and finish 'em off."

Moe hesitated when he saw Jesse Hightree look down, shaking his head. "What's your problem, Mac?"

Hightree did not look up as he forced a slow and feeble answer. "I guess it's the futility of war, Sergeant. It seems to resolve itself into butchery."

The fiery Chernikov stomped forward to confront the young Indian. "Listen Junior, you're a Marine rifleman now, not a prophet. I lost my big brother at Pearl Harbor. They never even found his dogtags. The Japs asked for it and we're payin' 'em back. Is that clear?"

Hightree was unabashed when he turned up his face. "I'll be OK, Sergeant. I too lost a brother, six months ago at Iwo Jima."

The crusty Chernikov was taken aback, inwardly touched with compassion for the young man. He stepped closer and put a hand on his shoulder. "I'm sorry kid, I didn't know. I guess that puts us in the same boat. You can stick with me anytime." He meant it.

Carter's shock treatment was working, showing in the eyes of the new replacements. Until now the war had seemed a great adventure. Casualty lists were only newspaper items, measuring in the thousands. By being reduced to the stark reality of man-to-man on a battlefield, the moment of truth was at hand. They had, at last, been sent to the famous FMF, the Fleet Marine Force, Pacific. It was their turn to ante but this was no poker game. The stakes were high and some of the players would never walk away. The fun and games of high school and college life would be expunged from their minds, perhaps forever.

Jake was now at the forefront again, holding a coil of rope. "From now on every scout group will carry a piece of rope like this. Believe it or not it may save your life. Sergeant Keeler will explain how to use it."

Russ Keeler advanced to take the heavy cord from Jake's hand. Russell's boyish looks and shy demeanor belied his cunning in dealing with the treacherous enemy for more than two years. As a heavyweight wrestler in college his skills had elevated him to team captain. Once, while grappling with Chernikov in a moment of frolic, he slammed him to the ground and pinned him in a matter of seconds. Moe never forgot his uncanny body strength and held him in great respect.

"Hiya fellas." Russ spoke in a soft monotone. The boys had heard about him but, until today, he had remained a face in the crowd. They were anxious to listen as he continued. "You guys know what ghoul hunting is by now. We search dead bodies. The problem is a dead Jap can kill you too. They even booby trap their dead, so when you turn 'em over they go kablooie." He gestured with both hands as though forming a cloud of smoke. "There's a lot of dead Marines who never knew what hit 'em. From now on, when you see an enemy body, take this rope and tie a slip knot around his heel. Then, you jump in a shell-hole and give it a yank. If he doesn't blow up you can frisk him."

A hurricane of questions came his way. Russ stood like a patient father explaining the birds and bees to his son. When he was finished he noticed Sergeant Stebbins had wedged himself between him and Carter.

"You guys are scarin' the hell out of me. This is one of the best training sessions I've ever attended. Lieutenant Chandler was right, out here we have to rewrite the manual."

Jake looked sideways and whispered from the corner of his mouth. "Stick around, Gunny, there's a lot more to come."

The Last Souvenir

CHAPTER EIGHTEEN

Down the street, with the warm morning sun on his back, Johnny Kovak sang lustily in baritone as he bounced along. "San Francisco, open your Golden Gate, dum tee dah dum..." He burst into the intelligence tent, raising both arms in salutation. "Greetings Leo, how goes the Great World War?"

Boston Leo sat hunched over his drafting board, a thick stack of aerial photographs under his elbows. "How come you're so cheerful? Ya been sippin' Jake's gin again?"

"Naw, if I sing about my hometown it keeps me from gettin' homesick."

Leo looked up. "Well sing about Boston once in awhile. I get homesick too, what's up?"

Johnny K lowered his voice as he gazed down at Leo's work. "Jake told me you were drivin' a truckload of Jap equipment to the village at 11:00. He needs an interpreter so I'm goin' too. Say, what's that contraption you're lookin' thru?"

"This gadget puts air pictures in three dimensions. I'm trying to sort out enemy positions in our next operation."

"No kiddin'? Do you know where we're goin'?"

"Yah, Kyushu, Japan."

"No shit, did you get the scoop from III Corps?"

"Naw, I got it from Tokyo Rose. She was broadcastin' on the Jap's radio last night. She ain't been wrong yet."

Kovak's face began to beam as he formed a mental image in his mind. "Ya know, I'd like to meet that broad after the war. I'm pretty handy with Japanese chicks. Maybe she'll invite me into her boudoir."

Leo put down his pencil and rose to his feet. "Yeah, sure,

and she'll probably give you a dose of the Jap clap too. Let's get outta here."

The two Marines walked shoulder to shoulder as they rounded the mess hall. Suddenly Leo burst into song in a scratchy New England twang. "Oh Bahston Town my Bahston Town, lah lee lah. . . ."

The disgusted Kovak turned his head. "Why can't you people pronounce it BOSTON like everybody else?"

"Whadda ya mean? We Bahstonians pronounce it right. It's you foreigners that are wrong."

"That's a real bunch of horse-shit. Besides, I've never heard that song before."

"I just made it up, it keeps me from gettin' homesick."

Quartermaster Sergeant Lang was stripped to the waist when they approached. He had just lifted and pressed an entire case of heavy M-1 rifles and loaded it on a truck's tailgate. Many men had attempted to duplicate this feat but none had succeeded. A warehouseman by trade, and a weight lifter by avocation, his oversized muscles rippled under a dark tan. He paused and took a deep breath. "Man, am I glad to see you guys. I've been holdin' this hot potato long enough. Moe and his boys loaded your souvenirs on that truck yesterday. It's jammed to the gills."

Leo nodded. "Thanks, Sarge, we'll shove off now."

"You're sure as hell welcome, and tell Jake thanks. He knows I don't drink so he gave me a couple of tins of them canned lobsters."

Leo checked the canopy as he pulled himself behind the steering wheel of the big ten-wheeled truck. From his pocket he extracted a contour map and unfolded it in front of him as Kovak watched.

"See these elevation lines, Johnny, we can take a perfect shortcut cross country." He manipulated the stick shift into four-wheel drive and lurched forward at exactly 10:30.

The map expert was flawless in his calculations. His journey took them in a hook-shaped half circle to the other side of the peaceful little village. As usual, bedlam broke loose when the children spied Kovak riding in the cab. Juvenile bodies emerged from doorways and through windows, chattering in Japanese as though a signal flare had been fired announcing his arrival. The young village girls dashed back inside to change into a prettier dress. Whatever charm or magic it took to mesmerize them, Kovak had it. Leo stopped in the town's center while Johnny K leaned over and gave each a traditional American handshake.

"There's Jake, by the warehouse, he's waving us over." Leo shoved the truck back into low gear and rumbled the last hundred yards with native children hanging on both sides. Carter was turned away from his men who were still perched on the stone wall. The replacements had an aura of over-saturated sponges that had absorbed too much for one day.

"Good show Leo, you're ten minutes early. Turn the truck around and back up to those doors. Kovak, see if you can find the mayor and fill him in on the master plan."

Jake turned and faced his men again. "OK boys, that's it for this morning. Set up a work party and start unloading that truck, and remember, this place is top secret. One big mouth can blow the whole deal. The Quartermaster General and his boys will come down on us like a pack of vultures. Savvy?"

His men acknowledged and began standing, happy for a welcome respite. Carter went on. "O'Malley, there's a jeep assigned to you at the motor pool. Call Sergeant Hicks and tell him you're coming with the loot. Sergeant Bowman will give you directions, and mind, I want you back in time for Gunny Stebbins' 2 o'clock lecture."

"Can I take Jesse with me, Sarge?"

Jake looked at the expectant Hightree and smiled. "Sure, take him along. He can ride shotgun."

The two new buddies took off and sprinted for the tent camp, their field packs jouncing wildly on their backs. Carter watched their vigorous departure and sighed. 'Am I getting old or did I simply lose something?' He turned back to the others. "Corporal Hull, see that a cot is set up inside and make out a nightly guard roster. Del, you and Russ stay and supervise. Make sure our goods are squared away and close up. Moe, you and Johnny B come with me."

"Hold it Jake." It was Kovak. "I just talked with the Mayor and he's happy as a pig in deep shit. There's something else. He says both his sons are first class carpenters. Does this mean anything to you?"

The opportunistic Johnny B moved his face close to Jake's ear. "Is he kidding? Does he know about the lumber yard heist yet?"

"Yeah, I told him yesterday. We'll need more room in the shed."

The three comrades were mentally drained by the intensity of the training session as they strolled slowly back to the camp. Once inside their tent the padded cots beckoned to them. Moe and Johnny B stretched out in prone position. Carter sat and reached for the phone.

"Hello, switchboard, get me the Officers Club at Yontan airfield." Following a series of clicking noises, a polite voice answered; "Yontan Officers Club, Sergeant Miller speaking."

"Hello Miller, this is Sergeant Carter, First Marines. I understand you called me, what's on your mind?" Jake listened while the fast-talking Miller spat out his story. "Yeah sure, we can come up with some captured Jap equipment. You what? When? How much are we talking about? I see, I'll send two of my best men, better give me some directions." Jake grabbed a piece of paper and started writing. "OK, I got it, my boys will be there in two hours." He placed the receiver back in its pouch, a stunned expression on his face. "My God, my fine-

The Last Souvenir

feathered yard-birds, me thinks we just hit the jackpot."

Bowman sat up with a jerk, revitalized by the prospects of a new scam. "Lay it on me, whatcha got?"

"Well boys, it seems Sergeant Miller runs the whole shebang for his officers club. Their tongues are hangin' out for souvenirs and they're crawlin' with bucks."

Chernikov joined in. "So what? Money ain't gonna do us any good where we're goin'."

"That's not the point ya big plow horse. Can't ya see? They've got supply planes flyin' in and out everyday. They've got real connections. We might've found Pandora's box!"

"Who's Pandora?"

"Never mind. Johnny, you and Moe hustle up to the mess hall for early chow. Then go to the motor pool and sign out one of those little recon trucks. I'll phone Dutch. After that, pick up a crate of Jap helmets. Feel 'em out Johnny, you know what to do. Here's the directions."

Bowman's spirits flew high as he squired big Moe through a fast lunch, the motor pool yard, and a bumpy ride back to the warehouse, sending Chernikov into a tail spin. When they hit the main road to Yontan Airfield the traffic was light for a change and Johnny B shared his thoughts.

"You know, I feel kinda honored that Jake trusts us to go alone on a big job like this, ya know what I mean?"

"Sure, I know what you mean. He knows ya got a big mouth and you're fulla bullshit."

"Thanks pal. Coming from you I consider that a compliment."

Moe clutched his seat with white knuckles while Bowman drove at an excessive speed. At last the big airstrip appeared and he eased off the gas pedal. Both men gulped when they viewed the two-storied bombers parked on the landing mats. The main gate was dead ahead.

Bowman pulled in and stopped by the guard shack. An

Air Force policeman in an over starched uniform came creaking over carrying a clipboard. "State your name, outfit, and who you're authorized to see."

"Sergeants Bowman and Chernikov from the First Marines to see Sergeant Miller."

"Oh yeah, you're the souvenir boys. Miller called about an hour ago. Take a right and go to the third quonset hut at the end of the runway. It's marked Officers Club."

"Did that guy seem like a smart ass to you?" Chernikov asked when they were twenty yards away.

"Who cares. We're in the Air Force drivers seat now, so play it cool, let them come to us."

They parked behind a string of brown jeeps and dismounted their truck. A large quonset hut, at least a hundred feet long, caught their eyes immediately. A small white sign with black letters made a simple statement: FLYING OFFICERS ONLY.

"Man, this looks like an exclusive joint." Bowman pushed open the door. "Wait'll they get a load of us raggedy assed marines."

Dim lights lit up over fifty tables inhabited by guzzling airman. On the left a long bar supported at least a dozen elbows. Behind the bar a four-striped staff sergeant directed the traffic of three corporals rattling ice cubes into empty glasses. The wall at their backs was lined with colorfully labeled liquor bottles.

"Wait'll I tell cookie about this paradise. He'll probably ask for a transfer."

"That must be Miller behind the bar. He's the only sergeant I can see."

It only took a moment for a hush to fall over the throng. Almost a hundred faces turned to size up the alien Marine riflemen. Sergeant Miller came bounding from behind the bar, rushing to greet his honored guests. The affable soldier pumped their hands rapidly while ushering them to the crowd at the bar. "You men will have to introduce yourselves. I don't know your names yet."

Johnny B was speechless. He hadn't seen this much brass since he attended his last band concert. At the risk of stammering he composed himself.

"I'm Sergeant John Bowman and my buddy here is Sergeant Moe Chernikov. We're from the First Marine Infantry Regiment."

All hell broke loose as the eager airmen pressed forward, extending their hands and jamming the two Marines against the bar. Moe and Johnny B never expected such exuberance and acceptance from a mob of high ranking officers. Moe's thoughts were clouded, turning to whisper, "I feel like I'm on another planet."

To maintain a semblance of order a full Colonel in his early thirties stepped in. At least a head shorter than Moe, he wore a leather flight jacket with pilot's wings imprinted on the chest. A thinly trimmed mustache pushed its way through his upper lip. Obviously nothing had escaped his eyes and ears. He remembered their names.

"Your name is Moe, right? I'm Colonel Wardlow, in command of this group."

Moe's giant paw swallowed his smaller fingers when they shook hands. "I feel like I should salute or somethin', sir."

"We don't allow saluting in here, Sergeant, it gets to be a pain in the ass." Wardlow turned to Johnny B. "Welcome to our club, Sergeant Bowman. It's customary for me to buy the first drink. What'll you have?"

Bowman's nimble brain was returning to normal speed. "We're both New Yorkers, Colonel, do ya have any rye whiskey?"

"You bet." Wardlow nodded to the bartender. "Sergeant Miller, two double rye and sodas for our guests." He looked back at Johnny B. "I'm from Chicago but you can tell I've made a few trips to New York."

Bowman slowly sipped his drink, feeling an inner glow spreading. Chernikov, on the other hand, moved down the bar, sucked into a whirlpool of questions.

The Last Souvenir

CHAPTER NINETEEN

The young daredevils who flew and manned the B-29 bombers over Japan proved to be a rare breed to the landlocked Marines. By their own admission their trips were ninety percent boredom and ten percent sheer terror. In the past the ground fighters always preceded them, wresting the airstrips from enemy hands and moving on. At last, and at first hand, the airman learned the truth about Banzai attacks and suicide squads crawling forward under darkness of night. The complexities of infantry perils held them in a state of disbelief.

The airmen, one by one, took their turns at storytelling.

They plowed through the air at altitudes of thirty-thousand feet or more, carrying racks of explosives weighing in excess of four tons. Flying in a straight line for twenty minutes over an enemy target, with fingers crossed, could take one's breath away. Cannons on the ground hurled salvos of time-fused shells at their formations. Puffs of grayish black smoke hung like shrouds over their flying coffins. The most electrifying was the infamous 'Baca' bomb, a word borrowed from the Japanese. Loosely translated it meant fool or idiot, but deadly was a more accurate description. Enemy bombers were dispatched to fly over the intruders with these winged missiles attached. When released overhead, a young maniac at the controls was bent on slamming into a fuselage or vulnerable wing tank. Most were shot out of the air by frantic turret gunners but a few were able to penetrate the hail of fire. A hit would send the bomber and its crew plummeting to earth like a flaming meteor. This was the airman's counter to the Banzai attack on the ground.

Chernikov listened intently. Many times he had watched the big ships sailing over him, but this was his first personal confrontation with the airborne gladiators. A lull came, returning him to the reality of the present. He had a caustic knack for brevity of speech. "Why hell, you guys are riding flyin' cows with bull's-eyes on 'em. I'll take a foxhole, at least I can duck when I want to."

Two long seconds passed, followed by a howl of laughter, reverberating from the metal walls of the big room. Whatever inter-service rivalry existed before was erased forever by the simplicity of his remark. Fear was the common thread that bonded them, but the word was never used. Instead, they found solace in humor and comradeship, a brotherhood of duty. The days of flag waving had long since passed and they were stuck there.

It was mid-afternoon and Bowman became nervous. He had come to the airdrome as a businessman, not a missionary. He renewed his rapport with Wardlow. "Colonel, that bombardier over there told me he makes over four-hundred dollars a month. Is that true?"

Wardlow took a moment to look. "That's right, he's a Captain."

"Well sir, I just got promoted to sergeant and I only get a hundred and twenty bucks."

"I know Sergeant, the disparity doesn't seem fair but that's not my department. I have an idea. Perhaps we can make it up to you. Would you and your buddy care to join us for dinner? We're having steak and onions, potatoes too. Wadda you say?"

Johnny B's quick brain began to click like a stop-watch. Money, steak, onions, and potatoes; a ticker-tape of visions flashed before his eyes. "Did I hear you right? Steak, Sir?"

Colonel Wardlow's eyes narrowed. "That's our little secret, Sergeant. An Australian transport pilot flies in twice a week.

The Last Souvenir

We bribe him with a few hundred bucks and he brings us Aussie beef packed in dry ice. This week he threw in six sacks of potatoes and onions."

Bowman became a hound sniffing at a new scent. "If you don't mind my askin' sir, how many bucks and pounds are we talking about?"

Far from gullible, the veteran officer was receiving a telepathic message. The paltry fare of the infantry mess halls was no secret to him. He had no desire to lie to these wonderful young men so he told it straight. "Two-hundred pounds of T-bones and three-hundred pounds of potatoes and onions for five-hundred bucks."

Sergeant Miller, an A-one scrounger himself, was leaning over with his belly pressed against the other side of the bar. Bowman turned his way. "Hey Sarge, can you have your boys bring in that crate from our truck?"

"Can do." He pivoted left and walked two paces. "Smitty, you and Zack hotfoot out to the Marines' truck. They've gotta box out there. Bring it in."

The crowd sensed new activity when the two corporals headed for the front door. Bowman and the Colonel were surrounded as Chernikov found his way back to his buddy's side. Within moments the door reopened. Anxious faces watched the two men deposit the big crate on the bar.

The container, made of white pine, was adorned with exotic oriental characters stenciled in black paint. Anticipation hung in the air with the little boys hovering around their new Christmas tree. Moe reached over and ripped off the top with his bare hands. He fished through the straw packing and produced a shiny new Japanese infantry helmet. A crescendo of shouts erupted.

"I'll give you fifty bucks for that."
"I'll make it a hundred!"
"A hundred and fifty."

The Colonel whirled to face his men, waving his arms desperately over his head. "Hold it, hold up just a minute. Let's hear what the Marines have to say."

The pieces of his plan had snapped together for the slick Bowman. He slowly and deliberately began his speech. "Gentlemen, we are here to trade, not sell. Cash will do us no good on an enemy beach. There are eight Jap helmets in this box, and what I have in mind is a fair swap."

"Name your deal. What do you want?"

"Gentlemen, to put it bluntly, I feel the steaks, potatoes, and onions will almost cover it."

"Wadda ya mean, almost? Hey Miller, throw in that case of Aussie steak sauce."

Sergeant Miller obliged, producing a tall cardboard box from a shelf behind him. He grinned, shoving the carton to Bowman and Chernikov. "It's kinda sweet but it tastes great on steaks. They use a lotta brown sugar."

Moe removed one of the fat bottles and read the label. "Hm, Outback Sauce, bottled in Sydney. We'll take it."

The calculator in Bowman's head was still spinning. He reasoned eight helmets at a hundred dollars each gave him eight hundred dollars to work with, yet he wanted the deal to be square. The hospitality and friendship they showed made a lasting impression on him. For the moment, the airmen and marines had one thing in common: money was not an object because there was no tomorrow.

Johnny B raised an arm and pointed his finger. "Is that a record player? That box with the wind-up crank on it. And what about that stack of records?"

"Yeah, but we never play it anymore. We've heard those records so many times we're sick of 'em. Take the damn thing."

To the astonishment of the two Marines, everything came easy. It dawned on them the airmen were sharing, not trading. They would never forget this memorable afternoon. The souvenirs had been removed from the crate, standing in a line on the bar. One of the pilots made a strong bid. "I got first dibs on the crate."

"Well Sergeant, is there anything else?" The Colonel's tone was apprehensive.

"There's just one more request, sir. If you could throw in ten quarts of that whiskey we'll call it even."

Moe turned his head away and looked at the ceiling, thinking to himself; 'Oh no, that greedy bastard is going to kill the whole deal.' To his surprise a wave of assenting noises filled the room.

Wardlow was galvanized into action. "Sergeant Miller, have your men load everything on the marine truck. The rest of you men find some paper and put your names in a hat. We'll have a drawing, a hundred bucks per helmet. That way we'll replenish the squadron fund."

The bombardier Captain stepped forward. "Sergeant Bowman, there's only eight helmets and almost a hundred of us. Can your people come up with any more Jap gear?"

"You bet, Captain. We've got rifles, bayonets, uniforms and a bunch of other stuff."

"Beautiful. Tell us what you need and we'll get it for you. Keep in touch with Miller."

The madcap drawing was about to start. The scribbling and tearing of paper ended with men crowding around their commanding officer. Moe and Johnny B shook hands all around and bade them good-bye. They pulled the door open and exited with Miller following.

The recon truck was surrounded by a flurry of loading activity. The steak boxes went in first followed by hundred-pound bags of potatoes. The efficient Miller issued a reasonable order. "Smitty, go up to the garage and get a tarp and some rope. I want that stuff lashed down tight."

In the fifteen minutes it took to finish the task the three

men stood chatting. Miller mentioned he had been a gunner on a B-25 bomber for thirty missions in the South Pacific. His reputation as a wheeler-dealer got him a transfer from Guam to take over the officer's club at Yontan. No more combat flying made him happy.

Smitty had just placed the record player on the front seat when a screeching siren sounded. CONDITION RED. CONDITION RED, came blaring over a loud speaker at the main hanger.

"Air raid? That's impossible. Intelligence has it that whatever bombers the Japs have left are confined to protect the Homeland." Miller watched his men scurry for the shelters.

"You're right buddy." Moe gestured across the runway to the China Sea beyond. "Ya see those four destroyers closin' in around that aircraft carrier? One of the Kamikazes must've busted through our picket line. Ya can't trust those sneaky little bastards."

"A Kamikaze raid! I've never seen one before. Have you guys?"

"Yeah, back in April or May they came over twice a day. If he got through he'll go for the carrier."

Bowman chose to speculate. "He's pretty close to shore, probably headed for the repair dock at Motobu."

"I don't want to miss this, what'll we do now?"

"If they start shootin' we'll duck under the truck. What goes up will sure as hell come down. Don't worry, you'll get a bird's eye view." Scarcely had the words left Moe's lips when the lead destroyer opened fire. The pom-pomming of 20 and 40 millimeter guns thundered across the water. A cannonade of 5 inch guns joined in the chorus, firing air bursting shells. The other ships spotted the diving black dot, unleashing their combined anger at the plunging lunatic. Five solid cones of orange tracers converged several thousand feet above the ocean's surface. An ugly garden of black puffballs dotted the blue sky.

The three spectators squirmed under the truck with Miller in the middle. Moe, next to the front wheels, was struggling to pull in his long legs and big feet. The din made conversation impossible, even at the range of five miles. Three sets of eyes peered from under the truck's metal running board, enraptured by the awesome firepower of the US Navy.

The show ended almost as fast as it started. A circular red flash, at least a hundred feet across, lit up the tortured sky, no doubt a direct hit. Johnny B edged closer to Miller and yelled in his ear. "In about five seconds that sound is going to hit us. Put your hands over your ears."

Miller responded, cupping his palms on the sides of his head. Bowman was right. Like a clap of thunder the explosion pounded down on the airstrip's runway. The guns faded and fell silent.

"Here comes the rain."

Gravity took over, pulling the spent metal downward. Tiny clouds of dust kicked up on the crushed coral, mostly .50 caliber slugs. One landed on their truck's floorboard, barely missing a stack of phonograph records. Silence returned and the three men crawled out and stood up, brushing the dirt from their dungarees.

"Well Miller, how'd ya like the fireworks?"

The airman was only slightly ruffled. "A helluva show. You know, the first time I saw a plane blow up it made me sick, but I feel nothing now. I do feel kinda sorry for the poor little son of a bitch flyin' that thing. He's gotta be scattered in a million pieces."

"Yeah, but they'll probably glue him back together when he gets to his imperial heaven." The biting bitter-sweet humor was actually spawned out of compassion and respect for the courage and dedication of the doomed Japanese pilot. Like all combat veterans, in their subconscious souls, they were putting themselves in his shoes, if only for a fleeting moment.

Moe bent forward and retrieved a red-tipped bullet from the floorboards and handed it to Miller. The colored marking proved it to be a .50 caliber tracer. "Here's a souvenir for you buddy."

"Thanks. I'm going to write a letter to my dad about today. I'll send this with it."

Johnny B had an itch to return to camp. The enjoyable afternoon with the Air Force took much longer than expected. "Sergeant Miller, nice meeting you. Thanks for everything, and I really mean it." They shook hands heartily and Miller stood watching their truck pull away and head for the gate.

Once on the highway Moe glanced back one last time. "Ya know, those Airedales are a great buncha guys."

"Yeah, and they've got balls too. After hearing their stories I feel better about being a rifleman."

The Last Souvenir

CHAPTER TWENTY

Master Gunnery Sergeant Stebbins strutted like a rooster in front of his baby chicks. Seated with their backs against the waist-high wooden wall that supported the mess tent, the replacements awaited his next command. With blindfolds hanging loosely on their foreheads, and rifles in their laps, they simulated a foxhole posture. For two hours the efficient Gunny had crammed their heads with facts about weaponry.

"Alright men, let's try it again. I want you to take off thirty seconds from the last time. It could save your life."

The precocious O'Malley raised his hand. "Hey Sarge, why can't we get pistols like Jake 'n Moe, and Johnny B?"

"I'll tell you why, because they ain't government issue for riflemen. You'll have to get 'em the same way they did."

"How's that, Sarge?"

"They probably took 'em off a dead officer or corpsman."

"Or off a dead Chaplain." Padre Turner had sneaked in to witness the show.

Stebbins snapped to attention. "Good afternoon, sir, I didn't hear you come up."

"At ease, Sergeant, for heavens sakes. What kind of a drill is this?"

Stebbins faced the men again, placing his hands on his hips. "I blindfold 'em sir. Then I teach em how to field strip and clean their weapons in the dark. It's Sergeant Carter's idea."

"That's right, it's my idea. How are they doin', Gunny?" Jake had arrived, taking a stance beside the Chaplain.

Stebbins was in his glory. His knowledge of gunnery was

practically limitless and he loved an audience. "This'll be the fifth time. I've got em under two minutes now, Jake, but I want em faster."

"OK boys fix your blindfolds and get ready." The Gunny eyed the secondhand on his watch. "OK, now!"

Nimble fingers pulled the trigger grips, removing the mechanism from its housing. The big rifles broke in half, parting the stock from the hand grip. Operating rods and springs came free of the recoil chambers. Metal parts from the firing apparatus were brushed into their laps.

The Master Sergeant watched them like a circling hawk. "Alright, put em back together."

The reverse process began with well-practiced dexterity. One by one the reassembled rifles were finished and held up for inspection.

"One minute and forty-five seconds. That's a little better."

The flabbergasted Chaplain gulped with amazement. "Well God bless you all. If I hadn't seen it with my own eyes I wouldn't believe it."

Smugly, the young men removed the kerchiefs from their eyes with the self-satisfaction of a job well learned. The urgency of their new existence was beginning to penetrate. Jake too, was satisfied.

"It's almost four o'clock, Gunny. We can knock off now. Great job."

"Thanks, Carter, same time tomorrow?"

Jake nodded and walked away. O'Malley followed, stuffing the handkerchief in his pocket. "Hey Sarge, did you really get your pistol off a dead officer?"

Jake did a double take and smiled. "Ya know kid, I hate to tell you, but that's a Military secret."

The dissertation was cut short by the loud honking of a truck horn in front of the mess hall. It could only mean one thing. The crass Muldoon had arrived and was demanding attention.

"Oh boy, Sarge, it's Muldoon with our Jukebox." O'Malley broke into a trot and yelled over his shoulder. "Come on Levine, you're up."

Chief Muldoon sat in the cab of his big gray truck, chewing on a gnarly cigar. The cargo bed was empty, save for a dolly supporting the large multi-colored music box. A swarm of gawking spectators closed in around the tailgate, elbowing to get a better view.

"Well kiss my ass, it's a Jukebox."

"Yeah, I ain't seen one of those things in two years."

"Wonder who it's for."

The old chief craned his neck to look above the sea of green dungarees. "Hey Jake, where are ya? It's me, Muldoon."

Carter pushed his way through. "I see ya. I'd recognize that map of yours anywhere. How ya been, Chief?"

"Doin' fine, pal. Say, is that Colonel of yours around? The last time I was here he acted like he'd fry my butt if I came back."

"Naw, he's up at HQ in Motobu. Been gone all day."

Muldoon, feeling relieved, led Carter to the rear of the truck bed. "Well there she is. You better have some of these young mules unload it. It's a heavy sucker."

Private Levine preceded them, sizing up his new project with a thin black tool box under his arm. "It's an old Wurlitzer, Sarge, just like the one my Pop has back in Brooklyn. Should be a piece of cake. I'll get 'er running."

Jake felt reassured by the young man's confidence. "Levine, I don't even know your first name. What is it?"

"They call me Ike, Sarge."

Muldoon was skeptical. "Are ya sure ya know what you're doin', sonny?"

The defiant Levine was quick to shoot back. "I can run circles around you, old man."

The two older men grinned at each other. Jake was besieged by volunteers eager to pitch in with unloading. Marine muscle prevailed as the awkward box slid slowly to the ground. Dolly wheels dug deep ruts in the soft soil behind the heaving bodies.

Cookie appeared in the entrance of the mess tent, holding open the screen door. "Put 'er in the corner over there. There's an extension cord rigged up." The cook scanned the following crowd with a sour expression. "The rest of you knotheads stay outta my mess hall. Chow isn't for an hour yet."

Once the box was in place Ike Levine wasted no time removing its back with a screwdriver. He rolled over on his shoulder and poked his head inside, carefully feeling the machinery. In a few minutes he extracted himself and looked up at Carter and Muldoon.

"It's a cinch, Sarge. The chassis is sheared off the frame and the rejector arm is bent. The motor looks OK. Can you get somebody to turn on the generator?"

Cookie turned his head and yelled at one of the mess men. "Hey Guido, go out back and start up the power plant." The suspense was high. "How much time are ya gonna need?"

"About thirty minutes."

The generator coughed and began running with its familiar thumping sound. Lights blinked on, signaling time for Muldoon to leave. Jake walked with him, exiting the mess tent and heading for the Navy truck. Many times before, comradeship had manifested itself in the odd mismatching of two men. The scruffy old Chief was rougher than a dry corn cob, while Jake was smooth talking and well groomed. The needle of fate had sewn them together in a true friendship.

O'Malley appeared from behind a front fender. "I put your rifles in the front seat, Chief. You're all set."

"Thanks kid. Here, have another cigar."

Sean thanked him and stood by Carter, waving good-bye.

The Last Souvenir

"Uh oh, Sarge, do you see what I see?"

"I sure do, it's a recon truck comin' the other way. Must be Moe and Johnny B." Jake had a second thought. "By the way, I forgot to ask, did you and Jesse pick up that load of gin and canned stuff from Sergeant Hicks?"

"Sure did Jake. We stacked it in your tent during noon chow." O'Malley looked at his sergeant with a tinge of hero worship. "Ya know, that tent of yours is startin' to look like a warehouse. One more load and you and your buddies will have to move out."

"Never think small, Mac. When our tent gets full we'll use yours."

The luck of the draw, in Sean's opinion, had placed him in the greatest outfit in the Corps. Every replacement, when he treads his way down the gangway of his troop transport, wonders what his next unit will be like. Imagination is never accurate. Only time will unravel the mystery. O'Malley thought happily about his new assignment. 'These guys are the best.'

Johnny B waved casually at the guard when he cleared the gate. The contents were piled high in the back of his little truck, its secrecy covered by a brown army tarp. It was almost top-heavy. Carter had no inkling of what was in the surprise package. With little regard for the camp speed limit, Bowman screeched to halt in a billowing cloud of dust. "Hello Jake, did you miss us?"

"Hell no. You two are like stray mutts. You always come home. Whatcha do, pick the Air Force clean?"

"Naw, not really, it's kind of a swap-donation. Come on Moe, gimme a hand with these ropes."

Bowman vaulted from the front seat in one bounce. Chernikov skirted the rear of the truck bed, bellowing in the direction of the mess tent. "Hey Cookie, ya better get your ass out here."

The overworked chef was in no mood to be yelled at, but curiosity was tugging him outside. It seemed to be contagious, drawing a crowd of men in his wake. "Well Jake, looks like you and the Boy Scouts have been at it again."

Carter denied any complicity. "Not me Cookie, this is Moe and Johnny B's show."

Bowman climbed back on the running board, seizing the tarp with both hands in a prelude to unveiling. He gave it a yank and simultaneously announced; "Gentlemen, I give you T-bone steaks, potatoes, and onions. Enough for the whole company."

To his chagrin there was no cheer, only the buzzing of shocked voices. Carter could not find words. His buddies had certainly topped all previous exploits. Cookie moved in to read the labels and feel a potato sack.

"How many T-bones are there?"

"I don't know Cookie, two-hundred pounds packed in dry ice."

"Dry ice? That stuff is worth its weight in gold nuggets. I can use it."

Chernikov was next. "Waddya say, buddy, can ya cook 'em up or is it too much work?"

"Hell no! It'll give me a chance to show you bums what real culinary magic is." To the astonishment of all, the inspired chef began barking orders. "You men there, start unloading. Stack everything behind the mess hall. Guido, get over to the engineers. Pick up ten steel bars, the kind they use to reinforce concrete. Ask 'em for a roll of baling wire, a hacksaw, and some wire cutters. The rest of you start breaking up empty crates for firewood."

"Wadda ya want the steel bars for Sarge?"

"Dammit boy, this ain't no debating society. Move out, and take Maxie with you." Cookie faced Moe and Johnny B with a wide grin. "Well, the 2 section has come through again. In the

The Last Souvenir

morning I'm gonna build a king size grill. Tomorrow night we'll have the biggest damn barbecue you ever saw."

Finally the suppressed elation blew up with cheering from over a hundred throats. A queue of men was moving away, shouldering their burdens. Bowman related the story of their trip to Yontan and the benevolence of the Air Force to the disbelief of Jake and the cook. After answering questions he held up his hand. "There's just one more thing." He rummaged through a box on the floorboard and withdrew a bottle of whiskey, handing it to Cookie.

"Here ya go, pal, a quart of bourbon for your trouble. Don't drink it all in one night."

"Are you kiddin'? I'll take this baby to bed with me."

The crunching of small tires on crushed coral caught their ears. It was Colonel Mason's jeep with Johnny Cobb at the wheel. The old man looked tired, most probably put through the wringer by the armchair Generals at III Corps. Men in the ranks had no idea of the trials of high command, and didn't care. To them, he was immediate authority, and they left it at that.

"Oh no, what now?" Mason gestured toward the milling mass. "Pull up over there, Cobb." With swagger stick whipping his leg, the Colonel came striding in to face his men.

"Well Carter, is this more of your hi-jinks?"

Jake dropped his hand salute. "No sir, we fell into a bonanza, thanks to Sergeants Bowman and Chernikov." He was not one to pass the buck but he gambled on the Colonel's acceptance. Credit for the coup belonged with his buddies. If the situation got ticklish, he would step back in and assume full responsibility. Gingerly he told the story while the Colonel shook his head.

"Carter, I'm too tired to wrangle with you now. I suppose you have enough to provide for the officers mess?"

"Yes sir, the works."

"Sergeant, you and your bandits keep putting me on the spot, but I'll let it slide. And, by the way, I'll take mine medium rare." He returned their salutes and made a move for the seclusion of his tent.

Inside the mess tent, Levine and his jukebox were ready. He selected a record and pushed the play button. The volume was too high, blasting music across the tent camp. Mason froze in his tracks. "What the hell is that?"

Carter stammered an answer. "It sounds like the Glen Miller orchestra sir, playin' 'The Chattanooga Choo Choo'."

"Dammit man, I didn't ask *WHO*. I want to know *WHAT*."

"Well sir, it's our new jukebox."

"Jukebox?" Mason stomped his way into the mess hall, confronting the startled Ike Levine. "Who authorized this? Did you get permission from a commissioned officer?"

"That's where I come in, Colonel." Padre Turner stepped in. "I authorized it for morale purposes, sir."

Mason was snookered again. "Well, Lieutenant, have you appointed yourself Morale Officer too?"

"Sir, you'll have to admit, morale is part of my job."

Mason never could resist the smiling Priest. "I guess you've got me there, Padre." He stared down at the record selection. "Can you get the Harry James Band on that thing?"

"Yes sir."

"Good, play him next. He's my favorite." The Colonel left abruptly, marching briskly past the smiling Marines. Carter and his men watched him disappear.

"Ya know, there's somethin' about that old man I like, but I'm glad I'm not in his shoes."

The Last Souvenir

CHAPTER TWENTY-ONE

With breakfast behind him, Carter strolled alone to the motor pool. His training schedule was prearranged with Kovak and his Japanese language lesson first on agenda. An impressive line of assorted vehicles appeared on his right. Far in the rear, the lanky figure of Lieutenant Van der Slice was moving between rows. Jake closed the distance and saluted.

"Good morning, Lieutenant."

"Hello Jake, you're just the man I want to see. Scuttlebutt has it we're having steak and onions tonight. Is that for sure?"

Carter reassured him of the fact, giving him a brief synopsis on the acquisition.

Dutch cautioned with his hand. "Hold it. Don't tell me too much about what you do with my trucks. I sure as hell don't want the Colonel climbing on my ass." Van der Slice was like his buddy, Chandler. He admired Carter and his conniving ways, and wished he could go with him on his junkets, but it wasn't in the cards. "What kinda wheels are you looking for this time?"

"I need something big, sir, probably a couple of days from now."

"Don't tell me any more, just follow me." Dutch led him to the end of the line and showed him two new long-bed models. "Are these big enough?"

Jake took his time, checking the high tarpaulin frame that covered the truck's bed. "This one is perfect, sir, I'd like to reserve it for day after tomorrow."

"You've got it." The Lieutenant was writing on a manifest form. "Shall we call it troop movement again?"

"Sounds good to me, sir."

The officer finished his notations and stuck the pencil in his pocket. "Hey, look at that." He pointed at the highway leading west. "It's an ambulance. He's goin' somewhere in a big hurry."

"I see it, sir, and I don't like it. This ain't no combat zone."

"Isn't that one of your men, Sergeant, running this way?"

"Yes sir, it's Del Stack." Jake watched him weaving through the parked vehicles like a halfback.

"Jake, ya better come quick! We've got big troubles."

"For gawd's sake what happened?"

"Don't know for sure. I've been lookin' all over hell and gone for ya. One of the guys from A Company is at your tent now."

Jake didn't even say good-bye. The former track star left in a sprint, leaving the puffing Del Stack behind. Covering the half mile distance in two minutes he rounded the corner to see a small group in front of his tent flaps. One of the men was waving. Carter walked to a halt, gasping for breath.

"Hiya Jake, remember me? Swanee? Corporal Swann from Able Company. You and your guys were with us in the big show at Wana Draw."

"Yeah, sure, hello Swanee. What the hell happened?"

"There's been a fight, Jake, a bad one."

Still gulping for air, Jake's pounding heart sunk in his body. "Who? Where? For god's sake, man, spit it out."

The corporal thought it best to start from the beginning. "Well, me and my squad was walking by your mess hall. We've got a new replacement named Bullard. We call him the Bully. He's an ex-convict from Mare Island Prison and a real psycho, a mean son of a bitch. He's always pickin' fights and nobody wants to tangle with him cuz he's big as a house."

Carter was anxious. "What about the fight?"

"Well, you got a sign on your mess tent that sez, 'HQ CO.

The Last Souvenir

STEAK TONIGHT, MEMBERS ONLY'. Two of your men were standin' there, readin' it. One was a redhead and one was an Indian boy."

"OK, that would be O'Malley and Hightree. Go on." Jake moved closer.

Swann fidgeted with his collar. "The bully couldn't resist a chance to mouth off. He walked up to 'em and said, 'How come a crappy Indian gets to eat steak when white men have to settle for beans?' The redhead was really pissed."

"Oh no, I can see what's coming. Then what?"

"The redhead lit into him and started swingin'. Hell, Jake, he wuz only half his size, he didn't even have a chance. The big guy hit him with a haymaker and knocked him flat. Then he jumped on him like he was gonna finish him off."

"Oh no, please God. He didn't kill him, did he?" Carter was horrified.

Corporal Swann continued, trying desperately to clear the emotion from his throat. "No Jake, he was lucky. Your big Moe saw the whole thing and jumped in. He pulled off the Bully and stood him up. I've never seen anything like it in my whole life." He stopped to cough.

"Like what? Come on man!"

"Big Moe plowed into him like a steamroller, and the other guy was bigger. He busted his jaw and caved in his ribs. They had to take the Bully to the hospital in an ambulance."

"What about O'Malley, the redhead?"

Frenchie Labeau had the answer, standing behind Carter. "He'll be OK, I've got him up at the aid station. I had to give him smelling salts but he came around."

"Frenchie, I'm glad you're here. What about the guy in the ambulance?"

"That's another story. His jaw is fractured in three places. It will have to be wired shut. He won't be able to chew anything for at least three months. I don't know about his broken bones. He'll be in X-ray most of the day."

"Shit, this is a real mess."

Swanee tried to console the crestfallen Sergeant. "Look at it this way. The crazy bastard has been askin' for it since he got off the boat. We've been trying to get rid of him for weeks but nobody listens."

"Well this is a helluva way to do it. By the way, where's Moe? Why isn't he here?"

"That's the bad news, Sarge. The Lizard's got him."

"The Lizard? What Lizard? What the hell are you talkin' about, Swann?"

"Lieutenant Lazarre, that's what we call him. He's one of the new replacement officers. Got a face like an Arizona Gila Monster and a disposition to match. He want's to court-martial Big Moe."

"Court martial? What the hell for? He was just trying to protect one of his men. This is bullshit, where did they take him?"

Swann pointed with his thumb. "Lazarre rounded up four guards and took him to Able Company HQ. He's there now, makin' out the charges."

Jake's breathing had returned to normal. A bully and a pig-headed shavetail Lieutenant were disrupting his life. To make matters worse, one of his best buddies was in dire trouble. To take off half-cocked was not a solution. If this thing got as far as the Division Legal Section the lawyers would cut Moe to pieces. A commissioned officer's word stands high above that of a lowly line sergeant. Quick action was required. If he had to put his own stripes on the line, so be it. The Lizard would butt heads with the veteran ram.

The wily sergeant took a firm grip on himself. The thought of loosing Chernikov this way was abhorrent to him. He felt no compassion for the battered man in the hospital. Corporal Swann was right, the damn fool asked for it and the outcome was inevitable.

A plan was forming in his mind, but it was only a long shot. He had connections but there was no time to pull strings. The approach was logic with pressure. He must face the green lieutenant now, before the matter got out of hand. He began by stroking his chin, and this was a good sign. Bowman noted this and stood ready to back him to the hilt.

"Come on Swann, take me to your CP." Jake pulled his fatigue cap down firmly on his forehead.

"I'm goin' with you." Bowman was adamant.

"No thanks, it's best I go it alone."

"Like hell you will! We're in this thing together and that's that."

Carter tried to force a smile, but it wasn't there. When he saw the determination in Bowman's jutting jaw he relented. "OK buddy, come on. But ya better let me do the talkin'. Too many cooks might spoil the soup."

Able Company Headquarters was four tent rows away. The three men covered the distance rapidly with Swann showing the way. "There it is, that second tent on the right." A small sign above the door read: HQ ABLE COMPANY. "You guys go ahead, I'll wait outside."

Jake and Johnny B pushed open both sides of the tent flaps. In the back corner a sullen Chernikov stood in a subdued slouch, surrounded by four armed men. Facing him, with his back to the door, a slightly built man was carefully scribbling on a clipboard. This had to be the Lizard. Seated to the right by a small desk was Captain Wannamaker, the company commander. Carter knew him, their paths had crossed before in combat. The two marines saluted.

"Good morning, sir."

The Captain turned and stood up. "Sergeant Carter, Jake Carter. Come in, come in. It's nice to see you again."

"It's good to see you too, Cap'n. I..."

"I know why you're here, Jake, but first, I've got something stuck in my craw." Wannamaker sat down and slid a piece of blank paper in front of him. "When we were pushing on Wana I heard you and your boys saved one of my platoons from being wiped out. The reports were sketchy, the lieutenant was killed. Fill me in."

Carter was taken by surprise and in no mood to tell war stories. Why did he start this? It might be the old salt had an ulterior motive. Was this a windfall that would open doors? He glanced at Moe and noticed Lazarre wasn't ready to face him, but at least he was within earshot. Like a quick change artist he redirected his momentum.

"Well sir, you're right, we were with 'em, spotting for the mortars. That was the day we had to cross those little railroad tracks. Sergeant Chernikov there, he was a corporal then, got a hunch something didn't smell right. He told me he was goin' out to take a look and I told your boys to hold up."

The Captain was taking notes. "Hold it, I want to get this down." When he caught up he asked Jake to continue.

Jake told the story from stark memory. Moe had crawled forward about two-hundred yards through a shallow drainage pattern. When he reached the railroad embankment he turned right and wriggled into a small culvert. Once on the other side he stuck out his head and peered through the brush. A squad of Japanese, well camouflaged and with light machine guns, had set up an ambush.

Wannamaker called another halt. "My God, if he'd been captured they would have hacked off his head. What did he do?"

"He was carrying a 'spamcan,' sir, you know, a portable field phone. He called me and directed mortar fire, blew 'em all to hell. Then he crawled back and told your boys it was OK to move out. That's about it. Your Corporal Swann is outside. He can fill you in with the rest."

The Last Souvenir

"Good grief, one of my rifle platoons could have been annihilated. Why wasn't he decorated?"

"Sir, you and I both know only Generals give each other medals. He was just doing his job." Jake was being facetious but the Captain agreed.

"Job hell, I'm going to recommend him for a Bronze Star. You say Corporal Swann is outside?"

"Yes sir."

The Captain arose from his desk. "I plan to get his full statement, and anyone else who was there that day. You'll hear from me, Carter, soon." Before he left the tent he spoke to Lazarre. "Take over here, Lieutenant."

Wannamaker had his reasons for leaving. In a dispute, protocol dictates support of a junior officer, and he wanted no part of it. Most of the reserve officers sent to him were excellent, but occasionally a bad one slipped through the cracks. The fact was, he must review the case, but Lazarre had the right to veto and could go over his head. Carter's reputation for being smart and tough had permeated the regiment. In vacating, the captain had gained neutrality, reducing the matter to a gut level where it belonged.

Inside, Carter was ready to face his adversary. "Sir, I respectfully request you read me the charges against this man."

For the first time the Lieutenant turned and confronted him. "And whom do you presume to be?"

Swanee was right. The man resembled a sketch from an encyclopedia on reptiles. His facial tissue was white and scaly from the weather of weeks on a troopship. Eyes were large and wide apart with thick lids blinking at random. A snubbed nose and pinpoint nostrils gave his face a pointed effect. The only thing lacking was a forked tongue darting from his thin lips.

"I'm Carter sir, platoon sergeant, Regimental Scout Section. Sergeant Chernikov is one of my men."

"Frankly I can't see that this is any of your business. However, there is no reason why I can't grant you a hearing." The hostile Lazarre, clearly pumped up by his new importance, read the charges. "Inciting to riot, striking a man of inferior rank, conduct unbecoming a non-commissioned officer, and attempted murder."

"Attempted murder? Why hell, sir you're going to ruin his life. He could get years in prison. Who in God's name do you think you are? The other man started it. He was only protecting one of his own men." Defying interruption, Carter went on to describe the entire incident.

"Sergeant, you had best be careful. You are walking a thin line. Discipline is the backbone of a combat unit and I'm going to see it's administered."

"Combat? What do you know about combat, sir, you just got here?"

"That's enough Carter. One more outburst like that and you will be brought up on charges of insubordination."

"Alright Lieutenant, let me put it this way. You can't start a precedent like this. When you get to the front lines you're gonna find out that half the privates up there are lookin' for an excuse to get sent to the rear. If startin' a fight gets 'em sent back, they'll do it. Facing Jap bullets is no fun." Carter spoke from experience. Once at the front, he watched two men squabble over the contents of a dead man's pack, of all things, a roll of dry toilet paper. Their punishment was extra duty, stringing barbed wire and digging a mortar pit. The unit had been cut down to half size and the lieutenant needed every man to cover the platoon sector.

"Sergeant, we're not here to discuss front line bravado. Discipline is the issue."

Johnny B was livid. Jake restrained him with his elbow. To them he was the kind of idiot that got men killed for no valid reason. Carter was far from finished, determined to see it

The Last Souvenir

through.

"Lieutenant, you're new here, so I'll give you some advice. I've served under two great Colonels, Puller and Mason, and neither one likes new lieutenants messing with their men. I've seen them both chew 'em up and spit 'em out. You're the one who's walking a thin line."

Momentarily, the Lizard changed his tune. "Puller? Do you mean to tell me you know the famous Colonel Chesty Puller?"

Bowman interrupted Jake's answer. "Know him! It was Chesty who recommended Jake for a Silver Star on Peleliu."

"I congratulate you on your decoration, Sergeant, but the charges still stand."

The man was ridiculous and Carter's patience was draining away. He decided to play his trump card. "Alright Lieutenant, we'll settle this front line style, man to man. You take off those gold bars and I'll take off my stripes. We'll go out behind the tents and square off, winner take all."

"That's right *LOO-TENANT!*" Bowman's face lit up bright red. "If he doesn't take you I will."

The impertinence of the two men launched Lazarre into a tirade. "That does it, you're both on report for rank insubordination and disrespect for a superior officer. Give me your full names and serial numbers right now."

"Lieutenant, I'll give you my hat size if you want it. You write it up and I'll carry it to Colonel Mason myself. When he finds out he's losing his Chief Scout and two of his best sergeants he's goin' right through the roof. You'd better be right. Knowing him he's liable to bust you down to buck-assed private and ship you to a line company."

Lazarre's thick eyelids closed and he shuddered. What if the veteran Sergeant was right? The silence came crashing down around him. Seven enlisted men stood in the tent with him and their eyes were on fire. Grim faces showed a profound dislike. These are the men I'll be asked to lead. Will they follow my orders? Will they face death for me? If I'm in trouble, will they rescue me? Probably not.

The disciplinary thrust had been broken. Lazarre slid the pencil in his mouth and sucked on it like a baby with a pacifier. He swallowed hard to alleviate the lump in his throat. "Men, I am perfectly capable of reconsidering this matter. Perhaps the charges are a bit overzealous, but I will have to write a full report. I'll need your statements for the record."

Carter snatched the opportunity and moved swiftly. "Come on Moe. Let's get the hell out of here."

Captain Wannamaker was standing outside and heard everything. In an unorthodox way they had done him a favor and he was grateful. Now there was a chance for the gung-ho Lizard to become a good officer. He spoke when they passed. "Is everything squared away, men? "Sergeant Chernikov, thanks for what you did for my men. I hope I see you again."

"Yes sir, squared a-way .So long Cap'n. Probably see you in Tokyo."

Heading for home, Moe fell into a silly mood. He raised up on his tiptoes, ballerina style. With his forefinger he forced a dimple in his cheek. In a high pitched feminine voice he asked Jake; "Was daddy really gonna fight for little ole' me?"

Jake flashed a wide grin. "Listen you big sap, that was close. One more hour and you'd be in the Graybar Hotel."

Johnny B had another question. "Ya know, I was wondering about something."

"About what?"

"I was just wondering. Is it possible to mate an iguana with a human?"

Bowman had lit the fuse of humor and they exploded with laughter. The final tension was over. With arms around each other they skipped down the road like three little boys playing hopscotch.

The Last Souvenir

CHAPTER TWENTY-TWO

At 1:00 in the afternoon, with noon chow over, Sean O'Malley stood in the center of the first aid tent. As ordered he reported back for a final check up. With a thumb, Frenchie Labeau held his eyelids open one at a time, staring into his pupils.

The young Marine's self esteem had sunk to a new low. That morning, with half the company watching, he suffered the disgrace of being knocked cold. Back home, he was considered the toughest kid on the block, but today was ridiculous. He had lost the respect of everyone.

"You suffered a mild concussion, Sean, but you'll be OK. Your pulse is good and your blood pressure is right on the money." The corpsman handed him a small bottle from the medicine cabinet. "If you feel a headache comin' on, take two of these."

O'Malley held the bottle in his hand and read the label. "What I need is a pill that will fix a busted ego, Doc."

Labeau grinned and gave him a reassuring pat on the back. "You've got the whole thing ass-backwards. I know these guys better than you do. I've patched 'em and plugged 'em up so many times I know 'em by their blood types. Why hell, they've even given you a new nickname."

"Oh no, what else?"

"From now on you're the Kamikaze Kid." Frenchie washed his hands in a white metal basin. "Listen, kid, you're only a middleweight, and you took on a super heavy. That wasn't the main event, it was only an exhibition bout. Your buddy was in trouble and you hopped in to protect him. The men respect that."

"I still don't get it, I lost."

"No you didn't. You showed 'em you've got guts. If they ever get pinned down in combat, you're the kind of marine who wades in and bails 'em out."

Labeau went on to describe the bizarre philosophy of men at war. Winning and losing took up a different connotation. If a man received a fatal wound, and was carried away feet first, he lost. If he survives, and goes home in one piece, he wins. To stay alive for just one more day is a minor conquest. These are the only criteria, everything else being trivial. The big picture began to loom in O'Malley's mind.

"Thanks, Doc, I think I feel a little better now. Is there anything else?"

"Yeah, one more thing. Today is Saturday so you have the rest of the day off. Go back to your tent and flake out on your cot for a few hours. I don't want you bouncing around, you could have a relapse. OK?"

"Sure Doc, will do, and thanks for everything."

O'Malley left the aid station with hands in his pockets. The corpsman had somehow put a bandage on his wounded pride. Men were working everywhere. A small party was raking and leveling the soil around the mess hall. Across the road, linemen from the communications section were stringing telephone wire along the tent tops. Eyes turned his way when he appeared, followed by waving arms.

"Hiya Mac, how ya doin?"

"What did the Doc say?"

"Ya gonna be OK?"

"How about joinin' us for chow tonight? We'll save you a seat."

O'Malley forced a smile and waved back. Labeau was right, these men are a rare breed. Drudgery and strife had matured them, and they were inviting him to join their membership. A new security found it's way into his make-up.

He was born and baptized Irish Catholic in Pontiac Michigan. Seeking a warmer climate, his family uprooted and moved to Texas when he was twelve. His father, mother, and three little sisters were all redheads. As a true big brother he was overly protective of the baby girls and they adored him for it. An evening at their dining room table had the aura of a rose garden, with blossoms of red hair everywhere. He remembered the tears on their cheeks when he boarded the train that would take him to the war.

Boot Camp training in San Diego was a breeze for him, and likewise the rifle range. He qualified as an expert rifleman and was assigned to the elite scout-sniper school, where he graduated at the head of his class. When he embarked on a troopship and steamed across the Pacific Ocean he felt he was trained and ready to fight. At last, he had been called to glory.

Today he had a whisper of creeping doubts, perhaps better described as apprehensions. This was no Hollywood movie set. The risks were too high. He was walking on a field of broken glass, wearing only a pair of sandals. He didn't know it, but the day was far from over and there were more encounters to come.

When he entered his tent, to his surprise, the fatherly figure of Del Stack was slouched on his cot, in a chat with Jesse Hightree. The usually stone-faced Indian was more than talkative, retelling the story of Sean's stab at gallantry, admiration for his buddy clear in the tone of his voice.

"Sergeant Stack, what brings you to the slums?"

"Hi, Sean. Come in and have a seat. You can knock off the formalities, just call me Del."

O'Malley parked himself next to the old vet and tossed the bottle of pills in his seabag. They exchanged smiles.

"You know kid, you remind me of Jake Carter when he first joined us." Stack's words were soft spoken and serious.

"He was full of piss and powder just like you. He was ready to charge out the first day and win the Congressional Medal of Honor."

Sean was intensely interested in the subject broached by the old timer. If ever there was a time in his life for advice it was now. "Let me see, is that a compliment or a warning?"

"Both. You have all the earmarks of taking over Jake's job someday, but you can't do it if you're dead. Trying to win the war in one day is out. I'm not trying to scare you, but there it is."

"I'll bet you sat down with Jake and talked to him like this too?"

Stack nodded. "I sure did. Moe and Johnny B too. They were just babes when I got 'em, and thank God they're all still alive.

O'Malley had a brainstorm. "Maybe I should follow you around, Del. I hear you're going into your fourth major campaign. You must have nine lives."

"Nope, It's too late my friend. I've seen too much. I think I'm coming apart at the seams. Every time a truck hits a bump I get the jumps. Lieutenant Chandler noticed it first and offered me a job at the Command Post where it's safer. If I make it through the next landing I'll probably take his offer."

"You've sure as hell earned it, Sarge. Ya got any suggestions for us?"

Del Stack was no a coward, he was simply close to the end of the line. The game of Russian Roulette had taken a toll on his sensitive nature. In three years he had sloshed through the rotting jungles of New Britain and Guadalcanal, sweated the carnage at Pelelin Island, and fought the grinding ridge battles of Okinawa. How much can a country ask a man to endure? He had some regrets, but his psyche was exhausted.

"Yes, I do have one suggestion for you and Jesse. Watch Moe Chernikov. See how he moves. He has an uncanny animal instinct. He walks like a cat and hides like a gopher. Every step is calculated, and when he's ready, he strikes like a rattlesnake. Yes sir, Moe is the best. He's the whole zoo." Del left the tent without another word.

"Waddya make of that old guy, Jesse?"

"Quite frankly, I consider him a legend in our times. If I can muster one half the fortitude he's shown, I'll be happy."

O'Malley frowned. "Naw, you know what I mean. Why did he pick me?"

"He likes you, and if you take foolish chances you'll be killed in the first week."

"I guess you're right. I always thought it was the other guys that got killed, not me."

"You're not invincible, O'Malley. Besides, you heard what he said. Someday you could become our platoon sergeant." Hightree inhaled deeply, folded his arms across his chest, and produced his best Indian accent. "Redtop heap big medicine now. Sioux boy carvem totem pole, makem you chief."

"Hey, that's pretty good. You sound just like Tonto with the Lone Ranger."

Jesse's trained ear turned to the sound of soft footsteps outside. The eloquence of his speech returned. "I think we are about to receive another guest."

Moe Chernikov's large frame brushed past the tent flaps and resumed its full height. His dark eyes scanned the surroundings and focused on O'Malley. "Howya doin' kid, how's the old bean?"

O'Malley raised his fingers to touch the sore spot on his head, and winced. "Aw, he caught me with a lucky punch, Sarge. I shoulda taken that big slob."

"Ya know, Sean, I like your grit. You reminded me of a flea takin' on a bulldog."

Sean tried to laugh but the throbbing in his temple would not permit it. "I guess I owe you thanks for pullin' him off me."

"Thanks hell, you got in some pretty good licks yourself. You just softened him up for me. Forget it."

Thoughts began to group and solidify in Chernikov's mind. The young Marine had an undeniable spark that intrigued him. Besides the raw materials, there was something else, often referred to as chemistry between men. "Ya know, we're goin' back into action soon. How would you like to be in my scout group?"

"Gee Sarge, do you really mean it, me? I was kinda hopin', that would be great, sure." The young man's spirits were flying. He would be under the wing of a real ace, and he felt a sense of belonging. The future was no longer an ominous black void. Chernikov had been there before, and would lead the way. But what if something happened to Moe, could he carry on alone? He gritted his teeth and shook the feeling off, knowing it was best not to manufacture problems before they happen. In the maturing process, the teenager felt he had just reached his thirtieth birthday. "I know it's not my place to ask, Sarge, but do you suppose Jesse can come with us?"

"I'm way ahead of you. I've already set it up. Jake's with the Lieutenant right now, making up the permanent assignments. Whaddya say Jesse?"

"Mr. Chernikov, I would be delighted."

Moe was tickled by the Indian boy's formal assent, pursing his lips in a simulated whistle. "OK, but there's just one more thing. We'll need a fourth, who do you recommend?"

Without hesitation, Sean answered. "Private Levine."

"Ya mean the boy mechanic?"

"Yes sir, Sarge, he's a tough kid. He was born in Flatbush, and from what I hear you have to be tough to survive and grow in that place."

"Good, that does it, I'll fix it with Jake." Moe clapped his hands on his knees and stood, checking his wristwatch. "We've got some time before the steak fry. What'say we go to my tent for some smoked oysters and a slug of gin?"

O'Malley's aching head was recovering rapidly. He reached for the canteen cup under his bed. "I'm with you Sarge, what say, Jesse?"

"I'm not averse to the oysters but I'll pass on the fire water. I'll tag along."

Chernikov glanced back as he led the way. "Do you suppose you can lasso Levine and bring him here?"

"Yes sir, Sergeant." Hightree broke away and steered for the mess tent. "He's still tinkering with the juke box. I shall fetch him post haste."

Moe's tent was a GI Garden of Eden. Piled waist-high in the corner were the cases of treasures extracted from the US Army. In anticipation he had prepared for a small cocktail party. In the center, next to the tent pole, a wide crate served as a makeshift table. Two stainless steel pitchers were there, one with ice and the other filled with powdered orange juice. Next to them, four tins of oysters awaited opening. Extra canteen cups and a box of toothpicks completed the array.

Chernikov pulled a full bottle from an open box and handed it to O'Malley. "Here ya go, kid. We've got a saying out here. If you're old enough to bleed you're old enough to drink."

"Thanks Sarge. Say, do you mind if I call you Moe?"

"Hell no. Before this thing is over we're gonna be closer than sardines in a can. Pour yourself a belt."

Sean took Muldoon's cigar from the breast pocket of his dungarees, saved for a special occasion. He lit it, choked twice, and blew a cloud of grayish blue smoke at the ceiling. Gin and orange juice sounded good to him as he filled his cup. Moe was right, he may not live to see the inside of an American saloon, so what the hell.

Hightree returned, ushering his prey inside. "Here he is,

Sergeant, your illustrious fourth."

Ike Levine entered with a quizzical expression. "Jesse filled me in. He says you want me to join your scout group."

"Well, how about it?"

"You're damn right. I always like to go with the best. When do I sign up?"

"Right now, welcome to murderer's row. Grab a drink and have a seat."

With cups filled they toasted the new comradeship. Jesse stuck to straight orange juice. Within a few minutes Chernikov was convinced the unusual mixture of men was excellent. The starch of combat was stiff enough, allowing no space for personality conflict. He chose to play host.

"Well men, what would you like to talk about, the war or the broads back home?"

"Broads, what else. Are you married Sarge?"

"Nope, but I had two on the string, both big. I was the only guy around tall enough. What about you, Ike?"

"It's the same old story. My parents are both from the old school. They want me to marry a nice Jewish girl but I like to play the field."

"Speak up, Jesse. Do you have a little filly staked out on the reservation?"

"No gottem squaw. Injun boy wait."

Terse but graphic, Hightree's verbal change of pace sent them into gales of laughter. The questioning of O'Malley had to wait, interrupted by the arrival of Sergeant Carter.

"This is a motley bunch. Am I missing something?"

"Come on in Sarge. We're just giving your gin a taste test. Have a drink."

"Later, I've got a news flash. O'Malley, you're promoted to Private First Class." Jake thrust a pair of chevrons in his hands.

"Me, a PFC, but I..."

"Never mind the modesty, you've earned it. But mind, this

is not an incentive for startin' fights. You've shown qualities of leadership and this stripe is the first step. Lieutenant Chandler just OK'd it so get 'em sewn on."

  Sean's buddies were in solid accord and hastened to congratulate him. The party ended with Levine offering him the use of a sewing kit. When the three young men retired to O'Malley's tent he walked like a zombie at twilight. Most certainly, this had been quite a day.

CHAPTER TWENTY-THREE

The screen door of the mess tent was securely hooked, denying access to the salivating Marines. Over a hundred and fifty sets of molars were poised and ready to chomp on the vulnerable T-bones. The boredom chain of camp life was broken. Chances were, the anticipation would be a greater joy than the taste itself, but it didn't matter. They were happy.

"Hey Jake. This time you've come up with a new high in scrounging."

"Yeah, thanks Jake."

"How'ja pull it off?"

Carter turned to the crowd and waved his hand. "Hold it, don't thank me boys. You can thank Bowman and Chernikov. They were the masterminds. I wasn't in on this one." He directed their attention to Johnny B, standing to his right.

Bowman took in their smiling faces. "Ya know, when we get home I think I'll go into politics. It looks like I've got over a hundred sure votes right here."

Cheers of encouragement filled the air. The throng pressed in, firing questions from four directions. Accepting their gratitude with modesty was his only recourse, the din was too much. Not until the enthusiasm subsided was a familiar figure able to weave its way through. Lieutenant Joe Lyons from Fox Company placed himself in front of Jake and Johnny B. The presence of gold bars caused the men to make room.

"Hello Jake, remember me, the historian from Oregon? I'm looking for another story."

After a quick salute, Carter received his handshake. "Sure I remember, Lieutenant, welcome to the political rally.

The Last Souvenir

Bowman's gonna run for President. How's that for news?"

"It might be a little premature for a press release, but I'll make a note of it. What the hell, why not? By the way, I have a surprise for you. I've brought an old friend of yours. He's just rejoined the company to take over the machine-gun section."

From behind Lieutenant Lyons the granite-block body of Corporal Chuck Courtney appeared. The square jaw and bushy black hair were unmistakable. The ever-present twinkle was still in his brown eyes. Through training together in the States the two men became, and remained, fast friends. A hearty hand clasp lasted for several moments.

Jake was stupefied, beginning to babble. "Chuck, Chuck Courtney, you're still alive. I heard you were hit bad, back in April. Clue me in buddy."

Courtney stepped back a pace and lifted the corner of his jacket, disclosing a revolting red scar. A piece of shrapnel had gouged a chunk of meat from his right side. "There she is. A few inches to the left and I'd be crappin' through a rubber tube."

"That looks nasty. You're lucky you didn't bleed to death."

"You can say that again, I did get lucky," Chuck replied reflectively. "The corpsmen were fast. They were pumpin' plasma in one side and I was bleedin' from the other. Those guys are great. I'd kiss their asses if they asked me."

"How come they didn't ship you back to the States?"

"If you mean the million dollar wound, forget it. The Navy doctors have their orders. If you can still walk and pull the trigger, you go back in the lines."

The listening veterans in the circle were well aware of this phenomenon, but not the replacements. The portent of their future turned grim and real. The good news was at least the wounded had a chance for survival. They would have to settle for that.

Courtney, the most fun loving of Jake's friends, eliminated the pall. "Aw, let's skip this bullshit. Tell me about steak dinners and how do I get invited? I see ya got four stripes on your sleeve now, ya got any pull around here?"

"I sure do. Come on, let's go around back and see what the cook's up to."

"Ya better not go back there, Sarge, he ain't allowin' nobody. He's meaner than an old bear today."

"We'll see about that." Jake motioned for the three men to follow.

Behind the kitchen, wielding a long handled fork with two prongs, the cook stared down at his new masterpiece. Stretched before him, like pages from a textbook on how to improvise, was the new barbecue grill. Steel bars wired together in a cross pattern were supported at the corners by empty metal ammunition boxes. A blazing fire licked its way through the checkerboard. To one side a stack of broken slats from ration crates waited to feed the flames. On a table to his left, trays of steaks, thawed and ready, were covered by wet white towels. Inside the kitchen, two long kerosene stoves, government issue, were placed end to end, all burners in service. Four ten-gallon pots of potatoes boiled, the steam forcing the lids to flutter and clank. A watery eyed messman reluctantly peeled and sliced onions, dropping the rings into deep frying pans of canned butter. Others worked in the empty mess hall, stacking trays, cups, and sliced bread. The excessive heat caused streaks of perspiration to seep between the shoulder blades of their green T-shirts.

Jake and Johnny B, with their two guests, peeked around the corner at the wondrous production line. Cookie's peripheral vision detected their intrusion into his private domain. "You jugheads were told to stay outta... Oh, it's you Jake. OK, come on back." He waved his fork like the baton of a symphony conductor. "Those Joes out front think I'm pissed off, but I'm not. I'm havin' the time of my life. How do you like my creation?" He pointed at the grill. "I figure she'll hold over fifty steaks."

"She's a beaut, Cookie, a real monster." Carter shifted to one side. "These are my guests from Fox Company, Lieutenant Lyons and Chuck Courtney."

"Now look here, I can't allow no strange officers eatin' in my mess hall. I'm gonna have to ship you to the officer's mess."

Joe Lyons promptly removed the gold bars from his lapels and dropped them into a side pocket. "How's that? I just demoted myself to Private. Can I enjoy your dinner now?"

"Ya know Jake, I like this guy. Sure, you can stay, I might even join you."

The chef, an element of pride in his delivery, was explaining the extent of his culinary plans when Moe Chernikov arrived, holding an empty pitcher in each hand.

"Here ya go, Cookie, I brought back your jugs."

"Dammit Moe, you know I don't do dirty pots. Put 'em in the kitchen."

Moe shoved one of the containers under the cook's nose. "Ya better look in this one first."

Cookie reached in to withdraw a full bottle of gin. "Now that's what I call a finishing touch." With no wasted motion he removed the cap and tilted the bottle to his lips, downing two big gulps of the perfumed nectar. His larynx was partially paralyzed when he wiped his mouth with a sleeve and croaked; "Ah... thanks Moe, you're not so bad after all." He handed the bottle to Joe Lyons. "You're next, Private, have a shot."

The glowing embers reached a perfect orange hue. The bottle made its rounds and the steaks hit the grill. The cook's prediction was close. Fifty-four T-bones sizzled before them with drops of fat spitting on the coals. The heavenly aroma recalled memories of backyard barbecue parties that seemed eons ago. The cook leaned over the grill and braved the smoke, applying steak sauce with a paintbrush.

"Them Aussies sure know how to make steak sauce. I'd like to get the recipe." Cookie held a quart-sized bottle in his hand and read the printing. "I'll have another swig of that gin now."

The curious mind of Joe Lyons hadn't missed a trick. He was scribbling on the fifth page of his notebook. Whatever drives a man to be a writer, he was blessed with the talent. The mundane events of ordinary living would bypass the average man, but not Lyons. He knew that someday they would have historical significance, and he was destined to record the story.

Cookie's curiosity finally overcame him. "Hey, whatcha writin' there? Lemme see that book."

Graciously, Lyons handed it over. "With pleasure, but let me warn you, it's in shorthand."

"Short - what? Hell, it looks like Nipponese. Are you sure you ain't a Jap spy?"

The remark made Lyons chuckle. He liked that one. "No, my friend, I had to take a special class to learn it."

"You sound like an educated man. Shit, I never made it past the ninth grade. I was a fry cook in a roadhouse when I was fourteen. Been cookin' ever since."

"And an admirable profession it is. Just for the record, may I have your name and hometown?" Lyons retrieved his notebook.

"Ya mean I'm gonna be in a book?" The old chef was honored. "The name is Watts but nobody calls me that. Just plain 'Cookie'. I was born in Idaho but I'm a regular Marine, the Corps is my home. I go where they send me."

Lyons noticed the six stripes on his dungaree jacket. "I see you're a Master Sergeant. I promise you, someday your name will appear before the world."

The Last Souvenir

One by one, the mess crew found their way outside, taking in every word. Watts turned and resumed his usual air of gruff efficiency. "Alright you buzzards, this ain't no tap dancin' school. Fill up the servin' trays and gettem out on the counter. Maxey, fish the potatoes outta them pots. Guido, stand by the front door and get ready to let 'em in."

The flurry of feet was instant and impressive to the spectators. His authority was never challenged. Being both tough and wise, he was consistently fair. The men respected him. He was a latent teacher, passing on his knowledge in bits and pieces on a daily basis.

Cookie was forking the steaks from the grill two at a time. In a sweeping motion he filled the open spaces with two more raw ones that hit the iron with a loud sizzle. "You guys better get in line first. When we open the door I gotta hunch the first wave is gonna be a wild one."

The five men side-slipped past the sweating mess crew and entered the empty dining room. The incredible feast had materialized. Deep rectangular serving trays lined the long table. First in sequence, a pile of steaming T-bones wafted their aroma throughout the room. Completing the lineup were ample portions of sautéed onion rings and unpeeled boiled potatoes. The serving crew stood behind like statues in white aprons, each brandishing a wide scoop-like metal spoon. The clamor outside was building.

"OK Guido, Cookie says open the flood gates."

Jake looked with horror at the thundering rabble. In a voice loud enough to be heard he said, "Lieutenant, you and Courtney are the guests, You're first."

Lyons blew a shushing sound through his lips. "I'm not wearing my bars, remember, you better call me Joe." This was the kind of excitement he was seeking. The thoughts of writing a novel came to mind.

They left the counter together with full trays of steaks

smothered in onions and a potato on the side. Carter selected a table in the center. On the surface, a one-gallon can of butter stood with a tablespoon plunged in it, ringed by salt and pepper shakers. Joe Lyons purposely sat between Jake and Chuck Courtney.

"I guess we'll have to rough it. No napkins."

Almost in the same motion, each man reached for his hip and withdrew a sharp blade. Unwritten tradition demands a Marine never venture anywhere without wearing his utility knife. The brutal carving began. The silence was punctuated by ums and ahs. Scores of men were seated by now, with more pushing through the door. The lack of conversation brought a smile to Joe Lyons' face as he savored the morsel in his mouth. How many times in history has a simple steak dinner been so thoroughly enjoyed?

Ike Levine was by the door, making final adjustments on his beloved jukebox. A self-made slug was hammered into the coin slot, allowing anyone free play. "You guys got any requests?"

With full mouths, and complete disregard for etiquette, the men made suggestions.

"Got any Benny Goodman?"

"How about Tommy Dorsey?"

"Start with number one and play the whole rack."

Ike liked the last idea. He punched the one button and delivered a piano medley of tunes by George Gershwin. The background music was perfect for the setting.

Courtney straightened and turned around. "My god Jake, don't tell me you people have a jukebox too. The guys in Fox Company ain't gonna believe this story."

"You just said the magic word, Chuck, story." Lyons wiped his mouth with a handkerchief and pushed away his empty tray. "I'm here for unusual tales. You and Jake have seen so much mischief together, how about it?" He tapped the eraser end of his pencil on the table.

"Chuck, should we tell him about the still we built in the jungle at Pavuvu?"

"How about the big beer bust on Banika?"

"Naw, that's not enough." A fiendish look came to Jake's face. "Let's tell him the big one, you know, the dud torpedo caper."

"Oh no! Not that one. If the Navy ever finds out it was us, they'll hang us from the yardarm."

With Joe Lyons in the middle, the two men bantered back and forth over the wisdom of retelling the incriminating event. At the end of the table an anxious Sean O'Malley voiced his eagerness. Any story about Carter was fodder for his admiration. Finally, Courtney relented and Jake told the yarn in his own words.

"The whole thing started when our invasion fleet assembled in the Carolines back in March. I never saw so many ships in my life, carriers, cruisers, transports, the whole damn Navy. We were anchored by the big island of Ulithi. Remember how hot it was? We were only a few points above the Equator. It musta been hundred and ten degrees in the troop compartments below deck."

"It was hundred and fifteen, I wrote it down." Del Stack, an amateur historian himself, had entered it in his diary.

Carter went on. "You're probably right, Del. Well anyhow, Chuck and I went up on the well deck about midnight to get some air. We were all alone. We were leanin' over the rail when Chuck pulled a couple of hand grenades out of his pockets. We decided to have a contest to see who could throw them the farthest. We pulled the pins and flung 'em as hard as we could, aimin' at a sliver of moonlight on the ocean. They splashed and sunk. Then the water jumped with a real soft kawumph."

Jake held his hands palms down over the table and raised

them an inch to illustrate the reaction of the water. "Up on deck ya couldn't hear anything, but we didn't know about sound traveling underwater. Down below decks, when the sound hit the metal plates, it was like a giant sledgehammer hitting a metal gong. All hell broke loose. Two thousand troops came up the ladders like ants, draggin' their life belts.

Bowman straightened his back and raised his eyebrows. "Do you mean to tell me that was you two crazy bastards? You scared the shit outta me. I thought we'd been sunk."

"So did everybody else. They woke up the Captain and told him we'd been hit by a dud torpedo. He ordered all hands to man their battle stations. Swabbies were runnin' everywhere, jumpin' in gun turrets and yankin' canopies off the barrels. You couldn't hear because of the noise from the bells and loudspeakers. Signal lights were blinkin' from every ship in the fleet. The whole damn bunch was put on condition red alert."

Chernikov thought the story was hilarious. "What the hell were you two jokers doin' in the meantime?"

"We were still on deck, surrounded by a buncha guys in their underwear. We decided to look innocent. Everybody was standin' by the rail watchin' the destroyers crank up. They were boiling around with their sound gear, trying to find the Jap submarine. I did feel sorry for the poor swabbies. They had to stand watch for the rest of the night, a hundred percent alert. They got no sleep."

Joe Lyons' right hand was a blur above his notebook. A creeping writer's cramp slowed him to a halt, and he began to digest his text. "The whole scramble started with a couple of lousy hand grenades. You two certainly didn't mean any harm. I wonder how many gallons of fuel oil were wasted, not to mention Navy sweat."

Courtney was fast to issue a warning. "We'd sure appreciate it if you left out our names in this fiasco. A Navy officer told us later they'd entered it in the ship's log as a dud torpedo. We better leave it at that. We don't wanna get our asses in a sling."

Lyons agreed. "Mum's the word boys, but still, that's a

The Last Souvenir

helluva story. I'd sure like to get my hands on that ship's log someday."

The mess tent crowd was thinning. Men with innards bulging over their belts filed by to pat the backs of Bowman and Chernikov.

"Thanks, buddy."

"If you ever need anything from us, just name it."

The scout section met outside to exchange final comments. Joe Lyons hastily replaced the gold bars on his collar. His mission for the day was accomplished, and then some. The reunion ended with the two men from Fox Company leaving together, heading back to their unit. A few steps away, Courtney turned to wave one last fond goodbye. Everyone waved back.

Carter felt a little emotional. "Ol' Chuck Courtney, there goes a great guy. I sure feel better now, knowin' he made it."

CHAPTER TWENTY-FOUR

The last few days of July ushered in the early traces of heat and humidity. Master Gunnery Sergeant Stebbins and his students stood in a cluster in front of the quartermaster's tent. Per schedule Sergeant Lang issued Browning automatic rifles to each of the eleven replacements. Like pack animals they squirmed under heavy burdens of oversized cartridge belts and extra bandoleers of ammo. Stebbins gave instruction on how to adjust the slings for carrying the light machine guns. At 8:00 AM, the sticky warmth in the air was already causing the leather straps to chafe their shoulders.

To one side, Carter spoke in low tones to Del Stack. "Del, about ten o'clock I want you, Bill, and Russ to break away and meet me at the shed in the village. Stebbins can take over. Keep this under your hat, buddy. I'll explain later."

"You're gonna knock off the lumber yard, aren't you?" Del was grinning.

"Shh! Not so loud, but that's it."

Without warning, Lieutenant Chandler rounded the corner and nosed his way into the scene. "Well done men, you're right on schedule. Where are they going?"

"To the new rifle range at First Battalion, sir."

"You sure have them loaded down. They look like Pancho Villa and his bandits. Move 'em out when your ready." Chandler was brief and left quickly. He did not notice that Bowman and Chernikov were missing.

Jake watched the file trail away and head east along the

main camp road. Stebbins, like the Pied Piper of Hamlin led the way with a Japanese rifle in his hand. This he would add to his repertoire. They were in good hands.

Over and over in his mind Jake turned the details of his complicated scheme. Timing had to be perfect. The clock was his enemy. He entered his tent to find Moe and Johnny B, fully clothed and ready. "You guys all set?"

Bowman's zeal for adventure was at its peak. "We're rarin' to go, buddy. Ya know, it's gonna be great to have wood floors. This place is turnin' into a real dust factory." He pointed at the powder on the deck.

Carter sat and pulled a bundle from under his cot. Wrapped in wax paper from an empty ration carton was the kimono and sash for Noonan's little sister. From his seabag he withdrew a shiny blue Japanese pistol, placing it on the package. Crimped on a clipboard under his pillow was a forged requisition form, courtesy of Sergeant Lang. As an added measure, he produced a Jap infantry helmet.

"What's the helmet for?"

"I'm not sure, just a hunch. Call it insurance." Carter rose and lifted his mattress, sliding a clean shirt into view. The old GI custom of sleeping on it all night had pressed it flat. The pinkish beige color and Captain's bars on the collar identified it as part of an officer's uniform.

"Whatcha gonna do with that?"

"I'm gonna wear it, soon as I get outta the camp. I just promoted myself to Captain for a day."

Johnny B loved it. "Hey, I get it. We'll be your aides, that'll work."

Carter had allowed for as many contingencies as probable, even the unexpected. His plan had four phases, which he methodically related to his cohorts. The three had been together so long they could almost read his mind. Johnny B was eager and Moe was fearless. Telling them once was enough.

"Well, that's it," Carter concluded. "Wear your pistols. Grab the stuff and take off for the motor pool. See Lieutenant Dutch. You better detour around the mess tent. I don't want you parading by the Colonel's tent. Park the truck by the Main Gate and wait for me. OK?"

"Your wish is my command, Captain." When they disappeared, Jake picked up the phone. "Hello, switchboard, get me the Army sawmill south of Motobu."

Several minutes passed while he endured an onslaught of clicking and strange voices. At last, the efficiency of Sergeant Eddie Gallo and the comm section paid dividends.

"Guard post, Sergeant Noonan speaking."

"Hello Noonan, does your little sister still want that geisha kimono? Yeah, it's me, we're comin' down for that visit. Sure, we've got what you said. OK, I'm comin' as Captain Manhoff, and the forms are signed by Colonel L. B. Puller. Anything else? OK, about thirty minutes. See ya."

He stuffed the shirt and a contour map in his jacket. A premonition told him to take his binoculars. Circling behind the headquarters tents, and climbing over the ropes, he made his way to the main gate. Bowman waited behind the steering wheel with the big truck idling. A cursory glance at his watch assured him of the timetable.

Jake scrambled into the passenger side. "Let 'er rip Johnny, and for God's sake, keep it under thirty-five."

The truck's cab, with a wide bench seat, easily accommodated three men, with Chernikov in the middle. Carter struggled out of his jacket and donned his officer's shirt, carefully tucking the tails into his trousers. He shoved the Jap pistol in his belt. It would be in plain sight. Leaving Noonan's present on the floorboards at his feet, he held up his clipboard and read it one last time. "This is a big load, boys, high priority merchandise. If anything goes wrong, it's phase three, we *SCRAM*. And remember, no names."

The Last Souvenir

Sergeant Noonan was anxious, waiting by the side of the road in front of the main gate. He was willing to forfeit the shade of his porch in his vigil for the Marine truck. Though their meeting was brief, he felt an instant liking for Carter and Bowman. Monotony and harassment from the General Staff officers had driven him to the brink of despair. To him, the war was an arid desert with nothing on the horizon. In his heart, he was seeking a combination of retribution and excitement, and it was on its way. A wide grin spread across his face when the truck pulled up to his gate. Once he spotted Jake, he worked his way to the passenger side.

"I see you've been promoted. Captain no less. That's a big jump."

Carter pushed the package through the open side window. "Hello again, Noonan. Here, this is for Melissa. I hope she likes it."

Noonan took the gift with both hands and clamped it under his arm. "Like it? She'll love it. I can't wait to see it myself. It'll go out in tonight's mail."

Jake hastened to caution him. "I put my real name and address inside like you asked. Stick it in your pocket. I'm too young to get the firing squad."

Noonan laughed, reaching for the clipboard. "This looks official enough. Captain Manhoff 'eh, and Colonel Puller too. Are these guys real?"

"They sure are, pal, but far away."

"This paperwork looks OK to me, but how are you gonna' get around the Lieutenant?"

Carter flashed the Jap pistol in his face.

"Wow! He'll cream in his pants when he sees that. He's a gun collector you know."

"I'm counting on that, buddy. There's one more thing. When you write down the ID number on our truck, can you transpose it? You know, garble 'em up?"

"I've already thought of that, you're covered." He waved them through. "Good luck you guys and thanks for remembering my little sister."

Fortune was with them when they entered the storage yard and parked by a mountain of lumber. The saw was shut down, with the work party at rest. A young lieutenant in army khaki came striding over as Jake dismounted. Military courtesy was observed when he saluted the Captain's bars.

"Good morning sir, has Sergeant Noonan checked your orders?"

Jake purposefully hid the pistol in his belt behind the clipboard, returning the salute. "Good morning, Lieutenant, you'll find everything in order here."

"We don't get any Marines in our compound, Captain, this is a bit irregular."

"Everything has been cleared through your 10th Army, Lieutenant. It's a special order." Carter could sense his resistance, knowing the time for a diversion had come. He handed away the clipboard, revealing the Japanese Lugar. The magnificent handgun caught the officer's eyes like a shock wave.

"Where did you get that, sir? That's a Japanese P-38."

"In combat."

"Captain, I'm a gun collector. I'd give my heart and soul to own one of those. Do you want to sell it?"

"Heavens no, this is my most prized souvenir. They're very rare."

"Sir, I'll give you a hundred bucks cash, right now."

Carter threw back his head with a sigh. "I'm sorry Lieutenant, I was offered more than ten times that figure at Yontan. It's not for sale."

"Can I see it, sir, just look at it?"

"I see no harm in that, but be careful, it's loaded." Jake handed it over.

The Last Souvenir

"Boy this is a beauty. It's brand new." Obviously a gunsmith, he pressed the release button and dropped the magazine into his palm. After clearing the breech he sighted down the empty barrel. "I can't believe it, it looks like it's never been fired."

"It hasn't. I had to clean out the cosmoline myself."

"Captain, I wish you could see my collection. I have the original colt revolver that Wyatt Earp carried in Dodge City. There's a certificate of authenticity that goes with it. I'll tell you what I'll do. I'll raise my offer to fifteen-hundred bucks. I have a lot of back pay coming. Whadda ya say?"

"You tempt me, my friend, but right now I'm thinking about lumber. When can we start loading?"

The pistol was back in Carter's belt when the officer lifted the board and read the requisition form. "Well, this is a big order and out of channels. I'll have to check with my colonel first." For five minutes he described the procedure.

"My God man, by the time this goes through my III Corps and your 10th Army it could take weeks of paperwork."

"I'm sorry Captain, but I don't see any other way."

"Well, I'm Colonel Puller's adjutant, and I'd do anything for the old man. He's desperate for this lumber, that's why it was cleared." Carter's instincts told him it was time to press. "Now, I'm going to tell you what I'll do. If you fill this requisition, get us loaded, and wait one hour before you start the paper mill, I'll give you the pistol. Call it a gift from Colonel Puller." He removed the weapon and handed it toward the Lieutenant, grip first.

The temptation was enormous, melting the young officer. "Just one hour? Well, you do have signed orders." He leered at the prize, wetting his lips. "I guess it's no skin off my nose, one way or another. All you need is 2 X 4's and 1 X 6's. I'll take it." He seized his new gem and held it with both hands.

Carter was galvanized into action. "Sergeant, back up the

truck to that lumber pile. You men over there, bear a hand."

In less than thirty minutes, with the aid of seven men, the truck bed was full. The stack of lumber on the ground was all but decimated. The three Marines climbed into the cab with Carter returning one last salute. The truck ground away in low gear. Noonan stood by the gate with both thumbs up. "Good luck, gyrenes, keep your powder dry."

Bowman turned North, according to the plan, with Chernikov shaking his head. "Jake, you're one slick-tongued sonuva bitch. We heard every word."

"Good, then you know we have one hour to get the hell outta here."

Bowman turned down his cap visor to protect his eyes from the blazing sun. His desire to be a speed demon was temporarily suppressed. Squinting his eyebrows, he peered ahead. "Hey Jake, looks like we got troubles. There's a traffic jam up there."

A long line of brown trucks was blocking the narrow road between the rice paddies. Johnny B pulled up and parked behind the last vehicle, a big ten wheeler. Nothing moved and they were stymied. Carter, as yet unperturbed handed the binoculars to Bowman.

"Here Johnny, take these and get out for a look-see."

Standing on the left of the road, Bowman adjusted the glasses and surveyed the dilemma. When satisfied he announced over his shoulder; "About a mile up there's a Sherman tank with a busted tread. There's a big crane next to it tryin' to fix it."

The last truck ahead intrigued him. He strolled over and lifted the rear canopy. "I can't believe it. This thing is loaded with folding chairs, arms and everything. You know, the kind movie directors sit in."

Now it was Chernikov's turn to be brilliant. He slid behind the steering wheel and put the gear shift in low, pulling their truck ahead with bumpers almost touching. In one bound he was out of the cab, scampering to a stance on the hood in front of the windshield. "Don't just stand there, start handin' them to me. Let's throw a few in the back."

There was no need for Bowman to be told twice. Hand to hand the chairs passed with Moe tossing them over the cab and under their own truck's canopy. The muffled clatter drove Jake out of his seat and onto the road. "You two bastards are crazy. Don't you think we're pressing our luck a little too much?"

Without breaking his rhythm Johnny B answered; "Aw come on Jake, they'll never miss 'em. There must be a thousand in here, we'll never get another chance like this."

"Well hurry it up, how many do you have so far, Moe?"

"Over a dozen. Just a few more and we can beat it."

Sensing something was amiss, the Army driver appeared, looking up in disbelief. "Hey, youse guys can't do that. Those chairs is goin' to the Officer's Club." His accent placed him from one of the New York City boroughs. When Carter faced him he brought up a sloppy salute.

"Captain, are you in charge here?"

"Stand at ease, private. Yes I am. We're on a foraging mission for our regiment."

"Foragin', sir? What's that?"

"Soldier, do you really care if the generals miss a few chairs?"

"No sir, not me. I'm just a driver. If it were up to me, ya could have 'em all. But I gotta account for 'em when I gets back to the QM dump."

Carter had one trump card left. "Do you have any war souvenirs?"

"Naw, sir, the only souvenir I got is a sore rump from drivin'. I ain't seen no combat."

Jake took the helmet from the cab. "Did you ever see one

of these?"

The driver's face registered mild surprise. "That's a Nip helmet ain't it? I never seen a real one, just pichers. That's worth a lotta bucks."

"Well, Private, it's yours on one condition. You climb back into your truck and keep your mouth shut about this. If your supply officer asks questions, make up a story. Any story. Understand?"

"Yeah, Sir, I got it, ya mean like a hijackin'. I always wanted a real souvenir." The annoyance ending on amiable terms. Carter read his watch again.

"Come on boys, we've got enough and times a wastin'. Moe, take the glasses and jump in the back. Keep a lookout. Johnny, you drive."

With Bowman at the wheel, Carter sat next to him and raised his contour map. "About a hundred yards back there's a dirt road. Put her in reverse and back up. Then turn right and put this crate in four-wheel drive."

As usual, Leo's map was accurate. For an unknown reason the dirt road was partially graded by the Army Engineers. It led through a series of gentle rolling hills, winding east, with expanses of sugar cane on both sides.

They had traveled almost two miles when Chernikov turned his head and yelled; "Hey Jake, we got company. An MP jeep just turned off the highway and they're headed this way, fast."

"How many?"

"One jeep with two men."

"Somebody must've blown the whistle on us." Jake went back to his map. "Johnny, see that crossroad down below? Drop me off there. Then go over the next hill, you'll see a little farmhouse. Park behind it outta sight, and wait for me."

"Shit Jake, we're out in the middle of nowhere, are you sure you know what you're doin'?"

"No time to explain now." Jake stood on the running board

and jumped into the intersection with a running dog trot. He watched his truck rumble over the hill and out of vision. With the coolness of a man on a Sunday stroll he held up the map, carefully examining the terrain. The Military Police also had problems with the rough road, arriving several minutes later. They seemed bewildered to find a lone man standing in such desolation as they pulled up beside him.

"Hey you there. Did you see a truck go through here?"

Carter lowered the map and spoke with all the arrogance he could summon. "Now wait one minute. Don't they teach you army people to salute a commissioned officer?"

"Sorry, sir." Both men sat at attention and saluted. "By the way, what are you doing here?"

"I don't see it's any of your business."

"We're Military Police, sir, it is our business to ask questions."

"Well, if you must know, my reconnaissance company is coming through here in a few hours on a night exercise. I'm laying out their line of march."

"That sounds peculiar to me, but feasible. Did you see a truck come by?"

Jake pointed south. "I sure did, they were in a big hurry. They turned here and took that road. According to my map it goes to the Yontan airstrip."

"Thanks, Captain."

When the jeep was out of sight he trudged over the hill and found his buddies. Behind the farmhouse they were surrounded by a native family of onlookers. Johnny B was relieved. "That was a close one, what's the story?"

"Sent 'em on a wild goose chase to Yontan. Come on boys, let's head for the barn."

CHAPTER TWENTY-FIVE

The early morning silence was shattered by the staccato of machine guns. Orange tracer bullets streaked across the open ground, pounding into the earthen butts at the base of a high cliff. A line of kneeling Marines braced their bodies against the recoiling weapons, slicing silhouette targets to pieces. Gunny Stebbins, with arms folded on his chest, watched intently as hundreds of empty brass cartridges were ejected and strewn along the firing line.

From a long table in the rear, a box of cotton balls provided stuffing for the ears of the spectating scout group leaders. Even the most seasoned veteran would flinch at the awesome display of firepower. A cloud of acrid smoke was beginning to swirl around the faces of the young replacements. One by one the magazines emptied and the rifle range fell into a temporary lull.

"That's it for now men. Pick up your brass and bring your weapons back to the table." Stebbins pulled the wads of cotton from his ears. "Well Sergeant Stack, I hate to admit it, but the boys look pretty good. They learn fast. Now we teach 'em how to strip and clean the Browning."

Del acknowledged with a nod of his head. "I'm impressed too, Gunny, but I'm afraid you'll have to go it alone. We have orders to report to Sergeant Carter and we're five minutes late now."

"Carter, eh? Alright, you've seen all this before. I'll take it from here."

Del Stack, a philosophical man, never shared the early dislike of Stebbins with the rest of the men in 2 Section.

Conversely, he admired his dedication. When the Gunny's demeanor adjusted to the laxness of rest camp discipline his respect grew. Stebbins had the power of knowledge sprinkled with deep consideration for new men. Not obvious at first, it gained momentum like a ground swell. The slovenly camp life and the urgency of training had taught him to wear two hats.

Stack gathered Keeler and Hull and herded them down the path leading away from the rifle range. The noise started again with new men taking their places on the firing line.

"What's all this about, Del? Where in hell are you taking us?"

"Don't worry, Russ, you're not gonna miss lunch. Jake wants us to meet him in the village."

"But that's over a mile away."

"Tell you what I'll do, if your little tootsies get tired I'll carry you piggyback."

"That I'd like to see, Pops, I'm back up to two-hundred-twenty."

There was no sign of Carter when they reached the warehouse. Del checked his watch. "Now I'm worried. You know Jake, he doesn't like to be late. Must have run into a snag."

"He's comin' now." The eagle eyes of Bill Hull picked up a cloud of dust on the horizon. "There's a truck headed this way, bouncin' like mad."

Bowman steered carefully between the little huts with his arm out the window, gesturing for clearance. Summertime on the island always meant a nightmare of dust, spurring the women inside to close their doors. Carter unbuttoned his shirt and shed his Captain's bars. "Turn 'er around Johnny and back up to those doors."

Once the truck was backed into the warehouse, Bowman cut the engine. In the rear, Chernikov was out, lowering the tailgate. He grabbed a folding chair and flung it to Keeler.

"Here ya go, muscles, plunk your ass down on this."

Russ caught it with an expression of delight. He removed the packing straps and squared it on the floor. Looking up from a sitting position he grasped the arms of the chair. "Hey, this is great. It's just like what those movie people sit in."

"That's what Bowman said. There's plenty for all of us."

Bill Hull joined the act. "Look at all that wood. Whatcha gonna build, Jake, a city hall?"

"Damn near." Carter was still fighting his time-clock. "Pile the lumber by that wall and stack the chairs over there. With six of us humping we can get it done before noon chow. I want it to look like we haven't been missin'."

Thanks to young sinew, the truck bed was emptied with surprising rapidity. Without work gloves, they acquired a splinter or two, but there was no concern. The wonderful future of flooring and furniture was uppermost in their thoughts.

"OK, boys, it's quarter of twelve. Johnny, you and Moe take the truck back and sign out. The rest of us can hoof it." Jake closed the barn doors behind the departing vehicle and led the way back to camp. His plan was to reappear from different directions, attracting little or no attention.

The mess tent was sparsely occupied when they straggled inside. The Comm Section was still out on a wiring problem. Cookie made one of his rare appearances in the serving line. When Jake saw this he walked behind the counter and whispered in his ear. "Hey Cookie, howdja like to have wood floors in your kitchen?"

"Are you kiddin'? I've sprinkled so much water on that crud back there I'm sick of it. Look at the mud caked on my soles. I feel like I'm walkin' in elevator shoes."

"OK buddy, you got it. Gimme a couple of days, and don't spread it around, the heat might be on."

"Jake, I don't know what the hell you've been up to, but

sign me up."

"There's one more thing. I'll probably need a couple of cases of franks and beans, the one gallon cans. Call it overheads."

"Seems like every day you pull a new rabbit outta your hat. Say when."

Carter held a tray while the cook spooned it with hot food. New rations of canned spaghetti and meatballs had come in. The spicy sauce smelled delicious, encouraging Jake to grab extra bread for sopping. He found his buddies at an isolated table and joined them. Kovak was there, along with O'Malley and Hightree. It was time for a conference.

"Kovak, you're just the man I want to see." With his fork he assaulted the short strings of spaghetti. "We're gonna need a five man native crew, so round up the carpenters. In the next couple'a days I'll draw up some diagrams. You're in charge of construction."

"I'm your man, Sarge. Woodshop was my favorite class in high school. Del just told me about the lumber. When do I start?"

Jake spoke through a mouthful of meatballs. "Can't say yet, the lid could blow off this thing. I'll let ya know."

O'Malley wanted in. "Is there anything I can do, Sarge?"

"Sure is, you can camp on that guard roster. Tell them to keep their traps shut. Right now that barn is hotter than a two dollar pistol."

Johnny B asked the obvious. "The Colonel's bound to find out sooner or later. What are ya gonna tell him?"

Carter dropped his fork and stroked his chin. "Been thinkin' about that."

"Looks like you're about to get your chance. Here comes Johnny Cobb."

The orderly stopped at the head of their table. "Sergeant Carter, Colonel Mason wants to see you in his tent right after chow." With his curt proclamation over, he spun on his heels and left.

"Well boys, I guess this is it. Keep your fingers crossed."

Colonel Mason sat slumped over his desk, bathed in consternation. "Why does everything happen to me?" He tried to make sense of the notes he had taken. A two-star general had just burned his tail feathers, threatening to court-martial every man in his regiment. 'Lumber and camp chairs? This is ridiculous.' In a few weeks it would be his responsibility to lead over two thousand men into combat. Many of them wouldn't be coming back. He wondered whether the General Staff had lost their minds.

Carter hunched over and entered the tent, saluting. "You want to see me, sir?"

"Yes, Sergeant, pull up that box and have a seat. I need your help."

"My help, sir?" Jake was expecting a blistering oration.

"Lieutenant Chandler just left. Thank heavens he can account for your whereabouts in the training schedule."

"My whereabouts, sir?"

Mason took the young Marine into his confidence. "This morning I received a phone call from no less than General Mueller himself. He's hopping mad. It seems that a Marine officer and two enlisted men stole a truckload of lumber and twenty-four folding camp chairs, all of which was exclusively slated for the new staff club. Their schedule has been pushed back a whole week."

"What do you need from me, sir?"

"Sergeant, you're the chief scout in my intelligence section. You and your gangsters have underworld connections. I want you to get to the bottom of this."

"Gangsters, sir?"

"You heard me. You have more connections than the division switchboard. Tomorrow the Shore Patrol and the

Military Police are coming to shake down the entire regiment. They're going to turn *MY* camp upside down."

"Colonel Mason, may I speak freely?"

"That's what you're here for, go ahead."

"Well, sir, the men have been talking. They think that exclusive generals club is a rotten deal."

Mason perked his ears. "Just exactly what do you mean by rotten?"

"Because they exclude you, sir. Why, you and the other regimental commanders are the real fighting officers, not them, sir. When the congressmen show up, they're gonna sit around and tell 'em how they won all the big battles. Why hell, Colonel, they sit back in the rear and draw lines on maps while you do the fightin' for them. They'll take all the credit. The men follow you, sir, not them."

"I appreciate your candor, Sergeant. Do the men really feel that way about me?"

"Yes sir, you're tops with us. We've done everything you asked us to do, haven't we?"

Emotionally stirred, the Colonel bowed his head. "This is none of your business, Carter, and off the record, but I had a call from Colonel Snedecker of the Seventh Marines. He said the same thing. He's miffed about it too."

"He should be, sir. Hell, you've been in my OP at the front lines a dozen times. Every time we get hung up on a tough objective you're right there, talkin' to the men. In all my foxhole time I've never seen a general at the front."

"Carter, God seems to have blessed you with a logical mind, twisted but logical. We have been through a lot together. I know you well, and I'm beginning to smell a rodent. You're behind this scam, aren't you?"

"Colonel Mason, I've never lied to you. Now I'm going to ask for *YOUR* help."

"Good grief, I knew it. This is not a pickle, it's a

catastrophe." He jolted upright and paced the floor.

The moment was opportune. Padre Turner poked his face through the flaps. "Colonel, may I come in? I just spoke with Lieutenant Chandler and I thought you might need me."

"By all means, Father, come in. I just turned my tent into a confessional and we need a priest." The chaplain had a calming influence on the beset old man. He returned to his chair.

"Alright Carter, spill it. I want the whole story from square one."

The intrepid Sergeant had allowed himself to be discovered by choice, not chance. There were no other options. New wooden structures in the camp would attract attention like a sore finger. To beseech Mason's support was imperative, yet had to be subtle. He loved truth, with a penchant for sniffing out fiction.

Carter's presentation would rely on the characteristics of the man himself. He used three known and simple facts. First, the Colonel had empathy for his men and their living conditions. He was forever haggling with superior supply officers. Second he was a tidy man, leaning heavily on neatness. Third, and best of all, he had a well-disguised sense of humor. Officer's training had not taken from him the recall of his enlisted days.

Carter began his story with the stakeout across the road from the sawmill, and the subsequent research that was necessary. Timing was next. From there, the tools of his trade: The kimono, pistol and enemy helmet. He meticulously fitted all pieces together, ending with the MP jeep chase and its diversion. Willfully omitted were the names of his buddies and the location of his warehouse, hoping the Colonel wouldn't ask. He didn't.

Mason was dumbfounded. He found himself in a hamstrung position. Carter was the only enlisted man in his unit with which he had rapport. Not to be confused as fraternization, it was hatched from mutual respect. Staring across the tent for several seconds, the words finally came. "Carter, I do believe, if you were given the chance, you could con the Devil out of his pitchfork. You know this is grand larceny."

"Oh no, sir, it's a donation. The Army wants to share their comforts with us, I just push 'em along. It's simple. Find out what they want and give it to 'em."

"Let's roll this thing back. What exactly were your motives for this farce?"

"Wood floors in our tents, sir, and you and the Padre too." Jake directed their attention to the floor. "We don't like eatin' or chokin' on this dust anymore than you do, Colonel."

The last statement rang a bell for the fastidious Mason. He wanted to relent, weighing the differences between accommodations for his men and a country club for the generals. If he reported the matter to the Adjutant General, Carter would be jailed and that would end it. However, his allergy for dust had plagued him relentlessly, and he wanted that floor. Sleepless nights are no fun. He sought more information. "Carter, you must have something up your sleeve. Fresh cut lumber is a dead giveaway, the MPs will certainly discover it."

"Not at all, sir, we have native labor lined up. We'll have the floors built in four sections during the day and install 'em at night. Sergeant Lang has twenty gallons of paint at the QM. We'll paint 'em green and stencil USMC on the sides. We'll work outside the camp."

"Sergeant, is there anyone on this island who isn't on your payroll? Besides, with all that pounding, the noise will be heard for miles."

"We have that figured too, sir. We'll make 'em in the morning when they're firing on the rifle range. Then we'll paint 'em in the afternoon. They'll look just like Marine issue."

Mason turned to the Chaplain. "Well Padre, what do you think about this insanity? I see you're writing everything down."

"I'm not writing, sir, it's a diagram." The priest held up his note pad for both men to see. "I was hoping, if there's any spare lumber, they could build a portable pulpit for me."

"Lieutenant Turner, are you trying to pressure me?" Suddenly, he sat erect, slamming a fist in the palm of his left hand. For the first time he erupted with laughter in front of his men. "Did you really forge old Chesty Puller's name to that invoice? I just received a letter from him. He's in Washington DC. I'll answer it today. He'll get a kick out of this."

Turner and Carter waited for the second shoe to drop. The suspense was immense. At last, the answer came. "Sergeant Carter, if you can make the MPs chase their tails, so can I. Tell your people to wait at least four days, I'll advise you through the Padre. I want two of those chairs. Paint them green too. Now, get the hell out of here before I change my mind!"

Jake shot to his feet. "Yes sir, thank you sir, I'm leaving sir."

With Carter gone, Mason paced the floor again. "Father, where do these fine young men come from? They're not regular Marines. You won't find them on the parade ground, or in a peacetime barracks. When their country is in trouble they enlist and come to us. They fight, and some of them die, but the rest keep moving on. All they care about is going home when it's over."

"Yes sir, they're a fine breed."

"Padre, it's more than that. A few weeks ago they brought in a young man on a stretcher. When he saw me, he looked up and said; 'Well Colonel, we took your hill for you.' Then he died. Those were his last words."

"I know, Colonel, I gave him his last rites, remember?"

"Well, I learned something today from Sergeant Carter.

Oh, I know, he takes care of himself, but did you notice how he shares with his men? He takes care of everybody. Sometimes I wish he could be my supply officer."

"Carter sir, a supply officer? May the saints preserve us."

In two swift moves, Mason snatched his swagger stick and put on his cap. His resolution was confirmed. "Turner, I want to see every man in my regiment, not a formal inspection, I want to catch them at their worst, see how they live. You will accompany me."

"That's twelve companies, sir, plus your attached units."

"I don't care if it takes two days, we'll leave now."

"Colonel, I think that's a wonderful idea. I'll be happy to tag along." The priest dropped to one knee. "I'm not praying, sir, I just want to tighten my shoe laces."

CHAPTER TWENTY-SIX

In the weeks that followed, the training schedule was intensified. Camp morale teetered between complacency and foreboding. To a man, the riflemen knew their time bomb was ticking. Ten new hospital ships arrived and dropped their anchors in Motobu Bay. The glistening white hulls, with red crosses painted on the sides, were harbingers of the future. Flights of B-29 bombers roared overhead, returning from their daily shuttle runs over the Japanese mainland. The Samurai people were determined they would die to the last man, woman, and child. By doing this, at least they would attain a spiritual victory. The unstoppable force was about to meet the immovable object.

The wooden floors had long since been assembled and put in place without a rumble. Padre Turner was ecstatic over his new green pulpit. Demands on his time were heavy as he traveled among the disconsolate infantry. Hearing confessions and lifting spirits, he was truly a magician with a magic wand.

Lieutenant Chandler saw fit to commandeer the mess tent for a morning lecture. With him was a man from JASCO, an acronym for Joint Air-Sea Cooperation. Attendance was mandatory for both the intelligence and communication sections. The highly technical procedure of directing naval gunfire and air strikes from an observation post on shore was being covered. Chandler had prepared a written examination, urging his men to take notes. They were interrupted.

"Hey, you guys better hear this!" A lone operator leaned from the radio tent. A passing platoon of riflemen halted and gathered around the excited man. A rousing cheer was lifted, disrupting the JASCO lecture. More men were attracted when the radio's volume was raised. Dancing and back slapping increased the crescendo.

Chandler's forum was in a shamble. "Carter, you better get over there and find out what's going on."

Eagerly, the men watched through the mess tent screen as Carter elbowed into the massed humanity. His short conversation with the radio man caused him to leap in the air, raising his arms with joy. Now he was shaking hands with everybody. Then he ducked inside the tent for more details. The suspense was pure torture for Chandler and his men. Finally, when the noise level dropped, Jake returned, almost out of breath.

"Well boys, the Air Force just dropped a monster bomb. Blew up a whole Jap city with one shot."

Now it was their turn to cheer. Questions came from every mouth.

"Was it one of those blockbusters like they've been droppin' on the Germans?"

"What city was it, Tokyo?"

"Is the war over?"

"Are they gonna drop anymore?"

Jake raised his hands. "Hold it boys, I'll tell ya what I know, which ain't much. They dropped it on a place called Hiroshima, which ain't no more. The whole city is flat, with about a hundred thousand dead. It went up with something they called a mushroom cloud. Has anybody here ever heard of an atomic bomb?"

All heads wagged negative except Jesse Hightree, who rose to his feet. "Perhaps I can answer that, Sergeant. I read about it in a new physics book. It's a concept developed by Albert Einstein called nuclear fission, a bombardment of neutrons. When an atom is split it releases tremendous energy."

"Aw, come on Jesse, lay it out so us dummies can understand."

"Well fellas, I'm sure not an atomic scientist, but it's at least ten times more powerful than TNT, maybe even more. Of one thing I'm positive, they've unleashed the energies of the universe. The repercussions could be horrible."

"Who gives a shit, I hope they throw the kitchen sink at the crazy bastards."

"Yeah, me too."

"Do the Nips still wanna fight, Jake, after all that?"

Carter could only speculate. "I've been fightin the Bushido Boys for a long time, and this is only gonna make 'em madder. As far as you guys are concerned, the war is still on."

Chandler's lecture was shot, and he knew it. "Men, in light of these new developments, you're dismissed. We'll reconvene this afternoon. I think it's best I confer with Colonel Mason on this matter. That's all."

A great debate was about to be launched. Bits and pieces of information trickled in via the Armed Forces Radio, confusing the men with a new scientific vocabulary. They stood in small groups, listening to a newly rigged loudspeaker. The gravity of the event began to register, and the terrible ramifications to follow. A formal education was a rarity in the ranks, leaving the boys in a state of bewilderment. Most had enlisted after High School, while others completed only one or two years of Junior College. They were trained fighting men, not scientists. History had thrown them a curve ball.

Carter's tent, the unofficial headquarters, drew people like a magnet. Squeezing themselves together on the four small cots, only standing room remained. From their ground level mentalities, they would hash out and digest this thing in their own way.

"Does anybody know what a megaton is?"

"Yeah, mega means a million, that's gotta be a million tons."

The Last Souvenir

"Geez, that much in one plane? How do they do it?"

"I don't know, but I was thinkin'. Suppose they drop a whole string of those bombs on our landing beach? They'd kill everybody. Then we wouldn't get so chewed up when we go ashore."

"Naw, didn't you hear what he said? When the atoms blow up they leave radio waves on the ground."

"Not radio waves, man, he said radioactive."

"Well what the hell's the difference? It sounds like the electricity ya make when ya walk across a new rug."

"That sounds OK to me. I'll take electricity to machine gun bullets anytime."

"Nope, you're both wrong. Radioactive is like an X-ray. It would burn us up."

"I wonder who pulled the lanyard on that baby?"

"Probably the President, he's the Commander and Chief."

"By the way, who is the President now? Who took over when Roosevelt died?"

"The Vice President. Some guy named Truman. What's the matter with you, don't ya read the newspapers?"

"Newspapers! Shit, I haven't even seen one in six months."

"This guy Truman, is he any good?"

"I think so. I heard he was in the artillery in the last war. At least he's seen some action."

"Well, it doesn't mean a rat's ass to me. I'm not old enough to vote anyway."

"The way I see it, things are lookin' up. If they drop enough of those bombs they'll blow the whole Jap Empire off the map. Then we can go home."

"You're dreamin', pal, this war could go on forever. Five years from now we'll probably be fightin' in Manchuria."

"Yeah, sure, by that time we'll all be up for a psycho discharge."

"Hey, I wonder if the Japs have any of them bombs. They

copy everything else."

"Good question, Mac. They could blow this rock to smithereens."

"Naw, I doubt it. If the sons a bitches did, they'd be usin' 'em on their Kamikaze planes by now."

"I hope you're right. We could all end up in one of them mushroom clouds."

"I can't figure out why our guys waited so long. Why didn't they start dumpin' those things years ago?"

"Who knows? The next time I'm invited to the White House I'll ask 'em for ya."

"You guys just reminded me of somethin'. The last time I got x-rayed they put a lead blanket on my chest. Maybe they'll issue us lead uniforms."

"Whyja hafta bring that up? We're like pack mules now."

"Don't laugh, he might be right."

It was perplexity, not boredom that terminated the bull session. Questions beget questions, resolving nothing. The specter of mass dying was ahead. This was their only certainty.

In the next three days they went through the motions of men at war, with a quiet and creeping elation filling their minds. Their nation had developed a new and powerful weapon, giving them an edge on the stubborn Japanese. Fear always manifests itself in the unknown, but this was a positive factor. It brought hope.

To the delight of the men, the Division Postmaster delivered a sack of stateside mail. Once distributed, they shuffled back to their tents, opening the perfumed letters first. Wives and mothers were notorious for clipping items from newspapers and forwarding them to loved ones. Because of shipping delays, it was far too early for them to read about repercussions from the States.

Jake sat on his bed, fingering five letters from his mother.

The Last Souvenir

He sorted them according to dates so he could read them in sequence. Del, Moe, and Johnny B sat across from him, relishing the same moments of nostalgia. The only sound was the anxious ripping of envelopes.

Their concentration was interrupted by a muffled cheer, traveling from tent to tent like falling dominoes. After a few moments passed, Mike Michaelson stood in their doorway.

"Hey you guys, they just dropped another one. It took out a whole city with one blast."

"Did they get Tokyo this time?"

"Naw, some joint named Nagasaki."

"Nagasaki? Never heard of it."

"That's great news. At least the Nips know we mean business this time."

"What do you think, Del? You told us you were a student of Jap history. Do you think they'll cave in?"

Stack knew he had been drawn into the big guessing game. "Well, I know the Japanese are big time gamblers, but this time the chips are stacked against them. When the people have had enough, they'll probably tell the Samurais to go to hell. The same thing happened in Russia in 1917. They revolted."

"Then that's the ticket. We keep hammering them 'til they give up."

"It's not that easy, Moe." Del's compassion swayed his military motives. "How would you like it if we were talking about New York, or California, or even Iowa? I can't see how two wrongs can make a right."

"Well, thank God us infantry slobs don't have to make that decision. They can have it."

The next day a general formation was called in front of the headquarters tent. The men lined up in double ranks with officers standing ahead of their platoon sergeants. No roll call was taken, indicating something was amiss. They stood at attention, but their eyes betrayed the looks of little children waiting for Santa Claus to come down the chimney.

Colonel Mason appeared and assumed his place, front and center. He held a piece of paper in his hand but his swagger stick was missing. His eyes scanned the long lines, returning the salutes of his section officers. "At ease, men."

The uneasy Marines spread their feet to a more comfortable standing posture. Holding the paper with both hands, Mason went straight to the point and began to read.

"From: III Corps Headquarters;
To: All units in this command.
Early this morning, the Imperial Japanese Cabinet transmitted in a message to the American Embassy in Switzerland their acceptance of the terms of the Potsdam ultimatum. All training units will stand down and remain confined to their posts until further notice.

The high level double talk had a disquieting effect on the ranks. This couldn't be a devious prank, it sounded too serious. It was typical of the General Staff to avoid plain English. Mason lowered the communiqué and folded it to tuck in his pocket. A smile of calm and relief spread across his face.

"Gentlemen, this is premature, and strictly unofficial, but it seems our war is over."

A piercing shriek rent the air. 'Yahoo!' followed by flying fatigue caps. The straight lines disintegrated with a lost regard for military discipline. Officers and men alike crowded together like bosom buddies. The flashing teeth were a credit to their fine dental care. Simultaneously, the rifle companies heard the same announcement, adding to the camp's vocal mayhem. This was their moment in history. Never again in their lives would so few words mean as much.

Through the writhing bodies, Carter caught the Colonel's eye. He was staring back. He forced his way through and faced his commanding officer. "Colonel, sir, would I be out of line if I asked to shake your hand?"

"Not at all, Jake, it would be my pleasure."

It was the first time he ever addressed Carter by his nickname. Because of the oddities of war, they had become the unusual melding of playing cards in a winning hand. Neither could have seen it through without the other.

Emotionally drained, the men started peeling away. It was time for reflection. The rainbows in their minds bore a variety of colors. To date, every day had been a maximum effort. Now, only peace remained. Being deflated like an old tire required thought.

Sean O'Malley wandered aimlessly south of camp and into the hills beyond. Myriad regrets twirled in his head as he stood alone. 'This damn thing is over and I've seen nothing. All that time, all that work, all that training. Why couldn't I have seen just one little battle? I know peace is great, but all I've had is a long boat ride. What do I say to the people back home? I can't tell stories like Sergeant Jake and Moe Chernikov. I know I'm being selfish. A million people are going to stay alive. I'll bet my family's dancing in the street by now. Why do I feel like somebody just pulled the rug from under me?'

Corporal Bill Hull reclined on his cot with his head deep in the pillow. Visions came of Solveig, a blond-haired Scandinavian girl with a round face and large breasts. 'Boy, was she happy when I scheduled her house for the last stop on my milk deliveries. She took me by the hand and led me behind the barn. Then she threw me in the grass and flung her blouse straight up in the air. Wow, watta woman! Now I'll see her again. In her last letter she said she's still available. She's in for a big surprise. Wait a minute, by now she might be hotter than me. Wow, watta woman.'

Jake Carter was also on his cot facing his three tentmates. "Well, Del, do ya have any words of wisdom, thoughts, plans?"

Del Stack looked down at the floor. "Yeah, I feel funny, like the condemned man in prison who's walkin' to the electric chair. When he gets there they slam the door in his face and tell him the whole thing's a big joke, that he can go home. I had my brain wound up that I was gonna be killed this time, so I wouldn't chicken out. I resigned myself to it, and that was that."

"That's weird, buddy, how do you unwind somethin' like that?"

Del raised his head and displayed a snapshot. "I can tell you in one word, Betsy. We've been in love since we were kids. The last time I saw her she was adamant about staying a virgin, but I'm going to change that in one big hurry."

"Maybe she's changed, it's been over three years since you've seen her."

"No, not *THAT* way. My first day home I'm gonna find a preacher and marry her. After that, the poor girl isn't going to see any daylight for six months."

The broad shoulders of Russ Keeler pushed through the flaps. "What's up? You guys talkin' about goin' home?"

"Come on in, Russ. Del's talkin' about getting married. Are you planning to look up your precious Joanne?"

He sat next to Stack with a forlorn expression. "Naw, that deal is off, a real bummer."

"Wadda ya mean, off? She's all you ever talk about."

Keeler hesitated before answering. "I didn't want to tell you guys, I thought you might rag me about it. I guess it doesn't matter now."

"What happened, man?"

"Oh, a while back I sent a hundred bucks home to my mother for an engagement ring. I told her to give it to Joanne

The Last Souvenir

and surprise her. Well, Mom just wrote back and said Joanne ran off with some sailor and got pregnant. When she found out she was knocked up she left town. Nobody's seen her since."

"Shit, that is a real bummer. Didn't she even send you a Dear John letter?"

"Nope, not even a crummy post card for months, but I'm OK now. I'm going back to college and find somebody else. There's lottsa pretty girls in Tacoma."

"Well Johnny, don't just sit there with a smug look on your face. You look like you just caught the brass ring."

Bowman dropped the letter he was reading. "Ya know, that lieutenant from Fox Company intrigues me. I think I'd like to be a writer like he is. I'll go to a big university on that new GI Bill they've been talking about. You know, a free education. The best part is, my Dad wrote me about an army of lonely co-eds. He said the ratio is fifty girls to one man."

"Oh, oh, here it comes. Our Lothario is going to strike."

Bowman extended his arms and flapped them like wings. "I shall swoop down like a predatory bird and cut a wide swath through a forest of skirts."

Laughter came from all but Chernikov. He only smiled.

"What's the matter, Moe? Aren't you thinkin' about those two big Amazon women ya got back home?"

"Naw, it's not that. What the hell am I good for now it's all over? The only thing I know is war, what else is there? You guys are all goin' to college, but I always hated school. I sure as hell don't want to be a mechanic, or a plumber. Maybe I'll get a gang together and rob banks. I'll wear fancy duds with wing-tip shoes, and have a babe on each arm. You know the old saying, 'Crime doesn't pay but the hours are good.' In the end I'll probably get bumped off by some G-man."

"That's bullshit. You don't really mean that."

"Yeah, I'm just kidding, but it does sound good, doesn't

it?"

"It's your turn Jake. We haven't heard from you yet."

Carter's thoughts were already crystallizing in his fertile mind. Painfully true, the war had affected him. "You all know I had a girl back home, the one from a Japanese-American family. Well, things have changed now. We've been killing off their cousins by the bushel for years. It's over, our families would be knocking heads forever."

"Ya mean there would be a wall between you now?"

"No, not a wall, let's just say a thin screen. I'll be movin' on. I was offered a football scholarship by the University of California. They've probably forgotten me, but I'll check it out anyway. I'll study business. You know how much I like wheelin' and dealin'. I'll stay single for a while, maybe even build an empire."

"That sounds great, Jake." Bowman heard the magic word. "When I get my degree I'll write advertising for you. Wadda ya say?"

"Sounds good to me, buddy, chances are I'll need someone I can trust. You're on."

A pensive mood ensued, but not for long. Chernikov turned his head and shouted into the next tent. "Hey, Hull, what are you, some kind of hermit?"

"No, I'm just dreamin'. My ass might be here, but my head is in Indiana."

"Well get your butt over here and play bartender. Pass the word too. It's time for a celebration."

The Last Souvenir

CHAPTER TWENTY-SEVEN

"Mason said *WHAT*? A patrol now? Leo, are you shitting me?"

"I'm sorry, Jake, but that's the scoop. He wants you to take a patrol up north tomorrow. It could be a long one. He wants to see ya right away."

"This is bullshit. The war's been over for a week. Now what?"

They were caught in the nebulous gray zone between the armistice and a lasting peace. An isolated enemy unit had been spotted on a mountaintop at the northern tip of the island. Civilian information was filtered through the Military Government and passed on to III Corps. Prisoners were needed and Mason's regiment was assigned the task. Explicit orders were to use peaceful means. No firing unless fired upon.

Every night at 7:00 the Japanese Emperor Hirohito conducted a broadcast from his palace. Once a docile man, he had broken away from his Samurai General Staff and taken the reins. His nightly instructions were for his people to surrender and lay down their arms. Any inclination toward guerrilla activity was forbidden. The Bushido code of absolute obedience was still in force.

The problem for the American rifleman was still deadly. The overlooked enemy usually had no radio contact. For all purposes he was still at war and ready to pull a trigger. He was unaware of his Emperor's decree that all should live and avoid further suicidal sacrifice. The last Japanese soldiers had to be overcome and dragged to a radio.

Carter's attitude vacillated from hostility to dejection as he marched to his rendezvous. Colonel Mason was in front of the intelligence tent, locked in conversation with Lieutenant Chandler. He stopped at attention and saluted. "You sent for me, sir?"

Mason returned the salute. "Yes, Sergeant, I want you to organize a patrol. A bypassed enemy unit has been sighted up north." He explained Hirohito's evening broadcasts. "Your job will be to take prisoners with no shooting."

"But sir, the nips don't know the war's over. We're liable to get our heads blown off for nothing."

"Carter, as long as you're wearing the globe and anchor insignia you're still in the Marine Corps, and Marines follow orders."

"You've got me there, Colonel, what's the set-up?"

"Lieutenant Chandler will be in overall command but you are in charge of all tactical decisions. I've seen you hoodwink the Army, Navy, and Air Force. Now it's up to you to con the Japanese. Take what you need but get me a prisoner."

Jake began his thought process by rubbing his chin. "Well, sir, the first thing we do is look at a map."

The three men entered the tent with Mason leading. On the left, fashioned from newly acquired lumber, was a wide table. Aerial photographs were predominant, supplemented by an enlarged contour map. Corporal Michaelson was at the far end holding a magnifying glass.

"Hiya Sarge, some detail huh? If you need me I'll go along."

"No thanks, Mike, I'll be traveling light. Besides, didn't they teach you never to volunteer for anything?"

Carter's interest in the aerial shot drew everyone into a ring around the table. The combined knowledge of the four men represented years of experience in map reading. Chandler bent over, peering through a small glass. With the tip of a pencil he pinpointed the objective. "There it is, that oversized hill."

"It looks like a biscuit, steep cliffs on all four sides."

Chandler bent closer. "It appears to be a solid coral outcrop with enough top soil to support a pine forest. There are irregularities in the foliage, which indicate very clever camouflage. I don't see any signs of life but I'm sure the Japs are there. It measures about a hundred feet in elevation."

"Let me borrow your magnifier, Mike." Jake reached across the table and slid the contour map closer. "I have an idea, Colonel. We'll have to scout it first, but it might give us a long shot."

Mason's confidence began to rise, knowing he had picked the right man. Carter's enterprising mind was in motion and he wasn't prone to making mistakes. "What's your long shot, Sergeant?"

"It's water, sir. Coral ridges don't have any springs. Can you see this little creek here?" Jake ran his finger along a dotted blue line. "It's about two hundred yards from the south cliff. If they have to come down for water we can set up a bushwhack."

"You're right, Carter. They probably come down at night. It sounds risky."

"Sir, we get paid for taking risks. I'll take my toughest boys. If it works, we'll jump 'em."

"According to estimates the enemy is in company strength, about two hundred men. You'll be over fifteen miles north of us. Suppose your scheme backfires?"

"We'll haul ass sir."

Mason smiled. "That certainly isn't a formal military tactic, but I like your description. That's what I have in mind."

"Here's the way I see it, Colonel." Jake turned to Chandler. "If it's OK with you Lieutenant. We'll set up a CP on the beach next to this little village. It's about two miles south.

There's a small hill between us and the Biscuit, so we'll be out of their observation. We can operate from there."

Chandler was relieved by Carter's acceptance of responsibility, trying not to show it. He brushed aside the maps, clearing an open space on the table while speaking to Michaelson. "Corporal, bring us that new piece of equipment."

Mike carefully deposited the paraphernalia on the table with the curious Carter watching. A carbine rifle had been fitted with a large stubby telescope. From it, a thick electrical cord connected to a battery in a leather carrying case.

"What's this gismo sir, some kinda ray gun? It look's like something from an old Buck Rogers movie."

"You're close, Jake. It's an infrared device that allows you to see at night. It picks up heat from a human body. It's still experimental, but the Army has had it for months. It works." Chandler clicked the switch and handed the rifle to Carter. "Here, take a look."

Jake sighted through the big round scope. "I can see the cross hairs, but everything else is light green. Are you sure it'll work, sir?"

"Here's the operating manual, take it and read it. If it can help us in night problems, we'll *MAKE* it work!"

"What do ya call this thing, Lieutenant?"

"It has a long technical name but we just call it the 'Millie'."

Colonel Mason wanted to move along. "Sergeant, I want you ready to shove off in the morning. How many men will you need? You can take a rifle platoon for backup."

"Oh no, sir, the fewer the better, just in case we have to cut out. I'll need Chernikov and Bowman with two new men, Hightree and O'Malley."

"But they're green troops, why them?"

"Sir, Private Hightree is a Sioux Indian and a damn good scout. He can track a mouse across a wool blanket. He's also a genius. I'll give him this manual and put him on the Millie."

"What about O'Malley?"

"He's a tough kid, sir, and a helluva Marine. Besides, right now he's ready to volunteer for anything. I feel good about him."

"Anybody else?"

"Yes sir. We'll take Frenchie Labeau in case we need a corpsman, which I hope not. For the radio jeep I want Sergeant Gallo and one of his best men. I'll take Corporal Kovak as an interpreter, and that'll do it."

Mason was skeptical. "That's only ten men to face a whole company, Carter."

"Colonel sir, we only need to catch one prisoner. The odds are pretty good. Once he listens to his Emperor on the radio we'll turn him loose to spread the word. Then we can round 'em all up without firing a shot."

"That's a daring plan, Sergeant, but a good one. Lieutenant Chandler, you will take over the details from here." Mason turned and walked out.

Chandler and his sergeant sat together for thirty minutes, categorizing and listing the necessary rations and field equipment to be taken. The men would carry fifty-pound transport packs and bedrolls. Extra socks and dungarees would provide a modicum of comfort on a prolonged mission. In case of an emergency evacuation, everything could be abandoned. The pressing motives of war were replaced by the prudence of peace.

Carter rose to his feet with the list in his hand. "I'll get on this right away, Lieutenant."

"Oh no you don't, I'm going with you. I don't want to miss anything."

"I'd like that sir, it'll be just like old times."

They walked together and turned the corner with Jake stopping in front of O'Malley's tent. "Hey Sean, are you and

Jesse in there?"

"We sure are Sarge, we're readin'. They just passed out some new Leatherneck magazines."

"No shit, I'd like to see one. Bring 'em along and get up to my tent on the double."

Carter entered his tent first, finding his buddies lying flat on their backs, enjoying tranquillity. Chandler followed, carrying the Millie with both hands. The sight of his silver bars catapulted them to attention.

"Good morning sir, watcha got there? It looks like a squirt gun."

Chandler responded with his usual deep belly laugh. "Gentlemen, meet Millie. She's your new blind date. Sit back down, Sergeant Carter has an announcement to make." He reached in his pocket and handed the manual to Jake.

With everyone seated, Carter asked for silence until he was finished. He outlined the patrol in detail, watching the astonishment on their faces. In their minds, the surrender had transformed them to a civilian status. The mixed reactions began to gel with each deciding to follow his platoon sergeant. Chandler had the authority and sought reassurance.

"Men, this is a volunteer job, what about you, Moe?"

"Yeah, I'll go too. I was gettin' bored anyway."

O'Malley couldn't wait to be asked. "Sir, this is great. Thanks for pickin' me. I can do the job, you'll see."

"You won't be so eager if we bring you back full of bullet holes." Chernikov liked the boy and was already worried. "You better stick with me, kid."

Hightree pre-empted their questions, holding the scoped carbine in his lap. He held the operating manual in his hand and examined the tuning knobs. "The mechanism is crude but simple. This is the transducer-receiver element. It transmits and receives infrared impulses. It's based on the density of heat."

The Last Souvenir

"This is no science class, Jesse, can you work it?"

Hightree looked up with a grin. "You betchum. Injun boy makem work."

Jake was satisfied but there was some unfinished business. "Well Del, that leaves you out. The scuttlebutt is they're shippin' you old timers home in a week."

"That's right buddy, Iowa here I come. Man, I can see it now. Beer, ballrooms, and Betsy."

"You're a lucky stiff pal, give her a kiss for me. Would you do one last job for me, as a favor?"

"Sure Jake, you name it."

"Thanks, I want you to liquidate that stash of souvenirs. Johnny B can help with the prices. Everything is on a cash basis now, no more swappin'."

"Hey, I'm no salesman, you know that."

"You won't have to be. Call Sergeant Miller at the officers club in Yontan. He'll take the whole load. Those flyboys could leave and take their money with 'em. Tell Miller to bring cash and an Air Force truck. He'll jump at the chance."

"That's a lotta cash, Jake. What do I do with it?"

"OK, here's what you do. Split it in half. Divide one half with the new guys and split the rest evenly with the old timers, yourself included. Consider it a wedding present."

"What about your share, Jake?"

"Del, when you get back to the States, would you mind stoppin' off in LA to see my mother? Give her the cash and tell her to start savin' a down payment for that house she wants."

"Buddy, it'll be my favorite detour." Stack's eyes were watering.

Jake stood and walked across the floor to Bowman. "Johnny, as soon as your pack is loaded help Del. Get on it right away. When you have a dollar number hop on the phone with Miller. Any questions?"

"Nope, what are we waiting for?"

"Well Del, there's only one more thing. The boys on patrol won't be here, so tell Leo to hold their cash until they get back."

There were places to go and people to see. The sergeant and his lieutenant walked together at a brisk pace, with the overweight Chandler huffing to stay even.

"Slow up Jake, I've got something I want to talk about."

"Sure Lieutenant, lay it on me." Carter reduced the tempo.

"This will surprise you. Colonel Mason authorized me to ask if you would like to fill out an application for Officer's Candidate School."

"*WHAT?*" Jake stopped and froze in his tracks. "Me? Mason said that?"

"That's right, his exact words."

"The old boy must be coming down with combat fatigue. I've been a thorn in his shorts for almost a year."

"I told you you'd be surprised. He said you are resourceful and intelligent. Most of all, he likes the way you inspire loyalty in your men."

"Lieutenant, you just hit me with a baseball bat. The only thing I'm lookin' for is a discharge. Me, a regular marine officer… I don't think so. Don't say anything to the old man. I'll tell him when we come back from this job."

"I can't see why not, Jake. You seem to be comfortable wearing Captain's bars."

Carter registered astonishment. "How'd you find out about that?"

"I'm the intelligence officer, remember? I just read the complaint and put two and two together. So did Mason."

"You're a real piece of work, Lieutenant. You both knew all the time and you didn't say anything. Why?"

"I told you, the Colonel's behind you all the way, and so am I. Think it over."

Jake's head spun with a new wrinkle in his mind. The communication section was their first stop. Sergeant Eddie Gallo was on the street in front, expecting their call.

"Hello Jake, good morning Lieutenant, Mike was just here to fill me in. Looks like I volunteered for a trip in the country."

"This is no boat ride we're goin' on, Eddie, but we're glad to have you. Did you pick another man?"

"I sure did." Gallo stuck his head inside the big tent. "Hey Ski, come out and meet your new boss."

A swarthy young man in faded dungarees appeared. His blond hair and wide cheekbones showed the features of a Northern European lineage. He walked up and saluted.

"Jake, this is Corporal Wisnewski. We call him Ski. He knows semaphore and morse code, and he went to Jap language school. Besides repairing radios, he handles a rifle like Daniel Boone."

Carter offered his hand. "I've seen you around before, Ski. With all those credits we can't miss."

"Thanks, Sarge, I hope I can help out. You want us in transport packs?"

"Yep, and bring your field mess gear. Pack everything so it doesn't rattle. You know the drill."

Next on their itinerary was Frenchie Labeau. A wooden sea chest stood on a table in the middle of his aid station. It was half full of medical supplies when they entered.

"Well Frenchie, I suppose Mike's been here too."

"You're right Jake, hello Lieutenant, I'm going ready this time. The last time I went with you guys I had to deliver a baby. Mike said there's gonna be civilians around. Maybe I'll get a chance to practice some family medicine."

"Labeau, I like your style. You're right, it might come in handy."

"Oh Jake, there's one more thing, Johnny Kovak was here.

He said to tell you he'd be ready too."

Quartermaster Sergeant Lang was no different than the rest. Busily stacking cases of rations and ammunition, he looked up when they approached. "You're in luck buddy, some of the new 10 in 1 rations came in. Canned pears and peaches and lotsa stuff. Cookie threw in some canned scrambled eggs, spaghetti, and pork and beans."

"Lang, do you remember tellin' me about those old boxes of C-rations, the meat and vegetable hash? Do ya still have 'em?"

"Ugh, Yeah, I still gottem. The men won't eat 'em, why?"

Carter ran his thumb along the side of his chin. "Toss in a few cases."

"What for, that junk tastes like dog food."

"It's just a hunch, but it'll give you a chance to get rid of it."

"Amen brother, they're all yours."

On a phone call from Mason, Lieutenant Van Der Slice had his men on standby at the motor pool. Dark green five-gallon cans of extra gasoline were in plain sight. He waved. "Hiya, Jimmy, I understand you've cut yourself a real piece of pie this time."

"You know me Dutch, the perennial volunteer. Sergeant Carter will tell you what he needs."

Jake's decision had been made hours before. The verbal carte blanche from Colonel Mason helped him in forming the big picture. He took one last look at the lines of vehicles. "Yes sir, we'll need two recon trucks for the personnel, a ten wheeler, and a radio jeep."

"When and where do you need 'em Jake?"

"Well sir, can you have someone take the big truck to the QM now? Sergeant Lang can have it loaded before dark."

"Can do Sergeant, what next?"

"Have 'em all parked in front of the mess tent by 8:00

tomorrow morning, sir."

"He gives orders pretty well doesn't he Jimmy?"

"You can say that again. Mason has given him the opportunity to be an officer, go to OCS, but he's balking."

"What's the matter Jake? You got something against lieutenants?" For fun the Dutchman put Carter in the middle. His answer made them both laugh.

"Oh no sir, it's just that the job doesn't pay enough."

"The kid's right," Chandler confirmed. "He makes more money on the side than we get paid in a year."

The patrol package was wrapped to their satisfaction. Hence, the script called for the uncomfortable theme of waiting. To men in the service this is always a distasteful practice. Carter had the answer. "Sirs, as long as I'm being considered for a commission that makes me at least half an officer. Would you two gentlemen care to join me in my tent for martinis before evening chow, say 4:30?"

"Sergeant, that's the one thing that makes real sense. We'd be delighted."

CHAPTER TWENTY-EIGHT

"We crank 'em up in fifteen minutes. Corporal, find Sergeant Carter and inform him."

Lieutenant Chandler's eyes examined the four vehicles, parked and pointed west. For the first time since the invasion he stood in a full regalia of fighting gear, from camouflaged helmet to field boots. 'Am I really qualified for command?' Every Marine, from general to private, is trained as a rifleman first and always. A young lieutenant, no matter his forte, must be prepared to assume infantry leadership. The carbine in his hand might be only a mythical baton of authority, recalling a dark secret from his past.

Just three months short of two years ago he received his first taste of battle on the island of New Britain in the Southwest Pacific. The enemy was put to flight and began a massive retreat in the tangled rain forest. Chandler was ordered to lead a small patrol and maintain contact, fully aware that sharpshooters would be left behind to delay their progress.

Two days out and early in the morning a shot rang out, impelling the men to cover. Jimmy spied the menace first and drew a bead on him. With the man's face framed in his front sight he froze, fighting to balance Christian decency with duty. Months of indoctrination failed, plagued by an inner conflict between the ten commandments and the military manual. In war, a second can be a lifetime and change the direction of a man's character forever. A burst from an American sub-machine gun startled him back to reality. He saw the dead man hanging in a harness of vines above the jungle floor, dripping blood on the leaves below. His trigger was never pulled, nevertheless, a man had been slain in the first third of his life. Soul and body were separated.

Even worse, what if the men, and especially the Colonel, gained knowledge of his lethal pause? He could be discredited and relieved of all duties. He thought back to the days prior to his enlistment, when the option of registering as a religious objector was available, but he chose to become involved.

The conscription of a civilian army brings a wide spectrum of ideologies. At one end the pacifists like Chandler, at the other warriors who simply carve another notch in their riflestocks. The in-betweeners are quickly driven to one side or the other, seeking their respective levels. The peacetime professional soldier is a trained assassin who accepts this as a fact when war comes. The rest are neophytes in uniform.

After the sniper incident Lady Luck placed her hand on Chandler's forehead. A draft of replacement officers arrived and he was called to the rear. Talents in aerial photograph interpretation and map maintenance were sorely needed, and there he would stay. His secret remained intact. Perhaps someday he might share it with his understanding wife, but not now.

Today's patrol was different. His mission was to bring peace and save lives, giving him a nobility of purpose. At last the days of darkness were behind. The idea of mending a shattered world and bringing an end to useless waste of life and property made him euphoric. The wheel of destiny had finally stopped on his number. It could be the Chaplain was right when he advised him to transfer into Military Government. Nonetheless, the time for hindsight was over and the future loomed bright as a new sunrise.

Sergeant Carter and his group arrived with an extra man. The afternoon before, Ike Levine had implored to be included with his comrades and Jake relented. Numerically it worked out better. Kovak and Labeau were straining to hoist medical supplies up and into the cargo truck. In the trailing radio jeep, Gallo and Ski were already seated, tuning and testing their equipment. A curious crowed was forming along the side of the little caravan.

"Looks like them scouts has drawn another shit detail."

"Yeah, a combat patrol with no shootin'. Can they do that?"

"Hell yes. We signed up for the duration of the war and six months, didn't we?"

"Sure, why?"

"Well the six months ain't up yet. That's where they gotcha."

"Ya got that right. By the short hairs."

One final consultation remained. Chandler was spreading a map on the hood of the first truck with Colonel Mason at his elbow. "Carter's plan can work, Colonel. Last night I picked up something new. There's a small trail cut along the south slope with two zigzags. It's the only access."

Mason pointed with his swagger stick. "I still want the entire position reconnoitered first. How do you propose to do that?"

"I think the answer is coming right now, sir."

A radioman was striding quickly toward them. He stopped and saluted. "Here's the weather report you asked for, Lieutenant."

Chandler returned the salute and thanked the man. "Ah, this is perfect, sir. Clear with scattered clouds for a week, and a three-quarter moon. Carter wants to work at night and so do I."

"Night patrols 'eh? They can be ticklish. Remember, I want every man back alive. You'd better get started."

Transport packs had been shed and tossed into the first two trucks. Prearranged seating called for Carter to drive the lead vehicle with Chandler at his side. Bowman took the second with Chernikov driving the ten-wheeler. At Jake's request, Kovak and Hightree rode with him, seated in the rear.

Mason backed away, listening to the whirring of starters firing the big engines. Father Turner stood next to him, giving the sign of the cross with his right hand. Carter released the clutch and turned to wave. "See ya, Colonel. Maybe I'll bring ya a Jap General or somethin'."

Tire treads bit into crushed coral as they trundled away. Mason was in a somber mood, watching his men exit the gate and wheel down the west highway. "Padre, do you believe in premonitions?"

"No sir, Colonel, I believe in faith. Why do you ask?"

"It's Carter, there's something about that boy that touches me. I have a feeling I'll never see him again."

The Chaplain was reassuring. "Don't worry about Jake, sir. He's like a cat. You throw him in the air and he still comes down on all fours."

"I hope you're right, Padre. I hope you're right." Mason headed for his tent to apply the soothing therapy of writing to his wife.

It was 8:45 AM, with the climbing August sun on their backs. Nearly eleven hours of daylight remained of their first day. In the China Sea ahead, cargo ships had begun the initial phase of reloading. The need for secrecy was long gone and a mass exodus was on its way. A traffic jam of supply vehicles clogged the beach by the bay.

For the veterans in the rolling patrol the plot was clear. Navy comrades were departing for peaceful endeavors, yet their war was still on. They were given a broom and dustpan and sent to sweep up the nasty little pieces that follow the end of a world conflict. If thoughts could be bundled and projected to future sons and nephews, the message would be succinct: "Never volunteer for the infantry."

The untested young men sat on the other end of the teeter-totter. Training had brought them to razor sharpness. At last they were about to plunge into their first great adventure. With complete disregard of the subliminal influences at work, the thought of a bullet in the chest was farthest from their minds, at least for now.

In the second truck Ike Levine occupied the right seat. Apprehension was high and he broke the silence. "Hey Sarge, ya got any idea what we're lookin' for when we get there?"

Bowman glanced half right with a sparkle in his eye. "I'll give you some advice, kid. When you go on a recon patrol you never know what you're lookin' for until you find it."

"Hey, I like that, short and sweet. They never told us that in training."

"Short yes, but I'm not so sure about sweet. Remember everything you see and bring it back. The map boys'll put it together. They like big pictures."

The basic conversations of war never seemed to change over the centuries. The veteran Chernikov was sharing the same topics with Sean O'Malley. The cast of the play remains constant: The patient Sergeant and the cherub. The dialogue will shift and vary, but the questions and answers are parallel.

Chandler sheltered his map behind the low windshield and pointed forward. "There's our turnoff."

A large sign on a high white post told the story: NORTH ROAD - PATROLS ONLY. Below the arrow someone had painted a skull and crossbones. Carter wheeled right to face a simple roadblock. A wooden sawhorse with red and white stripes stood in his path. An army MP officer wearing a pistol motioned a halt. "You guys got any traveling orders?"

With a new air of command, Chandler disembarked and faced the man, handing across the paperwork. "We're from the 1st Marines, Lieutenant, our destination is Hagachi."

"Hagachi! Hell, that's way up North. Our jeep patrols only go about ten miles. You'll be on your own the rest of the way."

"Wait a minute, you mentioned jeep patrols. What's the story?"

"We're not sure, but there's a rumor of a bypassed enemy unit on the northern end. Don't get me wrong, we're watchdogs, not riflemen."

Chandler had heard enough. "Well we are, Lieutenant, that's our mission. We'll be back through here in a few days, I hope."

"You can have 'em. Good luck Gyrene." He lifted the barricade and bade them to pass.

The narrow road twisted North, eventually bending in a slight westerly direction. The surface was partially graded, leaving a rocky center bordered by shallow ruts on either side. The spine of the mountain range on their right divided the island in half, East and West. The absence of crushed coral indicated an introduction to virgin territory. Cliffs and valleys appeared on the left with the sea for a boundary.

The wondrous sight unfolding took on the semblance of a picture postcard. Bleached white sand spread itself over dunes on the beaches and extended hundreds of yards into the water. A high visibility of coral heads gave an almost garish display of colors in the shallows. Orange, red, black, white, and other blending shades took on the appearance of an oil painter's palette. To end it all, a rocky cliff fell several fathoms, transforming aqua-green in the lagoons to the dark navy blue of the open sea.

"Lieutenant, did you ever see anything like this in your life?"

"You know Jake, it looks like someone threw a handful of colored marbles on a white tablecloth."

"You're right sir, maybe you shudda been a poet."

"See how clear the water is? It's like looking through a clean window. Back home in Philly, when we were kids, we used to swim in the Delaware River, but it was murky. We would have given anything to skinny dip in water like this."

"Know what you mean, sir. In Southern California we used to go to the beach and body surf the waves. It sure as hell wasn't this clear. Ya couldn't see the bottom."

Chandler, who had memorized his map the night before, jerked upright. "Stop below that next rise, Jake, I want to take a look first. Hagachi should be in the next valley."

The precarious incline compelled Jake to yank hard on the hand brake. The motor was still running when the two men climbed down, hanging field glasses around their necks.

Carter paused. "Jesse, you better come with us. Kovak, you stay and hold the fort."

The road was lined with bright red lilies and white-faced flowers they had never seen before. At the crest on the right was a clump of chest-high bushes with heart-shaped leaves, adequate for cover and observation. The three scouts sought refuge behind it with Hightree standing one pace back.

Like every motor patrol, a moment of decision hung in the balance: Go in or turn tail. Intense scanning of the landscape with binoculars was crucial. Five minutes passed while Jake and the Lieutenant carefully raked the terrain below, impressed once again by a breathtaking pastoral scene. A round-topped spur protruded west from the central mountain range, accenting a backdrop for the village in the valley. Dozens of hand-dug rice paddies etched the hillside like steps on an irregular staircase. Foot trails snaked everywhere, scrawling patterns in the greenery. The road fell away from the hillocks in a gentle arc, bisecting two rows of wooden houses with tile roofs. Horse drawn carts passed each other in slow motion, while natives on foot carried burdens of varying sizes and shapes.

Carter lowered his glasses. "Looks peaceful to me, sir."

"That's what Daniel said before he walked into the lion's den."

"That from the Bible, sir?"

"No, it's from me. Chandler's law."

Jake removed his field glasses and offered them to Hightree. "Here ya go, Jesse, take a look. Tell us what you think."

The young Indian took his time, breathing deliberately. This was no time for impatience. In one careful sweep he was satisfied. "There's a preponderance of humanity in that hamlet, Sergeant. You told us once the civilians have instincts. They seem aware in advance when the Japanese are preparing an ambush. In plain English, they scram!"

Chandler laughed with admiration. "Well spoken Private, I say let's go."

Bowman leaned against the steering wheel, his chin resting on a forearm when Chandler approached. "What's the scoop, Lieutenant?"

"We'll go in first, Johnny. It's downhill from here so we'll coast in. That means no noise. You hang back about half a mile. If there's any trouble, beat it, we'll fend for ourselves."

Calculated risk was typical of his lieutenant and Bowman knew it. He sat up straight and adjusted his helmet. "Ready when you are, sir."

CHAPTER TWENTY-NINE

The tense caution had been for naught. The inhabitants were more surprised than the squad of riflemen, viewing them as tourists who had somehow jumped the beaten track. Many months prior, a patrol of the 29th Marines had breezed through but that was the last of it. The green giants were back again with what must be peaceful intentions. The pounding of big guns in the south was silenced.

"So this is Hagachi. I must be in Wonderland."

"OK Kovak, do your stuff, start yackin' Japanese. See if you can find a mayor. Bowman, take two men and check the beach. Find me a spot for a CP. Gallo, radio the Colonel. Tell him we've reached our objective."

Chandler's attitude was more paternal than military. He was the head of a large family now, and it continued to grow. Nothing in the book of Military Science could explain it, but it was there. The man from Philadelphia had become a citizen of peace. Work was the only fuel for his passionate fire. His sadness of many yesterdays could never be erased, but he had control of the future, at least a small part.

Kovak returned leading a tiny old man. His head was domed with bushy gray hair and a matching beard. Wooden sandals made a clopping noise as he moved to face Chandler, bowing profusely.

"Here's your man sir, they call him the Ichiban. In Jap lingo that's the boss or big shot."

When Jimmy offered his hand the old man was puzzled and continued to bow. "Did you ask him if there are any Japanese soldiers around?"

The Last Souvenir

"Yes sir, and he said yes. They landed 'em by boat just before we invaded. They're on a mountain-top about two miles north. He thinks it's some kinda special base."

"Has he seen them since?"

"No sir. The little kids went up there to make friends and the Nips took pot shots at 'em. After that he made the place off limits."

"That's not much to go on, but it's enough. What do you think Jake?"

Carter and the men had dismounted and joined him, ringed by a growing throng of curiosity seekers. The miniscule people grinned with delight. A new circus had come to town. Jake's feelings were mixed, comforted by the friendly atmosphere and disturbed by an enemy presence.

"I think we'd better get to it, sir. After we set up we can crawl out and take a look."

Kovak stopped them. "The old boy says there are some lean-tos on the beach we can use. They keep their fishing canoes there. He'll have his boys move the boats out. But first, he wants to give us a tour of the town. I know this, it would be impolite to refuse."

Frenchie Labeau stepped in. "We'd better go with him. If he doesn't stop that bowing pretty soon he's gonna develop a bad sinus problem."

The Americans were on the brink of being introduced to a pure cooperative society, a commune where no money changed hands. Crafts and trades were passed along from father to son and mother to daughter. Oversized wooden houses stood on both sides of the road, with shops in front and living quarters in the rear. There were no signs or display windows, only open doors. The simplicity of their honor system was explained through Johnny Kovak: Take what you want but only what you need. Special orders were filled and put aside.

Their first stop at the far end of one row was a tailor and dress shop. A pretty young girl sat facing an antique sewing machine. Her dress was pulled up, fully exposing her thighs as they pumped the foot treadle. She rose to her feet and bowed, trying to hold back a demure smile. Noticing a torn pocket on Kovak's jacket, she advanced and aggressively tugged at his sleeve. When he spoke in her native tongue she gasped with feminine confidence. Her small hands deftly unbuttoned his coat and peeled him down to a green T-shirt.

Kovak turned and winked at his buddies. "Well boys, this is it. If I have the time I'm definitely coming back." Gaping with amazement at her dexterity. When the stitching and thread-biting was over she thrust back his jacket and stepped away. The smitten Kovak, in the process of rebuttoning, leaned toward her. "I'm coming to see you later," he said softly. Through half-shut eyes she smiled and nodded her agreement.

Ichiban, with the patience of the elderly, led them to the next structure. The absence of young men in the village was becoming apparent. The practice of drafting young males into servitude had reached far north into Hagachi. To date, not one had straggled back, closing a tragic chapter in their lives. Only boys in their early teens and men over fifty remained. Hardiness of mind and spirit was their greatest asset. Women stepped in willingly to accept the chores of everyday living without a grumble.

The wood shop was next. Carter entered first followed by the inspired Kovak. His love and knowledge of woodworking sent him on a fast inspection of the crude tools hanging from the walls. Bowls, spoons, sandals, and other assorted items littered a long table in the center. A stock of fresh cut pine was stored below it. In the rear, an old woodcarver and his wife tutored a young boy seated beside a low workbench.

A pair of hand carved wooden goggles caught Jake's

attention. He picked them from a shelf and ran his fingers along their smoothness. Two circles of glass were cemented by an odd waxy substance, completing the eyepieces. A piece of twisted string connected them. The headband was cut from a red inner tube and stretched with perfect elasticity.

The old lady, more than a head shorter than Carter, witnessed this and came to take them away. Momentarily, she held them against his eyes. She twisted the strings to adjust for the space across the bridge of his nose. When she replaced them, and slid the elastic above his ears, they were snug.

"Hey Kovak, these things musta been made just for me."

"She says they're for fishin', skin divin'. She wants you to keep 'em."

"Well tell her thanks, arigato."

The gracious woman bowed and returned to her pupil.

Bowman and his men had returned from the beach, reporting their findings to Chandler in the middle of the road. Even from afar the Lieutenant exuded optimism. Slowly nodding his head, he punctuated the meet with an occasional question. He was satisfied and they broke away.

The tour carried them through a leather works and blacksmith's shop. Because the town lacked electric power, operating equipment was propelled by hand or foot pedals. For the Americans it was a journey back into the eighteenth century.

Old Ichiban brimmed with enthusiasm when he waved them into a day nursery. It was his creation. Kovak turned parrot, interpreting his sentences word for word. Babies in rocking cradles lined the wall, attended by two hovering nannies. Through an open door in the rear one could see a bubbling cauldron and clothesline for drying diaper rags. The mothers were freed to work in paddies and vegetable gardens.

On a chair to the right, a young woman sat with her dress open, nursing a suckling babe in her arms. She smiled wistfully, gently stroking the black fuzz on its head. In the fields the procedure was simple and efficient. When the pressure of mother's milk filled her breasts it was nature's signal. She would simply drop her tools and walk to the village for mutual relief. At times, if necessity arose, she would feed the infant of someone else, assuming the role of a wet nurse.

Chandler, the only family man in the group, lingered to the last. The puffy cheeks and well-developed limbs assured him the babies were well nourished. His thoughts drifted back to his own little girl. Memories were interrupted by a shout from the street.

"Hey Frenchie, ya gotta see this. Come on in here."

Kovak had discovered the dispensary. Labeau mounted the steps with a corpsman's bag slung over his shoulder. The room was cleaned spotless, befitting a white glove inspection. Hanging on the wall, a colored chart outlined the human circulatory system and internal organs. From a medicine cabinet he removed a large bottle and sniffed its contents. The treatment table in the center was cut from massive timbers and stacked with clean rags. He was sad to learn the practitioner was gone, grabbed months ago by the Japanese army.

"I'm setting up right here boys. Tell everybody the doc is ready and open for business. How's about a couple of volunteers to bring in my medical supplies?"

O'Malley and Hightree hustled away. The old man disappeared in search of his grandson. Labeau's message was translated again, buzzing through the native crowd.

When everything was in place to his satisfaction, Frenchie rolled up his sleeves and washed his hands in alcohol. Ichiban brought him his first patient, a little boy with a lumpy bandage on his arm. When the corpsman bent down to examine him the scared child backed away.

"Don't be afraid little fella, I'm your new doctor."

The boy wasn't completely convinced, but he allowed

himself to be lifted on the table. Labeau moved mechanically with a pair of surgical scissors, snipping away the bandage. The lumps underneath proved to be globs of tree moss filling an open gash.

"Hey Kovak, check this. That's what I call early penicillin. Pretty smart."

Using disinfectant and a cotton swab he cleared off the debris. The child flinched at first, but Labeau's smooth bedside manner was contagious. He broke into a tentative grin. Non-styptic iodine and a clean compress finished the job, and he was handed back to his grandfather.

"Here ya go old man. He'll be good as new, bring him back tomorrow."

The grateful grandparent clasped the little boy's hand and bowed. The Marines didn't know yet, but there were many ways in the future he would show his gratitude.

It was well past midday. The task of arranging a command post was at hand. Bowman's report was accurate. The beach and its shed-like structures presented an excellent defilade. A slow-moving stream of fresh water flowed quietly into the lagoon on their left. By the mouth, the road ended and turned into sand less than a hundred yards from the village. A mile north, obscuring their objective, a round-topped hill stood with a crown of untended sugar cane.

Their new home at water's edge bustled with the activity of women and young boys. Dugout canoes were pulled away from the half-shacks and replaced by hand-woven straw mats. Hard round pillows and oil lamps were placed inside. Many of the afternoon fishermen were already in their boats, paddling for the distant reef.

Ichiban steered them to the final stop, a large low storehouse with no door. Stacked inside were sacks of rice and sweet potatoes surrounded by copious baskets of fresh vegetables. Racks of dried fish were nailed to a wall. With a nonchalant manner he casually mentioned everything was free for taking. Following a brief conversation with Kovak he departed after a low bow.

"Lieutenant, the old man says we can store our stuff in here and park next door."

Chandler was more than agreeable. In case flight was necessary, empty trucks were faster, and the faster the better. On his orders, Carter assembled the men and formed a work party. Thirty minutes was sufficient. They shouldered their packs and trudged single file to their new homes.

Never in the wildest dream could a bivouac area be more heavenly. The soft sand was stark white, lapped by crystal clear water. A cool breeze from the west carried the soft scent of the ocean. A row of lean-tos faced the sea, standing like right triangles. Open ends were fitted with roll-down blinds of hand tied reeds, shielding interiors from the afternoon sun.

One by one the Marines tossed their transport packs inside and broke down bedrolls. Chandler chose shelter at the extreme far end, positioning the radio jeep in front at an angle, reasoning that the headlights could illuminate the great expanse of beach beyond if needed.

Exercising the privilege of rank, Jake opted to bunk alone for the first time in years. He assigned Chernikov the ritual of guard posts and a duty roster. Every man, including the corpsman, would have a turn standing watch. It was no great surprise when the Lieutenant volunteered to take a stint. This is a front line custom and he never lost the habit.

Carter made up his bed by placing a navy sheet on the straw mat. Next, he spread a wool blanket and covered it with his waterproof poncho. When the necessary items were extracted from his pack he laid out spread-eagle with a contented sigh. Lying on his back he reflected on what was to come. In the morning an observation post would be established in sugar cane above them. Once satisfied, after scrutinizing the terrain

The Last Souvenir

ahead, he would dispatch two-man night patrols when darkness came. Time was not of the essence, only extreme caution. Again the responsibility of command fell on his shoulders. The good part was nothing was scheduled for the rest of the day.

Feeling no fatigue, Jake sat up and stripped to the waist. When his boots and socks were removed he strolled barefooted down the sand dune to the water's edge. He noticed the fishing canoes landing far down the beach where old women were busily unloading the catch of the day. He pulled the new goggles from his pocket and sat down to examine them, lapsing into a soliloquy of blankness of sight and sound. The voice of Johnny Kovak startled him back to awareness.

"Hiya Jake, I brought you somethin'. It seems like you made a conquest."

At first, Carter couldn't believe his eyes. Standing before him was a half-naked native girl, removing a scarf from her head. She was clad only in a pair of cotton panties supported by a knotted drawstring. Seawater still dripped from her ample breasts. She had to be one of the divers.

"She saw you in the village Jake. She thinks you're pretty, how about that?"

The air hissed from his lungs and he fought to clear the tightness in his throat. He glanced at the triangular pubic patch that was clearly visible through the thin wet fabric. To all intents and purposes she was nude. The symmetry of her hips and thighs sent his glands into a rage.

"She says her name is Wana, just like the little village down south. She's twenty."

"My God, she's beautiful Johnny, absolutely beautiful." Jake could only offer a stammer.

"Well she thinks you're beautiful too, pal. Ya better be careful, she speaks a little English."

"English?"

"Yeah, her parents took her to the Philippines when she was a little girl. She went to an English missionary school. When the war broke out the Japs sent 'em home."

The meaning of time and place had faded away. Spanning the chasm between war and peace was one thing, but this was something else. A man, living in an all-male world, loses his perspective. The frailties of females are somehow lost and replaced by the violence of conflict. A man, to retain his sanity, must stuff these memories somewhere in the dark recesses of his soul. They are held in a holding pattern at a different altitude, out of sight and mind. A letter from home is contact, but not a visual image. Jake's solitude had been doused by a bucket of cold water.

The young woman clearly had her own desires, seemingly transfixed by his handsome features, blue gray eyes and blond hair, melting any modesty she might otherwise have felt. She had never known deep love, but the abyss was near and she was wavering on its edge.

Gracefully she moved forward and sat by his side. Vibrations between the two were overwhelming. Her voice was soft and clear when she spoke. "I not know you name. What you name?"

Confidence ceased its ebb and began to flow. He gazed at her round face, captured by shining brown eyes and dark eyebrows. Long ebony black hair fell over her body, partially covering her bare breasts. The corners of her mouth turned up in a natural smile. "My name is Jake, and I know your name. It's Wana," he finally answered.

"Jaki? Is nice name."

He liked the native touch of adding an i to all names. Cute perhaps, but he accepted it eagerly. Small talk would come later.

"Wana, you are very beautiful. Can you understand me?"

"Yes, Wana get. I think you pretty too. I happy."

The Last Souvenir

Threes a crowd and Kovak wanted out. "You're on your own now, Sarge. I'll see ya later. Gotta date with a seamstress." When he left Wana moved closer.

Their conversation sputtered at first, eventually gaining momentum. She was far above average intelligence and Jake was enthralled by her knowledge of English and how quickly it came back to her. They spoke mostly about life in her village and the remorse they endured for the loss of their young men. Her charm was infectious and her bright outlook refreshing. Her accent was a challenge, however, especially the way she substituted 'l's with 'r's. This was Japanese tutelage; like was rike and love ruve. From both hearts this new encounter was exotic and wonderful.

Jake described California, its beaches and palm trees, confining his grammar to its simplest form. Immediately she asked about the girls but he adroitly ducked the subject. She persisted but he assured her she was prettier. A tiny white lie but she wanted to hear it. She moved even closer, her breast almost touching his arm. Suddenly she reached down and picked up his goggles.

"Jaki rike come swim with Wana?"

The warm water beckoned and he stood up, stripping down to his underpants. "My darling, I would ruve to."

Wana went first, wading ahead. She dived forward and cleaved her way with effortless motion. He watched the flexing muscles in her back and buttocks. It dawned on him that keeping pace might be a problem but he was undaunted. He donned his goggles and plunged in. In spite of his powerful strokes he still trailed in her bubbling wake. After two-hundred yards he was relieved to see her roll onto her back and drift with a slow kick. He swam to her side, breathing heavily.

"I show you fish now. See down."

Jake readjusted his goggles and immersed his face. Below

them a school of large round fish dawdled near the bottom. Their white bodies were adorned with a stunning orange band and a long filmy dorsal fin. The fat creatures seemed oblivious to their presence.

"Is good to eat, Jaki. Wana cook for you sum time."

Face down they paddled further. When they reached a wide blue reef she took a deep breath and surface dived. Her twisting body disappeared. A cloud of black ink developed, throwing him into a panic. Before he could dive to assist she emerged holding a small octopus. On the surface she exhibited her prize and released it. She swam away from the murky cloud, laughing at Jake's shocked expression. "Is good too. I fix for you. We go back now?"

The journey back was slow and relaxing. They constantly glanced and smiled at each other affectionately. Neither wanted the magic of the moment to end. In the shallow water their feet touched the sand and they pushed for shore.

"Jaki give Wana pig back?"

"Pig back? I think you mean piggyback." He reached for her to climb aboard. She slid her arms around his neck and clamped her legs about his waist. Every nerve ending in his back transmitted the softness of her curves. She reveled in his strength and the broadness of his shoulders. In ankle deep water, obeying a devilish thought, he fell sideways, both splashing into the soft sand. In a reflex action she bounced on top, straddling him with her knees. Her face drew close to his.

"Jaki want kiss Wana now?"

For Jake, this was not aggression, it was downright invasion, and he loved it. Their lips met with all the joys of a first kiss, lingering and tender. They touched each other and slowly rolled together, charged with the fires of eternal youth. A bolt of lightning had struck from another world.

"I'm sorry to break this up, Jake, but the colonel's on the radio and he wants to talk." Chandler was standing on the beach, an apologetic look in his eyes.

"N-now sir, right now?"

"Like I said, I'm sorry, but unfortunately we're still in the war business."

Wana wanted to restrain him but thought better of it. "Jaki go now, Wana come back." Reluctantly she arose and strolled for home.

When Jake stood and walked toward him, Chandler looked down and clucked his tongue. "Don't look now Sergeant, but your passion is showing."

Carter turned a light pink. "I know sir, the girl hit me like a ton of bricks. What in the hell does the old man want? His timing is murder." Mildly angry he almost ripped off his wet shorts and climbed into dry trousers. Chandler thought it best to stay silent as they walked to the radio jeep. Eddie Gallo held up the receiver with his hand over the mouthpiece. "That's a real dish ya got there ,Jake. Does she have a sister?"

"As a matter of fact she does. They live together next to the village. The parents are both dead."

"You're a lucky dog, buddy. Here, say hello to the ever lovin' Colonel Mason."

Carter took the phone and gathered his wits the best he could. "Hello Colonel, Sergeant Carter speaking."

Mason quizzed him on every detail. The old salt was openly worried and kept repeating himself. The big show was slated for the next day but the tenacious colonel was unwilling to terminate. Jake swore a solemn oath he would call back with a full report. The verbal joust was unnerving at this time, but Jake held his ground. Mason finally relented and clicked out.

"Come on into my tent Jake, we can shoot the shit for awhile." The Lieutenant was inviting him to step in the CP. Two boxes of rations provided seating. Carter's head was down.

"What kind of a world are we in, Lieutenant? First we're in peace and then we're back in war. We're out in the boondocks sweatin', everybody else is goin' home. Now, to make things worse, cupid comes along and kicks me in the head. I'm surprised we're all not in a booby hatch."

"Welcome to leadership, my old friend." Chandler's empathy was running high. "Now you know a little bit what it's like to have a girl back home. I haven't seen my wife in almost three years."

"I'm glad you said that, Jimmy, I mean really glad. We've been together a long long time. Do me a favor. If it looks like I'm feelin' sorry for myself, give me a swift kick in the ass."

Chandler knew his candor was not disrespectful. "Here, take my mess gear. I just heated a big can of pork and beans. Fill'er up and chow down, you'll feel better."

The man to man chat between two comrades continued long after sundown. Both men opened wide their emotions and the rough bark of their existence fell aside. The world was not perfect yet, but there was hope. The long day had taken its toll and they broke into a yawning match.

"It's time to hit the sack sir. I'll be here early tomorrow, thanks for everything. I'll be OK now."

The path to his lean-to was well lit by an oval moon. From a box of stubby matches he struck a fire and lit his oil lamp. He was tired but not sleepy when he lowered the blind. Once he was stripped he stretched out and pulled the blanket to his waist. With hands clasped behind his head he rested on the hard pillow. The flickering flame brought dancing shadows, encouraging a parade of reminiscences. The ghost of his swim in the lagoon came back to haunt him.

A slight rustling sound outside jarred his senses. Instinct made him grab for his pistol but he drew back his hand. It was Wana. She lifted the blind and stood before him. It was a vision of loveliness wearing a loose fitting white dress. Her narrow waist was circled by a purple sash knotted in front. Shiny black hair, neatly groomed and brushed, glistened in the dim light.

"Wana say she come back. Is good?"

"Sweetheart, if you only knew how good it really is."

She knelt beside him and placed her hand on his chest, leaning over to kiss him. Absence and anticipation made it even more exciting than the first time. His hand on her bosom discovered a palpitating heart.

"Wana stay with Jaki." She sat up, untying the knot in her sash. With both hands she lifted the hem of her dress and pulled it over her head. Without another word she slid under the blanket and nestled softly against his body. He turned and caressed her.

For her it was love at first sight, and she wanted that love fulfilled. On this night of nights her wish came true.

CHAPTER THIRTY

The imaginary alarm clock in Wana's head sounded its usual signal at sunrise. Through a combination of habit and duty it was her chore to rise at dawn and feed the goats. From a sitting position she felt her man stirring and fell back to touch his face. Without a second thought she decided the beasts could wait, affording her one more erotic hour.

Along the beach the setting was quiet and peaceful, lacking the sounds of a bugle and the bellowing Sergeant Stebbins. On the sandbank, Private Levine peered into the early light, standing the last watch. An occasional snore rattled the air but added to the serenity.

The concerned Chandler was up first, drying himself from a cold morning swim. A driftwood fire crackled beside the CP, warming a pair of gallon cans, both containing meat and vegetable stew. Inside, the blue flame of a hand-stove heated a container of instant coffee. He strapped on his wristwatch and called to the sentry. "You can secure now, Private. You better come down and have some hot coffee."

"Yes sir, thank you sir." The young Marine slid down the bank and joined him, sticking his rifle in the sand, bayonet first. Slipping a canteen cup from his cartridge belt he filled it. Nothing can equal the savory taste of hot coffee after night guard duty. It was without doubt the soldier's ambrosia. Two long sips were a good start, and then it was clear he had a dozen questions. "Lieutenant, do you mind if I ask where we're goin' today?"

Chandler was patient, knowing he would have to repeat the plan. "You're Levine aren't you? where are you from, Ike?"

The Last Souvenir

"Yes sir, I'm from Brooklyn New York, sir."

"I've never been there, but I hear it's a tough neighborhood. I'll give it to you straight. You're going on a night patrol tonight. You'll be with Sergeant Bowman."

"I won't have a problem with that, Lieutenant. If you ever spent a night on the streets of Brooklyn you'll know what I mean, sir."

Pride showed in Chandler's eyes. It was more than duty that placed him in command of such dedicated young men. It was a privilege. He shared his past experiences, stressing the pitfalls of working against the Japanese in the dark. They were halfway through a second cup when Levine pointed down the beach.

"Hey Lieutenant, do you see what I see?"

It was Wana crawling under the blind of Jake's lean-to. A cheery smile lit her face when she saw them, turning to wave. Barefooted she sped away, the white skirt fluttering in her self made breeze. Even the monogamous Chandler felt envy when he watched her turn the corner and disappear up the road to the village.

"Wow, she's really somethin', Lieutenant, how do I get me one of those?"

"Unfortunately, Private, that is not Government Issue and it's time to go to work. Tell Sergeant Carter to assemble the men at the CP in thirty minutes. No helmets or canteens, just fatigue caps, cartridge belts, and weapons. Tell them to bring mess gear."

Carter was wide awake when Levine relayed the orders. He raised the reed blind and appeared naked in the gray light. The morning sun had not yet cleared the mountains at his back. "Thanks Ike, do me a favor and pass the word. Roust 'em out." He waded knee deep in the cool water, splashing his face and body. Behind him, grousing men with shaggy hair showed themselves, stretching and rubbing their sleepy eyes, looking anything but a fighting unit, but he was confident they would shape up. They always did.

Chandler had the foresight to eat first. He was sitting on his haunches, scouring his mess gear with beach sand when his men and their appetites straggled toward him. Back home his friends knew him as the ultimate diner and gourmet chef. Nonetheless, his menu today was plain and plentiful. With six spoons filling empty mess tins the morning fare soon vanished.

"Save those cans and wash 'em out. We can use 'em for coffee."

The old adage, 'an army travels on its stomach,' rang true once again. The men were on their feet with color in their cheeks and determination in their eyes. Carter's plan was threefold. First, split up into groups of two, crawl unseen to the hilltop. From there, taking advantage of full daylight, they would examine the valley below and the Biscuit beyond. With three night patrols going out simultaneously, each sergeant would select the best cover and line of march. It was a tricky business, requiring stealth and coordination.

Chernikov and O'Malley would circle the west cliff while Bowman and Levine scouted the east. Carter and Hightree, with the infrared detector, would work close into the south slope, purportedly the only access. They had two advantages, surprise and dim moonlight. In the third phase, with morning surveillance completed, a final meeting at the CP would harmonize their timing. Dusk was still many hours away but moonrise would come early.

It was like old times for Jake as he watched Chernikov and Bowman split company and climb in two different directions. The two new men mimicked the cat like steps of their veteran partners.

"OK Jesse, you're the tracker, take the point. The Lieutenant and I will follow. When we get to the top we'll crawl the last twenty feet."

Hightree moved with the grace of a stalking lioness, scaling the gentle slope and reading trail signs. Near the crest he paused by the sugar cane and dropped to one knee. Turning his head he spoke in a low whisper. "There are footprints everywhere, Sergeant. The children have been here recently, but no adults."

"What about cover?"

"More than adequate, the grass is two feet tall. I'll worm the rest of the way."

Shoulder to shoulder the three Marines joined each other on the ground. Supported by their elbows they used field glasses to view the valley below. There was no sign of life. Dead ahead, at least a mile away they could see the Biscuit. Jake focused on a dry wash and trickling creek arcing near the south slope. It appeared to originate in the central mountain range. The arroyo wound its way west through the sand dunes and emptied into the sea. A Z-shaped path dropped down from the mesa and led across the field to a small pond. Access to the water was bordered by clumps of chest high shrubbery.

"That's our spot, Lieutenant, down in those bushes. We can work our way up the gully from the beach and set up by the creek."

"Then what?"

"It's a perfect place for a stakeout, sir. If we all meet there we'll have six men. If the Nips send a water party of more than six we'll pull out and head for the beach."

"Good God, Jake, you're talkin' about a helluva fist fight. What if something goes wrong.?"

"We'll have two things goin' for us, sir, the element of surprise and Marine muscle. Why, hell, sir, we've done it before. That's what takin' Jap prisoners is all about."

"Sergeant, I've got to give you an A-plus for balls."

"Sir, it's the only way."

The rudiments of training in Officer's Candidate School

had taught Chandler he must be willing to sacrifice men in combat. To become overly familiar with the people in his command was taboo. In sequence, he should calculate the risk-reward ratio and issue a reasonable order, resulting in matching body count with the assigned objective. His decision was nurtured by faith in his seasoned platoon sergeant and he went along with the format. After all, it was Carter who knew the procedure, having been through it many times. No matter the consequences, Chandler was still mentally crossing his fingers.

"Alright Sergeant, I'll go along with your plan, but there's one thing more. When we get back to the CP I want to review every contingency and discuss alternatives."

"Sounds OK to me, sir. Now I'd like to move right and get a better look at the east side."

Backtracking down, the three men moved eastward until the hill began to fall away. Bowman was below in the tall grass, studying the landscape with binoculars. Beside him, Ike Levine's side vision detected their movement and he held up his thumb.

The Biscuit was well named, a page from the textbook on geology of the Pacific islands. The coral head was uplifted from the sea in a million years of evolution. Perpendicular escarpments of dark green moss and razor sharp edges made mounting improbable. On its crown, the unlikely pine forest must have been God's afterthought. In the past, the Marines were accustomed to facing hand dug caves and gun pits, but here there were none.

"Looks spooky doesn't it, sir?"

"Took the words right out of my mouth, Jake, but at least you don't have any caves lookin' down your throat."

The rising sun was directly overhead and the scouts had seen enough. They withdrew to the southwest in single file with Bowman and Levine falling in line. The spring in Carter's step showed his confidence. Conversely, Chandler had a bad

The Last Souvenir

case of the jitters. They found Chernikov lounging on the beach, the bill of his cap shading his eyes. O'Malley was too keyed up for rest, deep in thought about the upcoming night. He had finally found his war, or what was left of it.

Chandler's anxiety ran high when he led his men to the CP. He sought opinions, questions, and answers from every man. It was his nature to overreact, imagining the smallest loose end could lead to disaster. This package of dynamite would be knotted securely before he was satisfied. Upon reaching his lean-to he was quick to retrieve his contour map and spread it on the sand. The men bent over to watch his moving forefinger.

"We'll start with the sergeants, you first, Carter."

Jake laid out the master plan in detail, attended by cryptic comments from Bowman and Chernikov. Their self assurance was sobering to the fidgety lieutenant, relaxing the tension. In the better part of an hour, Chandler's doubts were put to rest. He was impressed by the logical questions from O'Malley and Levine. Through it all, the straight-faced Hightree remained silent. One loose end needed tying and he found speech.

"Sergeant Carter, you mentioned we are to waylay and arrest these potential prisoners. Exactly how do we overcome them?"

Bowman laughed and nudged Carter with his elbow. "He's gotcha there, Jake"

Carter threw up his hands. "That's a damn good question Jesse, now listen carefully. We hide in the brush and wait 'til they get so close ya can smell 'em. Pick your man and jump him. Smash him hard on the temple." He tapped the crucial spot above his ear. "If he still wiggles put your arm around his neck and cut off his wind. For God's sake, no more than ten seconds. Any more than that and you'll kill him."

"What comes next Sarge?"

"We tie 'em up and gag 'em. You'll find the Jap is different. He's so ashamed of being taken prisoner he'll come quietly. At least that's our past experience."

The Lieutenant was horrified. "After all these months you never told me that's how you did it."

"This ain't no kindergarten sir, if you can think of a better way I'd like to hear it."

Chandler gave up. "I guess that's it. We still have over six hours before sunset so get some rest. That's all."

Moe and Johnny B were the first to stand and walk away. Jake edged closer to the water and raised his field glasses, staring hard at the outer reef. After waving his arm he lowered the binoculars and turned to his pals. "Where do you two think you're goin'?"

"Were goin' up to the village and look around."

"Oh no you're not! Come back and stick close."

"What's this shit? Ya pullin' rank on us or somethin'?"

"You know me better than that, Moe. I've gotta surprise for you. We're all invited to a barbecue."

"Yeah sure, and tonight the tooth fairy is gonna slip a dime under my pillow."

Curiosity overcame skepticism and the duo shuffled back, joined by the rest of the men. From the sea, two outrigger canoes turned their bows and paddled for the shore. It was Wana and her friends, three in each boat, with wooden goggles hanging from their necks. The sharp points of sling spears protruded from the snub-nosed prows. Barely audible, their paddles made a chunking sound, propelling the small craft forward. Their supple bodies drew the Marines eyes like a magnet.

"Hey, look at all them tits."

An embarrassed Bowman slapped his buddy's back. "Moe, ya got no couth, can't ya see there's ladies present?"

"OK, OK, but look at their nipples, they're brown. They

ain't pink like American girls."

"What are you, some kinda nipple expert?"

"Nah, but I'd like to be."

Shy giggles emanated from the native girls. Though unable to translate, they delighted in being the center of attention amid so many handsome young men. Wana was no exception.

"Jaki friends have food now?"

"All this and food too? Man, I think I just died and went to heaven."

Assuming acceptance, the women increased their cadence and went gliding away to the river's mouth. The trotting Marines could not stay even, unbuckling cartridge belts and stowing rifles in their lean-tos. Carter hastened to halt the rush.

"Wait a minute, who's got the guard duty?"

"Wisnewski, he's up the beach."

"OK, let's go."

A column of gray smoke lifted skyward beside the estuary, encouraged by a popping fire under a large square grill. Three old women in plain kimonos leaned over a raised chopping board, filleting fish and preparing fresh vegetables. A stack of wooden bowls and a pile of chopsticks occupied the far end. When the guests arrived the matrons smiled their greetings through weather-beaten faces.

Wana and the girls had already pulled the boats ashore, and were in the process of unloading their catch nearby. The Marines would soon learn they were marked men. The girls had made their choices the day before and the matching was predetermined. Wana had her man, freeing her to interpret and make introductions. The young men, so long isolated from distaff companionship, were astonished by the onslaught.

Chernikov was first, facing the willowy maiden who was tallest. She took his hand and coaxed him away. He followed with his eyes fixed on the gyrations of her exposed bosom, his breast fetish sending his long dormant libido in a spiral.

Wana whispered in Jake's ear, relating a feminine secret. He smiled. "Hey Moe, you won't believe this, but she has a thing about your hands."

"My hands? Are you kidding?" The big Marine looked down. His huge paw engulfed her tiny digits like a fist in a catcher's mitt. His latent strength made her ecstatic over the protection he could provide.

"Sergeant, would you step over here, please, and bring your lady."

It was the fluent Hightree. His scientific mind was engrossed in the contents of a giant metal pot, its sides blackened by years of fire and smoke. The bottom contained a residue of assorted gray and white crystals. When Wana arrived he asked her to explain. "Miss, can you tell me the purpose of this process?"

"We cook water. Water go way. Reave sart."

That went over Jake's head. "Reave sart? What's that?"

Hightree's mental reflexes were quicker. "I understand, Sergeant. Her diction prevents her from pronouncing her L's, she means 'leaves salt'. Of course, how stupid of me, it's distillation of sea water producing NaCL, sodium chloride supplemented by natural minerals. Excellent for seasoning and nutrition."

"Jesse, you amaze me. You're standing there with a beautiful girl and you talk about chemistry. If the Sioux Nation hears about this they'll drum you outta the tribe."

Jesse had no chance to respond. The young beauty seized her opportunity and dragged him away, skipping merrily down the beach. Wana's keen sense of hearing picked up the sizzling of fillets on the grill. One of the kindly old women spoke to her in a low monotone. She nodded and passed on the message.

"Jaki get frens. Eat soon."

The Last Souvenir

Carter's men were scattered in four directions. Three were stripped down to their underpants in knee-deep water, engaged in playful splashing matches with squealing adversaries. O'Malley sat nearby, drawing descriptions in the sand with a short twig. His counterpart paid little heed, touching his red hair with her fingertips. Jake called out through cupped hands.

"OK boys, the lollygagin' is over. Time to chow down."

A veritable feast was presented. Thick fillets were withdrawn from the grill, barely cooked beyond the raw stage, and sliced into bite-size cubes. These were placed in bowls on a bed of cabbage and bean sprouts. Cups of tasty cream sauce, concocted from goat's milk and chives, were distributed to outstretched hands. With chopsticks, Wana demonstrated by dipping chunks into the side dish. Those who were inept in the art of eating with sticks soon found competent teachers. The girls insisted on serving their men, returning for seconds and thirds when capacity permitted. They were not surprised to learn that big men supported bigger appetites.

Wana was bursting with wonderful news. Unable to contain it any longer, she took Jake's hand and steered him to a secluded refuge between two sand dunes. Once seated she snuggled close, bubbling with internal warmth. "Past days we talk Ichiban. He say is good you here. Is good we have babies. Wana want Jaki baby. Is good? Friends want too."

For once the nimble-witted Carter was stunned beyond words. Perhaps his ears were deceiving him. He was far from home in an exotic environment, experienced and trained for all contingencies, but this was a bombshell. Because of her naive sincerity it must be true. In the moment that passed he reached deep for composure, choking the first question. "You say the Ichiban *WANTS* this?"

Wana's smile grew wider. "Yes, Jaki. Young men go away, no come back. No babies Hagachi die. Mericas big strong pretty. Make Hagachi happy again."

Jake sensed the marriage ceremony was not an issue. It was purely a case of demographics, procreate or perish. The Japanese Army had subtracted an entire generation from their existence, with no way to replenish. Apart from which he felt he had no right to sit in judgment of these simple people. The seat of his cultural upbringing was thousands of miles away and had no bearing on local mores. His knowledge of history recalled the Crusades, where one group attempted to foist it's religion on another and failed. Travels in the South Seas brought memories of pagan fertility rites, placing population first. An open mind determined that morality is based on geography, or simply, where one lives. He vacillated between his perceptions of right and wrong, deciding in the end that, on a word-wide basis, he was too small to issue a verdict.

"Wana my love, you know I must go away someday. Maybe I'll never come back. What then?"

"Is OK. Jaki reave piece behind for Wana to ruve. Wana be much happy."

"Wana, I don't see how I can help loving you, no matter what happens."

"Wana ruve Jaki too, first time she see."

They talked well into the afternoon about everything and nothing. Jake hated the sun for seeking its rest over the horizon. Wana's astounding intellect brought back her fluency with every sentence. It did not seem possible the best and the worst times of his life could take place in the span of such a short time.

Jake could wait no longer. "Wana, my darling, you know I must go now. I have work tonight."

"Yes, Wana know. You go for Nipponese. They bad men hurt Jaki. Wana no rike."

"Don't worry about me sweetheart, I'll come back. I always do."

CHAPTER THIRTY-ONE

Darkness fell like a closing trapdoor. The last light refractions from a low lying cloud bank in the west cast an eerie lemon color on the sea. An odd shaped moon kept its early appointment, a hanging yellow eye in the sky smiling down on the mortals below.

The six-man patrol worked its way north along the shore and found shelter behind a bank on the rocky creek bed. The rolling terrain was turning silver from moonlight on its surface. Harsh black shadows provided havens for the prowling Marines. Only the sound of flowing water marred the silence, marked intermittently by a lonely birdcall. In the past, the night was filled with distant gunfire to smother their footsteps, but that was silenced by peace and they had to deal with a crushing quiet.

From here forward only a barely audible whisper could be issued to a waiting ear. Chernikov would wait an extra thirty minutes for perfect darkness before he and O'Malley scaled the embankment and crawled for the Biscuit. Carter, with the cumbersome Millie in both hands, motioned for Hightree to lead the way up the stream bed with Bowman and Levine in the rear. The intrepid Indian moved with the caution of a rolling mist, placing his feet in the soft sand between the cobblestones.

The side banks were slowly tapering lower, sending them into an uncomfortable slouch. Their objective, the beaten path from the mountain came into view after twenty minutes of light treading. Suddenly their point man paused and motioned a halt, dropping to his knees. Still clutching his rifle, Jesse moved his face to within inches of the ground. The marvel of young eyesight and the moon over his shoulder allowed him to read trail signs. Footprints pointing downward were shallow, probably made by smaller men. Those that returned were much deeper, denoting heavy burdens. The telltale signs left no doubt a small party of Japanese military had preceded them.

He inched upward as far as he dared for a final examination before he slid back to rejoin the men. Their faces almost touched, straining to hear his hushed tones. "You were right, Sergeant. They've been here, split toes and hobnails. Appears to be a small party, maybe three or four."

"Can you tell how recent?"

"No, but they're carrying something up the hill, probably water."

"I knew it!" Carter gave himself a verbal pat on the back. "We'll stay here, Jesse, and set up the Millie. Johnny, you and Ike can get started. Move in as close to the cliff as you can. You know the program."

Bowman leaned toward Levine. "What say, Ike, shall we give it a whirl?"

"Ya know Sarge, I thought I'd be scared stiff, but I'm not."

"That's good. Wish I could say the same thing. Let's go."

The stream bed took a gentle curve to the North and straightened abruptly. With Bowman in the lead they crept a few hundred yards, keeping the Biscuit on their left. When cover ran out they stopped and peered through a stand of high greenery, noticing a swail between two low hills. The moon made a feeble attempt to replace the light of the sun, but this was to their advantage.

"We'll crawl it from here, Ike. Stay on my heels. Once we make it to the cliff they can't see us."

Slithering on his belly across open country gave Ike Levine his first tinge of fear. He was convinced all eyes were watching him and every rifle on the hill was pointed at his back. His mouth grew dry and he tried to swallow, but his throat refused to function on his command. Beads of salty perspiration burned into his eyes, forcing him to wipe them away with the sleeve of his jacket. He had gone half way, unable to turn back and fearful of advancing. Like thousands of young Marines before him he gritted his teeth and told himself to keep moving. 'Hell, this is what they pay me for.' He was a civilian no longer, having tasted real fear of the unknown.

Bowman was a few yards ahead, crawling through a row of dirt mounds lined against the base of the cliff. Under cover of the mossy ledge he stood up, pressing his back against the steep hillside. When Levine finally reached the sergeant his eyes were bloodshot and his chest heaved, sucking in much needed oxygen. In spite of his apprehensions a feeling of calm swept over him, knowing he had overcome his fright. The stark reality of being a veteran was now more than just words. Now he understood that fear was the bond that cemented their lasting comradeship. Standing together they could conquer the monster.

Bowman tilted his head and spoke in a low whisper. "Well, we made it kid. You OK?"

"Sarge, I take back what I said about not being scared."

"I know what you mean. Take a look, we just crawled through a graveyard."

A cold shiver flashed the length of Ike's body. "Ya mean those piles of dirt?"

"Yep, we better count 'em. Might mean somethin'."

It was an ancient native custom to inter the dead in burial vaults and Bowman knew this. A crude cemetery in the open with no markings was highly irregular.

"I count twenty-four, Sarge."

"Yeah, me too. Sh! There's sumthin' goin' on upstairs. Back off quick."

The two men pinned themselves against the hillside, listening with every fiber of their being. In a training session, Carter told the men a scout must grow eyes in the back of his head and ears like a jack rabbit. Levine thought it was funny, and even laughed, but tonight the words were gospel truth. His senses of hearing and sight were expanding at an uncanny rate, feeding waves of signals into his muddled brain. He drew strength from the nearness of Bowman and found security in a new brotherhood. What he did not know, and probably would not have believed, was that Bowman's heart was beating just as fast.

The bustling noise above was too high for them to discern the nature of the activity. Suddenly, a few feet to their left, a rain of pebbles and mossy dirt clods tumbled down the cliff side and scattered between the graves. To their horror, a hurtling body followed and landed with a sickening thud not more than a few steps away. Pale moonlight accentuated the ghostly sight, with the men too surprised to look away.

Levine felt a rush of nausea and clutched his stomach. "My God, what was that? Is that harry carey?"

Bowman was steadfast. "Sh! They might be lookin' over the side. We'll wait awhile, then take a look."

The ticking seconds felte more like hours, and their eyes remained riveted on the grotesque corpse. The body was fully clothed in a dress uniform, complete with calf-length leather boots and a Samurai sword. Lying face up, the ribbons on his dark brown tunic indicated he was an old campaigner, probably decorated in many theaters of conflict. In his fall the jagged coral had torn shreds from his skin and clothing.

The cascading debris had long since ceased, replaced by a ghostly silence. Bowman was an old hand at ghoul hunting but to Levine it was a new ordeal. He had seen dead bodies before in the ghettos of Flatbush, but they were always carried away on stretchers by the police. This was different. Instead of being the end, this was just the beginning of a lurking danger.

They carefully sidestepped to a vantage point directly over the body. Bowman's quick scrutiny told him something was amiss. "This guy's been dead for hours."

"How can ya tell, Sarge?"

"Look at his face, it's gray.... and there's no blood anywhere."

"So the fall didn't kill him?"

"Nope, he was rolled off the top by his men."

Bowman bent forward and touched the collar insignia. "He's a Captain, ya can tell by his stars."

"Why didn't they bury him like all the rest?"

"That's the big question, Ike. We've got somethin' here. Remember everything you see, we'll put it together when we get back."

"Maybe the Japs are too scared to show themselves anymore."

"Yeah, that's possible, but they could be sick and weak too. Don't touch anything, we've got another mile to cover. Come on."

To the west, Chernikov and O'Malley had completed their circuit of the Biscuit and were on the return leg. The moon still hung to one side, shrouding the cliff with blackness. On the ground below, dark shadows pointed away from the steep precipice in a lazy half circle. An evening breeze was rising, stimulating a light slapping sound of sea water on the shoreline.

Thus far their mission was uneventful and fruitless. Their backtracking took them once again through a stretch of mushy underfooting. This time it piqued O'Malley's interest and he knelt to scoop up a handful. The Texas boy had a smattering of knowledge about farm soil and he pinched its texture with two fingers.

"Psst! Hey Moe, come back and take a look at this stuff" Chernikov obliged and retraced his steps. "Whatcha got?"

"This dirt doesn't belong here. It ain't native, and see how it's been spread around?"

"Yeah, you're right, it's ground up coral. In an air photo it looks like beach sand."

"How the hell did it get here, Moe?"

Chernikov pointed upward with his thumb. "Up there. The little bastards were diggin' somethin' a long time ago." He hesitated and looked up. "Caves, that's it. Seen it before. Good work, Sean, let's get over in those bushes and take a squint from a better angle."

From the new slant of observation a wide fan-like pattern revealed the results of extensive excavation, cleverly disguised as alluvial deposits. The May monsoon had washed the hillside, leaving an unmolested face. The masters of camouflage had probably installed moss covered doors, making detection impossible from afar.

"It's so damn dark, I'd sure like to get a closer look. "

"I can get up there, Moe. I used to be a champ tree climber when I was a kid."

"Naw, no way. After ten feet up your hands would be raw hamburger."

"I can make it, Sarge, watch this." O'Malley reached in his pocket and displayed a heavy pair of work gloves. "I got these from a buddy in the engineers, see, I even cut a hole for my trigger finger."

"You're crazy kid, do ya really think you can make it?"

'Sure I can. It's only about fifty feet, and look at all them knobs. It's like a ladder."

"OK, it's your ass, be careful. If they spot ya you're a dead duck.."

"Don't worry about me, I'm from Texas, remember? That makes me part lizard." O'Malley slung his rifle over his head and across his back while slipping into his protective gloves. His compulsion for adventure drove him forward and he began his climb. On rare occasions, war gives birth to a special species of fighting man, close to foolhardy and far from insecure. This he was. His own invincibility dispelled all thoughts of bodily harm, and he calculated risks to the brink and beyond. If he made it home, he would either ride in a ticker tape parade, bedecked with medals, or occupy a coffin.

Higher and higher he scaled, watched by the uneasy sergeant. His inborn agility and determination carried him near the crest where he paused. A shift in the breeze brought the stench of smoke, musty clothes, and human excrement to his nostrils. Like a fly on the wall he moved gingerly sideways, following the scent until he came to a large opening. There was a cave, and he was clinging to the edge of its mouth.

The moon was ninety degrees above, giving a better definition of light and shadows. A mottled door in the entrance was partially ajar, allowing the barest sliver of candlelight to show. He strained to hear a muffled conversation but the words were unintelligible. Back from the ledge, the pulleys of a large block and tackle caught his eye. In his training he was taught not to analyze, just remember everything and bring it back.

He suppressed an urge to climb over the top for a better look. Instead, he sidled in the opposite direction, feeling sharp blades of coral biting into the thick soles of his boots. If anything the traction was much better than he'd hoped. He found a second cave, far smaller than the first, but the pungent odor of dried urine drove him back. In a few more minutes the moon would spotlight his frame against the green. He decided it was time to return.

In the thicket below, Chernikov frowned with concern at Sean's precarious descent, groping blindly with both feet, at times swinging to and fro, supported only by his hands. The 'rungs' of his ladder were easier to spot on the way up than coming down. When he reached the bottom he slid on his rump part of the way, then trotted in a crouch to safety. Moe had witnessed but still could not believe the circus act. "Ya must have ice water in your gizzard. Did ya see anythin'?"

"I sure did. They're up there alright."

Moe noticed a tear in the boy's pant leg. "Hold it, ya got a bad cut there, your leg is all bloody. We'll have to go down on the beach so I can patch ya up."

In the security of a domed sand dune Chernikov went to work, unbuckling his cartridge belt to make his first aid pouch accessible. After sprinkling sulfa power on the open gash he clamped a wound compress above the knee and knotted it tightly. "That'll do it for now. We better get you back so Frenchie can take a look at it. Ya might need stitches."

"Oh no you don't! Sergeant Carter wants us to meet him and I'm goin'!"

Moe smiled at the stubborn redhead. "OK Sean, if you want to bite the bullet it's your biz."

Carter was in a nervous state, glancing constantly at the luminous dial on his wrist watch. Hightree had given him a crash course on the use of infrared equipment and it proved to be invaluable. Even though it was new and experimental he knew infantry warfare had taken a giant step forward. Unfortunately, for his war it was too late.

"I think I hear something, Sergeant, off to the right."

"Yeah, I hear it too." Jake slid down the bank and drew his pistol. The running water hampered his listening, but the sounds of soft footsteps in the sand came closer. The shadowy forms of Bowman and Levine appeared and he breathed a sigh of relief.

"Hiya Jake, did ya miss us?"

"Come on in Johnny, you guys had me worried. You're thirty minutes overdue."

"Man, it's pretty creepy out there, I'm glad to be back."

The three men sat together in the asylum of overhanging branches. Bowman removed his cap, wiped his brow, and inhaled a series of deep breaths. Levine lay on his back and stared at the sky, pondering his new-found manhood.

"Well Ike, what did you think about your first patrol?"

Levine sat up slowly, nervously pulling a burr from his sock. "To tell the truth, at first it was like goin' through a meat grinder but I got the hang of it, thanks to Sergeant Bowman. He's a cool one."

"Thanks buddy, maybe someday you'll know what it's like to wear three stripes."

"I doubt that Sarge, I'll be goin' home. But I know one thing, when I get back to Brooklyn I'll be a couple of inches taller."

Bowman gave his report objectively, purposely avoiding conjecture. Carter absorbed the facts with a nodding head and no interruptions. When he finished Bowman turned to Levine. "Did I leave anything out, Ike?"

"Yeah, one thing. We counted twenty-four, does that mean anything?"

Jake took over. "It sure as hell does, they're dyin' off like flies. They'll stay up there 'til they all kick the bucket. The Jap is Bushido trained, he can only follow the last order he was given. If his ranking officer is killed off he'll stay there 'til he rots."

"My God, ya mean he can't think for himself?"

"Shit no, that's one of the reasons he lost. Americans can improvise, think for themselves. They can't."

Johnny B added more. "That's right, if that dead Captain was their CO they're all frozen solid. Besides that they're probably too sick to move. They've been up there a long time."

"I wonder why they don't have any radio contact?"

"I think I can answer that." Jesse Hightree was eavesdropping. "In all probability their batteries expired."

"He's right... hey, hold it a minute, somebody's comin' up from downstream."

It was Chernikov and O'Malley outlined against the gloomy horizon. Moe dropped to his knees and returned his pistol to its holster. "Well, we're back, I see you guys made it OK."

"Yeah, we're all here now, what's the story Moe?"

"We had a long walk. I didn't see anythin', but ya better ask O'Malley. He was climbin' all over that cliff."

"He what?"

"That's right, the kid's got more guts than a fish cannery. Tell 'em Sean."

O'Malley dropped to a squat, favoring the tight bandage on his leg. His rhetoric was nonchalant and unassuming. It wasn't false modesty that made him minimize his bold exploit, he truly believed it was a simple assignment. The job had to be done and he did it.

Carter listened with respect, pride and amazement. "That's quite a story, Sean. Did you see any guns, grenades, weapons of any kind?"

"Naw, it was too dark."

"How big was the block and tackle?"

O'Malley held up his hands and formed a circle. "About this big, maybe eighteen inches. Does that tell ya anything?"

"I'll say it does, it tells me they get their supplies from the sea and haul 'em up. Now that they're cut off they're running out." Carter harked back to captured Japanese field rations. Sacks of rice with boxes of pressed fish and oatmeal cakes were the main staples. The fish was salty and unpalatable, but the oatmeal was tasty when well soaked in water.

"There's somethin' else Sarge, I picked up a word. Heard it two or three times. 'Mizu', doesn't that mean water?"

"Water it is. Kovak taught you well, anything else?"

The Last Souvenir

"Yeah, there's one more. When I got close to the top the place smelled like a country outhouse in the summer."

Jake smiled at his graphic description. "On top of everything else they have lousy head facilities. Must be a terrible place." He stroked his chin, every trail led to fresh water. Sickness and lack of food were important but only secondary. He crawled back up the sand bank and propped himself next to Hightree. "See anything yet?"

"Not a thing, Sergeant, not even a flicker."

"Jesse, do you believe in hunches?"

"Perhaps, yes, many studies have been pursued in extrasensory perception, and even in metaphysics."

"Where did you learn all this mumbo jumbo?"

Hightree looked away from his scope. "I am curious by nature, Sergeant. What's your hunch?"

"I have a feeling they're comin' down tonight. Dunno why, but I can feel it right down to my liver."

"Thus far your hunches have been accurate. Do we stay?"

"Yep, we stay for a while. I'll tell the men."

Bowman and Chernikov could sense a swing in Jake's mood. "What's the scoop, are we goin' back?"

"Not yet, we're here now so we'll stay a couple more hours."

"OK Jake, then what?"

"You guys can snooze if you want, but no snorin'. Be ready. If the Nips come down for water tonight, we'll jump 'em."

CHAPTER THIRTY-TWO

The faithful moon tagged after the sun across the sea like a dutiful child following its mother. A new shimmering light split the dark water, changing the western attitude. As always, a new family of shadows moved into the neighborhood, rearranging the features of the mountainside. Only the quiet remained unchanged.

"It appears we have been stood up by our guests, Sergeant." Jesse Hightree placed the scope aside and rested his head on folded forearms, a respite from accumulated eyestrain. Carter retrieved the apparatus and adjusted it to suit his visionary needs. He was joined by a snaking O'Malley.

"Sarge, I can't sleep like those guys. Mind if I have a look in that thing?"

Hightree raised his head, aroused by the sound of Sean's whisper. "You'll find a variance in reflection from the different sizes of foliage. It's tuned to adjust for that."

"Ya know, Sarge, half the time I don't know what the hell he's talkin' about. But that's OK, were buddies."

Hightree's regard for his friend took a new twist. In his culture the word 'brave' had lofty connotations. Courage was the backbone of his tribal heritage, and he could picture O'Malley riding bareback on a charging pony. Unusual circumstances created an unlikely comradeship that would last into the years ahead.

Sean's untrained eye peered through the cross-hairs in vain. "Can't see a damn thing. Everything's green, but I swear I saw somethin' move way up on top." He handed the rifle over Jake's head and into Jesse's hands.

"He's right Sergeant, it's set on the maximum range but I see figures."

"How many?"

"Four so far. They're starting down the path. Yes it's clearer now, I make it four."

Adrenal glands began to pump, stirred by an invisible stimulus. Carter was catapulted into action. "Moe, Johnny, get up here fast. We've got company."

Hightree was down to his final transmissions. "They're almost at the bottom now. Looks like an officer in the lead. The others are carrying buckets, about two hundred yards out."

"Moe, crawl up the path and hide in those bushes. You take the last man. Sean, go with him and take the next one. Johnny, we'll grab the first two, leave the officer to me." Carter held up both hands for silence. "Jesse, you and Ike are backup. If anything goes wrong, bash 'em with the butt of your rifle. And remember, we want prisoners, not dead bodies."

Within seconds the ambush was established with the professionalism of trained Marines. The unsuspecting enemy was unaware of the waiting hornet's nest, walking slowly in their badly weakened condition. They were bareheaded, following their leader in single file. He was larger in stature, with a mass of bristling black hair and a full beard, uncommon in the genes of an oriental race.

Tense vibrations permeated the night air when the officer hesitated, waving for his men to close ranks. Even the waning moon was impatient, sailing away to rob them of their advantage. Waiting at night was the scourge of the rifleman. If he moved too soon, or worse too late, it could spell disaster. In this game of cat and mouse, the mouse would fight back in a desperate reaction of survival. Carter's cap visor was pulled low on his forehead, giving better focus on his prey. Above

Jack Carroll

and to the left of the trail, Bowman had done the same. Together, they had been through this harrowing experience before, and each time seemed more electric than the last.

Closer and closer the forms moved into their trap, with Carter and Chernikov on opposite ends of the jaws. When the exact moment came, Jake sent an unspoken telepathic message. 'Now Moe, NOW.'

The mental message was received. Chernikov lunged from hiding, delivering a crushing blow to the head. His man careened away, landing on the grass in a motionless heap. O'Malley's adversary had a split second to recoil, taking a glancing shot to his forehead. A hard counter-punching left hand struck him above the ear and he dropped. Bowman had further to travel, closing the distance in a high-flying tackle. When his target fell to one side he circled his neck and squeezed hard.

A full three seconds elapsed from the first attack, giving the startled officer time to look back in disbelief. Carter clutched the front of his uniform and yanked him downward, both sprawling in the sand by the pond below. With the advantage of surprise, Jake slid his arm over the officer's head and clamped his larynx with the crux of his elbow. By sheer weight he overpowered the man, but he could feel hard muscle across the back and shoulders of the oversized Japanese, who continued to kick gurgle.

Ike Levine stood over them with his rifle poised. "Ya need any help, Sarge?"

Carter grimaced through clenched teeth. "No... Stay back." Tightening his grip on his wriggling foe. "Come on you sonuvabitch. Give up. The war's over."

Behind him the other three men dragged their staggering prisoners, each with an arm thrust up his back in a painful hammer-lock and a hand clasped over his mouth. They were dazed and shocked by the assault, too weak to resist. A long period of sickness and hunger had destroyed their will to fight. To them, submission was a happy ending, in spite of the rough treatment.

Carter eased his grip, heeding his own ten second warning, and rolled the Japanese over on his back. The man's face was speckled with coarse grains of river sand. He inhaled jerky breaths of fresh air and raised his hands in a gesture of surrender. It was obvious he wanted to speak but his vocal cords were slow to respond. He finally regained his senses, aided by a combination of oxygen in the lungs and blood in his brain, and sat up. His classic statement was an epithet that would stay in the memories of the six Marines forever.

"You dumb shits. All you had to do was ask me. I've been wanting to give up for four years."

"Hey, this guy speaks English. Almost perfect."

"Of course I do, you fools. I was born in the States. What have you done to my men?"

Carter helped the man to his feet, trying desperately to identify his collar insignia. A spotty cloud bank was creeping closer, turning the silver moonlight into a dark gray hue and cutting their visibility in half. Jake could only venture a guess. "If that's a star on your collar you must be a Lieutenant."

"That's right, Imperial Quartermaster Corps, and you guys must be Marines. I always knew you were a bunch of rough-necks." He spoke with a flawless American accent.

"OK, Lieutenant, since you speak our lingo I'll lay it out. You are a prisoner of war and I must have your unconditional surrender. The war is over. Ya got that? The Emperor wants you and your boys to lay down their weapons and come home."

The Japanese officer sat down and began brushing the sand from his face, unimpressed by the politics involved. "I'm not surprised, we have nothing left. All I've seen is American flags sailing by for weeks."

'Well tell your men to shut up and we'll turn 'em loose.

The officer looked up and turned to his men, issuing terse orders in Japanese. When released, the small men bowed from the waist, their token of absolute subjugation. They were never trained in surrender, only following orders, and they accepted their new master's with full compliance.

"Now, Lieutenant you can tell me what the hell you were doin' up there and how many men ya got left."

The man was both willing and anxious to tell his story. They were an isolated quartermaster depot waiting to supply a counter-invasion force with arms, food, and ammunition. They didn't know the plan was thwarted when their fleet sunk and they lost all communication. Of an original contingent of thirty four, only nine survived the malnutrition, sickness, and strafing by American aircraft. A half bag of rice was the last of their food supply, rationed out at a half cup per day.

In command was their Captain, a die-hard samurai bent on leading his men on a final suicidal Banzai attack when the rations were gone. Early in the war in the Burma campaign he contracted malaria and was forced to accept limited duty. Beset by fever and lack of medication he died the previous morning.

Bowman was quick to acknowledge the fact. "We met the gentleman. He dropped in on us tonight, right Ike?"

"Yeah, that's right. He was all dressed up with no place to go."

The Lieutenant searched his heart to find respect for the dead but it wasn't there. "I never did like the bastard, He was going to get us all killed for nothing." Carter remained silent while he watched the mannerisms of the Japanese soldier. There was something about the way he bowed his head and raised his face to make a point. Then there was the affectation of pointing his finger like a gunslinger holding a six-shooter. His voice was still hoarse from their tussle in the sand. The whole rounded image nagged at Jake's insides. He strove to fight off the darkness but clouds moved in overhead. He interrupted the man's story.

"Did I hear you say you were born in the States? Whereabouts?"

"Southern California, why?"

Carter reeled to his left and extended his hand. "Moe, do ya still have that skinny flashlight ya always carry?"

"Yeah, the batteries are kinda low but it still works."

"Well let me borrow it anyway."

Carter leaned close, shining the light directly in the face of the sitting man. The full beard and unkempt appearance could no longer disguise the man's identity. Jake stood straight and raised his hands above his head to accent his amazement. "Oh my God, it's Roy. . . .you're ROY. . . . Roy Sugimoto."

"How do you know that? I didn't tell you my name." The Japanese rose to his feet.

Carter shone the light in his own face. "It's me, Jake. Jake Carter. Hey man, we went to high school together."

The Lieutenant took a moment to gather his confused thoughts. "This is impossible. I can't believe it. No, it's better than that, it's ridiculous." With both hands they clasped each other in a pumping handshake and danced with glee on the unsteady footing of the stream bed. They were the stars of the show, leaving their supporting cast with nothing to do but gape in awe.

The other prisoners were specially stunned by their commissioned officer's loss of dignity, a sight never seen before in their army. Carter's men accepted the coincidence as another quirk in the insanity of war. In a global struggle with five continents involved, millions of displaced persons roamed the map in search of something. The law of probabilities was overcome by the intense weight of numbers, making miracles commonplace and the impossible a matter of time. War brought them a new vocabulary and they knew it.

The exhausted young men sat together, both mentally drained. Jake draped an arm around his buddy's shoulder. "Roy, would you mind tellin' me somethin'? How in the hell did you get into that Japanese uniform?"

"I was drafted."

"Aw, come on Roy, you're an American Citizen. They can't do that."

"Well they can and they did. You remember that last time I saw you in the summer of '41?"

Jake removed his cap and scratched the side of head. "Sure, I remember now, your grandfather in Japan was dying and your dad sent you over to represent the family at his funeral."

"That's right, when I got there the place was crawling with Niseis. Then the damn fools bombed Hawaii and grabbed us all."

"Just like that?"

Sugimoto was indignant. "You can bet your ass they did. Then they made me an interpreter at the British prisoner of war camp. The guys they captured in Hong Kong."

"How the hell did you wind up in quartermaster?"

"This is a good one, typical Nippon logic. When they found out I used to manage the family farm I was transferred to quartermaster and they made me a lieutenant. Can you believe that? Me, a lieutenant in the Japanese Army?"

Carter found a measure of humor in his question. "That is funny. You and I agreed that if a war broke out we'd join the Marines together. That was four years ago."

The lieutenant, overcome by remorse, dropped his face to his hands. "Man, four years down the drain. You know, those clowns told us we were winning, but I knew it was a bunch of horse manure. The sky was full of American planes. They bombed the hell out of us. The whole country is burned to the ground."

The Last Souvenir

"Well you're safe now Roy, the only thing left is figuring a way to get home." Jake decided to make introductions. "These are my two buddies, Johnny Bowman and Moe Chernikov. We've been together all the way. They're New Yorkers. It's too dark to see his red hair, but this is Sean O'Malley from Texas. This guy is Ike Levine from Brooklyn, and over there is Jesse Hightree, a full blooded Sioux Indian from the Dakotas."

Sugimoto stood up and shook every hand. "It's sure nice to meet you all and I really mean it. It sounds like the boys came from all forty-eight states to join up. The General Staff must have been crazy to think they could lick America."

"Lieutenant, ya better tell your men to stand at ease. They look like they're gonna bust a gut."

There was no doubt about the extreme discipline of these fine troops, awaiting their next command. The veterans saw them as symbols of a formidable adversary and showed the respect due to fellow soldiers. When an armistice finally comes it brings a mingling of victors and vanquished, an odd ritual of forgive and forget.

The towering six-foot-five-inch Chernikov made the first move, facing the Japanese. "What's this guy's name? I don't know whether to shake his hand or put him in my pocket."

"This is Kimi, he's our medic. He wants to be a doctor. I've been teaching him English so he can read American medical books."

"Well I'll be damned." Moe offered his hand. "Hiya doc."

The tiny man bowed first and broke into an infectious grin. He knew the Anglo custom of shaking hands and obliged. "Yes, speak English good. Maybe now go home. Be doctor."

Sugimoto beckoned O'Malley to join him and they stood opposite a larger man. "This guy with the muscles is Sergeant Ohashi. It may interest you to know that tonight you clobbered the judo champ of the 32nd Sendais."

"I did?" O'Malley registered his surprise. "Tell him it was a lucky punch and ask him if he'll give me some lessons."

The Lieutenant gave a brief translation and the champion bowed deeply. "He says you hit very hard and he would like a rematch."

Bowman took an interest in the third man. "What's this guy's name? He looks mighty skinny. Tell him there's plenty of chow where he's goin'."

"This is Private Nishigawa, a rice farmer from Kyushu. He's our cook. That'll be good news to him."

It was time for Carter to take charge. "OK boys, let's break it up. Roy, have your men fill up their buckets and head back up the mountain. Tell your sergeant to spread the word and tell 'em we'll be back tomorrow. It's too dark for a roundup tonight."

"What about me? I should go with my men."

"Oh no you don't, you're my prisoner. You're comin' back with me and meet my lieutenant."

"I guess it wouldn't do any good to pull my rank on you since we're in the wrong armies." Sugimoto issued explicit orders to his men and they obeyed without question. The Marines watched the haggard Japanese struggle away with heavy burdens, wending their way along the dimly lit path.

Back on the beach a nervous Lieutenant Chandler knelt on top of a commanding sand dune above the CP, switching a flare grenade from one hand to the other. Eddie Gallo, a radioman turned rifleman with his weapon at ready, lay by his side. Above and to the right Kovak and Wisnewski positioned themselves on a high vantage point while Labeau waited in the rear, his medical bag by his side.

"Dammit, they're way overdue, can you hear anything yet?".

"Don't worry about Jake, Lieutenant, there ain't been no shootin'. That's good news."

"Sure, but if they got jumped and had their throats cut we wouldn't hear anything either."

"Naw, sir, ya got the jumps. Now ya got me worried."

The dank night air and an encroaching cloudbank added to their curtain of gloom. In the far distance a night bird called to its mate in an off-key falsetto voice with no answer. Even the breeze had lifted, leaving the dark ocean with a tomb-like atmosphere.

"I hate night patrols. They take too long and ya can't see anything."

"Wait a minute Lieutenant, I think I hear somethin'."

"Yeah, me too, can you make it out."

"Yes sir, it sounds like singin'."

"Singing? Has Carter lost his mind? He'll wake up every Jap within five miles."

"Yes sir, they're gettin' closer. It sounds like 'California here I come'."

Chandler's nerves were almost shot. "Be careful you men up there, it may be a Jap trick. No firing unless I give the order." He loosened the pin on his flare grenade and prepared to throw. When his patrol became visible he sat back on the sand like a pole-axed steer, subdued by a breath-stealing sigh of relief.

It was an opportune moment when moonlight broke through the scattered clouds and lit the beach in both directions. The men approached in a tight group with the cool indifference of strolling through a peaceful plaza at midnight. The exuberant O'Malley was the first to speak. "Hey Lieutenant! Jake's got himself a Jap officer. He even knows the guy."

Chandler rose to his feet and wobbled unsteadily down the sandbank with his eyes fixed on the stranger standing with Carter. The sight of a docile enemy soldier grinning at him only aggravated his tortured neural condition. "Well I'll be hornswoggled."

Jake pulled Roy forward for his momentous introduction. "Sir, may I present Lieutenant Roy Sugimoto of the Imperial Quartermaster Corps. Roy, this is Lieutenant Jimmy Chandler from Pennsylvania."

Being an American, Sugimoto ignored the Japanese tradition of bowing and held out his hand. "Nice to meet you Jimmy. I was in Philly once when I was a kid. Have you ever been there?"

"Well... Uh... Yeah, sure... It's my home town."

"No kidding, I'm from LA myself."

"Lieutenant, I have a helluva story to tell ya," Jake cut in. "But first I want to build the biggest bonfire in history."

"A bonfire? Jake, under the circumstances that might be unwise."

"Don't worry sir, Roy told his men to hit the sack. They're up on the Biscuit right now, sleepin' like babies. We'll go get 'em in the morning."

Consternation was slowly leaving Chandler. "I guess that's that. I sure could use a drink about now."

A timely appearance by Frenchie Labeau carrying a straw covered jug solved the problem. "Try a shot of this native hooch, sir. It's brandy made from sweet potatoes. Be careful, it has a helluva kick. I prescribe it in limited doses." He handed the bottle away and noticed Sean's bandage. "O'Malley, ya better let me take a look at that leg. Let's go up to my dispensary."

"Aw come on Doc, ya pass out the booze and then ya ask me to leave."

The fatherly Chernikov moved to his side and issued a warning. "Let's go Sean. I'll come with ya. Either we walk together or I sling ya over my shoulder."

Bowman's mind was on arson. The wonderful idea of a giant fire compelled him to organize. "OK boys, spread out and start pickin' up driftwood. We're gonna give this beach a real hotfoot."

The gurgling in Sugimoto's stomach culminated from months of existing on meager rations. In addition, he found an instant link of friendship with the affable Chandler. "Jimmy, I know it's not polite for a guest to ask this of his host, but I'm starved. Do you have any grub to spare?"

The humanitarian in Chandler surfaced in a flash. "You betcha. How would you like to try our new issue of spaghetti and meatballs?"

"Spaghetti and meatballs! It sounds like heaven to me. Haven't had any American food in four years."

"Sure, join me in my shack, we'll scrounge up something. I have a little stove with hot coffee too."

"You have real American coffee? I've been drinking tea so long I never want to see another cup of the damned stuff."

Neither of the men knew at the time that a lifetime of comradeship was in its embryonic state. Years would come and go but distance could never completely separate them again.

Jack Carroll

CHAPTER THIRTY-THREE

Roy Sugimoto was more than a prisoner of war, he was also a victim. Every soldier, no matter the color of his uniform, has a personal dream of his homecoming. Perhaps it's a front porch crowded with waving family members or even a platform in a familiar train station. The wonderful embracing from his parents, wife, sister or sweetheart would renew the affection taken away so long ago. In Sugimoto's case the prodigal son would return home to nothing.

The declaration of war with Japan brought the paranoid threat of espionage to an entire nation. Patriotic citizens were imprisoned for no other reason than a surname or the shape of their eyes. Roy's family was no exception, scattered by whim to isolated internment camps with little hope for the future. By Federal proclamation their land was confiscated. As delicately as possible, he must be told.

In spite of the late hour Johnny Bowman kept his promise. The firebug lit two fires, one a blazing pyre of logs and a smaller collection of sticks for heating a late supper. The licking flames painted faces and beach sand with a pale orange tint. The delightful smell of wood smoke excited taste buds and delivered memories of a fireplace or campfire from the past. Simmering cans of spaghetti and stew added to the mixture of aromas, and the brandy jug found many sharing lips.

Roy sat between Chandler and Carter, working on a second helping and washing it down with cautious gulps of coffee. The lower part of his chin whiskers dripped with juices, his hunger driving away all intentions of good table manners. Jake stared into the fire, relating the details of Roy's capture and the

The Last Souvenir

unlikely coincidence of their lives together as schoolboys.

Chandler was a sports buff. "So you two were on the track team together? What events?"

'We ran the hundred yard dash and the two-twenty. I could always beat Jake in the short race, but he passed me in the longer ones."

"Come on Roy, why be modest?" Jake leaned forward to look around him. "We finished one-two in the All City finals, remember? We thought we were real hotshots that day."

"Yeah, we were just kids then. I won the hundred and you won the two-twenty. It was the first time we got our pictures in the newspapers."

Roy dropped his empty mess gear and stretched his arms in an effort to make room for the feast he consumed. "Jimmy, you're a terrific host. I feel great, but I'm worried about my men."

"I would be too, Lieutenant, but don't give it another thought. We have a whole truckload of chow just waiting for your boys."

"I guess they can wait a few more hours." Roy turned and placed his hand on Jake's shoulder. "By the way, did you know that Jake used to have the hots for my kid sister?"

"No, he said something once about a Nisei girl but I didn't know she was your sister." Chandler's eyes widened.

"Oh yeah, and I told him I'd kick his ass if he tried any hanky panky. Right Jake?"

"I remember alright, you used to get pissed off when we parked by the beanfields in my old Model A Ford."

"Well Jake, don't keep me in suspense, what do you hear from Tokiko. Has she been writing?"

Uneasiness crept over Carter, forcing him to hesitate. "I got one letter from her right after Pearl Harbor and that was it."

"What do you mean, it cooled off? Did she meet somebody else?"

Sensing the undertones, Sugimoto pressed for hard answers. "Come on Jake, we've been friends too long to play games. Spell it out."

Carter experienced a sinking feeling in the pit of his stomach, caught between compassion and the truth. The sins of war were brutal and could only be faced head on. Only perchance the pain would be eased if it came from the mouth of a friend. "I'm sorry Roy, but your farm is gone and your family was taken away. We lost track."

"Gone! What do you mean gone? How can that be? I can't believe that!"

Broaching the subject was one thing, but explaining was another matter. Telling your friend to forget his dreams and all was lost required the ultimate in diplomacy. On the other hand, to bandy words would only prolong the agony. Sugimoto's expression was one of dread and foreboding, like a man about to be sentenced for a crime he didn't commit.

At first Chandler remained silent, but he sensed Carter's loss for words and chose to intervene. To him it was a national shame, but not all shared his opinion. Slowly and deliberately he explained from the beginning of a country divided and the ensuing ramifications. When he paused it was clear the future held no resolution.

"Why, Jimmy, why? Jake, you remember my dad, he was a real patriot. Every holiday he used to stick the America flag on our veranda."

"Sure, I remember, he used to lecture me on voting and how great it was to elect your own President."

Roy had more questions as he gazed into the darkness across the sea. "Hell Jake, my mom and dad aren't spies, and neither are Tokiko and my uncles. Where are they now?"

"Like I said, I lost track. They got split up and sent to internment camps. That's the last I heard."

The Last Souvenir

"You mean like criminals? Stuck in prison four years?"

"I wish I could put it another way Roy, but I can't."

"Is there any brandy left in that jug?" The initial dismay was replaced by seeds of determination and Sugimoto decided to take the reins and deal with the circumstances. "What happened to our land? We built that farm with our bare hands. I lived there my whole life."

Not knowing the answer, Chandler could only respond with a summation. "The Japanese Americans were told to sell quick or abandon their assets. Just take what they could carry."

"That brings up another question. Did they round up the Germans too?"

"No, only a few."

"Jimmy, this is bullshit, you know that don't you? Where do I go from here? What am I supposed to do?"

The fact that the questions were turning positive gave Jake the encouragement he needed. "You know me buddy, I'll think of something."

"Me too," Chandler agreed. "They'll probably send you to a POW camp in Japan for processing. After that I have friends in Washington, maybe I can pull a few strings. I'll give you my address at home."

Roy lapsed back into discouragement. "That could take months, maybe even years. You know the government and its red tape."

The campfire clique dissipated leaving the three men alone in a mute state. The channels of their thoughts were equal, each believing that even the greatest of questions had a simple solution. With a single exception, Sugimoto was pessimistic, a feeling for which he had every right. In his semi-catatonic condition he feared he was having delusions.

"Am I seeing things or is that a woman coming this way?"

It was Wana, trotting along the shore with her skirts held

high above her knees. In her restless sleep a nightmare had awakened her and she bolted upright. Quickly, she donned a black kimono and sped away, hoping to find her man safe and allay her fears. The sight of a dwindling fire increased her heartbeat. When her eyes found Jake sitting unscathed she knelt by his side and caressed him affectionately, placing her face on his shoulder.

Sugimoto revealed his first broad grin of the night. "Well Jake, I see you've been busy. Wait till I tell Tokiko this story."

The mention of a feminine name stung Wana like a bee. She loosened her grip and straightened her body. "Who Tokiko? What he mean? You have Tokiko?"

The dour mood changed leaving Carter with new problems. "Roy, you just stuck your big foot in it." He spoke softly to the anxious girl. "No sweetheart, she is someone I knew a long time ago. She's gone now."

Before Wana could react she noticed the uniform of a Japanese officer and jumped to her feet, trembling with fear and respect. The men rose to face her as she backed away. Jake began the introductions. With her palms turned inward along the sides of her thighs, Wana bowed from the waist and spoke in Japanese. Her manner and speech contained the elegance of a seasoned courtier.

"I am most humbled to be in the presence of such an honorable personage."

To honor the oriental tradition Sugimoto returned her bow. "I am happy to make your acquaintance, but please, I am no longer in the army of Nippon. Consider me Jake's friend and we can speak English from now on."

Decades of subjugation by the Japanese Empire left Wana filled with apprehensions. Harsh discipline and rigid respect had left a mark on her gentle ways. However, this man was different, with the accent and attitude of an American masquerading as a Nipponese officer. Just in case, with defer-

… ence to her confusion, she returned to Jake's side, seeking the comfort of his protection. The plot needed more unraveling before she was convinced.

To Roy, Wana was an omen. For years his life had been devoid of affection and the wonders that feminine companionship can provide. Memories of his past came back. Even though the future was vague, it was now within reach. The envy he felt for his friend was a natural impulse and he voiced a frank opinion. "That's quite a lady you have there, Jake. She talks like a queen and looks like an angel. How come you always have all the luck?"

"Wish I knew. It just happened." Carter could sense the strain fading, replaced by congeniality. "She has a sister too, but I haven't met her yet."

That was Wana's cue. "Yes, have sister. Her name Koko. She cut hair for Hagachi. You rike haircut?"

Roy was impressed by the simplicity of her speech. "All this and a haircut too. You bet I would. I think I've stumbled into the Garden of Eden."

"That's exactly what you've done, Roy." Jake put his arm around Wana's waist. She listened intently while he told her about the plight of Sugimoto's men still occupying the Biscuit. As a favor he asked she and her friends would prepare a Japanese lunch for the hungry survivors.

The kindhearted young woman almost danced her assent. "Oh! We cook fish soup, have sushi, everything." Her day was complete. She turned her face upward and looked into Jake's eyes. "Wana happy now. We go to bed Jaki?"

There was no way Carter could resist the uncomplicated suggestion. "Well gentlemen, I guess that means good night. Lieutenant, you put Roy up at your place?"

"Took the words out of my mouth, Sergeant." Chandler was delighted to share the company of his new friend. "How about it Roy? I have an extra straw mat and blanket."

"Lead the way, Jimmy." He watched Jake and Wana disappear in the shadows. "You know, I've known that guy since we were kids. We used to run through our bean fields together, making my father mad when we trampled his crop."

"I know what you mean, he's a helluva man. Come on, let's hit the sack, we've got work to do tomorrow."

CHAPTER THIRTY-FOUR

Malnutrition and dysentery can best be described adequately by those who are afflicted, and this was the case for Sugimoto's men. National pride and patriotism can be stretched to the limit, but ultimately the basic needs of the flesh will prevail. Hunger is a grim reaper, capable of striking down the mightiest of armies, and even the loyal Japanese soldier can lose his effectiveness and will to fight. One way or another death was tugging at their sleeves.

They were advised by their Captain, when he was alive, that a glorious charge would end it all and they would be deified. But they were not of the Samurai class, only simple farmers and factory workers conscripted to rally around what was now a lost cause. Lieutenant Sugimoto had issued the final official command and it tasted sweet. The human instinct of self preservation is the highest emotion and it began to sweep through their ranks. They would be assigned to new masters but it had no consequences, and their need for a higher authority would remain uninterrupted. In simple terms they would live long lives and not lose face.

Sergeant Ohashi, in temporary command as a non-commissioned officer, knew his job and did it well. His unit rose at sunrise and assembled field equipment, readying themselves in full marching order to leave at a moment's notice. They felt no disgrace or disillusionment, only the gnawing in their stomachs. Knowing that hot food and fresh water awaited actually lifted their spirits a notch.

On the beach below and to the south, the two lieutenants were the first to rise in the early light of dawn. In spite of the limited sleep they were restless and drawn to their duties. Chandler insisted on providing a meal of canned scrambled eggs and hot coffee like a father sending his children off to school. The reluctant Sugimoto was guilt-ridden and anxious to collect his men but he was given no choice.

The industrious Wana was long gone on her way to organize the women of the village and the feast to follow. Carter sat naked in the lagoon with a cake of soap in his hand, trying in vain to create suds in the salt water. Prior to his dip he dispatched Bowman and Chernikov to rouse the hard sleeping Marines and they were greeted with the usual profanities.

In the next half hour the scouts dragged themselves to the CP, joined by Kovak and Frenchie Labeau. Hot coffee and youthful stamina brought them back to the semblance of a military unit. Chandler had his way and the men were fed but Sugimoto could not control his skittishness. The Americans would soon learn the dire condition of his men.

"Lieutenant Sugimoto will lead and I'll be with him." Chandler buckled his pistol belt and gave it a hitch. "Sergeant Carter, follow me, Chernikov and Bowman will bring up the rear. We'll move out in single file."

They crossed the creek bed, remembering last night's scuffle. Open ground and the Biscuit looming dead ahead made the veterans leery, remembering Japanese trickery from the past. If hell broke loose they would seek the scant cover available. For them old habits were difficult to reform, and yet they accepted their new world of trust and peace. Puffing his way to the crest, the overweight Chandler was relieved to see an end to the steep path.

The mesa divulged the magnificence of a dwarf pine forest where low hanging branches spread like umbrellas over mossy green soil. White coral outcroppings reared their heads intermittently, rendering monuments to the creativity of nature. An absence of man-made structures made aerial detection impossible. The Japanese, in their typical fashion, lived underground.

Sugimoto's men stood stiffly at attention in a perfect line with Sergeant Ohashi four paces in front. He raised his hand in salute and held it. Their pomp and carriage was a marvelous sight to behold, befitting the finest of royal guards, yet the haggard expressions in their eyes told the pathetic truth. Frenchie Labeau ignored all protocol and strolled down their line, his experienced eyes searching for impending medical problems.

"Lieutenant, ya better let me look these guys over, and the sooner the better."

Roy ordered his men to stand at ease and Ohashi dropped his salute. The miniscule Kimi spied the red cross on the corpsman's bag and stepped forward.

"I medico too. Speak English. I rike work with you. "

Labeau was startled by the little man's abruptness. "Who is this guy, Lieutenant, and how old is he anyway?"

"His name is Kimi." Roy was about to relax many of his military formalities. "He's our medic, and believe it or not he's probably older than you are."

"OK Kimi, you can pitch in. Just call me Doc, that should be easy."

"How do Doc. I rike see you bag, can do?"

"Sure, take a good look." Frenchie watched him rummage through the contents, trying desperately to read labels. A large bottle caught his attention and he removed it from the bag.

"What this Doc?"

"That's sulfa powder. Can you say sulfa powder?"

Kimi gave it a stab. "Surfa porder."

Frenchie laughed in admiration at his tenacity. "You'll do fine Kimi, just fine. We'll work together."

O'Malley approached Ohashi and offered to shake hands. Instead, the Japanese sergeant reached across to feel the muscle in Sean's arm, after which he motioned for Sean to touch his biceps.

"Gawd almighty, this guy's built like a brick shithouse."

"You're lucky he didn't tear your head off." Roy said it and meant it.

"Hey Ike, come over here, I wanna show ya somethin'." Bowman and Levine stood together on the edge of the cliff, gazing down on the land they had traversed the night before. "They were here and we were there. It makes ya feel kinda funny when ya look at it the next day."

"My God, they cudda plugged us easy."

"When we get back to the village ya better find a shovel, then come back and bury that poor guy down there." Bowman made it sound more like a suggestion than an order. "You can grab that samurai sword. He won't need it where he's goin'. You'll have a first class souvenir."

"Oh boy, thanks Sarge, I'll take it home with me. I can't wait for my Pop to see it." Levine had a new idea. "Maybe I can get one of the Japanese to help me with a marker."

An open excavation drew Carter's interest. A moss-covered hatch was open, normally closed to seal the entrance of a square shaft leading downward. Two wide wooden ladders provided access and egress. "Roy, as long as we're here I'd like you to take me down and show me the layout. Ya better tell your men to sit in the shade."

At first Sugimoto hesitated, but he soon realized the Marines had every right to request a full inspection. "Sure Jake, you're going to be surprised, it's quite a setup. It was built for us by the 32nd Engineers."

They scaled down the rungs together and landed in the main corridor that traveled in a North-South direction. A tomb-like darkness was defeated by lighting, provided by a series of oil lamps sitting in carved niches along the walls. Laterally spaced hallways led to the amenities of a barracks, kitchen and laundry facilities, and the beds of a small infirmary. On the south end a huge cavern contained the officers quarters which doubled for an office and radio room.

Roy led the stunned Marine sergeant through the labyrinth, patiently explaining its construction and the aspects of everyday living. Carter was speechless. His eyes were becoming adjusted to the dim light and he could only acknowledge the marvels by nodding his head. In his combat days many such honeycomb complexes were captured and quickly sealed forever by demolition teams. In this way the threat of booby-traps and bypassed enemy soldiers was eliminated. Today, for the first time, he was able to see first hand why these subterranean bulwarks withstood the pounding of air attacks and naval gunfire. A cold shiver travelled down his spine and he thanked God the thing had ended.

"Well, Jake here we are. The reason we got stuck here." A rectangular wooden door blocked the northern end of the passageway. Sugimoto translated the oriental characters painted boldly across its face: 'STORAGE ROOM, AUTHORIZED PERSONNEL ONLY.'

The door swung inward and they entered the cave, by far the largest room in the network. White pine wood cases were stacked from floor to ceiling, each identified by Japanese writing. Regardless of the fact that he could not read the characters, Carter recognized the boxes by their sizes and shapes. A final confirmation would clear up whatever mystery remained.

"What is all this stuff, Roy?"

"All that's left is field equipment, mostly small arms and ammunition. We ate all the rations."

The waves in Jake's brain made his scalp tingle. He stroked his chin, lightly at first, accelerating into vigorous rubbing mode.

"Uh oh, you used to rub your chin like that when we were kids. Every time you did it, we got into some kind of mischief."

"Let me think, pal, let me think. Do you have an inventory list around here?"

"Yeah, sure, it's in the office, why?"

One by one Sugimoto turned off the lamps and they climbed upward into the bright sunlight. Bowman waited expectantly by the opening above ground. "Whatcha got, Jake?" Seeing the light in Carter's eyes.

Jake shielded his eyes from the sun and handed him the list. "Here, take a look at this."

"I can't make it out, it's all in Japanese."

'Never mind that, Ray's gonna translate it. It's the key to a gold mine."

'No shit, ya mean souvenirs."

"That's right Johnny boy, by the bushel." Carter made one last request. "Roy, ya better send a couple of your guys to collect extra blankets. O'Malley, you and Levine go with 'em." His master plan was already taking shape in his mind.

He watched the men descend one by one, and in the minutes that followed his thoughts began to crystallize. A cache of this size was a bonanza with mind-boggling possibilities. The average soldier would walk away and leave the problem for his officers to solve, but Carter was far above the average. When Sugimoto had been told of his misfortune the dejected look in his eyes had cut Jake to the core. Now the new pieces began to fall in place. Cash was the answer, on a scale never before attempted. It could be Roy's ticket home.

"We got your blankets Sarge, do ya want me to close the hatch?"

"Yeah, sure, thanks O'Malley." Jake snapped out of his soliloquy. "Get your men ready to move out, Roy. O.K. Lieutenant, we can shove off now."

Lieutenant Chandler took the lead of his strange detachment and began their descent. The proud Japanese refused to betray their weak physical state, squaring their packs and marching like the soldiers they were. To a man they glanced back to bid a dismal farewell to their incarceration. The prison that held them so long had no gates or guards, but just the same the walls were there. The claustrophobic existence of the past gave way to a wide blue sky and the open fields ahead, and they could smile again. Once more the war brought an abnormal convolution and they viewed the Americans as liberators, not a conquering enemy.

Wana was waiting expectantly on the beach in front of the command post. With her was her sister, making a first appearance. When the men approached they had mixed feelings about the different uniforms, but they knew that something new and wonderful was happening, and regardless of old fears they wanted to be part of it.

"Roy, you can have your men bivouac above us. There's a grassy spot up there." Chandler was apologetic when he added; "I'm sorry, we don't have any tents for them."

Sugimoto grinned back. "Don't worry Jimmy, they've been living in caves so long they would rather have the sky."

O'Malley, Levine, Kovak, and Labeau had volunteered to carry the extra blankets, which they quickly deposited in the short grass. The Japanese soldiers bowed as they passed to show their appreciation.

"Hey Kovak, tell these guys they don't have to bow anymore. Tell 'em in America we don't bow to nobody."

"I can't tell 'em that you numbskull. It's their tradition, like we shake hands."

Sugimoto was so mindful of his men he did not notice

Wana move to his side, holding her sister's hand. She spoke in her native language. "Honorable Lieutenant, may I presume to present to you my humble sister? She is called Koko."

The sound of a feminine voice was still foreign to Roy after months of solitude and he looked startled. Koko was wearing a white kimono with a red sash around the smallest waist he had ever seen. The features of the two sisters were like carbon copies, both with round faces and long raven hair. Roy's tastes leaned heavily toward oriental women, making Koko the impossible dream. He was known for his glibness and a natural command of any situation, yet this time the silence was proof that cupid's arrow had zinged him hard.

His buddy Jake watched with a quizzical expression. "Come on Roy, you're supposed to say something. I've never seen you lost for words before."

Sugimoto recovered and stammered his way through a formal introduction. In the past he was judged to be a man among men, but mostly this was just a cover for his basic shyness. Now Dame Fortune smiled on him in that Koko, like her sister, was self-confident and aggressively willing to cross the boundaries of timidity. In his traumatized state he could not believe she was interested in him. She, on the other hand, wanted to get her hands on his beard first and remove it, followed by a stylish haircut.

Koko made her move and stepped forward, holding up the bag she was carrying. "Roy sir, may I offer you my services? I am the barber of Hagachi."

Before Roy could respond Carter interrupted, urged by an insistent Wana. "After lunch pal, take a look down the beach. The women are wavin' like mad. Tell your men soup's on."

A light breeze blew from the South, wafting scents of woodsmoke and simmering pots. Outwardly, Sugimoto's men waited politely and mute, but the salivation in their mouths was tormenting them. They were rid of their packs and cartridge belts and could sense their time to eat had come. When the order came they followed their Lieutenant along the beach, knowing the suspense was over.

Wana sprinted ahead while Carter hung back, collaring Chandler in a private conversation. "Lieutenant, when you report to the colonel, would you do me a favor and stall him about all this?"

"Stall him, what for?"

"Well sir, there's a lot of money on that hill and it's gonna take me a few days to set up my plan."

"Not a chance Jake!" Chandler disagreed vehemently. "We're Marines not merchants. If the Colonel orders us back, we're going."

"But sir, the money is for Roy, not me. He's lost everything and when he gets back to the States, he's gonna need all the cash he can lay his hands on to buy back his land."

"So that's your scheme, what kind of money are we talking about?"

"Thousands, sir."

"Thousands!" The lieutenant stopped dead in his tracks. "My God, Jake, this is more than just one of your little peccadilloes. You're asking me to condone one of the biggest scams of the century."

"But sir, look at it this way. Not only did Roy get screwed by Japan, but his own country as well. He has nothing to go back to."

"Damn you Carter, you make everything sound so logical and easy. I don't know what to say."

"Sir, when ya talk to Mason tell him we ran into a snag. Tell him we need a few more days. Tell him anything, you'll think of something."

"Jake, you told me once that when those rear area guys take over contraband they sell it and pocket the money. Now, just the thought of it pisses me off. If anybody ever needed a helping hand it's Roy Sugimoto. How much time will you need?"

"A week would be great sir."

"Jake, every time I get involved with you I seem to be putting my silver bars on the line. What the hell, we're all going home anyway, but I still want to think it over."

"That's good enough for me Lieutenant, let's go to chow."

On this landmark day the ladies of Hagachi outdid themselves in providing a bountiful menu for their honored guests. Ichiban had declared a holiday to celebrate the peace and harmony the American Marines had brought to his village. The old magistrate assumed the role of an official greeter, circulating with a complete disregard for bygone days. Freedom had returned to his hamlet at last, accounting for the frivolity in the air. The northern land was safe once more for farming and children at play.

Straw mats were placed end to end on the beach in a makeshift seating arrangement. Sugimoto sat cross-legged at the head of his men while the Marines stood to one side, opting to spectate the orgy of indulgence. The gracious women had placed a colorful array of steaming bowls before them. A selection of soups, fish, vegetables, and sauces supplied many temptations. As was their custom, the soup came first, bringing a symphony of loud slurping. Flashing chopsticks were next, adroitly pinching strings of bean sprouts and sushi from bowls held close to their chins. On and on they went in a marathon of stuffing to satisfy their bottomless pits. The wonderful doting women hovered above, furnishing refills to empty bowls. Roy was constantly showing his gratitude, thanking them profusely.

The Marines aligned themselves beside the smoking grill, cafeteria style, many carrying GI mess gear and forks. With choices made, they sat together on the sandbank with high expectations.

"Geez, this stuff tastes pretty good, especially when ya dip it in the sauce. Wonder what it is."

Kovak spoke through a mouthful of cabbage. "That's raw fish you're eating, Mac."

"Raw fish? No kidding, it tastes good. I'm gonna write my Mom about this. She won't believe it."

Frenchie Labeau had a particular interest in Kimi, the smallest of the lot. His gargantuan appetite did not fit his size and he was the last to finish. When he looked up and smiled, Labeau could sense he was almost ready for the impending workload in the dispensary.

Legs were wobbly at first when the Japanese stood up, supporting the heavy onus of over-full stomachs. They burped and bowed simultaneously, giving thanks to their hostess, unaware that the meal was only the end of phase one. Koko slipped her hand around Sugimoto's elbow and whispered in his ear. Startled at first, Roy nodded and passed the word along.

"Men, the ladies have prepared a bath for us. Our uniforms are to be laundered and temporary civilian clothing provided. Follow me."

Koko led the men upstream to a freshwater pond especially widened for community bathing. Piles of resurrected men's kimonos were stacked neatly on the bank with rows of wooden sandals available. Bath towels and large fiber sponges completed the facility. The water was barely tepid, heated only by the sun, but the townspeople were fully aware of the Spartan life on the Biscuit. The heavenly sight lured the Japanese to their next pleasure and the disrobing began. To the surprise of none, Koko removed her kimono and sash to follow Roy, intent on scrubbing his back. Soon there were more girls to round out the pairings. This was their milieu and it was a common courtesy.

For the next half-hour the slow moving water flowed past their bodies and washed out to sea. The filthy uniforms disappeared and the sounds of rinsing came from above. The pleasures of a clean skin and full belly were written clearly on the faces of the Japanese soldiers, accentuated by the promise of fresh clothing.

Roy was the first to exit and dry himself. After slipping into a light gray kimono Koko led him back to the beach and plunked him down by the fire. Her gentle persistence was making his heart beat faster as he watched her withdraw a bucket of lukewarm water from the grill. Deftly she trimmed his beard and lathered his face. The scratching noise of a long straight razor in her experienced hand made him flinch, but she tamed him with reassurance.

Carter arrived in time to see Koko put the finishing touches to his haircut. The old Roy was back from the past. "My God, Roy, you look human again."

The lady barber backed away to admire her masterpiece. "Yes, he is quite handsome." From there she bent over and placed her face close to his. "I would rather say very handsome."

Jake did not understand the Japanese but he got the gist. "Uh oh buddy, it looks like you've got yourself a girl-friend."

The Last Souvenir

CHAPTER THIRTY-FIVE

The burden of decision was on Chandler once more. In falsifying a report to Colonel Mason the day before at Carter's request he had bought a few hours and postponed the final reckoning. Thousands of dollars and Roy Sugimoto's future life hung in the balance, teetering between the legal and moral aspects of a judgment of such magnitude it could not be ignored. The Lieutenant hoped it would dry up and blow away in the wind.

In the past, as a combat officer, he had sent his men into life or death assignments. Many times they were carried back from the battlefield mortally wounded in the wasteful deadly game. In reality, he was only a subaltern, passing along orders from a higher authority. He could rationalize the losses by blaming a loftier source. Today was different. He sat at the top, experiencing the true loneliness of command. In every letter of the law Carter's proposal was wrong, but it was also morally right, leaving Chandler alone with the decision to either squelch or sanction. A negative response would be safe, and yet it could return to haunt him forever. On the other side, an assent could bring all of the perils that law and money entail.

Unaware of Chandler's dilemma, Sugimoto stroked slowly through the clear water of the lagoon with Koko by his side. His shyness was fading, gaining reassurance from her ever-smiling face. The majesty of a new love is rarely a simple affair, yet it flowed through his heart like a river of hope. The futility and despair that had frozen him in the past were thawed by every touch of her fingertips.

The young native girl had long since looked past the uniform he wore and into the human being beyond. She saw him not as a gentleman, but as a gentle man. In her life, the dominating Japanese officers had demonstrated arrogance and superiority in the presence of females, but Roy had none of these attitudes. Instead, he treated her as an equal, or better yet, a goddess. It was the first time her heart had been touched and she could not resist a desire to be with him.

Far out, near to the inner edge of the protective reef, Jake and Wana were engaged in a serious swimming race, with Wana in the lead. Their consummated love had moved them to higher pinnacles of frolic and confidence with each other. The disgruntled athlete was struggling in vain to match the free-kicking young girl. Not only was he losing, he was learning to laugh and breathe between strokes. In knee-deep water Roy and Koko formed a rooting section and cheered for their champions with all the gusto of a stadium crowd.

Strolling on the beach above, a solemn Chandler was attracted by the sounds of merriment and headed their way. His muddled mind had reached a decision, tentative as it was, and it was time for a confab. Standing on dry land by the waterline with hands in pockets, he broke through their laughter and invited them ashore. The sight of young women with naked breasts was unnerving for the puritanical man from the Quaker State. He was not carved in stone, and experienced a tinge of envy for the young men, yet the memory of his wife and daughter shone like a beacon in the darkness of his wartime chastity. The oath he had made at the altar was still valid.

"Jimmy, I have a news flash for you." Roy's statement had happy overtones. "You just lost a roommate."

"How's that?"

"Koko asked me to move into her house with her."

Chandler's overloaded mind was too full for domestic matters. "Well, technically you're still a prisoner of war, but I can waive that. I have something a lot more important. Come on out and sit down. You too Jake."

Koko was quick to comprehend. "Men tark. Wana and I go home, get dress. After then we make food."

"What was that? This is the first time I've heard you speak English. Why didn't you tell me?"

Koko and her sister were already headed homeward when she yelled over her shoulder. "I go same schoor with Wana. Speak good Engrish."

"Well I'll be damned, what do you think about that, Jake? I think we're tied in with a couple of sharp girls."

The unusual trio sat together facing the sea, not knowing their conversation would soon take on epic proportions. Sugimoto had been kept in the dark and had no inkling of what was coming. Carter, on the other hand, resembled a fused bomb awaiting ignition, impatiently waiting for Chandler to make known his decision, warned by his intuition that it would be a green light. Chandler cleared his throat twice.

"Roy, Jake and I've been talking, and we've decided we can send you home with some money. Maybe enough to buy back your family land."

"Money! When? Where? Here? Is this some kinda rib?"

"This is no joke my friend. Jake, you better take over."

Carter willingly took center stage, starting from the beginning. His explanation of the souvenir mania running rampant through the fleet was crisp and informative, leaving very little to the imagination. A wry smile spread across Sugimoto's face when he heard tales of mattresses, steaks, jukeboxes and whisky. The purloined lumber story was the best. The methodical Carter could only spin a perfect web when every strand was in place, and he finished by saying; "Well, Roy, waddya say?"

"Jake, this is incredible. First, you save me and my men

from that lousy mountain, then you introduce me to the most beautiful girl I've ever seen. Now, you're telling me I can go home a rich man. You better pinch me, I think I'm dreaming."

"You're not dreaming, buddy. If my connections are still around, I can do it."

"Back up a second, Jake. How much money are we talking about?"

"Somewhere between forty and fifty grand."

"Fifty thousand dollars! For that kind of money I could buy a whole square mile and two tractors. You wouldn't shit me, would you? You know I've never been gullible."

"My old friend Roy hasn't changed a bit, Lieutenant. I offer him the keys to the mint and he wants to go over the books first."

Chandler was also over his head. "Can't say I blame him, Jake, that's a lot of money. I paid twenty five hundred for my house in Philadelphia, and that was back in forty-one during the housing shortage."

The word '*if*' was not the question, simply '*how*'. They each conceded there were no checking accounts in the fleet or on the island, and a cash transaction would amass a mountain of greenbacks. The three high IQ's battled between conservative and aggressive, or perhaps avarice and caution, and yet the decision was definite.

"That's strange." Carter interrupted and pointed out to sea. "See that landing craft? He went by earlier, now he's circling outside the reef."

"Yeah, I see him, it looks like he's using signal flags. Can you read it?"

"No, but I know somebody who can." Jake shouted loudly up the beach. "Hey, Ski! Get your ass down here on the double. We need ya to read semaphore."

The half-asleep Wisnewski was on duty, seated in the radio jeep when he heard the call. It was the urgency in Carter's yell that caused him to bolt upright and bound out of the jeep on a dead run. "What's up, Sarge? What do ya need me for?"

"Take a look at that swabbie in the boat out there. What's he sayin'?"

Wisnewski advanced to the water's edge and placed his hand to his forehead to shield his eyes. "...CAN...YOU...READ...CAN...YOU...READ..." Without the use of flags he stood at attention and extended both arms in the R for roger. "He's comin' back, Sarge. Wait a minute... IS...CARTER...THERE. Hey, Jake, he's lookin' for you!"

"Well, find out who he is and what he wants."

The radioman held his cap in one hand, a handkerchief in the other, and began wig-wagging the query. "He's comin' back,Sarge. REQUEST.. PERMISSION.. TO.. COME.. ASHORE.. and he signed it, Muldoon."

"Good work, Ski. Tell him, yes. There's an opening in the reef by the river mouth, he can beach there." Jake placed his arm around Roy's neck. "Well, buddy, it looks like providence just dropped in your lap. It's one of the scroungers I told you about. Come on, let's go shake his hand."

A bubbling sound from two big diesel engines echoed across the empty bay, propelling the landing craft through a gap in the coral. Muldoon braced himself high on the forward ramp, signaling port and starboard directions to his coxswain. Even in calm water and a rising tide, the coral heads were fraught with dangers for the shallow draught vessel. The old salt knew his trade well, and the snub-nosed craft crunched to a safe halt in the granular sand.

"Hiya, Jake. I've been lookin' all over for ya." Muldoon vaulted over the gunwale and lit on the beach, lighting the fresh cigar in his mouth. "One of your boys told me ya wuz here, so I decided to take a boat ride and find ya."

"It's good to see you, you old barnacle." Jake meant it when he moved to shake hands with his naval counterpart.

When Muldoon noticed Chandler he turned his head. "Hello, Lieutenant. I'm sorry, I don't salute nuthin' but Admirals. I think it's all those snot-nosed ensigns we got in our Navy that did it."

Chandler learned his military courtesy in front-line service and acknowledged with a smile. "That's OK, Chief, in the Marine Corps, we call them Second Lieutenants."

The old chief's hard-nosed manner was only a partial facade, while his piercing eyes scanned every detail of his new surroundings. "Who's this guy, Jake? He looks like a Jap in a bathrobe."

Carter ignored the slur and introduced his old friend. "You're half right, Chief. This is Lieutenant Roy Sugimoto of the Imperial Japanese Army."

"No shit! Are you really a Nip Officer?"

Roy took no offense. On the contrary, he was happy to be among fellow Americans again. "Not Nip, my blunt friend, I'm a Nisei. I was born in L.A. How do you do."

"Well blow me down. He speaks better lingo than I do." Muldoon clasped his hand.

The two sisters remained quietly by the grill in the background, preparing a meal of boiled rice and vegetables. At the most propitious moment, Wana came forward holding a jug of sweet potato brandy with both hands. "You Jaki friend. You rike drink, is good?"

"What the hell's goin' on here, Jake? Good lookin' broads and booze too." The sailor took the bottle and guzzled at least a half a pint with one swallow. "Man, this stuff kicks like a mule. What'll ya take for the rest of this bottle?"

"She has her eye on your knife, Chief."

"Ya mean my GI K-bar? Ya gotta deal, baby." Muldoon unbuckled his belt, removing the knife and scabbard. "Jake, I gotta a whole box a these back on my ship. What kinda swap can we make?"

The Last Souvenir

Carter shook his head. "You're talkin' about peanuts, Muldoon. That's only a sample. Let's go up there and have a seat. Bring your jug."

With Carter and Muldoon in the center, flanked by Chandler and Sugimoto, the four men sat by the river watching the clear water merge into the brine. The coxswain had switched off the engines and joined the girls by their cutting board. Carter was so happy to see his crusty friend, it sent him into a jocular mood.

"Chief, do you play poker?"

"Of course, I'm a sailor."

"What would you do if I dealt you a pat hand royal flush?"

Muldoon's greed clicked in gear. "I'd probably bet my ass and one ball. Why?"

"In a minute, Chief. But first, what brings you up here?"

Not usually long winded, Muldoon began an oration. "It's kinda sad, Jake. The Navy decided to give all those swabs shore leave a few days ago and they draws out their back pay. Then, a whole mess of 'em goes ashore and heads for the old battlefields, lookin' for souvenirs. Well, three of those damn fools got blown up by booby traps and dud shells, and the Admiral called 'em back and canceled their leave. I'm lucky, I always had a special pass. Then I figured ole Jake was up to somethin', so here I am."

"Muldoon, if I hear you right, those swab jockeys are sittin' aboard their ships on a wad of cash."

"That's it in a nutshell."

Jake nudged Roy with his elbow and turned back to the Chief. "Do you suppose you could unload some brand new .31 caliber Arisaki rifles and bayonets?"

Muldoon's face lit up with all the colors of a Christmas tree. "What are you up to, Carter, you know friggin' well I could."

"How much are they worth right now?"

The old conniver stroked the stubble of his two-day beard and hesitated. "Well, maybe a hundred bucks for the rifles, and twenty-five for the bayonets."

"OK, Chief, that's what I'll take. You can keep everything you make above that, but it's gotta be cash."

"Oh, no ya don't! I can't be runnin' all over that ocean for a few measly rifles."

"That's fair enough, I'll start out with three hundred of each."

Muldoon's eyeballs clicked like three bell signs in the window of a slot machine. "*THREE HUNDRED!* Did you say three hundred?"

"That's right, buddy, COD, with more to come."

"Wait a minute." The chief made hasty calculations with his finger in the sand. "My Gawd, that comes to thirty seven thousand five hundred. That's a lot of moolah."

"You're gettin' the picture, Muldoon, and I know you'll sell 'em for at least a fifty dollar profit each, and that's over fifteen grand. Are we in business?"

"Jake, I've always liked your style. I guess ya know that's over eight years' pay. You're damn right were in business. I gotta set up an organization tonight, but don't worry, I know every chief and radioman in the fleet. By God we're gonna shear some sheep."

Sugimoto was dumbfounded. He was accustomed to higher levels of finance, but this was ludicrous. His memory took him back to a day in his youth when Jake won fifty dollars in a poker game. They both counted it twice to make sure it was real. Here and today his old friend felt no qualms about adding zeros and moving decimal points with the acumen of a master mathematician. At first it was frightening, but he settled down to the realization it was for his welfare and he was happy to have such a comrade.

The plan was exact in Carter's mind and he carefully outlined it for Muldoon. "When you shove off, take a ride up the shore. You'll see a small mountain that looks like a biscuit. We'll need more block and tackle to lower the stuff from the caves. Now, ya better haul ass, times a wastin'."

Muldoon stood quickly and took another healthy swig from his jug. "Carter, ya sly sonuva bitch, I still wish we were shipmates."

The trademark thumping of Navy diesels began again with the coxswain slamming the twin screws into reverse gear. The churning froth sent waves of water and sand high on the beach, leaving a deep furrow in its wake. The native girls backed away, threatened by the sea monster reincarnated from the deep.

Jesse Hightree appeared in time to watch Muldoon clear the reef and turn north. The sight of the young private gave Chandler's thoughts a prod. "Where in the hell are all my men? I haven't seen them for hours."

"I can only give you an approximate answer, Lieutenant."

"All right, Hightree, speak up."

The sober Indian delivered a concise report. "Well, sir, chronologically, Sergeants Bowman and Chernikov are cohabiting with two ladies in the village. Corporal Kovak is with the seamstress, taking sewing lessons. Private First Class O'Malley is with Sergeant Ohashi in the warehouse receiving Judo instruction, and Private Levine took Private Nishigawa on a burial detail for the dead Captain. Sergeant Gallo is off duty and asleep."

Sugimoto came to the same realization. "What about my men?"

Jesse was apologetic. "I'm sorry Lieutenant, I thought you knew. Those who aren't watching the Judo match, are still in the dispensary with our corpsmen. He's treating them for open sores and fungus. Kimi is there too."

"My God, Jake. I'd better get up there right away. I'll see

you later."

Chandler grimaced and looked down. "I must be the world's worst commanding officer. I mean, how lax can I be? If Colonel Mason were here, he'd skin me alive."

Carter did not agree. "You're still tops with me, sir, you're doin' fine. The boys have earned a rest on both sides."

"Maybe you're right, Sergeant. At one time I thought about being promoted to Captain, but right now I don't think I'd qualify for regimental dog catcher."

"That's a good one, sir, funny I mean. Cheer up. Let's have some chow, the girls are wavin' us over. Come on, Jesse, you too."

A special treat awaited the hungry Marines, concocted by Wana and her sister. Koko lifted the lid on a steaming casserole, revealing a lightly scented creamy delight. She spooned out bountiful portions in large wooden bowls and distributed them to eager hands.

"Man, this stuff is great."

"You can say that again. Wonder what it's made of?"

Wana reached for a box at her feet and lifted an empty, dark green can. "Is your food, see?"

"Oh no, it's that cat food. Meat and vegetable hash, I can't believe it."

Chandler was on his feet like a coiled spring. "This I've got to see."

The gourmet learned a lesson on how to improvise. The girls showed him the goat's milk cream sauce first, followed by scallions, bean sprouts and cabbage hearts. The true secret was in the native spices.

Chandler's final comment summed up the magic. "Even when I know what I'm eating, it still tastes good. It's remarkable."

Roy was the next to arrive, followed by a line of sniffing chow hounds. When the large pot was emptied to the last crumb, the generous girls were already working on a second batch. Knowing they were backed up by a truckload of unwanted rations, it would be put to good use.

Carter was finished and on his feet, stroking his chin again. "Come on, Roy, we've got work to do. Let's take a walk to the radio jeep."

"You mean there's more to come?"

"That's right, a helluva lot more. I want to make sure I keep time on my side." Jake walked to Wana and kissed her cheek. She smiled back lovingly, returning to her chores.

Roy was not to be out done. "Hey, I can do that too." He advanced to Koko and did the same. She turned and whispered in his ear, "Don't forget tonight." He was on a soft cloud when he departed. No matter what came to pass, the whole scenario was too good to be true.

When they reached the radio jeep they found Sergeant Gallo back on duty, sitting in the driver's seat honing his utility knife. "Hello, Jake, thanks for droppin' in. I was beginning to feel like a hermit. What's up?"

"Eddie, is there any way you can get me through to Yontan Airfield?"

"Are you kidding? I'm a communicator, remember? Who do ya wanna talk to?"

"See if you can get me Sergeant Miller at the officers club. There's a phone there, can you handle it?"

The radioman had enough confidence for ten men. "Sure, I can patch a phone-radio hookup together. May take a while so you better have a seat."

The wonders of advanced communication techniques in the hands of the Americans bewildered Sugimoto. For the sake of secrecy, Gallo went through his buddies in the camp's radio tent, relaying from switchboard to switchboard until he found his man. The process took less than five minutes, and he handed the phone to Carter. "Here ya go, Jake, talk nice and loud, it's kinda fuzzy."

Carter took the phone and cupped his hand around the mouthpiece. "Hello, Miller, this is Carter from the first Marines. Yeah, me too, I've gotta make it short. Are you guys still interested in Jap Souvenirs? Good, that's what I thought... What, you're leaving for Guam in a week? OK, I've got about a hundred rifles and bayonets plus ammo. No, I'm not shittin' ya." Jake listened to Miller's offer and returned an answer. "That's fair enough, look on your map, I'm way up north in Hagachi. There's about a mile of dirt road east of the village. It's narrow, but it's straight... OK, let me know."

Carter handed the receiver to Gallo. "Eddie he wants to know your direct frequency, he'll radio back in about twenty minutes."

"What's all this about, Jake?" Chandler was on the edge of his wits. "What have you gotten me into now?"

Carter gave him a twisted grin. "Hold onto your hat, sir, it's gonna be raining bucks around here pretty damn quick. Miller says he can get two hundred a piece for a whole package. He means a rifle, bayonet and ammo to go with it. He wants ten percent of the deal and I said OK."

The math was easy for Sugimoto. "Jeez, Jake, that's close to twenty thousand dollars. What are we going to do with all of that cash?"

"Buy land in California, what else? There's a wrinkle in it though. Miller wants a sample to take back to the airstrip. He'll be flyin' up here in a Piper Cub later. Told him he could land on the east road."

"The east road?" Chandler was close to a fit. "Oh my God! Hightree, go find Kovak. Have him warn the natives to get their carts out of the way, and the kids too. Carter, are you sure he can do it?"

"Don't worry, sir, he said he can land that little kite on a dime and give you a nickel in change."

The fast changing patterns were a kaleidoscope in Sugimoto's mind. He was an organized man, believing in one slow step at a time, but this was taking on the elements of a horse race. A wave of caution advised him to pull on the reins, yet he could not resist a surge of elation. In the four years of their separation, his boyhood chum had matured into a fast-thinking wizard and he was now swept up with it. The fireworks were dazzling and his reactions were adjusted upwards.

"Jake, it sounds like someone has to go back up to our supply dump on the mountain and pick up what you need." Roy cleared his throat. "I'd like to volunteer, if it's all right with you."

"Don't mind it a bit, buddy." Jake knew he must wait for Miller's call. "You can take off now. Take Jesse with you."

If you don't mind, I promised Koko I'd show her the place. Is it OK if I take her instead?"

Carter smiled and placed his hand on Roy's shoulder. "Sure, that's all right with me, but remember, we don't have any time for grab-ass. Save it for later."

"Aw, come on, Jake, you don't think I'd do anything like that. Do you?"

CHAPTER THIRTY-SIX

The 'shot heard round the world', is a quotation every citizen knows, stemming from the American Revolution. It was heard again when Sergeant Miller announced the market for Japanese rifles to the Yontan personnel. Spreading like a fire through dry grass, it traveled from the top down to the ears of the lowest private. The Sergeant's popularity skyrocketed to new heights, bringing a stampede of clamoring freaks to his officers' club. After all, they were going home with nothing but a chest covered with ribbons to prove they were in the fray. The money in their pockets was only paper and soon to be frittered away, but a prime souvenir was a very tangible object. Fighting a modern war in the clouds, with the enemy thirty thousand feet below, is hardly conducive to the collection of mementos. It was their last chance.

"Lock that front door, Smitty, I gotta have time to think." Miller ducked for safety behind the bar, hounded by a host of flying officers. "Hey, Zack, go up to the intelligence section and find me a map of the north island area. Use the back door."

"OK, Sarge, but what kinda map do you want, contour or road map?"

"I don't care if you bring me a cartoon. Find out what they have. Get going."

The decibel count in the big room fell back to a normal audible range, eventually tapering down to an expectant silence. Miller had the floor and was on the brink of telling the details of his story when a pounding on the door interrupted him. His attempts to ignore it were frustrated by the persistence of the intruder.

The Last Souvenir

"Damn it! Open this door immediately, it's your commanding officer."

"Uh oh, ya better let him in, Smitty."

The red-faced Colonel Wardlow strode onto the scene, followed by the squadron paymaster. "Miller, what the hell's going on? My phone has been ringing off the hook. I'm supposed to be running a Bomber Group, not a gun shop."

The Sergeant was not guilty of any misdemeanor, yet he felt as though he was being treated as a criminal, convicted without trial. Wardlow was out of character. In the past, his state of mind was always calm and fair. The redeeming factor of the moment was that Sergeant Miller was an A-1 operator, experienced and capable of taming a tiger. For him, the head on approach worked every time.

"Colonel, I'll give it to you straight. My buddies from the First Marines called me from up north. They're sittin' on a supply dump of Jap rifles and they want to know if we're interested."

The bomb of shouting burst again with comments and bidding, returning the Colonel's color from crimson back to natural. The crowd pressing in around him was not a rabble, they were his favorite boys and he was inclined to heed their requests, and why not? Time and again he had sent them away on nearly impossible missions and they went without a whimper. Now it was their time.

"All right boys, hold it. I've heard that captured enemy equipment is contraband and should be turned over to proper authorities, but I've not been notified officially. Let's say for now I'll turn the other cheek. Spell it out for us, Sergeant."

A muffled cheer filled the room and quickly subsided, allowing Miller to tell his version of the plan. The dull routine of a peacetime airdrome was broken and the airmen were ready for anything new. However, the varied range of temperaments brought up questions.

"Wait a minute, I ain't gonna buy no pig in the poke for two hundred bucks. I'd like to see what I'm gettin' first."

"What the hell do you care, Scrooge? You're over paid anyway."

"Yeah, that's what I say. Miller's come through for us in the past."

Miller held up his hand to stop the friendly wrangling. "Sir, I'm checked out in Piper Cubs, will you authorize flying orders for me? Sergeant Carter told me there's a road I can land on up there. I've made arrangements to fly up, grab a sample and bring it back."

Wardlow took a few seconds to consider his proposal and shook his head. "Absolutely not. The Cub is a two-seater. I'll fly it and you can ride in the back."

"But, sir, you're a bomber pilot, the Piper's only a ninety horse power."

"Listen, Sergeant, when I was only nineteen years old, I was a stunt pilot for a flying show in the Midwest. You put a propeller on a box kite and I'll fly it. Besides, these guys have been having all the fun. It's my turn to fly a mission." He turned to the paymaster. "Mayor, see to it my boys get the money they need. If it's a special allotment, have it on my desk and I'll sign it." His humdrum life had been punctuated and he was excited about the prospect of flying by the seat of his pants again.

A handful of maps arrived and they were quickly spread on the bar. The chart with contour lines was the favorite and everybody had an opinion, pointing fingers and suggesting routes.

"The Marine is right, Colonel, that east road looks pretty good. What do you think, Mitch?"

"Yeah, but I'd fly over it first and check for potholes."

"What about wind direction?"

"I checked it this morning, it's comin' from the west."

"Ya know, Colonel, ya don't really have to fly up there. I trust those guys. I'll buy one of those rifles blind."

"Oh no you don't. You're not gonna cheat me out of a joyride. Besides, I like those young Marines and I want to see what they're up to. Miller, get on the phone with our mechanics. Tell them to service a Cub and roll it out on the line immediately."

"Yes, sir. I'll radio the Marines and tell them we'll be on our way within an hour."

Wardlow's name was solid gold with his mechanics. His decades in aviation had taught him that the man with the wrench was king, and to be treated with the highest respect. Mutual admiration is contagious and his service crews would happily work overtime to insure perfection. The little plane was gassed, oiled, and ready when he and Miller crossed the tarmac, wearing their flight overalls. Flying the big, two story bombers for so many months had thrown their perspectives out of kilter. The tiny aircraft resembled a model airplane from a kit purchased at the corner hobby shop.

Wardlow related to the trim little bird with sheer delight. "Sergeant, this is wonderful. It brings back memories of the day I first soloed. I was sixteen, flew a biplane then." He knew he was from the old guard and probably one of the last complete pilots. The days of bailing wire and canvas had been X'd off the calendar, and science had swallowed them whole.

Miller entered first, climbing through the side door under the wing of the brown monoplane. With the map clenched between his teeth, he fumbled for his seatbelt and adjusted a set of headphones over his ears. Wardlow followed, high kicking his left leg and springing into the pilot's seat with the agility of a teenager. After a routine check of ailerons and rudder bars, he shouted, 'Clear, and closed the door.

The little engine started on its first cough and the propeller ticked quietly before their eyes. The Colonel's conversation with the control tower was that of a bomber pilot, yet it was a Piper Cub that passed them and took off, airborne in less than two hundred yards.

"Are you secure back there, Sergeant?"

"Yes, sir."

"All right, you're the navigator. We'll use the hogback ridge on our right as a reference point."

Gaining speed and altitude, he banked right over the Bishi Gawa River and flew over the famous Yellow Beach. Ironically, it was the same beach the First Marines had stormed ashore almost five months ago. The wounds of battle were healed now, and it resembled the sands of a beach resort. Following the shoreline they soon hopped over the Motobu Peninsula, keeping the west road on their right. A rainbow of colors greeted them when they viewed the coral heads in the clear water, displayed like bouquets in a flower shop. The picture was framed by lush green sugar cane and rice paddies on the right, and the dark blue of the China Sea on their left.

"My God, Miller, this place is breathtaking. Wish I had a camera."

"I brought one, sir."

Wardlow tilted the plane on its side and flew lower. "Well, start snapping. My wife's gonna love this. She thinks we fly so high we never see anything." His touch on the controls was as precise and as gentle as a skilled surgeon with a scalpel as he dropped to a wave-hopping level.

"Colonel, that looks like Hagachi dead ahead." Miller tapped him on the shoulder and pointed to the spur headed west, away from the central mountain range.

"You're right, Sergeant, I think I see some people on the beach. Let's take a look." He shoved forward on the throttle, giving the engine full power. "Hang on Miller, we'll do a little showboating. Show those Marines what the Air Force can do."

The Last Souvenir

Wana was first to hear the droning motor and she gestured wildly to the south. Carter and Lieutenant Chandler rose from their seats in the sand and shouted to Sugimoto, who was swimming with his men in the lagoon. Gallo swung out of the radio jeep and awakened the snoozing Wisnewski, just in time to see the little plane scream by.

"Hey, that's them, they're wavin' at us."

"The crazy bastard is goin' like a bat out of hell."

They watched in awe as the tiny craft jerked upward in a half loop, rolling out at the top. Gaining speed on its return trip, it executed a sharp snap roll barely fifty feet above the water.

"Wow! Did you see that, Jake? That guy's a real hotshot."

"Yea, I saw it. I'd give anything to be able to do that. Maybe I'll take flying lessons when I get home."

Wardlow banked his ship inland and kept the main road on his left for a view of his landing area. Children danced everywhere in the street, straining for a closer glimpse of their Phoenix risen from the dead. The airmen could see a Marine recon truck parked east of the village with two men standing on the floorboards, each clutching the windshield and waving with the other hand.

"Look Colonel, that's Chernikov, I can tell by his size, the other looks like Bowman."

"You're right, Sergeant, let's put on a real Air Force show for them."

The master pilot flew in a wide circle, intent on making his approach from the sea. Back he came at rooftop level while slowly reducing power. Midway down the road he suddenly maneuvered the little craft into a climbing bank and partial stall, falling away and pancaking lightly on the road below. The feather-light landing was so perfect he rolled to a stop in less than one hundred feet.

"Gawd almighty, Moe, who is that guy? I can't believe my

eyes."

"Man, he came down like a seagull landing on the beach. Come on, let's go pick him up."

An open goat pasture on the right presented an ideal parking spot, and Wardlow spied it. He taxied off the road and into the short green grass, cutting the engine immediately. The lethal propeller rotated to a stop not a moment too soon. A swarm of children materialized from every cranny of the village, smiling and crowding close for a better view of the visiting giants. Ichiban clopped behind the throng issuing warnings like a worried father, to no avail. A dark brown bird with stars on its fuselage had fallen from the sky, and the curiosity of youth was overpowering. When Wardlow and Miller squeezed through the narrow door, an overture of young voices and the bleating of frightened goats greeted them. Like a groggy fighter saved by the bell they were rescued by the honking of a truck horn.

"Hey! You guys want a ride?"

Wardlow led the way through the leaping little bodies, removing the dark flight glasses, which disguised his features. Bowman was the first to recognize the high-ranking officer.

"Well I'll be damned, it's the Colonel himself. Hello, sir, welcome to Shangri-La. Hiya Miller."

"You two can forget the salutes, I'd rather shake your hands." Wardlow couldn't hide the pleasure he felt from being in the company of the young Marines again. "Let's see, it's Sergeant Bowman and Chernikov, right? How's that for memory?"

"On the button, Colonel. Ya better hop in the back before ya git mobbed. Our Lieutenant wants us to bring ya to our CP on the beach."

Bowman steered slowly through the village, carefully avoiding the gawking spectators jamming the main street. The airmen took in the sights like tourists on a cruise warmed by the

The Last Souvenir

rustic nature of the native architecture. Viewing a small town from the cockpit of a bomber at high altitude was a big dose of nothing compared to seeing real life up close. They would never forget this memorable day being recorded by the shutter of Miller's camera.

When the truck turned north and found the wet beach sand, Bowman shifted into four-wheel drive. "There they are, Colonel, that's our bunch."

"You call this is a command post? It looks more like a holiday resort in paradise. You Marines really now how to live."

"Believe me, sir, it hasn't always been this way. Ya see those little guys coming out of the water? Those are Jap prisoners."

"Jap prisoners! They're not even under guard."

"No, sir, we let'em run loose. They're just as sick of war as we are. There's our Lieutenant."

Chandler and Carter advanced to greet the oncoming vehicle, with Sugimoto one pace to the rear. Jake was first to sight the silver eagles on the shoulders of Wardlow's leather flight jacket. "Check that, Lieutenant, we've got a real bird Colonel comin' to visit."

The two Marines snapped to attention and saluted with Chandler stammering a salutation. "Er, good afternoon, sir. I'm Lieutenant Chandler... In command here... and this is the Platoon Sergeant Carter.

Reluctantly, Wardlow returned the salute and offered his hand. "Let's knock off the formalities, just consider me another guest at your beach party. You're Jake, aren't you? I've heard a lot about you."

"Yes, sir." Jake looked past him. "And you must be Sergeant Miller. We meet at last."

Miller stepped up to shake his hand. "That's right, Jake, we've talked on the phone, but that's it. You're just like I had you pictured."

"That good or bad? Come on over and have a seat. We've got a lot to talk about."

"Hey, what am I, an orphan? How about introducing me!" Roy moved in with a captivating grin.

"I'm sorry, buddy, Colonel, Sergeant Miller. This is Lieutenant Sugimoto of the Japanese Army."

"The Japanese Army! I've always known the Air Force was informal, but this is a new wrinkle. How do you do, Lieutenant. Where's your uniform?"

"It's still in the laundry, and I'm in no hurry to put it back on."

The Colonel was intrigued by the new turn of events. "You're the first enemy officer I've met. I'd like to swap stories with you. Miller, bring that bag you've been carrying."

The men seated themselves on the sand before Chandler's lean-to while the obliging Sergeant retrieved a small traveling bag from the back seat. He placed it gently on the beach and emptied its contents. "Here you go, compliments of the Army Air Corps. Three bottles of scotch whisky."

"Now that's what I call hospitality." Carter looked up and spoke to O'Malley.

"Sean, see if you can scare up some cups, and bring a jug of that native booze. How about it, Colonel, it's sweet potato brandy. Do you want to try it?"

"No thanks, Jake, maybe just a taste." Wardlow was disciplined. "Miller can have all he wants, but I'm driving, remember?" He noticed a smile spread across Chernikov's face. "Did I say something funny, Sergeant?"

"No, sir, I was just thinkin'. The way you fly, you remind me of a guy that drives a bus for a living and has a hot rod to play with on his day off."

The blast of laughter that erupted was not derogatory and meant as a compliment. The old pilot sensed and accepted this.

"Well, I go way back. Used to fly a crop-duster and learned how to land in an alfalfa field before we had blacktop. We sure did piss off the farmers."

Miller had flown with Wardlow as a gunner and couldn't wait to confirm his prowess. "I'll vouch for that. He brought us home once on one engine after a bombing run over the Rabaul. We pitched out everything that wasn't nailed down to lose weight. Man, I was scared that day, but we made it."

The smoky flavor of scotch whisky gave a mixed sensation to Sugimoto's unprepared taste buds. Although the beverage was imported, it was still an American drink in his mind, and thoughts of home returned. He listened intently while Miller continued his yarns of air combat in the Pacific War, knowing he was hearing the truth at last. The Japanese propaganda machine had led him down a thorny path of distortions and lies for the past four years, but he was too intelligent to buy the rubbish. The Air Force Sergeant was laying out hard-boiled facts, and he loved it.

The strange blend of Japanese and American warriors was drawn together in an eerie comradeship, attracted by Bowman and O'Malley building an unlikely bonfire in mid-afternoon. They sat in a circle on the beach like brothers in a family reunion, circulating the straw-covered bottles of native liquor and smiling in peace. Their languages were different, but they shared a common thought - how ridiculous the war had been. Sugimoto sought and was granted permission to translate for his men. He broke into the airmen's stories and related them back in Japanese, greeted by bewildered oohs and ahs from the stoic survivors. Combat soldiers can always face the truth, no matter how bitter. It's lying they abhor. Miller had the highest respect for the skills and courage of the Japanese pilots who opposed him, and they were grateful for that. Perhaps history would be kind in recording their valiant deeds, regardless of the insignias on their wings. Some had lived and many had died, but that was that. It was over.

The advantage of daylight was holding, but Colonel Wardlow had his eye on the sun. He could sense an uneasiness in Carter's shifting body and he summoned him away. They climbed together to the seclusion of a high sand dune, hardly missed by the laughing men below. The two veterans sat side by side like two old friends, with the difference in rank fading away.

Carter fed the whole story into Wardlow's hungry ears, beginning with Roy's capture and ending with the fate awaiting on his return home.

"My God, Jake, the poor man's been screwed from beginning to end."

"I know, sir. It may seem altruistic, but I propose to do something about it."

"Well, God bless you, Sergeant. He's lucky to have a friend like you. I'm behind you one hundred percent. What's next?"

"Sergeant Miller and I have a deal, sir. Roy has the rifles and your men have the cash. It's that simple. Are your boys still interested?"

Wardlow reared back and slapped his knees. "Interested! Why hell they're rabid, this is a sweet deal all around, let's set it up."

"OK, Colonel, we'll need Miller and Sugimoto to hammer out the details. We'd better get 'em up here."

Fetching the two men was no problem. Both had been glancing over their shoulders, straining to pick up traces of the discourse. When called, they popped erect in unison and trudged up the sand hill.

Carter was the first to speak. "We're all set boys, the Colonel's given us a carte blanche. Roy, do you suppose your men can help us get that stuff down to the beach with your block and tackle? We'll need to load it on a truck."

"Sure, Jake, first thing in the morning." Roy smiled with

another thought. "As a matter of fact, I think they'd be happy to help. One of them told me he hadn't been treated this well since he joined the Army."

Miller laughed. "Know what you mean. I guess all Armies are the same, no matter what kind of flag you follow. How many rifles and bayonets can you let us have?"

Roy turned pensive and stubbed his toe in the sand, carefully calculating his numbers. "Well, after what we've promised the Navy, I'd say about one hundred and fifty."

"One hundred and fifty. Sold, man, sold. To hell with the Navy, we'll take em all."

"Hold it, Miller." Wardlow stepped in. "The boys made a deal and it's their store. As I get it we're talking about thirty thousand cash. The paymaster is going to blow his cork as it is."

"I'm sorry, sir, I just got carried away. Where do we go from here, Jake?"

"All right, here's the deal. Come back tomorrow with a big truck and a couple of muscle men. You'll need a pass. There's a guard gate just north of Motobu. And for Gawd's sake, don't tell anybody where we are. We'll have every GI on the island up here before you know it."

"Mums the word, buddy, you've got a sale."

Bowman and Chernikov were waiting by the truck when the four men returned to the beach. "Taxi, Colonel?"

"Sergeant, you were right when you called this place Shangri-La. I hate to leave but duty calls. By the way, is it possible to take a bottle of that native booze with us? There's going to be a hell of a party at our officers' club tonight and I'm sure my boys would like to try it."

"Already thought of that, sir. There's a jug in the back seat with the rifle... and thanks for the scotch."

The entire contingent stood and waved good-bye as the little truck sped toward the village, kicking up a rooster tail of wet sand.

Chandler felt like a forgotten man when he walked up to join Carter and Sugimoto. "I realize I'm only the commanding officer around here, but would you mind filling me in on this caper?"

"Hell no Lieutenant, I think we just bought a couple hundred acres of California land. Is there any of that scotch left?"

"Sure, I'd figured you might want some so I stashed half a quart in my lean-to."

"Good thinking, Lieutenant, let's break it out and I'll tell you the whole story."

Chandler sat in the middle and sipped his drink, listening to the wild tale unfold. Within thirty minutes the humming of an aircraft engine interrupted their conversation. They watched the little plane gain altitude and bank their way, wagging its wings in a victory salute as it passed. The pilot circled out to sea and headed for his home in the south. To Jake, the day was a great success, yet Chandler could not suppress his doubts. It was all happening too easily.

"Jake, I've got to hand it to you, you certainly have some wonderful friends."

"No, Roy. It's you that has wonderful friends now, and they're all in the right places."

The Last Souvenir

CHAPTER THIRTY-SEVEN

Sunrise in Hagachi was a sight that would remain in Jake Carter's memory for the rest of his days. Perhaps the hand of civilization had waved over the little colony, but it only cast a shadow and moved on. Their primitive and permanent arrangement with nature was like an ancient treaty, signed and sealed by their forefathers centuries ago. Any drastic change could be a violation and the pact would be nullified. Basic necessities sprang from the earth, ranging from the wood in their structures to food on the tables. They had achieved a balance with the changing elements of four seasons and that was enough.

The early rays of morning sun were blocked by the eastern mountain range, leaving the valley in a pale orange hue. The curling smoke from the chimneys refused to give up its pastel gray as it spiraled upward, as yet untouched by a morning breeze. Dawn's first light signaled goat-milking time as sure as a bugler's reveille. A chorus of bleating from a score of demanding nannies filled the air, a plea to be relieved of the pressure in their swollen udders. Off key as it was, it was their morning music and the beasts refused to be denied.

Jake and Wana hurried through the village and turned right into the outskirts where she and her sister dwelt. The sensitive noses of her two goats picked up her scent and they joined the raucous crescendo. At first, the city-bred Carter found humor in the concert, but it was soon replaced by the urgency of the moment. No more would he wonder why Wana insisted on rising so early.

Their house was a masterpiece of craftsmanship, built by

her grandfather and his brother in a prior decade. In that year a devastating typhoon had swept in from the China Sea, literally lifting the little village and blowing it to points unknown. Modern times had presented the girls with a new word, and they laughingly referred to it as 'Kamikaze Manor', or the true translation of 'Divine Wind'. In their hemisphere the threat was always there. It was Mother Nature's way of showing her dominance, either a warning of her continuous presence or the process of spanking naughty children. To the people it was only a factor added into their equation of life and they simply dropped the subject.

Odd jobs in construction had gifted Jake with a higher level of awareness, and he marveled at the obvious use of hand tools alone. Sturdy upright beams supported a tile roof, with hand-hewn planks completing the sides. The sliding doors were latticed with opaque panes, allowing more than abundant lighting. On his right and beyond the access path was a chest-high fence guarding a tempting plot of green vegetable tops from hungry marauders. He slowly circled the residence with curiosity, hoping he could commit the details to an everlasting memory for future reference. He couldn't explain to himself why he was so strongly drawn to the tiny abode. He just was.

The busy Wana reappeared, carrying a wooden bucket of warm goat's milk in each hand. From the doorway of a nearby house a young boy ran to face her, bowing from the waist. She extended one of the buckets and he took it, scurrying away to turn left on the main road.

"What was that all about, sweetheart?"

"He go big house. Others no have goats. I give."

"I think I get it, it's a trade. If you want something you just go to the big house and get it... for free." As soon as the words left his lips, Jake knew it was a foolish statement, but it was too late for retraction.

Wana's brief stint in the outside world had given her understanding, and she strove to soothe his ignorance of their communal customs. "Yes, Jaki, we give, we take, we trade work. Is good."

"Wana, I think you're wonderful." Jake reached down and removed the remaining bucket from her hand, placing it on the ground. He drew her close and kissed her tenderly. Her body trembled from the morning surprise and she circled her arms around his neck. Love and lust combined to fire their embrace with electricity and the world was theirs, at least for the moment.

The busy schedule of the day prevented them from slipping away to pursue their swelling desires. Wana could sense her man had many irons in the fire and she reluctantly terminated the intimacy. Her brown eyes were half-closed and watery when she looked up to speak.

"Wana ruve Jaki too. Is so nice, I happy." She paused and placed her cheek against his chest. "Jaki must work. We go in house now, Koko cooking."

"Wana, my love, for two bits I'd chuck the whole thing and whisk you away somewhere."

"Jaki tark too fast. What two bits mean?"

He laughed and reached out to hold her tiny hands. "It's just a saying we have. It just means you're right."

Wana led the way, sliding the door aside and negotiating the high step from the ground to the wood flooring inside. She carefully removed her sandals and motioned for Jake to do the same with his GI boots. Sugimoto was seated on a stool, clad only in his underpants. He sprawled over backwards against a low table with his face fully lathered while Koko shaved away his day old beard.

"Oh, brother, if I only had a camera. I'd send a picture of this home to your Mom and Dad. They wouldn't believe it otherwise."

Before Roy could speak he was cautioned by his barber

against any sudden movement. He gently pushed her hand away and sputtered through the soapsuds. "Buddy, I wish I could shout this to the whole world. She treats me like a king. This is the first time I've ever really been in love."

The power in the announcement was actually a milestone in his life, but only Jake could recognize its significance. In his school days, because of his colossal shyness, Roy was dubbed a perennial wallflower. Lunchtime in the cafeteria would find him in the company of fellow athletes, unable to break the circle and mingle with the opposite sex. Saturday nights he spent alone, tinkering over an engine or reading volumes of print on the advancements in agriculture. His genius carried a penalty with it, and shyness was the fine.

On this day, the bud of his personality had blossomed into a magnificent flower, and he stood on the threshold of a completed manhood. Koko had discovered a way to kick-start his character, without knowing how or why. Her blithe instincts told her to turn the doorknob, and she beheld a gold mine of understanding and passion. Roy hadn't changed, in the true sense of the word, he had simply been found.

Oriental custom rejects public displays of affection and demands demureness, but Hagachi lived in a world of its own, unencumbered by a forced system of outside mores. Throughout breakfast they chatted happily in a combination of English and Japanese, revealing their true feelings with a kiss or touch of the hand. Jake winked knowingly at his pal, acknowledging his new-found happiness. This day had to come sooner or later, and here it was. Roy grinned back with the radiance of a shining light, reading the thoughts of his old friend.

The mystique was broken by the booming voice of Johnny Bowman, standing somewhere in the neighborhood with his hands cupped around his mouth. "Hey, Jake, where the hell are ya? Stick your head out, man." He was answered by the bleating of a dozen frightened goats and an instant mob of curious children, all pointing around the corner.

Without a doubt something was in the wind. Jake rose and strode for the open door in his stocking feet with Wana beside him, breaking into laughter when they sighted the clowning Bowman, marching like a drum major leading a parade of giggling children.

"Mornin', Jake, sorry to break up your little tête-à-tête."

"What the hell are ya wearin' a pistol for, Johnny? Haven't ya heard, the war's over."

"Dunno. I've been wearin' it so long it sort of grew on me. Habit I guess."

"Well, ya might be right. One of these goats might get pissed off and attack. OK, what's the story?"

Bowman's inquisitive nature couldn't resist a peek inside. With eyes wide open he scanned the neatness of the feminine interior. "Man oh man, what'a layout. You guys are really cuttin' a fat hog. How can I sign up for this kinda duty?"

"Stow it, buddy. Find your own Fun House. Come on, what's on your mind?"

"OK, OK. Muldoon just radioed you." Bowman backed away from the door and handed Carter a written message. "He says he's on his way up here with the first installment. What does he mean by that?"

"At this hour? He must be eager, but I smell cash. Come on, Roy, get your pants on. We're in business."

Roy's uniform was cleaned and ready. He pulled on a pair of modified Jodhpur breeches, reaching for his socks and hobnailed boots. Forsaking his uncomfortable tunic, he slid into a pullover shirt donated by the sisters, a holdover from the days when men also occupied the house. When the three men stood together on the road outside, Bowman moved in to admire the conglomerated attire.

"Now that's what I call fashionable, Lieutenant. Back

home we call 'em 'Zoot Suits'."

The girls waved tentatively from the doorway as Roy matched strides with the two Marines. Wana felt a foreboding in her heart, the ominous dread that her love was a puff of smoke awaiting a powerful wind. Her choices were minimal. She could grasp for it now or wait for the breezes of her destiny to blow it away. She knew the good fortune of having a sympathetic sister, and Koko, because of a common language, had learned the entire narration from Sugimoto the night before. She sat with Wana and related the quandary of her new love for the Nisei boy. In the end, optimism prevailed and sadness was lost, bringing a unanimous decision. They would enjoy the gift of the moment and allow the consequences to manage themselves.

The young men rounded the corner and walked together on the main road, a three-way mix of old and new comrades. Roy was choked with emotion and bursting with questions. "Would you mind slowing up? I need some advice."

"Sure, Roy, shoot."

"Well, I'm in love and I'm not sure what to do about it."

Bowman waved a casual hand. "That's easy, the whole thing starts with the birds and the bees, and then ya..."

Sugimoto interrupted, mildly confused by Bowman's cavalier attitude to the tender subject of romance. "No, I'm serious. I'm trying to figure a way to take her home with me. You know, back to the States."

"You what? Man, you've really got it bad." Jake stopped to look in the face of his friend. "Hey, I'm in love too, but we're out here a thousand miles from nowhere. Ya gotta spend more than twenty-four hours to think that over."

"I know it sounds crazy, Jake, but she's the most wonderful girl I've ever met. I'll never find another like her."

"OK, pal, let me put it this way. You want to take her away from this island paradise and transplant her in the big city.

Why hell, it might ruin her, did you think about that?"

In the pause that followed, Johnny B interjected his own candid viewpoint. "There's another thing. Those little Nisei gals back home would get jealous if a handsome dog like you brought back imported stuff."

"Johnny's right, Roy. What about your family and friends? And what about Koko?"

"Jake, you should know by now, you've been around Japanese-Americans most of your life. We encourage people to immigrate from the old country. It's a new world."

"A new world, eh? You can say that again. With a little luck, you're goin' home rich. You'll have women climbin' all over you. I'm glad I'm not in your shoes, at least for makin' that kind of decision."

The most important question had not been answered, but it occurred to Bowman. "What about your girl, have you asked her yet?"

"No, I haven't. I'm afraid she'll say no."

"Roy, you've got a mighty big cud to chew on. Let's head for the beach, we can talk more about it later."

"You're right again, Jake, and I thank you for listening. You too, Johnny. It's about time I started thinking about my men."

As long as the subject was being changed, Bowman was first to speak. "They're all there, Lieutenant, down by the firepit, and they're back in uniform. Our boys are with 'em. It's too bad the guy who started this war can't be here to see this buncha jokers."

The barriers of language and culture had toppled. Marine riflemen and Japanese soldiers rubbed shoulders with all the off hand delights of youth. Snapshots from home were produced on both sides, bringing the usual admiring comments. The subject of pretty girls transcended the walls of language and bonded them together in a new brotherhood.

The lesson they were learning was a universal creed in which all men were basically alike, regardless of dividing boundaries. It was a friendly plague worth spreading.

Private Nishigawa was the center of attention, assuming his roll of chief cook and lord of the outdoor kitchen. The farmer from Kyushu was showered by helpful hints from two old village ladies who insisted on being present. The grandmothers had lost their males in the conflict, but their maternal instincts were rejuvenated by the voices of young men with healthy appetites. Nishigawa had two assistants whether he liked it or not.

The most unlikely scene was unfolding by the open doors of the warehouse. Two Sergeants wearing different uniforms were directing a small work-party of men hefting cases of Marine C-rations on their shoulders. Ohashi and Chernikov had fallen in together in a mutual respect of a common rank. A month ago their kind was leading men against each other in a hell-bent destructive showdown in the flames of combat. Today, the invisible handshake of truce had thrown them into a new ideology, and citizenship of the world. An eraser had moved across the blackboard of animosity and wiped it clean.

Chernikov broke away from the group when he saw Carter, his long legs eating up the yardage between them. "Hey Jake, I gotta tell Cookie about this one. Roy's boys can't get enough of our hash. I'll betcha even Lang wont believe it."

"I'm glad you're here, Moe. Get the big truck unloaded and drive it to the CP. When Muldoon gets here we'll move it up to the caves."

"Consider it done, Jake. By the way, the Lieutenant's lookin' for ya."

"Did he say what he wants?"

"Naw, 'cept it was good news and bad news. Sounded important."

"Shit, what now?" Jake's mind was a jumble of loose ends.

"Roy, you and Johnny better see to it that the men get plenty of chow. I'm takin' off."

A speck on the southern horizon caught his eye when he reached the water's edge and turned up the beach. It had to be Muldoon. Chandler was waiting in front of his lean-to with a worried expression furrowing his brow.

"Sergeant, you better have a cup of coffee and take a seat. We might have a problem."

"Sounds like a bribe, Lieutenant, but I'll take you up on the coffee."

Chandler sat next to him with both hands surrounding a canteen cup. "Colonel Mason called last night and again this morning. I can't hold him off anymore. He's given us three more days to clean up this patrol, no matter what, and come back."

"What's the big hurry, Sir?"

"Well, sometime between ten days and two weeks from now he's taking the regiment to North China and there's a lot of work to do."

"North China! What the hell's up there, Sir?"

"I don't have the foggiest idea, Jake, but you know the Marine Corps. They tell us what to do and we do it."

"But I don't understand, Lieutenant. The Division's been fightin' in the Pacific since forty-two. Why don't they send us back to the States?"

"I can only guess on that one. We're loaded with new replacements that just came over, and they'll need the old timers to take 'em along."

"Pardon my French, Lieutenant, but that's really chicken shit."

"Now hold on, Sergeant, it's not as bad as all that. You're going home."

"Home! Me? Why me?"

Chandler fished in his pocket for a piece of paper and studied the notes he had written. "This morning, Colonel Mason handed the phone to Padre Turner and he told me about a new rotation system for veterans. Stack and Keeler are already on their way home and you're next."

"What's a rotation system, Sir? I don't get it."

"It's simple enough, Jake. They give you points for months overseas and add in more for citations."

The initial shock waves were over and Carter could sense a dawning of new ideas. He knew every puzzle had a missing piece and he was set on finding it. "Points for medals? That sounds weird to me, Sir. I still don't get it."

"Who knows what the top brass is thinking. The Padre said your second Purple Heart put you over the hump. The points are there, you're going, and that's it."

"Well I'll be damned. What about Moe and Johnny B.?"

"Tough luck, they came up a few points short, and me too. We're going to China without you."

Carter had never seen the medals he was awarded, only pictures on the wall where he went to boot camp so many eons ago. In his mind, they were scraps of tin and brass with little tangible value, but suddenly they became his ticket for home. In a way it didn't seem fair. Bowman and Chernikov, and the rest of his buddies, had performed incredible acts of courage without a flinch. Their only reward was survival. Now, decorated heroes were being singled out for special treatment, and yet they were the same as everyone else in the struggling infantry. Another blow of Military madness had been struck, leaving a trail of prostrate victims in its wake.

"Lieutenant, do you have any idea how much time I have left?"

"I think so, Jake. According to the Padre, about two weeks."

Carter was torn between sadness and elation. "Jimmy, if ya don't mind me callin' ya that, I'm startin' to miss you guys already."

The Lieutenant choked down the lump in his throat. "Same with me, my old friend, but don't start packing your sea-bag yet. You're still a Sergeant in the US Marines and we have a job to finish."

"You mean Roy, Sir?"

"That's right. I put my ass on the line for this project and we have three days left. We'll see it through together."

Jack Carroll

CHAPTER THIRTY-EIGHT

It was a confused Muldoon who landed his craft on the beach near the river's mouth. A crowd of enemy uniforms gathered, sprinkled with the green of Marine dungarees. He released the cables retaining the high landing ramp, and the big door dropped with a heavy thud on the sand. The absence of a bow created a gaping mouth, exposing the innards of the little boat and its contents. Coils of rope and pulleys were piled on the deck, with three sailors already in the process of unloading.

For the Japanese, their first glimpse of an American sailor was hardly an exemplary experience. The old Chief's sea garb was badly faded and spotted with engine grease, and the worst was the frayed condition of his trouser legs. The usual two-day beard on his square jaw surrounded an unlit cigar and he spoke with the voice of a mature bullfrog. "Waddya say O'Malley, where's Jake?"

"He's up there, Chief, with our Lieutenant. Look, he's headed this way now."

"Yea, I see 'im." Muldoon's rough exterior and impolite manner belied the core of the man himself. The Japanese could sense the power of his confidence and his innate qualities of leadership. "Where'd ya pick up this collection of characters, O'Malley?"

Sean took umbrage to the question. "Hold on, Chief, we walked 'em in. We're all on the same side now."

"I gotta get used to that. First we fight 'em for four years and now we're buddies. Where's that Nip Lieutenant?"

Sugimoto was unabashed but he still shook his head with mild disgust. He tapped Muldoon on the shoulder. "That Nip

Lieutenant is right here behind you. How many times do I have to tell you I'm not a Nip. I'm a Nisei Californian."

Muldoon whirled to face him, noticing the unusual blend of clothing. "Have it your way, Lieutenant. I know nuthin' about polyticks. I'm Navy. Here, I got somethin' for ya."

Carter walked up in time to see Muldoon hold up a navy blue bag with canvas handles. The little cloth traveling case bulged wide with its overload, and Muldoon struggled with the zipper on top. Jake was too engrossed with the contents to say hello, and his mouth dropped open. The bag was crammed full of greenbacks, resembling an overstuffed turkey. Wads of bills in various denominations were wrapped together by black electrical tape, and the neatness was a credit to Muldoon's integrity.

"There she is, boys. Twelve-thousand-five-hundred in cash. Sorry but it's mostly in tens and twenties."

"Chief, that's quiet a boodle you got there." Jake removed a stack and thumbed through the notes. "If I didn't know ya so well, I'd think ya had your own printing press."

The dreaming was over for Roy Sugimoto. Lip service had been overtaken by reality and the arrows of his mind began pointing towards visions of plowed land and happy days ahead. Right there, under his nose, were the seeds of the future, and he fought back the moisture in his eyes. His old friend Jake had come through again in a way unmatched in the annals of comradeship. Suddenly, it didn't seem right not to share it with his buddy, and a new plan was formulating in his head. However, and for the time being, he would reserve a shift in direction until the picture was clear. Now was not the time to rock the boat. He would remain conservative and save the punch-line for a later date.

Sergeant Ohashi marched up to confront Sugimoto. He stood at stiff attention and snapped up a rigid salute. "Lieutenant, the men are ready to go to work for you on the mountain." Loyalty to his officer was high virtue in the training of the old Samurai. For years the merchants of propaganda in Japan had depicted the American Marine as a forked-tail monster with a dagger in each hand. Ohashi believed the Marine to be a hand-picked Chicago gangster who murdered on whim, paving the way to rape and pillage, and he must be slaughtered. Imperial soil had to be protected from these ogres by the sacrifice of his own life, and he would climb to his heaven over the bodies of dead Americans. But now the lies had been washed away in a changed venue and he viewed men like Chernikov and O'Malley as peers. They laughed and cavorted like the boys of his school days, and the sweet smell of life and home came back to his nostrils. The trial was over, the jury was back, and the gavel had rapped out its final verdict.

Sugimoto addressed Ohashi with a casual wave of his hand. "Thank you, Sergeant, we can dispense with formalities now. Have the men load this equipment in that truck, then take them up to our supply dump. Move the rifles and bayonets to the exit doors. We'll lower everything over the side."

"Yes, Sir." Ohashi turned and spouted the orders. The furious activity began.

Muldoon's ears picked up the long dissertation in Japanese, leaving him spellbound. "Hey, that's the first time I ever heard Nippo talk. It sounds like pig Latin. What did ya tell 'em?"

Roy answered with the patience of a Saint. He knew the old sailor meant well in spite of his crass remarks. "Chief, did anyone ever tell you that you have a way with words? If they did, don't believe it. I just put our business in motion."

"That's good enough for me, Lieutenant." Muldoon and his sailors tramped up the beach to the truck where Bowman and Chernikov waited. O'Malley and Ike Levine opted to join the Japanese for the trek up the hill and a climb down into the bowels of the Biscuit. Lieutenant Chandler would stay in the background, ready to accept radio traffic from regimental headquarters. Kovak and Ichiban arrived on the scene in time to catch the tail end of the exodus.

"Look's like we're just in time." Kovak encouraged the old man to join them. "The old guy told me he wants to hear more about your plans to irrigate the north acreage. Are you some kinda farmer?"

"You bet I am, thanks, Johnny." Roy stood before the Mayor who was locked into another one of his bowing modes. "Good Morning, Your Honor."

Ichiban was, as usual, the epitome of humility. "Most honorable officer, your presence brings grace to my humble village."

"Copious thanks to you, Your Honor. It is gratifying to be at peace once more, and to be among your generous people." The active mind of Roy Sugimoto had not been idle. During his months of boredom on the mountain he found solace in gazing on the land below. He chose a secluded spot on the cliff between two rocks and under a tree, drawing sketches and diagrams for an agricultural miracle. Thoughts of accolades and glory had not crossed his mind, it was only an avocation. But this was the hour that the footprints of fate had overtaken him. How wonderful it was he could share his dreams with these simple people who were enterprising enough to put them to use.

At first he told the story to the Mayor in his own language. The plans were in a desk in the headquarters cave, and he invited the old man to come along. From there he repeated the conversation to Carter in English, unaware that Jesse Hightree was soaking up every word.

"Well, that's it, Jake. When our work is finished I'd like to sit and talk with Ichiban."

Carter folded his arms and spread his feet. "You've done it again, Roy. Every time I think I've got ya figured out, ya come up with something new."

"OK, did you figure this out? I'm going to count the money before I do anything else."

Jake beamed and shook his head. "Nope, that much I know. There's a clipboard in the truck, ya can start your record-keeping on that." He turned away to include Hightree. "What's the matter Jesse, has the cat got your tongue?"

"No, Sergeant." The serious Private took time to come out of his shell. "It's just that now I have two principles that arouse my curiosity."

"Two?"

"Yes, two. First I shall observe the Navy men and their employment of ropes and tackle. With my knowledge of Physics, and the advantages of torque and leverage, perhaps I can contribute. Of course I don't want to intrude."

"That's quite a mouthful, Jesse. What's the second?"

"Secondly, Mr. Sugimoto has a wealth of information and I would like to listen, if he will permit me. I plan to seek a degree in mechanical engineering, but my minor studies will be in agriculture. My tribal elders have endowed me to further the comforts of our people."

The lengthy discourse from the normally tacit Indian left his audience in a state of shock. Through the ages, in the search for education, it is inevitable that two scholars will eventually find each other. If words could be music, Hightree was playing a whole symphony for Sugimoto. A new lifetime friendship had popped up as sure as Isaac Newton discovered the falling apple.

The meeting of two great minds began with four simple words. "Please, call me Roy." Sugimoto invited Jesse to sit with him and assist in tallying the money, and they isolated themselves in a world of scientific gibberish. The spark of a few sentences had ignited the flame, and a new dictionary was opened. Currents of learning flowed together like two streams forming a mighty river of ideas, and they fed on each other.

Distance had separated them in the past, but it would never be a factor again.

It was one of those few times in Jake Carter's life when he felt he had nothing to offer, and he slipped away unnoticed. It was also a feeling of jealousy, as though Hightree had horned into his exclusive friendship. He walked slowly up the beach, staring at the sand and sorting out his emotions. His strength of character clicked in and his confidence returned. There had always been a small gap in his amity with Roy, and that was science. It had to be nourished by a third person, and none could be better than the intellectual Hightree. He quickened his step and began to whistle.

The long stretch of beach was a happy tonic for Jake and he commenced singing aloud. He had learned something about himself today but the full meaning escaped him. A Freudian analyst might call it 'self realization', but the subject was too deep. For a fact, a new chapter was added to his book of life, and the rewards would come in future relationships with males and females alike.

Muldoon was the first to hear Jake's singing and he waved. In a daring bit of driving, Bowman had backed the truck between the sand dunes to a site almost directly below the caves. He relied on ten wheels in four-wheel drive and it worked. The sailors were busily rigging two rope slings in parallel lines, anchored at the base by the rear bumper. High above, O'Malley and Levine made use of two big metal eyebolts sunk in concrete by the exit doors of the caves. Stacks of wooden cases were building on the two ledges, ready for transport. The muffled voice of Sergeant Ohashi could be heard, shouting instructions from the inside of his man-made anthill. Muldoon tested the tension on the ropes and pulleys by hanging with both hands.

"We're ready now. Put one of those little crates in a sling and lower it down."

Hightree came trotting up to join Carter in watching the elaborate spectacle. All eyes were on Levine as he slid a box carefully into the rope cradle and slowly pushed it over the side. Height and gravity took over and the merchandise came roaring down out of control. The box shattered on impact, strewing bayonets and packing in four directions behind the truck bed.

"Sonuvabitch, whatta mess!" Muldoon spat out his cigar stub. "Levine, ya gotta get a better grip on that line. We don't wanna be here all day."

Ike's rebuttal came fast and clear. "Shit, Chief, the angle's too steep and it's burnin' my hands."

"That's OK, Kid." Muldoon yelled to one of his men; "Hey you, loan him your work gloves."

"Do you mind if I make a suggestion?" It was Jesse in a polite interruption.

"Sure, Mac, it don't cost nuthin' ta listen. What's on your mind?"

With one last glance at the ample supply of equipment, Hightree made his statement. "You need a second line attached to your load. Loop the other end twice through the eyebolt and the friction will have a breaking effect. The rate of descent can be regulated manually."

"You took the words right outta my mouth, Sonny." The Chief set about performing the task himself. "Ya know, you're pretty smart for a Gyrene, ya shudda joined the Navy."

The five-minute delay was time well spent, and the process began again with the efficiency of a production line. Crate after crate slid down in perfect tempo, a coordination of Sailors, Marines and Japanese Soldiers. The last to arrive was Sugimoto, and he made a beeline for the clipboard in the cab. For bookkeeping purposes he prudently drew in columns and made notations at the head of each one. Muldoon was relieved to see him.

"Lieutenant, I'm glad ya got here. I can't read the hen scratchin' on those boxes."

"First, Chief, I congratulate you on the money count. You're right on the button." He led Muldoon to the crates and pointed at the oriental characters with his pencil. "These are the symbols for rifles, and this means five. There are five rifles in a case. This is the symbol for bayonet, and there are twenty in each box. This sign is twenty."

Once more the Chief's crude demeanor had fooled the gentry. The steel trap in his brain clamped down hard on every word. "OK, pal, I gottcha. I get twenty cases of those pictures and five of dese. We didn't say nothin' about ammo. How about it?"

"That we have plenty of." Roy shouted instructions to Ohashi and turned back to Muldoon. "I just told my Sergeant to send down five cases of .31 caliber cartridges. They're on the house, but they're your responsibility."

"Don't worry Lieutenant, those swabs out there don't know nothin' about loadin' rifles."

"That's what I'm afraid of."

The Navy Chief, a Platoon Sergeant and the Japanese Army Lieutenant stood together to one side, admiring the slick operation and its joint effort. In their silence, each man had his individual thoughts and they were different, yet they came to the same end. Their war was over and this was living proof. Headlines and peace treaties were far above their heads and much too distant, but this was graphic and easy to grasp. Even the moldy Muldoon was able to put aside his greed and reflect on the picture.

"Da boys are workin' great together. Don't ya think so, Jake?"

Carter nodded without looking away. "They sure are. It's like one big free spirit."

"I wouldn't say free." Muldoon reverted back to his character. "I'm payin' my boys twenty-five bucks apiece."

"Twenty-five bucks?"

"Yeah, that's over a weeks pay for those wharf rats. It'll keep 'em in butts and pogey bait for a month."

Roy had been out of touch too long. "What the hell is pogey bait?"

"That's Navy lingo for candy, Lieutenant. They can buy it at the ship's store."

A nagging point had come up, and Sugimoto decided to tie off the loose ends. "Jake, I think we should give our men something too."

"Don't look at me, buddy." Jake abstained. "It's your money, do what ya want."

Before Roy could commit himself Muldoon spoke up. "Let me give ya some advice, Lieutenant. Those guys are like cab drivers. Ya pay 'em too much and ya spoil 'em."

"Good point, Chief, I shall take it under advisement."

They all agreed on one element. The unloading of the storage cave would continue to the last crate. It was ten o'clock in the morning and the whole crew was there. Muldoon's lading came first, and the balance was stacked between two sand dunes. Hightree's retaining lines, with help on the pulley ropes below, made the project complete. When Ohashi signaled from above that he was finished, Sugimoto hastily began a new inventory count. He strolled between the neat stacks and scribbled on his clipboard, translating into English.

Two sailors yanked simultaneously on the ship-knots and freed the rope and tackle from the rear bumper. The strong hands of Chief Muldoon lifted the truck's tailgate and slammed it shut. Bowman and Chernikov were already parked on the bench seat in the cab, and the engine was running. Carter and Sugimoto hopped to the running boards on each side and took firm grips. Suddenly, a voice from the rear halted their departure.

The Last Souvenir

"Ya better hold it, Mac. Look at that."

All heads turned to watch Nishigawa dangling from the loose ropes still hanging on the face of the cliff. He worked his way down hand over hand, yelling frantically in Japanese.

"What's he saying, Lieutenant?"

Roy couldn't resist a smile. "He's in a hurry and he wants to join us. He says he wants to get a head start on fixing lunch."

The panting chef ran up and joined his Lieutenant on the running board. A large gold incisor dotted the wide grin on his face, topping off his gratitude.

"OK, Johnny, let 'er rip."

The ten-wheeler moved away slowly in granny-gear and turned left on the smooth beach sand. Bowman gleefully shifted into second gear and stomped on the accelerator, creating eight pairs of white knuckles, all clutching for the nearest stability. The wild ride was short. Eddie Gallo was ahead, standing by the radio jeep and waving his arms frantically. The radioman dived for safety as Bowman slammed on the brakes, reappearing and brushing the sand from his dungarees.

"Hey, that was pretty good, Johnny. I'm a speed nut myself. Next time you go anywhere take me along."

Chernikov released his grip on the dashboard. "Man, you can have him, and good luck. Every time we go anywhere it's like drivin' in the Indy 500."

Carter was more interested in information than speed. "What's goin' on, Eddie?"

Gallo circled the hood and looked up. "Jake, your boy Miller just called. He said he'll be leavin' Yontan in about an hour. That should put him here about two o'clock."

"Thanks, Eddie." Jake turned to caution Johnny B. "OK, hotshot, see if ya can get us to Muldoon's barge without a major wreck."

The short trip to the river mouth was uneventful, and the

passengers were more than happy to bail out when Bowman stopped. His light touch on the steering wheel had no relation to his lead-footed treatment of the throttle. He backed the cumbersome truck over the landing ramp and partially into the boat as gently as a mother pushing her baby carriage. Muldoon watched with satisfaction and directed his boys to begin unloading. By his manner it was obvious he was impatient to be gone. There were deliveries to be made and more money to collect. Carter walked up to stand beside him.

"You're makin' a bundle on this deal, aren't ya, Chief?"

"Ya know me, Jake, I do nuthin' for nuthin'. Now don't get any ideas about raisin' the prices on me."

Carter assured him the verbal contract was solid. "Where do ya go from here? What's your schedule?"

Muldoon stuck a fresh cigar in his mouth and searched his pockets for a match. "I'm goin' back to my ship. My boys'll be waitin' to pass out this stuff and pick up some more cash. I got three Chiefs workin' for me."

"Three sounds like a big organization."

"Listen, Jake, I opened a case of those rifles and I'm gonna use 'em for samples. When those swabs get a load of those beauties they'll jump overboard to get 'em."

"Ya still haven't answered my question, Chief. How much time? We've only got two days left."

"Stop worryin', Jake, der's a big aircraft carrier anchored in Motobu bay. I'm goin' der dis afternoon. The chief mechanic is a buddy of mine."

It didn't take long for Carter to read his mind. "Now you're talkin', who is this guy?"

"His name's Langer and he's a jarhead like you. A real con man. Youse guys could be brudders."

There was no doubt left that the tough old Chief would produce. Muldoon had seen his chance to make a killing and he pounced on it. In this case, Muldoon's one-track mind was an asset, and Carter was confident enough to turn back his stress.

Jake was so busy watching Bowman drive away in the truck that he didn't see Wana and her girls glide their canoes on the beach behind him. The two boats were brimming with freshly speared fish, and the half-naked divers stepped out to slide the prows higher on the shore. The bug-eyed sailors rushed to the rail and leered over its side.

"Hey, Chief, why can't we hang out here for awhile?"

Muldoon exploded with authority. "Knock it off, you bubbleheads. This ain't no liberty port. Get those engines started and stand by to shove off." He turned and waved with one last promise. "I'll see ya tomorrow morning, Jake, and ya can count on that."

Jack Carroll

CHAPTER THIRTY-NINE

Reading an aerial map was a simple matter for the flying Sergeant Miller, but ground level was different. There were two many details in the topography. A trained infantry scout would welcome myriad contour lines, but the airman saw it as an oversized rat maze. The Air Force truck pressed steadily north redeemed by the fact that there was only one road. According to his destination on the map, the road turned sharply left and dropped off in the China Sea. That was fair enough and he sat back to relax. Hagachi would still be there.

When Miller passed over the last rise and saw the valley below, it all came back. He recognized the landing path where Colonel Wardlow had set down their plane and he issued a warning to his driver. "Be careful, Smitty, this place is crawling with little kids."

He was right. Their progress was stopped midway through the village by a screaming mob of youthful citizens. Miller had the foresight to buy two cartons of chocolate bars from his post exchange and he passed them around. Within seconds, the grinning little teeth turned dark brown. They were saved by the bell when Ichiban came out to shoo them aside.

Frenchie Labeau leaned against the door frame of his dispensary, attracted by the young laughter. Behind him an old lady sat patiently on a table with a thermometer in her mouth. "If you guys are lookin' for Jake, he's up at the CP."

"Thanks, Doc." Miller leaned over his seat and found a bottle. "Here you go, a jug of bourbon for medicinal purposes."

"Thanks, Sarge, I'll remember you in my will."

Miller gave a friendly salute and motioned for the journey to continue. For his two-man crew it was their first view of Wonderland. Life in a massive airdrome was a sharp contrast to the real world of an island culture. In their boring environment all objects were painted khaki brown, whether mobile or stationary, and surrounded by an endless barbed wire fence. Only authorized visitors could come and go, under the watchful eye of a posted sentry. They enjoyed three square meals and posh living quarters but it just wasn't enough. The splash of natural colors that greeted them was too real to be faked. On their left, the clean water of the river had a lime green tint, which quickly gave way to the light blue of the waiting lagoon. A boundary of white beach sand stretched for hundreds of yards both north and south. An ebbing tide allowed small patches of coral to poke their black and orange heads through the surface and into the sunlight.

In the bathing pond a group of Sugimoto's men washed away the grit of their morning toil, assisted by two young girls. Lunch was over, and Nishigawa sat with his old ladies, munching on a fare of sushi and cream sauce. Up the beach a boat race was in progress, encouraged by a gang of cheering Marines.

"Man, these Marines really have it made." Zack stood in the truck bed for a better view. "Hey, ain't them Jap soldiers down there? They have a better life than we do."

"Maybe I can get you transferred." Miller gave directions. "Turn up there, Smitty, that's their CP."

Carter glanced at his wristwatch and waved his hand. "Hiya, Miller, you're right on time. Park it and climb down."

Miller was an avid hand-shaker and proved it by greeting everyone. He invariably brought smiles wherever he went. "Any of you guys want some chocolate bars? I've got half a box left, I gave the rest to the kids." Outstretched hands, followed by the sound of tearing candy wrappers answered his question. The round of thanks came from their hearts.

"There's more to come, boys." Miller asked Zack to hand down the surprises stashed in the rear of the truck. "Colonel Wardlow sends his compliments to the US Marines. Twenty five T-bone steaks and a sack of fresh corn from Guam."

"Real T-bones, like we had before?"

"Ya mean corn on the cob like ya eat with your fingers?"

"You got it." Miller wasn't finished. "Here's a case of bourbon and a gallon of steak sauce. The Colonel likes you guys and he said say 'hello'. Oh, I almost forgot. There's a gallon of canned butter for the corn."

The deluge of gifts left Chandler tongue-tied, yet he recovered in time to offer his gratitude. "Tell the Colonel we send our thanks, and we wish there was some way we could reciprocate."

Miller's outward mood changed, and he faced Chandler like a fox with a bushy tail. "Oh, but there is a way, Lieutenant. The Colonel wants us to bring back some fresh fish and a bottle of that native hooch."

When the pendulum swung in Chandler's direction he knew exactly what to do. Wana had brought in two boat loads of fish and the girls were busy gutting them on the beach below. The natives had a taste for American spaghetti and meatballs and they would probably swap. If the steaks were packed in dry ice, the fish could be refrigerated for the trip home. He even knew the right man for the job.

"Sergeant Carter, you heard the man. That's your department. You know what to do, get going, and take Kovak with you."

It didn't take a jab with a sharp stick to motivate Jake. Just a chance to be with the love of his love was enough, and he went striding away with Kovak struggling to keep pace. Wana was alerted by the giggling girls that Jake was on his way. She hastened to wade into the lagoon and wash the fish scales from her hands and body. Most probably he would embrace her and this was the only way she could prepare herself. Cleanliness and vanity were the twin sisters in her grooming habits.

Sergeant Miller was keyed for business and he pulled a long duffel bag from its place on the floorboards. The weight of cash in both ends caused it to bend in the middle, and he presented it to Sugimoto. "Here's my end, Roy. Let's sit over there. You'll probably want to count it."

The windfall was turning into a bonanza for the Nisei boy, and he summoned his new pal for assistance. "I need your help again, Jesse. More mathematics."

Once again the accounting began with the serious duo sitting on a sand bank, thumbing through the currency under the watchful eye of the Air Force Sergeant. The denominations were mostly twenty dollar bills, bound in stacks by rare rubber bands. When a recount divulged the same number they were satisfied.

"We get an even twenty seven thousand, Sergeant."

Miller nodded and patted the bulges in the side pockets of his jacket. "I've got my cut right here. Jake and I agreed on ten percent. That makes it an even thirty thousand bucks."

This was Hightree's first venture away from science and into business, and he chose to delve into the subject. "With your permission, are you saying you have three thousand dollars in your pockets? What happens if your Colonel learns of this profit?"

"Hell, Jesse, he already knows. All the men know. In some circles I'm known as 'old ten percent' Miller."

New vistas opened for Hightree and the welfare of his Dakota tribe. "Of course, I see it now. You are an agent and entitled to a prearranged remuneration. It's legal and profitable. Interesting, very interesting." Destiny, or perhaps a guardian angel, had placed Jesse smack in the middle between Carter and Miller, the two master money makers.

Gathering a fortune was a knack, not a university subject, and his thoughts of the Sioux people became more profound. There were so many ways he could make them a powerful nation again. To begin, in the algebraic equation of living, he would eliminate the 'S' for survival and replace it with a 'P' for profit. This was mathematically correct and positive.

"What's the matter, Jesse? Are you day dreaming again?"

Hightree's exhilaration brought back his comedy routine. "Ugh. Injun boy make big magic, bring down wampum from sky."

At first, Miller and Sugimoto were speechless. When they looked at each other they burst into laughter over the unlikely comic. They were driven out of their momentary doldrums and back into action.

The eyes of Johnny Bowman did not miss a trick, and he watched the trio break up their conference. He waited beside the Air Force truck and offered his services. "Mind if I drive, Miller? I know the way."

Miller had no objections. "That's OK with me, how about it, Roy?"

Sugimoto had his doubts. "It's your truck, buddy, but you better hang on, he's a frustrated fighter pilot."

The bench seats were in place and they all climbed into the truck's bed. The fiendish expression on Bowman's face was frightening to say the least. He tromped on the gas pedal and covered over a mile in less than a minute. When he finally came to a halt he backed slowly between the sand dunes with the caution of an inch-worm.

"Ya know, if this thing had wings I could take 'er off."

Miller got more than he bargained for. "Johnny, we have a saying in the Air Force. 'Any landing you can walk away from is a good landing'."

Roy and his clipboard were the first to dismount, followed by Miller and Hightree. An explanation of the oriental characters on the crates was next, and the loading was a simple process. Miller's men stripped to the waist and revealed the strength in their young muscles.

Jesse noticed the Sergeant back off and place his hands on his hips. "Is something bothering you, Sergeant?"

"Hell no. I was just thinking, I can get another ten bucks apiece for those boxes, maybe more."

Hightree was hooked on making money, and he stood beside a full professor with his doctorate in finance. No doubt the institutions of higher learning wouldn't accept Miller's degree, but Jesse could. "If you don't mind my asking, how do you figure that?"

Miller was willing to share the rudiments of operating. "It's simple, anything with Jap writing on it is a souvenir. Those guys back at the base will buy anything."

It came to Hightree that buying and selling was a philosophy, and had no connection with a tangible science. "I see. One must recognize an opportunity when it arises. It is actually a mind-set."

"Jesse, you have a funny way with words, but that's about it. A buck's a buck."

For many years a deep dark void had existed in Hightree's plans, and today the gap was being filled. The answer was wealth. Wealth and comfort walk hand in hand down the path of happiness. Acquiring a technical education was a wonderful thing, yet worthless if not properly applied. It would be like a sophisticated tool in the hands of a stupid mechanic. Yes, indeed, today was a beautiful day.

A curious Miller interrupted the private's muse. "Jesse, there's somethin' I've always wanted to ask. What the hell is wampum?"

"You're not kidding me are you, Sergeant?"

Miller was dead serious. "Naw, I really mean it."

"If that's the case, I shall explain." Hightree took a deep

breath. "Wampum is a very old medium of exchange. It used to be beads and shells in the form of necklaces and belts. Today, the word has evolved to mean money, or in your vernacular, bucks!"

"Hey, I really like that." Miller's mind was moving ahead. "From now on I'm going to call myself 'ten percent of the wampum' Miller."

"Sergeant, I believe we both learned something today."

The truck was ready. Miller climbed into the front seat next to Bowman and the rest of the men piled in the rear. The passengers prepared themselves mentally for the worst, and it came. Smooth sand and an ebbing tide provided an excellent drag strip for the maniacal driver. In a way, they were fortunate, Bowman's uncanny hand-eye coordination took them in a straight line to the CP like a speeding bullet.

Lieutenant Chandler was waiting, holding a carton in his arms. When the truck stopped he walked to the passenger side for a few last words with Miller.

"Here's your dry ice and wax paper, Sergeant, and thanks again. You'll need it to pack your fish."

"Thanks to you, Lieutenant, and I have one more thing for you." Miller reached into his hip pocket and withdrew a piece of folded paper. "Colonel Wardlow wants you to have his home address in Chicago. He's leaving the Air Force and he wants you to look him up when you get home."

"By George, I'll do that. I'll even write to him from North China." Chandler was delighted. "What about you, Miller, are you going home too?"

"Yes Sir. I've got rotation points coming outta my ears. I'm gettin' out soon."

"We've heard about your Air Force point system." Chandler couldn't resist putting the rumors to rest, and he asked in a joking way. "Is it true they pass out medals in the chow line?"

Miller smiled, not in any way offended. "That's pretty

The Last Souvenir

close, Sir. You fly a few missions and you get another Air Medal. I've got four clusters on mine."

"It's a crazy world, Sergeant. In combat my boys go on two patrols a day, and they don't even get a pair of dry socks."

"I know, Sir, it doesn't seem right. Maybe in the next war you and your boys can join the Air Force."

"That's impossible, haven't you heard? We just fought the war to end all wars." Chandler held out his hand for a last good-bye. "So long, Sergeant, and give my regards to your Colonel." He backed away and pointed down the beach. "Carter is down there. He has a mountain of fish for you. May God go with you."

When Bowman pulled away, Miller sat back to reflect. "You know, Johnny, that's one hell of a fine officer you've got there."

"Ya better believe it, buddy. He's the best."

Carter was ready for them, giving explicit directions on where to park. The fish were piled on thin straw mats with moistened cloths protecting them from the sun. The women had carefully cleaned and scraped the fat creatures, and the next step was a hot grill. The trade was a happy one. Eight large cans of spaghetti and meatballs to them was a delicacy and would probably constitute their evening meal.

Wana and her friends had finished a few minutes ago, and now were busy sponging off their arms and bodies in ankle deep water. The tantalizing picture of bare bosoms and clinging wet panties was almost too much for the celibate young airmen. Their rude gawking was a tribute to the highest form of voyeurism.

"Hey, Sarge! How about us takin' a break and goin' swimmin'?"

The distraction had not escaped Sergeant Miller but he had a schedule to maintain. "I see what you mean, boys, but forget it. The cook's waitin' for us. Spread out a tarp in the truck bed and start loading, and pack 'em in this dry ice."

The mumbling and groaning that followed was not fit for print. Smitty and Zack climbed out of the other side of the truck and stared at the pile of dead fish. With the tarpaulin in place they began their lackluster chore.

"How do you like that, Smitty? Naked broads only thirty feet away and we get stuck with a load of fish."

"Yeah. War is hell, ain't it?"

Miller walked over to join Carter and Sugimoto. "I think my boys are pissed off, Jake. They want to run amuck in your harem."

"I can't say that I blame them." Jake knew their final parting was near. "I don't suppose I'll ever see ya again, Miller, and I don't even know your first name."

"Well, I don't spread it around, but my name is Earl. I'm from Nebraska." Miller stumbled verbally in a short pause. "Jake, I wish we could have met sooner. I have a hunch we would have made some beautiful music together. If you know what I mean."

"Damn right I know what you mean. I have post-war plans and I can't let a brain like yours get away. Ya got a piece of paper?"

Miller produced a note pad and they exchanged home addresses. Many wartime friendships are fleeting, but this one would stick in a most unusual way.

When Smitty and Zack finished their job they squatted by the water and washed their hands. Their Sergeant was urging them to make haste and they slid back into their khaki shirts. They walked slowly away to mount the truck, glancing over their shoulders for one last close look.

The giggling females stood in a group on the beach. They weren't blind. Their coy facades couldn't hide the fact they had noticed the muscular physiques of the youthful Americans. When the truck pulled away the men waved, and the eager girls waved back, exposing the fullness of their pulchritude. All thoughts were the same. The plot would have taken a dramatic twist had they spent time together, and that would require many more pages of description. Instead, it was just another tale of woe to be taken back to the base and shared with the mechanics.

The exit of Miller brought down the curtain on the second act of Sugimoto's financial drama. The time had come for him to take a hand and rewrite the final script. Miller had taken his cut, and so did Muldoon, but thus far Carter wanted zero. It wasn't equitable, and Roy was convinced a subtle change was necessary. In Jake's character traits he had the generosity of a true benefactor, yet he could be as stubborn as a thirsty mule. There was a way around this and Sugimoto had it figured.

"Jake, it's been a busy day. How about going up and sitting in front of your lean-to. The money is stashed there. We can shoot the shit like we used to do."

"Sure, why not? It's all down hill from here on."

The lifelong friends walked together in slow motion and found their seats in the warm sun, facing the sea. Roy began his dialogue with a very casual approach.

"Do you remember when we were kids we used to go to the beach every Saturday?"

"Yea, Hermosa Beach. We used to ride the waves all day. That was a million years ago, and I remember you checkin' out the babes in their new bathing suits."

Roy nodded, confessing his guilt. "Remember how we always went back to your house. Your Mother would be baking a roast and making mashed potatoes and gravy. Then she would always ask me to stay for dinner?"

"She cared for you, Roy. She liked the way you always tried to finagle an extra slice of her French apple pie."

"We never talked about this before, Jake, but your Mother

is different. A lot of Caucasians didn't accept my people, but your Mother treated me like I was just another kid on the block. I never forgot that."

"Aw, come on, Roy. Your folks were always good to me too. So what?"

"OK, OK, I was just thinking. That old house you lived in. She said once she was tired of renting, and she dreamed about buying that big house around the corner."

"I can remember that. They wanted thirty five hundred bucks for that place. It seemed like shootin' at the moon." When the message hit Carter he sat up in shock and grabbed Roy by the wrist. "Wait... a... minute! You sonuva gun. You're settin' me up for something."

"That's right you stubborn jackass! If we get this loot home I'm going to build a custom house for your Mother. Take it or leave it."

Carter was in a vise, and yet it was a pleasant feeling. He honestly wanted no part of Roy's money. Every cent would be needed to correct the sins of the past, but the rest was academic. The jutting jaw and fierce determination on Sugimoto's face showed no way out. Meditation brought out some interesting points. Jake removed his cap and rotated it between his hands. "If I know you, Sugie, you've been hatching this idea for a while, right?"

It was the first time Roy had heard his nickname since the athletic fields of High School. Now, more than ever, the old memories were racing back. "For at least two days, Jake. Listen, we have almost forty thousand dollars in our kick. If Muldoon comes through tomorrow we'll have over sixty four grand. That's way more than we expected and I'm not going to hog it all. It isn't right."

Even the Devil has his price and Carter was relenting. "OK, pal, what's your program?"

The trigger was pulled and Roy let fly with a verbal

fusillade. He picked up a stick and drew a large square in the sand. "This is the land I hope to buy. Way up in this corner your Mom gets one acre. She always wanted a place with a view in the country. My cousin Ito is a builder. I'll make a deal with him if I can find him. She'll have a porch and a garden and everything."

"Wow! Take it easy, you're mowin' me down." Carter's side vision detected movement and he turned his head. "Well, well, look who's comin'."

A very determined Ichiban was marching their way, flanked by Koko and Wana. Tagging along behind was Jesse Hightree. Roy's promise to hold a lecture on technical farming was not forgotten. His chat with Carter would have to be postponed. He stood up and lifted his shirt, exposing several rolls of graph paper tucked in his belt.

"I'm sorry, Jake, we'll have to break it off. I've been looking forward to this meeting. There's a lot we can do with his land up North."

Carter had no desire to return to the Biscuit, much less sit through a session on the wonders of contour irrigation. He sat back and stretched his arms. "You guys go ahead. It's time for me to take a nap. I'm going to need my strength for those steaks tonight."

The high energy level of Roy Sugimoto was no fluke, it was his gift. The foursome hiked away with Roy holding his diagrams. He turned left to speak in Japanese and right to translate for Hightree. Wana elected to stay behind and join her sleepy lover in his afternoon repose. She crawled inside the lean-to and held up the blind for Jake to follow.

Carter wanted one last word and he yelled up the beach. "Hey, Roy! I like your idea. About the house I mean. I'm all for it."

Roy heard him. He turned to talk and walk backwards at the same time. "OK, buddy, we'll go for it. If you get a chance to write to your Mother, tell her I said thanks for the roast beef."

CHAPTER FORTY

A pot of trouble was brewing on the stove of military judgment but Muldoon had no way of knowing. The old pirate had said his last good byes to Carter and his men, and he pulled away with his second boatload of treasure. Jake's calculations were close. After paying bribes and wages his net profit exceeded fourteen thousand dollars. This tidy sum was prudently tucked away in a locker aboard his mother ship. The Captain, his commanding officer, was ecstatic over his new Arisaki rifle. He was most willing to turn his head and look the other way. The clever Chief and his Irish shenanigans in the past had brought harmony to the vessel and it's crew. The US Navy was no different from any other branch of the service. 'Midnight operating' was a way of life, perhaps better described as maintaining the balance of nature.

Distribution was the final phase. Muldoon's LSD, an abbreviation for Landing Ship-Dock, was anchored off the point of the Motobu Peninsula, and it was there he would meet his cohorts. By design, the repair ship was accustomed to landing boat traffic, bringing help for broken propellers or twisted drive shafts. This turned out to be excellent cover for his covert movements. Two small landing craft were waiting when he arrived, each tied to the port side bulkhead of his LSD. Both crews were under the direction of a Chief Boatswains Mate. Skullduggery, like water, seeks its own level and the two chiefs were clones of their salty old ringleader. They even smoked the same brand of cigars.

Muldoon was steering, and he pulled up abeam of the first boat. When they were securely tied together he yelled across. "Hey Louie, bring that boat over here on my starboard. Lash it tight, we'll hand ya your boxes."

The erratic China Sea was kind to them that morning and provided a smooth working surface. Muldoon, unlike the methodical Sugimoto and his clipboard, kept the numbers in his head. With his incredible memory he was able to store figures like marbles in a jar. His only written notations were the scribbled signatures of the souvenir recipients on the other end.

It could not be said that Muldoon was a super salesman. He wasn't. It was organization that made him shine. He had assembled his midget Mafia through contacts and cunning, and satisfied demand with supply. The word 'souvenir' has a different meaning in a peacetime curio shop. In war it becomes a trophy, or even an heirloom to be passed along to a grandson. It is tangible proof that the fighting man was really there and saw a great battle. A large ship in the armada provides luxuries and accommodations for the combat mariners, and yet it is also a form of confinement. He can tread the steel decks from bow to stern and never see the face of the enemy. This certainly doesn't minimize the terror he experienced from diving planes, enemy warships, and torpedoes fired from two thousand yards away. Death had been stalking these men for months, and for some, even years.

Now the war is over and they will return home to tell their stories to the eager ears of family and friends. A Japanese rifle or bayonet will cap off these tales like icing on a cake. Accumulated back pay was only paper. This was their last chance and they clamored for the services of entrepreneurs like Carter and Muldoon. There was no bilking involved. It was a willing transaction between buyers and sellers and nothing else. If the question of profit arose the answer was simple. 'Who cares?'

Muldoon's lesson in reading Japanese characters had stuck like flypaper to the fingers of his mind. One by one he scrutinized the crates and ordered them passed over the gunwales in both directions. A soft breeze was rippling in, bringing low ocean swells and a gentle rocking motion to their parallel boats. The working sailors took this in their stride. To them it was just another dance floor in their everyday waltz with the sea.

"OK, Louie, ya can shove off now. Ya got those two transports and that big cargo job." Muldoon scaled the rungs to the coxswain's turret for a better view. "Shorty, take the sub-tender first, then head for those two mine sweepers."

"Wilco, Muldoon. We'll meetcha back here and settle up."

Muldoon's code of honor was rigid and he shouted an afterthought. "Youse guys got your lists. Make sure all those swabs get what they paid for. I don't want nobody squawkin' about gettin' gypped. It's bad for business."

The three chiefs had an inkling their customers were anxious, but they didn't know to what extent. Crewmembers lined the railing of every ship on their circuit. Anticipation ran high, a welcome break in their tedium, and they crowded together like sheep at a feeding trough. The clients ranged from ordinary seamen to the ship's Captain himself. Loading cranes stood ready with cargo nets dangling from the cables. Rope ladders were tossed over the side to accommodate the visiting Messiahs.

Muldoon had only one stop, a CVL at anchor in the middle of the bay. This fast light carrier was only one third the size of its bigger brothers, weighing in at fourteen thousand tons, but capable of speeds in excess of thirty knots. Forty-four fighting planes were stored below its flight deck, all supported by a small floating city. Demand was so high for Muldoon's merchandise a lottery was arranged by throwing names in a bucket. This drawing was organized by Staff Sergeant James 'Wheels' Langer, the chief mechanic and member of the seagoing Marine contingent. Muldoon's prices were firm, giving Langer latitude for his own mark-up. The extra profit was never divulged, being of no concern to the Chief. One thing was sure. Langer lined his pockets too.

When Muldoon steered toward the formidable giant he could see the huge open doors of the hangar deck one level down. A cheering rabble of sailors stood on the edge of the cavern, shouting and encouraging him forward. Langer was already directing the crane operator to lower his cargo net. It had to be a humorous sight watching the mouse sidle up to an elephant. Once the boxes were safely inside the net, Muldoon jumped on and grasped the ropes with both hands.

"OK, Wheels, hoist away."

Up and up he twisted until he was softly deposited on the deck inside. "Hiya Wheels, it's all there. Tell your boys there ain't no more. I'm outta business after this run."

Langer shook his hand. "It's a damn shame, Chief. We cudda sold another five hundred at least."

Crowbars and claw hammers appeared from everywhere. Pine slats and straw packing were strewn on the deck in messy piles as the eager hands grabbed their prizes.

"Man, look at this here rifle. It's even got Jap writin' on it."

"Yeah, and check this bayonet. I'll betcha you could shave with it."

Langer offered a caution. "Alright you guys, this is an honor system. If anybody snatches somethin' he ain't paid for I'll personally kick the crap outta him."

Langer's popularity ran so high on his carrier the crewmen paid little heed to his outburst. He was generous to a fault, and would probably give the blood from his veins if asked. In his travels across the Pacific, island to island, his light fingers had lifted everything from carburetor jets to rotary engines from warehouses on shore. When a pilot cleared the flight deck in his aircraft he was secure in knowing that Wheels had double-checked every moving part. For the flying officer, Langer was

The Last Souvenir

more than a mechanic. He was a mascot to some and a magician to others.

"What the HELL is going on down there?"

Leaning on a railing above the hangar deck was Commander Alvin S. Shaffter, the Intelligence Officer on the staff of the Fleet Admiral. The silver oak leaves on his collar denoted a rank equivalent to a Lieutenant Colonel in the ground forces. He was thoroughly disliked by everyone. To him, military service was not a popularity contest, and he made that perfectly clear. When his question was met by stuttering he yelled again.

"You there, Sergeant Langer, get up here on the double. And bring that sloppy looking creature with you."

Langer climbed the ladder with the reluctant Muldoon on his tail. When they faced the fuming officer on the platform, Wheels brought up a snappy salute. Muldoon's right arm was motionless. The Commander had never seen this lack of military courtesy before.

"Well, don't you salute a superior officer?"

"No, sir. I only salute Admirals and Generals. It's a habit I got into."

"You *WHAT?*" Shaffter turned beet red. "That's gross insubordination. I'll have you court-martialed."

The obstinate Chief decided it was best to humor the man and he lifted a limp arm. "Alright, sir, I'll salute if it'll stop you from beatin' your gums."

The prissy Shaffter was too shocked to recover immediately and he returned their salutes. He was more interested in Muldoon's appearance. "What branch of the service are you in?"

"The Navy, sir."

"Our Navy? You look like a ragpicker from the slums. You're a disgrace to the Armed Forces."

The Chief grinned, reflecting his highly unorthodox

confidence. "Ya got me there, sir. I never did win no beauty contests."

For the moment, Shaffter decided to bypass the slovenly sailor. He was out for bigger game. "Sergeant Langer, what are those men doing down there? What kind of equipment are they handling?"

"Those are souvenirs, sir." Langer went on to explain the lottery and the Chief's ingenuity. "Some of the pilots are in on it too, sir."

To the mentally warped Commander this spelled trouble with a capital T. He was furious. "Sergeant, do you mean to tell me you're running a black market operation right under my nose? That's captured enemy equipment and the property of the United States Government. Somebody is going to jail for this."

The men below stood frozen in their shoes, bedazzled by the intensity of his rage. Their experiences with Shaffter in the past told them the bulldog wasn't going to let go. Using the privilege of a high rank, the officer took full charge of the situation.

"You there, find the ship's armorer. Tell him to store that gear immediately. The rest of you stack that equipment against the bulkhead. As of now, everything is confiscated and the lottery is canceled."

Langer took a firm stand. "But sir, the men put up a lotta money for those souvenirs. That's not fair."

"I don't give a damn." Shaffter was rapidly launching his crusade. "I want the money too. Have it brought to my office."

"I'm sorry sir, we don't have it. It's already spent."

"What? Where is it? Who has it?"

Wheels did his best to cover up. "I can't really answer that, sir."

"Well, I have ways to find out." Shaffter looked with

disgust at Muldoon. "You, ragamuffin, tell your crew to tie up and come aboard. Langer, I want everyone concerned in my office in ten minutes. We'll get to the bottom of this if it takes all day."

The machinery of doom was in motion and Commander Shaffter relished the power he felt by pushing the starter button. The egomaniac had delusions of achieving fame and recognition at last by busting the first post-war black market ring. He had been passed over three times for promotion in rank. The footnote on his fitness report stated he was - 'unfit to command,' - but this time he would show the world. He would take full charge of the case and direct it through from indictment to sentencing. New laws and regulations would be written, all based on the precedents he set. He even imagined a death penalty for piracy on the high seas. He decided not to seriously pursue the underlings. No, he wanted the crime boss himself. History would probably record it as the famous 'Shaffter Case'.

He was brimming with vindictiveness when he entered his office and sat behind his desk. His first move was to call for his aide in the next room. "Lieutenant Adams, come in here and bring a note pad. You're going to take dictation."

"Yes sir. Will you need any special forms?"

"No, you're going to type an arrest warrant." Another idea came to Shaffter. "What's the name of the officer in charge of the Marines on this ship?"

"Lieutenant Brandt, Sir."

"Well get him on the intercom. Tell him to be in my office in thirty minutes."

"Yes sir."

The aide had his notes and was busily typing when there was a knock on the door. It was Langer. He cracked the metal hatch ajar and poked his head through the opening. "Sir, I have the men you want to see."

"Well tell them to get their butts in here and line up."

Muldoon entered first, followed by two baby-faced seamen. The young sailors saluted, but not Muldoon. The set of the Chief's jaw evinced the Commander he had been down this street many times before.

"You men will write down your names, ranks, serial numbers, and the name of your ship." Shaffter shoved a paper and pencil across his desk and spoke to Muldoon. "In the meantime, you will tell me the name of the man who is behind this syndicate."

The Scrounger's Code of Silence was one of the few laws that Muldoon obeyed. Irate officers had badgered him before, and a lapse of memory was always a good defense. If necessary, he could blame it on combat fatigue.

"Well sir, I don't rightly recollect de name of those guys." Muldoon paused to scratch his graying temple. "Ya see, it was dark and there was a buncha guys hangin' around."

"Hanging around where?"

"Well sir, I remember there was a beach." The chief went on to mumble vague descriptions of sand and coral.

"That's enough." Shaffter was more determined than ever. His intelligence training had taught him to look for the weakest link. If the chain of muteness was broken the whole structure would collapse. He pointed his finger at the youngest looking of the lot. "You.... you stay. Sergeant Langer, take the others outside and wait, and close the hatch."

The snake was coiled and ready to strike with all the venom in its jaws. The frightened young sailor stood alone with visions of a hangman's noose around his neck. With his hat in his hand he began to squirm under the pressure. The Commander had set the stage beautifully, and he was resolved to grill the young man until he broke.

"What's your name sailor?"

"Seaman Henderson, sir."

"Well, Henderson, do you want to go home?"

"Yes sir."

Shaffter's eyelids narrowed. "Well you're not. You're going to prison."

The boy's heart sank to a place behind his belt buckle. "Prison, sir? But I don't understand, sir."

"You'll understand this. You are an accomplice in this gang and I intend to press for maximum sentences for everyone involved."

Henderson was crushed by the intimidation, and his voice quivered. "But I was only following orders."

"That's not good enough, sailor. However, if you're smart, there might be a way out."

"A way out, sir?"

Shaffter was ready to spring his trap. "If you cooperate with me, and give me the names of the ringleaders and where they are located, I'll see that your name is withheld from the indictment."

The youngster was hooked, and he tried one last feeble plea. "But sir, Chief Muldoon will skin me alive if I snitch on those guys."

The cruelty was working and Shaffter reveled in his success. "You are making a lifetime decision right here in this room. Either you go home with honor, or you will be dishonorably discharged from the Navy and spend at least five years in jail. Make up your mind, now, I don't have time to dawdle."

It wasn't much of a choice for Henderson. He thought of his mother and father and how they would react to the disgrace. After months of association with Muldoon he knew most of the salient details. Suddenly, he lost his taste for wheeling and dealing, and he wanted to walk away with a clean slate.

"I guess you'll find out sooner or later, sir. There's a Marine

Sergeant and a Japanese Army Lieutenant. They're up north in a little village named Hagachi. Sir, I'm gonna hate myself for ratting like this. They're a great buncha guys."

"No they're not, they're criminals and should be brought to face justice." Shaffter was wringing his hands with the joy of knowing his plan was moving along so well. "Seaman, go into the next room with Lieutenant Adams. Write down everything you know. He's preparing an arrest warrant. That's all."

Another tapping on the door introduced a new member to the cast. A young Marine officer stepped in wearing starched and pressed khaki. He stood straight and tall and presented a perfect hand salute. "Lieutenant Brandt reporting, sir. You sent for me?"

"Oh yes, Brandt, come in." Shaffter moved directly to his point. The Marines on board were trained as guards and Military Policemen. Brandt would issue MP armbands to himself and four men, forming a shore party. With Henderson as a guide, they were ordered to go in search of Carter and Sugimoto in a shore boat. Utmost importance was in retrieving the money and bringing it to Shaffter's office intact. From there, the prisoners would be incarcerated in the ship's brig. The written order was ready and a signed copy was handed to the Lieutenant.

Henderson stood in front of the desk across from the Commander. "Sir, can I speak to my Chief?"

Shaffter snapped back with annoyance. "Alright, you can talk to him on your way out, but make it brief."

The door was purposely left open a crack by Langer, and the men outside heard everything. Henderson stepped out with a hangdog expression. "Gee, Chief, I'm really sorry I squealed on those guys, but he scared the shit outta me."

"That's OK kid, forget it." Muldoon placed a fatherly paw on the boy's shoulder. "He was just bluffin', but ya had no way of knowin'. Ya just ain't played enough high stakes poker."

"Then you ain't sore at me, Chief?"

"Naw, listen, rats like that always gets poisoned in the end."

The teenager rebounded from the bottom but he still had a long way to go. "Can we still have chow together like we used to?"

"Sure, kid, the sooner the better."

Custody of Muldoon and his men was remanded to the Captain of their own ship. They would wait in open confinement for further orders as the case developed. Sergeant Langer sought permission to join Brandt's shore party and it was granted.

Now was the time and Shaffter was off and running. He ordered a second shore boat and headed for the Judge Advocate's office in Motobu. The coxswain manned the tiller while he stood in the bow, striking the pose of General Washington crossing the Delaware River. This was truly his finest hour as a reserve officer. The world would soon recognize his latent talents of discipline and command. Yes, it was a wonderful day for him.

The longboat pulled easily against the dock with the driver reversing its engine. A gray Navy jeep was waiting with SHORE PATROL clearly stenciled on its side. The occupant was wearing an SP armband and he swung to his feet with a smart salute.

"Sir, are you Commander Shaffter?"

"I most certainly am. Do you know the way to the Judge Advocate's Office?"

"Yes sir. I helped them move in yesterday."

Shaffter was over-anxious. "Well drive me there on the double." He tossed his briefcase in the back and barked instructions to his coxswain. "You will wait right here until I return, no matter how long it takes."

"Yes, sir."

The Commander looked scornfully at the landlubber's world as they drove along the crushed coral road. A long Quonset hut loomed before them and the driver screeched to a halt. "He's in there, Commander. He ain't even had time to put up his sign."

Shaffter disembarked and grabbed his briefcase. "He won't have time for signs when I get through with him. You will wait here."

Clomping inside like he owned the building, the tyrant noticed a startled young Lieutenant spring to his feet.

"Good afternoon, sir.... er, Commander, what can I do for you?"

"Are you a Navy lawyer?"

"Yes sir, I'm Lieutenant Pappas. Please excuse the mess, I just flew in yesterday from Pearl Harbor."

Shaffter advanced and placed his briefcase on the lawyer's cluttered desk. "Here's your first case, and it's a big one, a black market ring. I have nipped it in the bud and I expect to get a letter of commendation for this. The criminals are being arrested at this very moment."

Pappas resented the pushy manner and fought to retain his patience. "If I may interrupt, Commander, there are many things I must do. First I must familiarize myself with protocol and the chain of command. Second, I must present my credentials to the legal sections of both the Army and the Marines. Then, there's authorization, notification, legal boundaries...."

Shaffter cut him off abruptly. "Just a minute, Lieutenant. I'm your superior officer and I order you to take swift action. Stop the legal double-talk and cut through the red tape."

"What's the big hurry, sir?"

Shaffter squared his shoulders and decided to confess his motives. "This coup could mean promotion for me to Captain, and I *WANT* that fourth gold stripe on my sleeve. Are you reading me yet?"

"Alright sir, let me see what you have."

For the next twenty minutes the attorney took his time and read Shaffter's typed forms and hand-written notes. He read them a second time for his own edification, and shook his head. "Commander, with due respect to your rank, it is obvious you don't have a legal background. All you have here are suspects, allegations, and hearsay. Where are the witnesses, depositions, evidence, inventories.... shall I go on?"

Shaffter stormed back. "Dammit man, it's your job to set up a list of charges. I want you to arrange a quick trial and prosecute it yourself. That's an order!"

"Sir, our business is law, not tar and feathers."

"That's insubordination!" Shaffter was livid. "You and I are going to put this case together if it takes the rest of the day."

The young lawyer was outshouted, outflanked, and outranked. "Alright Commander, we'll go to work. I'll see what I can do."

CHAPTER FORTY-ONE

The beach at Hagachi was calm and serene, and the scouts had finished their packing. Orders came through, and they would return to their main camp early the next morning. The big truck was unloaded to accommodate the transport of Sugimoto's men. All excess rations and medical supplies were left as a gift to Ichiban and his gracious villagers. The air was filled with sadness and gratitude on all sides. The simple little people were truly inhabitants of another world and they would not be forgotten.

Carter and Sugimoto sat together on the sand facing the sea, each with an arm around his 'lady fair'. Wana and Koko fought valiantly to hold back their tears and face the reality of separation. One last night remained for love and closeness, but it was only an anti-climax. Even the greatest memories cannot ease the pain of farewell.

Parting was only one of Jake's problems and he ended the silence. "I'm worried, Roy. When we get back to camp they're gonna split us up. I've been trying to figure an angle, but it just doesn't come."

Roy was resigned to his fate. "Perhaps because there isn't one. I'll be sent back to Japan and that's it."

"Dammit, Roy, you could be stuck there for months. maybe even years. There's gotta be a way."

Wana's keen ears picked up the sound of a droning motor. "Funny boat come, see?" She pointed to the outer reef.

The sight and sound attracted the other Marines, and they gathered in a group on the beach. The afternoon sun caused a twinkling effect on the water, slightly impairing their vision.

"It's one of those Navy shore boats."

"Yeah, the ones they use to float Admirals around."

"Wonder what they want. They lost or somethin'?"

"Hey look, one of Muldoon's men is standing in front, he's bringing her in."

"Look at the rest of 'em, they're all MPs."

"Yeah, I don't like it. Somethin' don't smell right if ya ask me."

The longboat coasted to within a few feet of the shore and drifted to a stop. Lieutenant Brandt leaped over the side and waded ashore in knee-deep water. 'Who's in charge here?"

That was Chandler's cue. He walked forward to face the Marine officer of equal rank. "I am, Lieutenant Chandler. What's on your mind?"

"I'm looking for a Sergeant Carter and Lieutenant Roy. I have warrants for their arrest." Brandt handed him the orders.

Chandler was stunned, his worst fears realized. "Are these the charges, Lieutenant?" he asked in a shaky voice.

Before the man could answer, Jake elbowed through and grabbed the papers. "I'm Carter, let me see that." He read the printing and reacted with disgust. "This is ridiculous, and who in the hell is this Commander Shaffter?"

Brandt himself was fed up with the pompous Commander and he answered with an apology. "I'm sorry, Sergeant. He's a fleet officer, stationed on our carrier. You are wanted for questioning."

Roy was next to chime in. "If you are looking for me, you can address me as Lieutenant Roy Sugimoto of the Imperial Japanese Army, not Lieutenant Roy!"

Wana and her sister had heard enough. They rushed forward to clutch their men and offer protection. Because their village was devoid of policemen they could only assume these were bad men. "You no take. We no rike you."

The erratic Moe Chernikov had his own way of dealing

with the situation. He drew his pistol and held it by his side. "Hey, Jake, want me to blow this cop's head off?"

The MP officer recoiled in disbelief. The stories he'd heard about psychotic combat riflemen must be true. He turned to Chandler for succor. "Lieutenant, tell your men I'm just another Marine like they are.... following orders."

"He's right, Moe, put that damn thing away." Chandler wanted another look at the paperwork. "I'm afraid I can't help, Jake. You and Roy will have to go with him. This Commander outranks me by a mile."

Brandt's men were ashore and stood in a half circle behind him. "Lieutenant, you'll notice the order also says I'm to confiscate the money. Tell them to bring it along."

This was too much for Carter. "That's a lotta bullshit!" he exploded. "Who does this guy think he is, God or somethin'? There's a lot at stake here."

"Those are the orders, Sergeant. It's evidence now. Where is it?"

Jake and his men were ready to fight when Chandler intervened. "You men *BACK OFF*! I'm still in command here. Now then, we're still in the service and we obey orders." He turned to Brandt and pointed. "It's up there, Lieutenant, in that lean-to."

"Alright Jimmy, I've never disobeyed you before and I'm not gonna start now. I'll get it, but this whole thing stinks." Carter started up the bank and stopped. "How long is this gonna take?"

Brandt was relieved the ordeal seemed to be over. He faced a tough crowd and knew it. "It could be a few days. Both you men better bring your packs."

Jake crawled into his lean-to and was not surprised to find Wana by his side. She was sobbing now, and she squeezed her body tightly against him. Their last night together was suddenly reduced to a few moments. The young girl simply could not understand the workings of the outside word. He held her in his arms, but it only made matters worse.

"Oh Jaki, I never see you no more. I ruve you. This no good for Wana."

It was tearing his insides apart but there was no solution. He tried to console her, but it only brought tears to his own eyes. A voice from below interrupted their embrace, and he pushed her away with all the strength in his being. No, it was not right. Nothing is right when two lovers are forced to part.

When Jake emerged from the shelter his pack was slung over one shoulder. In his other hand he held the big duffel bag, bulging at the seams with cash. By now, his priorities were so mixed he walked like a man in a dream. A forlorn squad of his buddies was waiting by the water's edge. Jake began a series of short handshakes.

"So long Frenchie.... Kovak.... Sean.... Ike.... Eddie.... Ski..... and you too Jesse."

Carter saved the oldest for last. Chandler, Chernikov, and Bowman stood to his left and he turned to them. "Well boys, we've seen a lot of shit together in the last two years."

"Ya got that right, Jake, enough to write a book.... maybe two."

"Well Lieutenant, you'll be needin' a new Platoon Sergeant. Either one of these guys can do the job, just flip a coin, but make sure you put it back in your pocket otherwise they'll steal it."

Jake's quip eased the tension for Chandler and he smiled. "Goodbye Jake, and good luck. I'll say a prayer for you."

Bowman had his own parting advice. "You taught me when the goin' gets rough there's always a way out. When we get back to camp I'll start beatin' the bushes for help, you'll see."

"I know you will. Thanks Johnny."

Wana appeared by his side again and threw her arms

around Jake's neck, kissing him so hard it took his breath away. When she released him, she ran away as fast as her bare feet could carry her. In that split second of time, he knew she could be strong; knew also that he would never see her again.

Carter and Sugimoto tossed their gear into the boat and swung in after it. When everyone was in place, the coxswain pushed the throttle and spewed an ugly cloud of gray smoke in their wake. The pungent smell of a mixture of sea water and carbon monoxide filled their nostrils. The tide was high, eliminating the danger of sharp coral razors beneath them. Once in the open sea the power was increased, and they plowed ahead to their destination of gray ships and strange uniforms.

Langer crossed the boat and took a seat next to the sullen Platoon Sergeant. "You're Jake Carter, right? Been waitin' a long time to meet ya."

"You have?"

"Yeah, I'm Sergeant Langer, but everyone calls me Wheels."

"Wheels? How did ya get that name?"

"Guess it's because I'm always in motion, ya know, puttin' deals together. Muldoon told me all about ya."

Carter was not in the mood for making new friends. However, this one might be useful, so he made an exception and they shook hands. "OK, Wheels, what's the scoop? Where are they takin' us?"

"Back to our carrier. Ya had some bad luck, got fouled up in the net of Shifty Shaffter."

"The son of a bitch that signed that warrant?"

"One and the same. He's the biggest horse's ass in the fleet."

The machinery of Carter's mind was running again. The infection of Langer's wide grin was enough to cement a new comradeship, and he was probably a fountain of information. Even adversities were necessary pieces of his puzzle. When they all fit together the big picture would emerge. Langer was happy to supply everything from fact to ship's gossip. Just a simple opinion might lead to an idea. "How much have ya got in that bag, Jake, if ya don't mind me askin'?"

Carter glanced at the duffel bag carefully tucked under the feet of Lieutenant Brandt. "About three hundred acres of California land."

"What?"

"I'm sorry Wheels. I'm still pissed off. A little over sixty four grand."

"Sixty four grand! Wow, that's gotta be a new fleet record."

"It's not for me, it's for my buddy." Jake directed his attention to Sugimoto, seated on the other side.

Langer was confused. "Ya mean the Jap officer?" Roy was in full uniform and there was no doubt of his affiliations.

"He's no Jap. He's as much American as you and me." Carter was at last lowering the barriers of his anger. He related the incident of Roy's capture and the hopeless jam he would face when he returned home. The answer was in the duffel bag in the bottom of the boat.

"Geez Jake, that's a helluva story. Ya jumped him on a night patrol, and he turns out to be your old High School pal?"

"That's right."

"And ya wanted to send him home with the money. I wonder if Shithead Shaffter knows about this? I'll tell ya one thing, the whole crew is gonna know. They'll all be on your side, if it means anything."

"It might."

They finally rounded Motobu Point and the anchorage was spread before them. Three of the white hospital ships were still there, surrounded by a few smaller vessels. In the outer bay their destination became obvious. The carrier sat like a mountain above the foothills, and the nearer they came the more it ballooned in size. It measured a thousand feet in length, with the majestic flight deck perched over a hundred feet above the waterline. On the starboard side, the superstructure and radar equipment extended upward another hundred feet or more.

"My God, Roy, look at the size of that sucker. It's gotta be over three football fields long, at least."

"Yeah, she's a whopper. A man could get lost up there."

Wheels added a footnote. "Right now we've got about two thousand men on board, give or take a platoon either way."

The longboat pulled even with the camel dock, a nautical term for an airtight floating platform. Angling up from the camel a gangway led to the hangar deck, over seventy feet above the water. Lieutenant Brandt was the first man out, leading the way up the steps and hugging the duffel bag against his chest. Langer was next, followed by Carter and Sugimoto.

Langer paused at the top, awaiting permission to come aboard, while the Marine Lieutenant strode away to salute the Deck Officer. The conversation was muffled, but Jake caught bits and pieces. It seemed that Commander Shaffter had not returned from his trip ashore. The money was to be taken to his office and placed under guard. Jake's heart was sinking fast. The whole plan had blown up in his face.

Finally Brandt returned and issued a crisp order. "Sergeant, deposit the prisoners in the ship's brig. They will not be allowed visitors."

They began a trek below to the bottom of the ship with Wheels in the lead. Hatch after hatch and deck after deck swallowed them like a giant whale. At last they leveled off in a long passageway that took them to another Marine guard. He was armed with a pistol and stood in front of an oblong metal hatch.

"Hiya Wheels, whatcha got?"

"Hello Lefty, open up."

The depressing atmosphere inside was appalling to Jake and

The Last Souvenir

Roy. They beheld a long line of one-man cells, each sealed by a door with steel bars. Unhappy incarcerated sailors peered at them with glum faces. On the right, another Marine sat behind a desk reading a magazine.

"Ah, I see we got a couple more mice for the trap."

Wheels was quick to snap off the man's attitude. "Knock it off you jughead. These guys are special."

"OK, OK, they're all special. I'll put 'em in adjoining cells, seven and eight." He noticed their baggage. "Drop your packs by the desk. They gotta be impounded."

The turnkey opened two doors and gestured for them to enter. When they stepped inside he slammed them shut with a sickening clang. Jake took his first look around his new home. The cell was six feet long and six feet wide, with a small bunk on one side. There were no portholes or toilet facilities. He turned to the door and grabbed the bars. "Roy?"

"I can hear you."

"I'm sorry I got you into this mess, buddy."

The guard heard it. "Shut up down there. There ain't no talkin' allowed in here."

Langer was filling out a form on the desk, and he stopped writing. "I told ya to take it easy, they're friends of mine."

"Aw, come on, Wheels, you know the rules."

"To hell with the rules." Langer walked back and spoke through the bars. "Listen you guys, I'm gonna volunteer for Sergeant of the Guard. Maybe I'll be able to make things easier for ya. I gotta go now. I'll see ya later." His exit began the silent monotony.

The nightmare intensified for Jake, and he struggled with his claustrophobia. Either night was day, or day was night, and now he wasn't sure. He paced his little square like a caged animal, constantly glancing at the slow moving hands on his watch. Minutes became hours, and hours turned into years until exhaustion overcame him. He fell onto his bunk and sank into a deep sleep.

    The thought waves of Jake's anguish reached across the water and back to the beach at Hagachi. Johnny Bowman sat up with a start. "Wake up Moe, Jake's in trouble."

    "Yeah, I know, I cain't sleep either. It's like a phone ringin' in my ear."

    "Well we can't do anything sittin' on our asses. Let's get outta here, now."

    Less than an hour remained before the sunrise, and the moon had drifted away leaving an ebony sky. Even the goats were quiet. A bonfire up the beach outlined another sleepwalker. It was Chandler. He moved his head and spoke to the night watch, Sean O'Malley.

    Bowman's purpose lay somewhere between pilgrimage and vendetta. He pulled on his trousers and laced his boots tight with a determination he had never felt before. Action was the answer and adrenaline was the fuel. Right now, his comrade was calling and he heard the cry.

    Chandler, too, was beset by vibrations, and he wasn't surprised to see his Sergeant emerge from the darkness. "I know what you're going to say, Johnny. We should leave now."

    "That's right, Lieutenant. Jake's bein' railroaded and we gotta stop it. Do I have your permission to wake the men?"

    "You certainly do. Tell them we're moving out." Chandler knew he should have initiated the order, but was happy to watch the fluency of Bowman's movements, and the way he exercised authority. It was like seeing the ghost of Jake Carter return. He was leading the men, not driving them. Heads popped out and packs were pitched on the sand. Kovak was dispatched to interpret for the Japanese, and Hightree left for the village to alert their corpsman. During this flurry, the Lieutenant was convinced he had found his new Platoon Sergeant. He would cut the order on his return to camp, and Chernikov would have to wait.

The Last Souvenir

When the men mounted their trucks, rations and can openers were passed around. They would eat on the way. The sound of the engines awakened the goats when they drove by, and a handful of villagers leaned out to wave goodbye. The eastern skyline was turning gray, heralding the dawn of a new and desperate day.

Bowman drove the lead truck without his usual reckless abandon. His face was grim and determined when he passed the Army check-point and viewed the familiar sights of Motobu on his right. He knew down deep there was a solution and he was the emissary. This was his mission.

The convoy pulled up directly in front of Colonel Mason's tent. Chandler stepped out first and stood outside the flaps, requesting permission to be heard. There was no answer. Bowman's premonition urged him across the road to seek advice from the Chaplain. Padre Turner knew secrets about the regiment that not even the Colonel would hear. The tent flaps were partially open, and he caught the Priest in his underwear. He was seated on his cot, holding a rosary and reading his Bible.

"Johnny Bowman, this is a wonderful surprise. Come in, come in."

"I'm sorry to interrupt you, Padre, but this is important."

"By the look on your face I'd say so." Turner put down his bible and began to dress. "Have a seat on that marvelous folding chair you boys gave me. We'll talk it out, that's what I'm here for."

Bowman sat across from him and told the whole story from the amazing beginning to the bitter end. The Chaplain absorbed every word, shaking his head and clucking his tongue.

"Jake is a fine young man, Johnny, and he doesn't deserve this kind of treatment."

Bowman had another problem. "Where's Colonel Mason?

He's got to know about this."

"He left early. Said something about having breakfast with Colonel Snedeker over at the Seventh Marines. He should be back soon." Turner rose to his feet. "Sergeant, let's take a walk. I do my best thinking when I'm moving."

Bowman lost his concern for the patrol. He knew his buddy Chernikov would get the men squared away. They walked a few paces and he was impatient. "Got any ideas yet, sir?"

The Padre stopped and looked at the sky. "Thank you God for answering so soon.... I certainly do. We'd best head for Able Company and look up Lieutenant Lazarre."

Johnny B was aghast, and couldn't believe what he'd just heard. "Aw, come on Father, you can't mean the Lizard?"

"Yes, my son, many things have happened since you boys left. Since that confrontation with you and your pals he's a changed man."

"But sir...."

"Now hear me out, Johnny. He was a crack criminal lawyer in civilian life. He even spent time in the Judge Advocate's office in San Diego. You know how people talk to me.... I learn things."

"OK, Padre, I'll go along. You always tell us God moves in mysterious ways."

"That's right, and I do believe he's on our side. Let's find Captain Wannamaker."

The first link in the chain of freedom was forged and Bowman could sense it. The Chaplain was right. Not only did Lazarre have a brilliant legal mind, he owed a debt of gratitude to Sergeant Carter. Lazarre had felt so strongly about this he'd sought advice from the Priest. He had walked into the Regiment as a replacement officer with a big chip on his shoulder, and immediately acquired a horrible nickname. Carter had stormed into his life and risked everything to protect one of his men. The transplanted lawyer learned more in that fifteen minutes than he had during his entire legal career. Leading an infantry platoon required a lot more than a book of regulations and a mule driver's whip. Carter understood that his men had their problems too, and staying alive was the biggest. He worked hard to gain their respect without becoming too familiar, which is a very delicate balance.

Lazarre's opportunity came one day when an outsider was wrongfully harassing one of his men. He jumped in the same way Carter would react, and saved the man from injustice. His riflemen were so impressed he heard one of them say; 'Man, when he strikes he's just like a Cobra.' The old nickname faded away. He was now 'The Cobra,' and he loved it.

Johnny and the Chaplain found Captain Wannamaker standing in front of his headquarters, drying his face with a towel. "Well, good morning Padre, and you too Sergeant. What brings you to Able Company so early in the morning?"

It seemed fitting for the Padre to speak first, rank to rank. "We need your help, Captain, and especially, we need advice from Lieutenant Lazarre."

"Sure, Father, for you, anything." Wannamaker called to one of his men. "Corporal, find Lieutenant Lazarre. Tell him to report to me as soon as possible." He invited them inside the tent for privacy.

In a few minutes, Lazarre arrived, looking different; face tanned and new muscle filling out his jacket. He shook hands with Turner and smiled when he acknowledged the presence of Johnny Bowman, remembering the last time they'd met. "You're Sergeant Carter's buddy."

"Yes sir."

"Well, Padre, you didn't come here to pass the time of day," Wannamaker said. "What can we do for you?"

The Chaplain told the story in his own words, wanting to include the flavor of compassion. Lazarre listened intently, nodding his head occasionally to confirm his understanding.

When Turner finished he sat back. "You know, Father, I owe a lot to that young rooster. Of course I'll help." He turned to Bowman. "Sergeant, first I'll need some answers."

Bowman was more than agreeable, he was eager. "I'll tell you everything I know, sir."

"Good. First, was he represented by counsel?"

"No, sir."

"Was he summoned before his Commanding Officer to answer charges?"

"No, sir."

"Was he granted any kind of hearing?"

"Not that I know, sir, they just took him away."

Lazarre fired a barrage of questions with all answers negative. He was licking his chops like a hungry hound. He made a decision and spoke to Wannamaker. "Captain, this case has more loopholes than a hand knit sweater. Not only can I set Carter free, I might even have his accuser's ass in the brig." Lazarre saw the need for expediency. "Captain, may I have permission to leave camp and pursue this matter? I'll need to research the case first."

"You have it." Wannamaker reached for his pen. "You'll need my written order, and take the company jeep."

When Bowman and the Chaplain left, they felt like they were walking in the eye of a hurricane. Their champion had picked up his legal lance and sped away to the jousting. Perhaps better put, the Cobra would strike again, and leave the mark of his fangs in the rump of Commander Shaffter.

The Last Souvenir

CHAPTER FORTY-TWO

Colonel A.T. Mason was an organized man. Contentment to him was a neat row of pins or an orderly closet. Only clutter and surprises could arouse his irascibility. Commanding a regiment of enlisted civilians was a challenge for the regular Marine, and that was putting it mildly. Their deeds in combat were unsurpassed. On the other hand, his treasured Book of Regulations walked a tightrope between mayhem and disaster. This would be one of those days.

On that beautiful morning, he was returning from a conference where peers of his own age group and circumstances had met. Most of the high ranking officers from other regiments were there, and he thoroughly enjoyed the rapport. Their move from the big island to the far reaches of North China was the topic, and he was satisfied with the logistics. The only task remaining was a smooth delegation of authority.

To his horror, when his jeep passed through the main gate, a large crowd of vociferous hooligans blocked the road. The word about Jake Carter's misfortune had spread and every man had something to say. The milling mob extended from Mason's tent to the mess hall without a break. And even worse, a squad of Japanese soldiers stood far to his left, completely unguarded. Johnny Cobb, his orderly and driver, honked the horn in a series of loud beeps. A semblance of order returned and the palaver stopped, bringing more than a hundred hand salutes.

"Oh my God, Carter's been at it again," Mason muttered as he slid out of the jeep and waved his swagger stick to return the salutes. Instinct told him he needed Chandler, and he wanted him now. "You men disperse and return to your duties. Someone find Lieutenant Chandler and get him up here, and place those prisoners under guard."

The Colonel entered his command post office and took a seat at his desk. He thought he knew the exact direction the rest of his day should go. Planning a major move required every minute of his time and dedication. A folder he'd been given contained directives and suggestions that needed to be carefully studied.

Minutes later, the Chaplain, Chandler, and Bowman pushed through the tent flaps in tandem.

"Colonel, there's been some trouble."

Mason could surmise that much. "From the condition of my camp I would say so. Did somebody bomb Pearl Harbor again?"

This was Chandler's cue and he edged forward. "Sergeant Carter has been arrested, sir. We think he's being held on one of the Navy ships."

"What?" Mason shot to his feet. "You think? What happened? Why wasn't I told about this?"

"Sir, you were away until late last night, and you left again early this morning."

"That's not good enough."

"Well, Colonel, this is as much as we know." Chandler spilled out the details and Mason sank back into his chair. Marine officers are not prone to having favorites, but Jake was clearly his, in spite of the constant headaches he caused.

Padre Turner had his way of calming the old man. Optimism was the best medicine. "Sir, we have taken the liberty to retain the best lawyer on the island. He left camp about two hours ago."

"And who might that be?"

"Lieutenant Lazarre, sir, from A Company."

Mason paused to think back. "Oh yes, I read about him in the Company reports. He's a good man.... an excellent man. Where's he gone?"

Turner was only guessing, but he knew he was close. "Most probably to the legal section at III Corps, sir. He said something about research."

Mason did not care much for lawyers. This was nothing personal, but they always seem to complicate his life. In this case, he was heartened by the news and concurred with the decision. "You men can leave now, but stay close by. I want to see Lazarre as soon as he returns. Bowman, you stay. I want to hear the whole story from ground level."

The next two hours of waiting were back to back eternities for Chandler and the Padre. Doubts were wearing their patience thin. Chandler especially had a bad case of the fidgets. Relief finally came when Lazarre wheeled his jeep through the gate, and they flagged him to stop.

"Lieutenant! Colonel Mason wants you to report to the CP right away."

"Will do, Padre, but first I'm going to report in to my Captain and change into my dress khakis. I'll be back in fifteen minutes." Lazarre drove away without waiting for comment.

Heartened by the confidence in his smile, and the set of his cap, the fifteen minute wait was much easier than the previous two hours. Lazarre had actually been away four hours, but the last two seemed more critical.

After being briefed, Mason walked across the road to join Chandler and Turner. "Gentlemen, in my opinion, lawyers are a necessary evil, but it certainly is nice to have a good one around when you need him."

Lazarre kept his word and came striding back, carrying a narrow briefcase. A perfectly knotted necktie topped off the splendor of his khaki uniform. With him was Wannamaker, sporting a shiny pair of Captain's bars on his lapels. His dungaree jacket was buttoned to the top, for which he had his own reasons. Mason ushered the four officers into his CP tent and they stood at attention before his desk.

"Well, Lieutenant, let's have it."

Lazarre stepped forward a pace and withdrew a handful of papers from his briefcase. "Colonel, I'd like to start from the beginning. Sergeant Carter is in the custody of a Commander Shaffter on an aircraft carrier." He gave the name and the size of the small carrier fleet. The ship's Commander was a Navy Captain Kelly Turnbull, the flagship for a Rear Admiral RM Ofstie. "Sir, the real villain here is this Shaffter."

So far, the Colonel was impressed. "Alright Lieutenant, do we have a case?" Lazarre shuffled his papers and began to read. "Sir, Carter has been denied counsel and there's been no arraignment. Also, legal jurisdiction has been violated with no notification or authorization. Pre-trial confinement is not justified. Commanding officers have not been summoned for any hearing. There's no evidence and no witnesses. The whole fleet has gone deaf and dumb."

"Lieutenant, I appreciate your legalese, but could you give it to me in plain English?"

Lazarre responded with a delighted grin. "Sir, in straight American, this Shaffter has been carrying the ball down the sidelines, and he's already stepped out of bounds six or seven times. There's no way he can score a touchdown."

Colonel Mason was a football fan and the light went on. "Well why didn't you say so? Where do we go from here?"

"Sir, III Corps and the division legal section are hot under their collars. They're preparing a motion to dismiss and summons for the officers involved. Also, I can have Carter released to your custody.... today. I'll need your permission to see Major General Mueller for his signature."

"Mueller!" The Colonel was delighted. "I just saw him

The Last Souvenir

yesterday. He said if there's anything I need to just call. I'll do that, what else?"

Lazarre turned serious. "Sir, there is one fly in the ointment. I stopped to see Lieutenant Pappas in the Navy Judge Advocate's Office. With due respect to the Commander's rank, Pappas thinks Shaffter is an idiot."

Mason raised an eyebrow. "Let's not get too drastic, Lieutenant. I'll let that slide for now, what does he propose?"

Fact was truth to Lazarre and he had no apology. "Sir, Commander Shaffter has influence in a high place. That's how he got such a high rank. His older brother is a Senator, and sits on the Military Appropriations Committee. When he pulls strings, Generals and Admirals jump."

"Why that son of a bitch.... pardon me Padre." The Colonel vehemently hated nepotism in the military. "Now he's picking on one of my Sergeants. That does it! Do you have any ideas, Lieutenant?"

"Yes sir." The lawyer had that base covered too. "There's a way I can tie him up and pluck him like a chicken." Lazarre gestured for Wannamaker to step forward. "My Captain has volunteered his services in a very unique way."

Captain George Thomasen Wannamaker walked forward, unbuttoning the top of his jacket on the way. His open collar revealed a gold star hanging from a light blue ribbon around his neck. He was one of the extremely rare recipients of the Congressional Medal of Honor. The Awards ceremony, and an unusual trail of events, led all the way to the White House itself. To put this in perspective, the regiment had been committed in the Pacific War for three and a half years, and only six men received this honor. Four of those were posthumous. They had seen four major island campaigns, hundreds of daily skirmishes, and thousands of Marines were engaged. The man and his Medal of Honor required a salute from the President down to the ranks.

Colonel Mason snapped to attention to salute the Captain and the others followed his example. Wannamaker's embarrassment was eased when Mason offered his hand. "It's always a pleasure to be in your presence, George."

"I know you mean that, Colonel." The Captain added his own bit of trivia. "I miss the pinochle games we used to play on the troopship."

Mason reacted with a happy grimace. "You should, you took all my money." He wanted to move along. "Alright, Lazarre, where does this sojourn take you? How many people are going?"

"The Captain and myself, sir.... and the Chaplain wants to come with us." Lazarre knew the Colonel was a stickler for regulations. "With General Mueller's signature we can get permission to board the carrier and serve the papers. I can bring back Sergeant Carter with a signed release from III Corps."

The procedure was clear in Mason's mind and he gave a thought to transportation. He startled everyone by shouting through the canvas walls. "Sergeant Bowman, I know you and Chernikov are eavesdropping out there. Get up to the motor pool and bring back a small recon truck."

From outside there came a loud, "*YES, SIR,*" followed by pounding footsteps on the crushed coral. The second guessing of Lieutenant Dutch Van der Slice, the transportation officer, also came into the picture. Various vehicles were gassed and ready. They could take their pick.

Bowman's return with the little truck probably set a new regimental record. He offered his services as a driver but Chandler wisely refused. The three officers left the tent with the Chaplain last to exit. Mason stopped him.

"Padre, I want that boy set free. You know how much he means to all of us."

"Yes sir. In my prayers I've asked God to come with us....

just in case."

Out in the bay, Sergeant Langer had kept his promise. He was Sergeant of the Guard and had a relatively free run of the ship. Carter and Sugimoto were still in the ship's brig, but at least they were out of their tiny cells. The cooks and bakers in the officer's galley had sent down two trays of catered food. It was part of the silent rebellion against Shaffter's inquisition. Even their fellow inmates enjoyed watching through the bars. The entire crew had closed ranks and stood solidly behind them.

They were seated around the guard desk, finishing a tasty lunch. It was the best the ship's larder could provide. The rule of silence was waived, but this was a far cry from freedom. They were not to know of the drama unfolding several decks above. A Marine Corporal wearing an MP armband burst through the big entry hatch.

"Hey Wheels! The Officer of the Deck sent me down here. He wants you to bring the Marine Sergeant and the Jap Officer to the pilots' briefing room right away."

"What's going on?"

"I don't know, but it sure looks official. Three Marine officers just came aboard with two armed MPs. Ya better hop to it."

After almost two years at sea, Wheels knew every unusual break in the daily routine. "Jake, I've gotta good feeling about this. I'll bet it's your buddies comin' to bail ya out. Follow me."

This time freedom led straight up. They climbed on ladders and stepped through open hatches until they came to a long passageway under the flight deck. The briefing room was in the center of the ship, and Langer pulled the long latch. Once inside, they walked past a lectern to behold a ship-shape nautical motif. Polished brass fittings and upholstered chairs were everywhere, and the far end contained a long table flanked by more chairs. It was there they found their visitors. It was a homecoming for Jake and a surprise for Sugimoto. Padre Turner stood first, and then Lazarre. Captain Wannamaker was the last to stand, with his jacket rebuttoned to the top.

Carter stepped forward to greet his old friend. "Padre! I've never been so glad to see someone in my whole life." Their handshake was forehanded and vigorous. "Father, this is my buddy, Roy Sugimoto. Roy, this is Chaplain Turner."

The Priest's greeting was hearty and well meant, and he turned to present the rest of the team. "Jake, you know Captain Wannamaker, and you should remember Lieutenant Lazarre."

Jake looked at Lazarre with dread in his eyes, almost too shocked to speak. "Oh my God, you're the liz.... er, I mean.... you're Lieuten...."

Lazarre cut him short. "That's right Jake, it's me, the Lizard." A grin stretched his lips wide. "I'm your defense counsel now. In that short altercation we had a few weeks ago you made a Marine out of me. Today it's payback time."

"He's sincere, Jake," Wannamaker added. "Between your saving the lives of half the men in my Company, and giving me the best Platoon Leader in the Regiment, we're both in your debt, and that's why we're here."

"Amen." The Padre briefly bowed his head. "And there's a lot more to it than that."

In the past, the men always looked to Carter and his agile brain, but today Lazarre was the main man. His talents ranged from the knowledge of a District Attorney to the daring of a riverboat gambler. His analysis was complete and his remedies were lethal. They sat together and listened enraptured, knowing their star quarterback was starting the game.

"Well gentlemen, I've only given you a thumbnail sketch, but the case is ironclad." Lazarre turned his head and spoke to

The Last Souvenir

Sugimoto. "I'm sorry, Lieutenant, you are out of our jurisdiction. I can't help. You will be turned over to the Military Police."

Roy took this the only way he could. "I understand."

Wannamaker stood up to stretch his legs. He walked to a far corner and gazed with curiosity at a Navy chart of fathoms. He was not needed now, but he was ready to play his ace if the necessity arose.

Finally, the inevitable happened. Commander Shaffter blustered into the room carrying a huge briefcase. His uniform jacket was bedecked by two rows of combat theater ribbons. An experienced eye could detect this as fruit salad. The lowest seaman in the fleet was authorized to wear the same decorations. His manner was overbearing and rude and he took over with the subtlety of a ramrod. The other men rose and saluted the three stripes on his cuff.

"Who's in charge of this farce?" Shaffter dumped his briefcase on the table with a resounding thump.

"I am sir, Lieutenant Lazarre."

"A mere Lieutenant, eh? What makes you think you have any authority around here?"

Lazarre forced a paper into the Commander's hand. "This is for you, sir. Consider yourself served. It's an order to appear and show cause. It's signed by Major General Joseph Mueller, United States Marine Corps."

"Mueller? Never heard of him." Shaffter read the long list of complaints with little comprehension. "I've never had much respect for the Marines. To me, they have the same mentality as a roving band of gypsies."

The remark made Carter furious and he started to rise. The Padre quickly placed his hand on Jake's arm and wagged his head. On the other side of the fence, Lazarre was the sagacious spider, inviting the fly into his dining room.

"Commander, for your edification, I shall read a notice

from the FPO.... the Fleet Post Office." Lazarre read with clear and perfect diction. The memo described the disposition of souvenirs. They could be mailed home if crated and addressed properly. Firearms must be unloaded and no explosives allowed. "So you can see, sir, possession acknowledges ownership, and ownership can be transferred until further written notice."

There was a gray loophole. The peace was new, and orders would come in the future. For now, Shaffter's case was falling apart, but he clung tenaciously to his arguments. When Shaffter lunged, Lazarre would parry. It was a duel between the clumsy hand and the master swordsman.

Shaffter's illusions of fame and promotion were fading, leaving only self preservation. His big brother was chummy with the Chief of Staff, the lord and master of all military personnel. A simple whisper in the right ear could countermand most anything. His security blanket was still warm.

"Well, Lieutenant, you think you've gone over my head, but it won't work. This is still my case and I intend to keep it." The Commander was nervously sorting his papers. "I have contacts in very high places.... and I expect to use them."

"Yes, Commander, we know all about the Senator, now, there's someone I'd like you to meet." Lazarre and his homework would soon deliver a decisive blow and end the matter.

Far in the corner, Wannamaker heard everything. The snide remark about the Marine Corps had really rattled his cage. He moved to the end of the table with his collar open. Shaffter and his tunnel vision had missed his presence completely.

"Who in the hell are you and where did you come from?"

"The name is Wannamaker, Captain Wannamaker. Commanding Officer of Able Company, First Marines."

"Captain, eh?" Shaffter walked up to face his adversary. "Can't you Marines learn to salute a superior officer?"

"If you'll look closer, Commander, you'll see it is I who rates a salute."

At least Shaffter had enough recall to recognize the star and ribbon at throat level. "Is.... is that the Medal of Honor?"

"Very good, Commander. You will salute and hold it until I've finished the story that goes with it." Wannamaker's recitation was brief and to the point. President Franklin Roosevelt in the White House awarded him the Medal. Vice President Truman was there and took an instant liking to the hero. Truman was also a Captain who served during the First World War in France. They lunched together for two hours, swapping stories and becoming friends. Formalities were dropped. They parted on a first name basis, Harry and George. "So you see, Commander, I have clout of my own, not to mention Harry's private phone number.... if it's needed. You can drop your hand now."

Shaffter was fully deflated when he slumped in his chair. "And now he's President of the United States."

"That's' right Commander. We Marines are a close-knit family. Next time you'll think twice before you pick on one of us. The rest of us don't like it."

CHAPTER FORTY-THREE

Two new players were about to join the cast of characters. High above the flight deck, on the officer's bridge, Navy Captain Kelly Turnbull surveyed his domain below. He wore silver eagles on his lapels, a rank even with an Infantry Colonel. Command of the ship was his. He was the absolute monarch.

The vessel was the flagship for a small carrier task force, pruned down to two carriers and four destroyers for escorts. Rear Admiral Ralph Ofstie brought his flag aboard Turnbull's carrier to make it his headquarters. His scope of command was the entire task force. Ofstie wore a star on his collar and pilot's wings on his tunic. Both men were graduates of the US Naval Academy at Annapolis, and longtime friends, dating back to the peacetime Navy. This was their world.

"Captain Turnbull."

"Yes, what is it?"

The executive officer, his second in command, joined him on the bridge. "Sir, this man has a paper for you. It's signed by a Marine General."

"A Marine General, eh?" Turnbull accepted the written order and began to read. "What the hell is this! I'm being summoned to a board of inquiry? This is outrageous." The Captain had every right to go into orbit. First, his record was spotless. Second, a ship's Captain must be made aware of all events transpiring on board. "Why wasn't I informed of this before now?"

His aide pointed to the lower corner. "Sir, you will notice the Admiral and Commander Shaffter received copies too."

"Shaffter! That…… I'm going below to see the Admiral.

The Last Souvenir

Take over here." Turnbull fumed and sputtered his way down the ladders in the superstructure. The hatch to Ofstie's office was slightly ajar. The flag compartment was larger than most rooms, and he found the Admiral seated at his desk. "Ralph, do you have any idea what's happening on my ship?"

The Admiral was reading his own copy of the bad news. "Come on in, Kel, have a seat."

They hashed out the printed details together. The axis of distress pivoted on their sailing orders. The fleet was scheduled to leave for the States in two days. The hearing was set for one week hence. To complicate matters, Captain Turnbull had purchased a Japanese rifle for his son in San Diego. He practically had to bribe Sergeant Langer to circumvent the lottery. Now, his rifle was impounded and he was in the middle of a legal whirlpool.

The Admiral found a ray of hope. "Look, Kel, this order is signed by Joe Mueller. Hell, we went to the Academy together."

"You mean Stud Mueller, the football player?"

"On the nose." Ofstie sat back and grinned. "I see he's a two star General now. He's tougher than a pine knot, but he's fair. We might have a break."

Captain Turnbull was a man of fast action. He spoke into the ship's intercom in an effort to locate Shaffter. When the answers came, he was disturbed to learn the ship's crew knew more about the situation than he did.

"Can you believe this, Ralph? Shaffter's in the briefing room with a Japanese prisoner." Turnbull grabbed his cap and jammed it on his head. "I'm going down there. Do you want to come along? He's your man."

"You bet I do. Lead the way, Kelly."

A guard was posted by the entrance to the briefing room. With him was Sergeant Langer. The sound of heavy footsteps and the sight of top brass stirred their instincts, and both men

saluted. The Captain had compassion for his men. He had no quarrel with them, and he politely returned their salutes.
"Sergeant, is Commander Shaffter in there?"
"Yes sir."
"Open the hatch, the Admiral and I are going in."
Langer's training sent him in first and he called attention for all hands. The occupants stood erect with more saluting. Turnbull touched the bill of his cap and they all dropped their hands. They were standing stiff before him like a row of mannequins in a store window.

It was Turnbull's nature to inspect everything. They were, after all, in his kingdom. He walked slowly down the line. 'Hm, a Japanese officer.... a Platoon Sergeant, obviously a rifleman.... a Navy Chaplain, I wonder what he's doing here?.... an Infantry Lieutenant, he looks fit.... and a Captain, probably a line officer.' One irregularity caught his eye.

"What's that around your neck, Captain?"
Wannamaker was embarrassed again. He had forgotten to rebutton his jacket. "Well sir, it's.... ah.... I'm wearing my Medal of Honor, sir."

"The Congressional Medal of Honor! Good Lord, Admiral, you'd better come over here. We are in very distinguished company."

Ofstie walked up to see for himself. Both officers raised their hands in salutation. In unison they wanted to shake his hand. "This certainly changes the complexion of things." The Admiral asked everyone to be seated. "I'll take over now. Shaffter, show me what you have."

Shaffter rounded the chairs and placed a pile of paperwork in front of his Admiral. "There's more, sir, a big bag of money."

"Well, go get it. I want to see everything."

Ofstie was a rapid reader. One of the papers was pushed to one side and Jake craned his neck to see it. Something bothered him, an itch he couldn't scratch. It was very strange.

The Last Souvenir

The Admiral had a similar nagging aggravation in his subconscious mind.

Jake could hold back no longer. "Admiral, sir, I know it's a bad time to bother you, but may I ask you a question?"

Ofstie thumbed his way backwards through the reports. "Let's see, you must be Sergeant Carter. I don't see why not, you're the accused."

"Well sir, is that your name.... Ofstie? It's a very unusual name."

"That's right, Sergeant. Why?"

"Sir, since I was a little boy, my mother has told me stories about an Admiral Ofstie in our family. He's from Seattle. Of course he was a Captain first."

"What? I'm from Seattle. What's your mother's name?"

"Helga, sir, Helga Carter."

"Good Heavens, you must be Helga's boy Jake?"

"Yes sir, I am, and I suppose that means you're my Uncle Ralph?"

Padre Turner's eyes looked up and his lips moved silently. This time the power of prayer had brought a genuine miracle. No doubt he had a subject for many a sermon to come. Roy Sugimoto beamed like a full moon. His buddy's infallible luck was back. Out of sight and under the table, Lazarre and Wannamaker shook hands. Kelly Turnbull was already considering the possibilities. No coincidence is impossible in time of war. They all had the same question. Was it fate, destiny, or the hand of God? Ralph Ofstie was experiencing a warm surge of paternalism. His baby sister, Helga, was only twelve years old when he ran off to sea. He was the oldest in a family of four children, and Helga was the last. Since then, their only contact was a sporadic letter or a furlough home. At last, the war, age, and maturity had mellowed him, and an urge to retire was calling him home. He never married, and yet he still sought the refuge of a family. Perhaps, Jake would be that beginning.

The privilege of rank allowed the Admiral to monopolize the conversation. He put his nephew in the spotlight and became fascinated by his exploits. Ofstie invited the others to add their comments, and they did so willingly. Padre Turner appeared to be Jake's most earnest devotee. Even Sugimoto came out of his shell and spoke of their boyhood days. Captain Turnbull was especially gratified to see his old classmate's spirits lifted again. The hands on the clock stood still.

In parallel to his interest in Jake's 'travels' he had a further interest in the fate of Roy Sugimoto. The deplorable treatment of Japanese Americans was an obsession with him. In the pre-war days he had befriended Frank Goto and his family. These third generation Niseis owned a large pineapple plantation on the island of Oahu. Ofstie had spent many afternoons on their veranda, lavished with food, drink and kindness. Goto's favorite vein of discussion was statehood for Hawaii, and he was one of the first to lobby. He was fiercely loyal to the Stars and Stripes.

The bombing of Pearl Harbor had destroyed Goto's world. A Federal order hustled them away to an unknown spot on the globe. Ownership of the land changed hands, and the proceeds of the sale, if there was one, were mysteriously misplaced. Sugimoto, like Goto, would return home to zero.

Ofstie and Turnbull had discussed this malady at length in the confines of their privacy. High-ranking officers are forbidden to voice their opinions on political matters. However, this edict did not preempt them from thinking. In the years of war, Ofstie's squadrons had destroyed property and lives in enormous proportions. It was time to rebuild and patch up the hemisphere. The Sugimoto situation was beginning to find a place in his mind. It might be a good place to start. However, first things must come first.

Shaffter was back and the Admiral lit into him.

The Last Souvenir

"Commander Shaffter, you have bungled this lash-up into a fine mess. You are permanently detached from my staff and this ship. You will gather your gear and seek quarters ashore, where you will cancel every scrap of paperwork you have generated."

Shaffter was reduced to begging. "But Admiral, I was only...."

"That's all." Ofstie's tone was even and firm. "You've broken every regulation in the book. You'll have written orders as soon as my yeoman can type them. When you're finished here, you will find transportation to Pearl Harbor for reassignment. You're dismissed."

Exit Shaffter. Ofstie looked at Turnbull, and the Captain winked. They were finally rid of their bad apple. The attention turned back to Carter.

"Well Jake, your Chaplain just told me you hold a Silver Star and two Purple Hearts. That should give you enough rotation points to go home."

Jake's relief was fast becoming elation. "Yes sir. All I have to do now is wait for another troopship to come in."

"Nephew, how would you like to go home on a fast carrier? You could be in California in ten days, give or take."

"California? Ten days?" Jake was flabbergasted. "But Admiral, what about my regiment.... my custody?"

Ofstie looked at Lazarre. "Well, Lieutenant, you're the lawyer, can this be arranged?"

Lazarre did not hesitate. "Admiral, with that star on your collar, you can do anything you want."

Carter leaned close to the Chaplain and whispered. "What do you think, Padre? Does this sound kosher to you?"

The Catholic had to laugh. "Jake, kosher is not in my line, but prayer is. Every rifleman on the island would love to be in your shoes right now."

The thought of an ocean voyage, and a chance to get

Jack Carroll

acquainted with his nephew, combined to make Ofstie anxious. Protocol was important, and he spoke to the Captain. "Well Kelly, do I have your permission to have Sergeant John H. Carter transferred to your ship's company?"

Turnbull had long ago learned the art of smiling only with his eyes. "Let me see.... my crew could use a small arms instructor, an expert rifleman. Permission granted."

"Then that's settled. Jake, you're a sea going Marine now." The Admiral dropped his clenched fist on the table. "Do you play gin rummy?"

"Yes sir, and Pinochle and black jack, but poker's my favorite."

Roy shook his head. "You better watch out, Admiral, he's a real card shark."

Lazarre was asked about the next step. With notes to General Mueller and Colonel Mason, the matter would be closed. The slick lawyer had tied the case like a slipknot. A yank on one end would pull it apart. The whole thing was a magnificent bluff, legal but loose.

Ofstie was happy but not satisfied. He rose to his feet and walked across the steel deck. For two long minutes he stared through a porthole, his hands clasped tightly behind his back. A circle of faces watched him in silence. He returned to the table. "I can't just let Mr. Sugimoto be sent back to Japan. It doesn't seem right. Do you have any ideas, Lieutenant?"

"Yes sir, I guessed that might come up." Lazarre was closing his briefcase. "We can have him resign his commission in the Japanese Army. When that's done he'll be a civilian and an American citizen. He can join the Marines as an interpreter. That makes him eligible to be part of your ship's company. You can take him home with you."

A burst of joyous laughter filled the room, with the exception of Ofstie and Turnbull. They looked at each other in addled amazement. The thought of a Japanese prisoner joining their Navy was ridiculous, and yet it made a certain amount of sense.

"Lieutenant, that is the most devious scheme I've ever heard."

Lazarre countered confidently. "Look at it this way, sir. You submit the documents to your Judge Advocate. From there it goes to the Military Police and III Corps. By the time they figure it out, Sugimoto will be in San Diego and discharged. Red tape can be beautiful."

Nothing in Navy regulations would cover this pioneering event, and Turnbull was reticent. New challenges require new rulings, however, and Ofstie was more daring. He was a naval hero, checking out of the service with a long list of citations. The opportunity to heal a bleeding nation was more important than a dusty book of rules.

"I say full speed ahead, Kelly. Will you back me on this?"

"Well Ralph, like the man said, you're the one with a star on his collar."

Ofstie wanted a last opinion from Roy. "Mr. Sugimoto, how do you feel about this?"

"Admiral, I'd join the Girl Scouts and wear a skirt if it meant going home."

The Admiral's features were glowing as he continued. "Lieutenant Sugimoto, you are hereby demoted. You will join my staff as an assistant to the Language Officer, a set of Corporal stripes goes with it." He made a facetious addition. "That's providing you can pass the language test."

"Hot damn, Roy." Jake was beside himself with delight. "Do you realize what this means? We can stay together."

"What about the money?" Father Turner was an active Catholic, and not a stranger to the fine art of fund raising.

Ofstie glanced down at the duffel bag on the deck. "Oh yes, I almost forgot, how much money do you have, Jake?"

"A little over sixty thousand, sir."

"That much! You have been busy. Does all that go to Sugimoto?"

Jake was eager to explain. "Yes sir, most of it. Roy wants to build a new house for my mother, it's kind of a gesture."

"And a nice gesture it is." Ofstie could picture his little sister in a brand new dwelling. "This is a tough problem. I'll have to think it over. It's going to require pulling some long strings. I don't know." He looked back at Lazarre. "What about our lawyer? Do you have any ideas?"

Lazarre was back in his bailiwick. "Sir, doesn't the Navy have special funds? You know, widows, orphans, crippled seamen.... if you go high enough you might find a sympathetic ear, and a loophole."

"Son, you're a helluva good lawyer." The Admiral deliberated the probabilities. "I think I know just the right man. With a little luck, and a prayer, Padre, we'll have the money deposited in a San Diego bank, in Sugimoto's name. Mind you, I can't make any promises, but I'll do my damnedest."

Jake blurted out his suggestion. "Captain Wannamaker knows the President."

"We'll see, Jake. Heaven knows we might need him, and I'm willing to go that high."

Sergeant Langer was ordered to escort Roy below to the ship's quartermaster, and Jake went along. Because of Sugimoto's average build, an ample supply of his size was in stock. The fun began when the souvenir hounds started bidding for his Japanese uniform. His Cinderella story made him an instant celebrity, and the crew accepted him into the open arms of comradeship. Roy was outfitted from the inside out, including stitched on corporal stripes. He was a new man, and Jake was bursting with pride for his pal. The loyal American was finally serving his country, if only in a small way and short on time.

Admiral Ofstie invited the others to his office for coffee and

The Last Souvenir

fresh doughnuts from the ship's bakery. There was typing to be done. The adjoining room was filled with the noise of clicking and sliding carriages. Lieutenant Lazarre excused himself to assist in the legal wording. Turnbull turned his attention to Wannamaker. Meeting a man who was awarded the nation's highest honor was a blue ribbon day, as a punster would put it. Uncle Ralph was pumping the Padre for information about the friends and exploits of his nephew. He too was proud to learn the family line had produced a fine Marine. The fiasco of yesterday was straightening into a smooth sailing future.

"Don't forget Roy, you're a Marine now. Salute everything with brass on it." Sugimoto struggled up the ladders with a new sea bag on his shoulder. Wheels led them to the Admiral's office and pushed open the hatch. Roy caught the spirit and stepped through.

"Corporal Sugimoto reporting, sir."

Captain Turnbull couldn't believe the transformation, but the others were pleased, especially the Admiral.

"Come in, Corporal. Your enlistment form is ready for your signature. I shall personally administer the oath of allegiance."

A formal ceremony like this could hardly be described as solemn with so many smiling faces. Roy signed his resignation first, and then committed himself to his country. Tears came to his eyes but they were tears of pride not shame. Years later he would try to relate his feelings of that day, but the superlatives weren't strong enough just yet.

Padre Turner was the first to advance and shake his hand. "Congratulations Roy, and may God bless you." The new Corporal wiped the dampness from his face. "Thank you Chaplain. I know you mean it, even though I'm a Buddhist."

When the felicitations ended, the Admiral clapped his hands together once. "Now then, what about this souvenir business? Everybody has a souvenir but me. Why wasn't I let in it?" Roy was slowly pulling himself together again. "Sir, I have a Japanese officer's pistol in the bottom of my pack. I would be honored if you would accept it as a gift from a grateful American."

Jake broke into the tribute. "Ya hit the jackpot, Admiral. That's the best souvenir on this island."

Roy promised to deliver the prize and the Admiral accepted with one final word. "I will treasure it always. It will remind me of this day. I'll say one more thing.... let this be the last souvenir."

Lazarre had his documents signed and the Marines were ready to leave the ship. Jake asked permission to go back to camp with them and retrieve his belongings. He also wanted Roy to come along. The Admiral was hesitant, and so was the Captain. The fleet was sailing early the day after tomorrow. The departure time was carved in stone. As always, special situations require special decisions, and the Admiral relented. He could see that his nephew wanted to say goodbye to his foxhole buddies. He gave Jake and Roy twenty hours and not a second more. A longboat would be waiting for them at the warehouse dock. The Admiral gave instructions to radio the Shore Patrol to provide round-trip transportation. In other words, the Navy Cops would camp on their tails.

The thrill of seeing a Marine tent camp for the first time gave Roy a feeling of reverence. It was the joy of belonging again, and his new uniform made him a part of the wondrous scene. It was far from drab, it was beautiful. Jake asked the driver to stop in front of Colonel Mason's tent, and the riders disembarked. Lazarre and Carter went inside to present the new orders, along with Captain Wannamaker. A small crowd was already massing in the road.

Mason was his old self, seated at the desk organizing plans. They saluted and he took the papers. After reading the last

The Last Souvenir

page he looked up with a half smile. "Sergeant Carter, this is a helluva way to come back from a patrol. Somehow you've managed to involve a Major General, a Navy Captain, and a Fleet Admiral. You've converted a Japanese prisoner into a Marine Corporal and arranged your transportation home. Just out of curiosity, how in the hell do you do it?"

"It's a long story, Colonel. I owe a lotta thanks to Lieutenant Lazarre and Captain Wannamaker .... and the Padre too."

Mason could not resist the young man's grin. "Alright Sergeant, is there anyone on this island who isn't involved? If I had your connections I'd be Commandant of the Marine Corps by now. You'd better get out of here and say goodbye to your gang of thugs."

Word of Jake's homecoming traveled fast through the canvas jungle. Bowman and Chernikov were waiting to steer them back to their tent. Del Stack was on his way home, leaving an empty cot for Sugimoto. Bill Hull was mixing gin and vermouth when they arrived. They were late for the evening chow and had to settle for lobster and smoked oysters. The whole platoon gathered with other assorted comrades until the mob bulged out into the Company Street. In part, Roy was a center of attention, enjoying a happiness he had not known for four years. Sleep came early to their drained minds and bodies.

After breakfast the next day, Jake took Corporal Sugimoto on a tour of the installation, shaking hands and saying goodbye to a score of riflemen. Time was passing like geese flying south. The faithful Shore Patrol was due in a few minutes.

A lusty throng of waving men greeted them when they approached the headquarters tent. There were too many hands to touch, they would have to be satisfied with a wave. Chernikov had Jake's sea bag and Bowman stood with him. The truck pulled in and Carter saved his two best buddies for last.

"We've been down a long road together my friends. I guess this is goodbye."

"We'll write ya from China, Jake."

"Yeah, I'd like that. I'll be seein' ya Moe... So long Johnny."

One last wave and he was driven away, gone from the ranks of the First Marines forever. It was bitter, and yet it was sweet. That's the way it always happened.

The clockwork efficiency of the US Navy took Jake and Roy to their new way of life. Wheels was waiting at the top of the gangway, and he showed them to their bunks in the Marine quarters. They had been supplied with mattresses, clean linen, and the luxury of a private locker. The rasping intercom was constantly crackling on and off, giving the crew instructions for getting under way. They were immune from this, and took their time unpacking.

The night passed uneventfully, but the next morning was another story. The metallic sounds of the anchor chains vibrated through the steel hull. Soon the ship shuddered under the power of its monstrous engines, and made a half circle into the vast China Sea. They were heading south to skirt the island and turn into the wide Pacific Ocean.

Langer was back and filled with enthusiasm. "Come on you land turtles, I'm going to show ya a real sight."

They climbed up the gray tunnels and out to an observation deck where they could view the majesty of the morning. Four destroyers, flexing their muscles against the rising swells ringed the ship. A second carrier fell in behind them. The sharp prow knifed through the water, creating foamy waves on either side. A playful school of porpoise jumped and plunged in the illusive froth, showing off like precocious children. Astern of the fantail, a sleek Albatross soared in the wind currents without once flapping its ten-foot wingspan.

The three men leaned against the railing for several minutes of wordless admiration. A kindly thought came to

The Last Souvenir

Sugimoto. "You guys are going to think I'm crazy, but we shouldn't be mad at Shaffter. We should be shaking his hand."

"Are you nuts?"

"No, if it wasn't for him we wouldn't be here."

"I suppose that's one way of looking at it."

Jake was experiencing a ripple of euphoria. He moved sideways until the railing curved and he could look forward. The breeze hit his face full on, and he closed his eyes to dream while he gripped the steel bar. Fantasies filled his mind. "Hey Roy, come on up here. This ya have to see."

Roy moved next to him and held the railing. "I can't see anything but ocean."

"Well close your eyes and concentrate."

"OK Jake, they're closed, now what?"

"Can ya see it? It's California out there waiting for us. The beaches, the palm trees, the pretty girls, the hot dog stands along the Strand."

The flight of imagination was contagious, and the Nisei saw a different picture. "I can see my mother with a blue bandanna on her head, going through the house with a dust cloth, and my father in the fields."

"We're goin' home, Roy, we're really goin' home... at last."

For sales, editorial information, subsidiary rights information
or a catalog, please write or phone or e-mail
ipicturebooks
1230 Park Avenue, Ste 8a
New York, NY 10128, US
Sales: 1-800-68-BRICK
Tel: 212-427-7139 Fax: 212-860-8852
www.BrickTowerPress.com
email: bricktower@aol.com.

For sales in the UK and Europe please contact our distributor,
Gazelle Book Services
Falcon House, Queens Square
Lancaster, LA1 1RN, UK
Tel: (01524) 68765 Fax: (01524) 63232
email: Sales@gazellebooks.co.uk

For Australian and New Zealand sales please contact
Bookwise International
174 Cormack Road, Wingfield, 5013, South Australia
Tel: 61 (0) 419 340056 Fax: 61 (0)8 8268 1010
email: karen.emmerson@bookwise.com.au